£8.99

D0795081

Laurence Gardner, a Fellow of the Society of Antiquaries of Scotland, is a constitutional historian and Professional Member of the Institute of Nanotechnology. Distinguished as the Chevalier de St Germain, he is attached to the European Council of Princes (a constitutional advisory body established in 1946) as the Jacobite Historiographer Royal. In the artistic domain, he has been Conservation Consultant to the Fine Art Trade Guild, and in the world of music his libretto compositions have been performed at London's Royal Opera House. He is also Executive Producer for a Hollywood movie company. Prior of the Knights Templars of St Anthony (1561) and of the Sacred Kindred of St Columba, he is the internationally bestselling author of *Bloodline of the Holy Grail*, *Realm of the Ring Lords*, *Genesis of the Grail Kings*, *Lost Secrets of the Sacred Ark* and *The Magdalene Legacy*.

THE LEARNING CENTRE
TOWER HAMLETS COLLEGE
POPLAR CENTRE
POPLAR HIGH STREET
LONDON E14 0AF

The Magdalene Legacy

Class: 229 GAR
Accession No: 108795
Type: 3 WKS

Also by Laurence Gardner:

Bloodline of the Holy Grail
Genesis of the Grail Kings
Realm of the Ring Lords
Lost Secrets of the Sacred Ark
The Shadow of Solomon

Class
Accession Number
Type

The Magdalene Legacy

The Jesus and Mary Bloodline Conspiracy

Revelations Beyond The Da Vinci Code

Laurence Gardner

THE LIBRARY
TOWER HAMLETS COLLEGE
POPLAR HIGH STREET
LONDON E14 0AF
Tel: 0207 510 7763

HarperElement
An Imprint of HarperCollins*Publishers*
77–85 Fulham Palace Road,
Hammersmith, London W6 8JB

The website address is: www.thorsonselement.com

and *HarperElement* are trademarks of
HarperCollins*Publishers* Ltd

First published by HarperElement 2005
This edition 2005

4

© Laurence Gardner, 2005

Laurence Gardner asserts the moral right
to be identified as the author of this work

A catalogue record of this book
is available from the British Library

ISBN-13 978-0-00-720085-6
ISBN-10 0-00-720085-4

Printed and bound in Great Britain by
Clays Ltd, St Ives plc

All rights reserved. No part of this publication may be
reproduced, stored in a retrieval system, or transmitted,
in any form or by any means, electronic, mechanical,
photocopying, recording or otherwise, without the prior
written permission of the publishers.

To Rose
A dear mother, sadly missed

Nothing is secret that shall not be made manifest; neither anything hid that shall not be known and come abroad.

Luke 8:17

CONTENTS

Colour Plates   xiii
Maps and Illustrations   xv
Acknowledgements   xvii

Introduction   xx

1   SAINT OR SINNER?
     The First Lady   1
     Restoration   2
     Seven Devils   8
     Magdalene Heritage   12
     Academia   16
     Fear and Trepidation   20

2   PERSECUTION
     Towards Oblivion   22
     Heirs of the Lord   25
     The Revelation   30
     Brothers and Sisters   37
     The Forbidden Tomb   41

3   APOCALYPSE
     Fruit of the Vine   44
     Fertile Allegory   47
     Magdalene Emblems   51
     Armageddon   58
     Agony and Torment   63

4   THE OTHER MARY
     Heritage of the Nazarene   65
     Gabriel   69
     Marriage Regulations   73
     Immaculate Conception   81

5   SEPULCHRE OF THE MAGDALENE
    The Holy Balm   86
    A New Emphasis   92
    Zachary's Deceit   95
    Living Waters   101
    A Gothic Bequest   105

6   GUARDIANS OF THE RELIC
    Daughter of France   109
    Faith Wisdom   114
    Breath of the Universe   116
    Inquisition   121
    The Baphomet Cipher   125

7   REMARKABLE TEXTS
    Martha   131
    Suppressing the Evidence   135
    The Great Heresy   141
    The Magdalene Archive   145
    Forgotten Gospels   148

8   WOMEN AND THE CHURCH
    A Matter of Dates   155
    Jesus' Birthday   159
    Consort of the Saviour   162
    Selecting the Gospels   167

9   THE SACRED MARRIAGE
    Aspects of Translation   177
    The Scarlet Woman   182
    Female Ministry   185
    Dynastic Wedlock   190
    The Betrothal   193

10 THE INHERITORS
    Marriage of the Magdalene   198
    Kingdom of Heaven   206

	The Order of Melchizedek	211
	Time of Restitution	215
11	THE GRAIL CHILD	
	Separation	219
	The Magdalene Voyage	221
	In the West	226
	Revelation of the Lamb	229
	Beloved Disciple	231
12	REALM OF THE *DESPOSYNI*	
	The Fisher Kings	238
	House of Bread	243
	Divine Highness	247
	The First Church	250
	The Bishops' Debate	254
	Secret of the Lord	257
13	THE HOLY BALM	
	Romance of the Grail	260
	Mount of Witness	264
	The Alabaster Jar	268
	Nascien and the Fish	275
	The Great Luminary	278
14	KINGDOMS AND COLOURS	
	The Holy Families	283
	Arthurian Descent	289
	Queens of Avallon	293
	The Magdalene Colours	297
15	LEONARDO DA VINCI	
	Mona Lisa	305
	Virgin of the Rocks	317
	Madonna of the Rocks	322
	Notre Dame	326

16	THE LAST SUPPER	
	A Tragic History	330
	The Adoration Dispute	335
	The Da Vinci Code	337

17	SACRED ALLEGORY	
	A Mysterious Panel	348
	The Bedroom Heresy	356
	Rod of Jesse	360
	The Repentant Courtesan	364

18	A SECRET PRIORY	
	Conspiracy of Sion	370
	The Saunière Mystery	374
	Commandery of the Revolution	378
	Suspect Dossiers	379
	The Original Prieuré	382
	God and the Magdalene	385

Notes and References	305
Genealogical Chart	
Bloodline of the Holy Grail	424

	APPENDICES	
I	Son of God – Son of Man	431
II	Trial and Crucifixion	435
III	Jesus and India	451
IV	Saint Helena	455
V	Three Tables of the Grail	458
VI	Downfall of the Merovingians	462

Bibliography	465
Picture Credits	478
Dan Brown and *The Da Vinci Code*	479
Index	487

COLOUR PLATES

1	*In the House of Simon the Pharisee*
2	*Penitent Magdalene*
3–4	*Mary Magdalene Renouncing Vanities*
5	*Noli me tangere*
6	Black Madonna of Paris
7	*Christ Falls under the Cross*
8	*The Life of Mary Magdalene*
9	*Mary Magdalene*
10	*Mary and the Bishop of Marseilles*
11	*Mary Magdalene Carried by the Angels*
12	*The Holy Grail*
13	*The Wedding Feast at Cana*
14	*Mary and the Red Egg*
15	*Mary Magdalene Ashore in Provence*
16	*The Magdalene Voyage to Marseilles*
17	*Magdalene and Fra Pontano*
18	*Mary with Saints Dominic and Bernard*
19–20	Studies for Mary Magdalene
21	*Allegory of Leonardo*
22	*Philip the Apostle* – study drawing
23	*Head of a Girl* (for *Virgin of the Rocks*)
24–25	*The Last Supper* – details
26	*The Redeemer* – study of Jesus
27	John (restored) – from *The Last Supper*
28	*The Last Supper* – restored detail
29	*The Last Supper* – detail variant
30–33	*The Last Supper* – details
34	*La Gioconda (Mona Lisa)*

35   *La Gioconda* – study
36   *A Visit by Raphael* – showing Leonardo's studio with Lisa Gioconda
37   *Rest on the Flight into Egypt*
38   *Mary Magdalene Reading*
39   *Mary Magdalene*
40   *Jesus and Mary Magdalene*
41   *The Three Marys at the Tomb*
42   *Tempi Madonna*
43   *Cowper Madonna*
44–46   *Virgin (Madonna) of the Rocks*
47   The *Arnolfini* double portrait
48   Magdalene window – Kilmore church
49   *Sacred Allegory*
50   *Eucharist of the Last Supper*
51   *Mary Magdalene Preaching in Provence*
52   *Jesus Maria* Stone at Glastonbury
53   Magdalene relics at St Maximus la Sainte-Baume

MAPS AND ILLUSTRATIONS

1	*Map* – The Gospel Lands	14
2	1st-century Roman standard	34
3	Grail watermark from 13th-century Provence	47
4	The engrailed black and silver shield of Saint-Clair	51
5	*The Annunciation*	70
6	Emperor Constantine gains Messianic approval	94
7	*Map* – Medieval France	112
8	Templar effigy of the Baphomet–Sophia	129
9	*The Raising of Lazarus*	134
10	Fragment of the *Gospel of Mary Magdalene*	152
11	*The Three Marys at the Empty Tomb*	164
12	The bishops submit their Gospel selections	168
13	Mary Magdalene anoints the feet of Jesus	181
14	Mary Magdalene anoints the head of Jesus	201
15	*Map* – Course of the Magdalene Voyage	222
16	Angels of the Sangréal	241
17	Josephes passes the Lordship of the Grail	258
18	1st-century alabastron designs	270
19	*Mary Magdalene at the door of Simon the Pharisee*	274
20	Aedàn the Pendragon	287
21	The Davidic lion of Léon d'Acqs	296
22	Leonardo's *Vitruvian Man*	310
23	Leonardo da Vinci	318
24	Detail of *The Last Supper* (copied in 1524)	342
25	*The Last Supper* from *The Grand Passion*	346
26	The 'double portrait' signature of Jan van Eyck	349
27	The Magdalene window legend at Kilmore church	359
28	Priory of Sion headers from May 1956	371

29   Commanders of the Temple of Carcassonne   376
30   *Marie Madeleine preaching to the King and Queen*
        of Marseilles   388
31   Rectangles of the Golden Mean   459
32   The Three Tables of the Grail   461

ACKNOWLEDGEMENTS

For their valued assistance in the preparation of this work, I am indebted to archivists and librarians at the British Library, the British Museum, Bibliothèque Nationale de France, Bibliothèque de Bordeaux, Devon County Library, Birmingham Central Library, the Ashmolean Museum, Bodleian Library, Congregation des Soeurs de Saint Thomas de Villeneuve, the Palazzo Ducale of Mantua, the Cathedral Museum of Gerona, the Samuel Courtauld Trust, the Russian Orthodox Convent of St Mary Magdalene in Jerusalem, the National Library of Wales, the National Library of Scotland, and the Royal Irish Academy.

For information concerning artwork, my acknowledgements are due to the curators and administrators at the National Gallery in London, Graphische Sammlung Albertina in Vienna, The Fitzwilliam Museum in Cambridge, Galleria Doria-Pamphili in Rome, Galleria degli Ufizzi in Florence, Musée des Beaux-Arts in Caen, the Church of San Francesco of Assisi, the National Gallery of Art in Washington, The Louvre Museum in Paris, Museo di San Marco dell'Angelico in Florence, Pinacoteca di Brera in Milan, Brooklyn Museum of Art in New York, the Philadelphia Museum of Art, Musée des Beaux-Arts in Nantes, Santa Maria delle Grazie in Milan, and Musée Conde in Chantilly.

I am most thankful to my wife Angela, whose tireless support has helped bring this work to fruition, and to my son James for his continued encouragement. My express gratitude is similarly due to my literary agent Andrew Lownie, publicity agent Jennifer Solignac, foreign rights agent Scarlett

Nunn, website manager Karen Lyster, technical advisor Tony Skiens, and business manager Colin Gitsham. Special thanks also to commissioning editor Katy Carrington, the directors and staff of HarperElement and HarperCollins*Publishers*, and the book's editor Matthew Cory. Additionally deserving of my appreciation for their professional help are Charlotte Lorimer and Tamzin Phoenix of The Bridgeman Art Library.

I am also grateful to the Royal House of Stewart, the Sacred Kindred of St Columba, the European Council of Princes, the Order of Knights Templars of St Anthony, and the Noble Order of the Guard of St Germain. Particular recognition is due to HRH Prince Michael of Albany for affording privileged access to Household archives, while my respects are conveyed to the late Chevaliers David Roy Stewart and Jack Robertson, whose research was of such value to this project.

As always, I thank Sir Peter Robson for creating the inspired allegorical paintings that accompany my writings, while also acknowledging composer Jaz Coleman and artist Andrew Jones for their collaboration in the Magdalene Oratorio. Appreciation is also due to all those concerned in Hollywood for adapting my work for cinema production. For their ongoing support in aiding my work internationally, my special thanks to Eleanor and Steve Robson of Peter Robson Studio; to Duncan Roads, Ruth Parnell, Marcus and Robyn Allen of Nexus; Adriano Forgioni of Hera; JZ Knight and all at Ramtha's School of Enlightenment; Christina Zohs of *Yes News*, Nancy and Mike Simms of Entropic Fine Art, and all the media hosts and journal editors who have been so supportive of this series.

ACKNOWLEDGEMENTS

Since this book is very much a synthesis of interrelated subject matter, I am greatly beholden to those specialist authors whose individual scholarship in their respective fields has facilitated the coverage of specific aspects. Their personal expertise and pre-eminent published works have been invaluable.

Finally, I must convey my gratitude to all those readers who have followed and encouraged my work over the years, especially those who have written to me with so many useful comments and contributions.

Laurence Gardner
The Graal Studio
http://www.graal.co.uk

INTRODUCTION

In 1996 *Bloodline of the Holy Grail*, the first book in this series, introduced the most comprehensive table of Jesus' family descendants to be published in modern times. In this context, the marital status of Jesus was detailed and, contrary to orthodox teaching, his wife Mary Magdalene was brought to the fore as a woman of considerable status. The revelation led to shocked newspaper headlines in America, a national press serialization of the book in Britain's *Daily Mail*, and very quick entry into the bestselling book charts. As a result, *Bloodline of the Holy Grail* became something of a worldwide institution, with a large number of foreign language translations and a variety of subsequent English language editions.

Having commenced as a book that rocked the establishment, *Bloodline* gradually settled into a more mainstream classification. It gained me a 1997 Author of the Year nomination from Hatchard's of London and the Dillons Bookstores chain, and began to appear in college libraries, with its genealogical charts used for coursework. From the outset, my media appearances with priests, bishops and other religious leaders were reassuringly amicable, and I discovered why when on television in 1998 with a Dominican friar. He summed up the situation by explaining to the programme host, 'Laurence Gardner comes to this subject as a matter of history and documented record. The Church comes to it as a matter of belief and faith. Do not confuse the two; they are different things.'

Conventional recognition of the book became even more apparent in the year 2000, when it was suggested that the Jesus and Magdalene story should be set to music. In this regard, I was commissioned to write the libretto for a gnostic oratorio based on *Bloodline of the Holy Grail*. The extensive musical score for the work was undertaken by Jaz Coleman, composer in residence for the Prague Symphony Orchestra, and we entitled the two-hour performance *Marriage at Cana*. It premiered at London's Royal Opera House, Covent Garden, in December 2001.

In recent times, the subject of Mary Magdalene and her nuptial relationship with Jesus has reappeared in a new format – that of an internationally bestselling novel, *The Da Vinci Code* by American author Dan Brown. Consequently, I have received an extraordinary number of requests to expand on some of the information contained in *Bloodline of the Holy Grail*. By virtue of Dan Brown's novel, there is now a widespread interest in the pictorial depictions of Mary Magdalene and, since fine art conservation was my field of professional occupation before becoming an author, I have therefore compiled *The Magdalene Legacy* with Renaissance artwork as its primary focus.

This book is not intended to support or challenge *The Da Vinci Code*, but to take up some of its more controversial aspects, and to comment on them where appropriate. Dan Brown's engaging novel is a work of fiction, and should be regarded as such. However, it does include certain historical facts, and introduces some themes that are relevant to the *Bloodline* story.

As with all the works in this Grail-related series, *The Magdalene Legacy* has been designed as a stand-alone edition, and it is in no way necessary to have read any of the other books first.

Laurence Gardner
Exeter 2005

Saint or Sinner?

The First Lady

In the New Testament Gospels, various female companions of Jesus are cited on seven occasions.[1] In six of these lists, Mary Magdalene is the first named. The seventh entry gives Jesus' mother as first in the ranking,[2] and elsewhere Mary Magdalene is featured alone.[3] In her relationship with Jesus, she is introduced as a woman who 'ministered unto him',[4] and she makes her final Gospel appearance as the first person to speak with Jesus after his Resurrection at the tomb.[5]

In the literature of the early Christian era, it is plain that Mary Magdalene held a special place in the life of Jesus and in the hearts of his followers. In later times, however, the Church bishops decided that Mary must have been a whore. Ostensibly this was because one of the biblical references classifies her as 'a sinner'.[6] This, in the minds of the bishops, signified a woman of loose virtue. But in the very next Gospel verse, Mary is said to have been a woman of substance and one of Jesus' personal sponsors.

Later in the Gospel accounts, Mary Magdalene is seen as a close companion of Jesus' mother, accompanying her at the

Crucifixion. Prior to that it is stated that Jesus loved Mary.[7] So, for what possible reason did the Church of Rome turn against this devoted woman, vilifying her name for centuries? Did the bishops really believe that a female sinner must necessarily be a whore, or was this simply an excuse related to something else they preferred to conceal?

In the following pages, we shall consider the overall legacy of Mary Magdalene – her biblical portrayals, her appearances in non-canonical Gospels, her life as it was recorded by chroniclers, her clerical and academic status, her depictions in the world of fine art, and her relevance in the world today.

Mary's position is in many ways unique in that, despite her apparent supportive role in the Christian story, she emerges as one of its primary figures. As stated in some of the Gospels that were excluded from the New Testament, Mary Magdalene was 'the woman who knew the all' of Jesus. She was the one whom 'Christ loved more than all the disciples', and she was the apostle 'endowed with knowledge, vision and insight far exceeding Peter's'.

Restoration

My first personal close encounter with Mary Magdalene occurred in the 1980s. I was then running a picture restoration studio, and was a conservation consultant for the Fine Art Trade Guild in London. A painting entitled *Penitent Magdalene* came in for cleaning and repair – an 18th-century Italian work from the Bologna school of Franceschini

Marcantonio. In a past restoration attempt, it had been crudely stuck (lined) onto a secondary canvas from which it had to be removed (*see* plates 3 & 4).

As part of a picture preservation course I was running at the time, I wrote up the details of this particular restoration in the Guild *Journal*. But, at that stage, my interests were in the physical aspects of the restoration procedure, rather than in the subject matter of the painting. It was not until later, when I was inspecting photographs of the completed work, that I began to wonder about certain features of the image itself. The Magdalene was portrayed with jewellery and a mirror, and yet was entitled *Penitent Magdalene*, which seemed rather incongruous. Holding her hair with one hand, and a pearl earring with the other, she looked content enough, and there was nothing to convey that she was in any way repentant. So, why the title?

What I discovered, on checking the painting's provenance, was that its documented title, *Penitent Magdalene*, was rather more a genre classification than a title given to it by the artist. To him, it had simply been a stylized portrait of Mary Magdalene.

Genre categories are common in the world of pictorial art since, although artists often signed or personalized their paintings, they did not normally write titles on them. Romantic titles were generally attributed later by owners, galleries and dealers – titles which the artists would perhaps never have known in their lifetimes. The *Mona Lisa*, by Leonardo da Vinci, is a good example. She is known by that name in the English-speaking world, but is known in France (where she hangs in The Louvre) as *La Joconde*, and in Italy as *La Gioconda*. (We shall return later to this fascinating Renaissance masterpiece.) Another more recent example is James AM Whistler's painting, entitled by him *Arrangement in Grey and Black*, but which since his death has become commonly dubbed *Whistler's Mother*.

Paintings of Jesus fall into a series of familiar categories, and not too often outside them. They begin with 'The Nativity', which sub-divides into such themes as 'Adoration of the Shepherds' and 'Adoration of the Magi'. They continue with 'Madonna and Child' portraits and scenes of 'The Rest on the Flight to Egypt'. Then there are depictions of Jesus' 'Presentation in the Temple', followed by various other high-point scenes throughout his ministry to the Crucifixion, Resurrection and subsequent Ascension.

A number of romantic portrayals exist too, such as Jesus with his lantern in William Holman Hunt's *The Light of the World* (1853), and John Spencer Stanhope's *The Wine Press* (1864). But such paintings are still firmly based on Gospel tradition: 'I am the light of the world' (John 8:12) and 'I am the true vine' (John 15:1). The great majority of Christine depictions are related to recognizable Gospel events, but with Mary Magdalene the scenario is different. Many of the popular subject areas depicting her have nothing whatever to do with any events related in the New Testament, and among these is the enigmatic 'Penitent' classification.

A majority of religious artists painted or drew Mary Magdalene at some stage, and she appears frequently in sculpture, stained glass and other media. She is, in fact, one of the most depicted of all classical figures. There are numerous portrayals of her at the cross and at the tomb, with a favoured scene of Magdalene and Jesus being the *Noli me tangere* ('Do not cling to me') drama from John 20:17.[8] In addition, images of the Penitent or Repentant Magdalene abound, even though they are quite unrelated to Mary's appearances in the Bible. In these scenes, she is generally alone at a dressing table, or in the solitude of a wilderness grotto. The recurring props of these scenes include a mirror, a candle, jewellery, a skull and a book.

Jewellery and mirrors were made popular during the 17th-century baroque era and the Italian school of Luca Giordano. They were introduced to symbolize Mary's renouncement of earthly vanities. In opposition to vanity, the candle and book represent the importance of light and knowledge, and the skull (*see* plate 2) is synonymous with the inevitability of death.

The most favoured and constant item in Magdalene art-work – the object that makes her personally distinctive, especially when seen in the company of other women – is an ointment jar. Mark 16:1 explains that when Mary Magdalene arrived with others at Jesus' tomb, they 'brought sweet spices, that they might come and anoint him', but the jar does not relate to that scene in particular. It is essentially pertinent to the most poignant of all events, when Mary anointed the head and feet of Jesus at the house of Simon in Bethany, shortly before the Crucifixion.

Despite all historical convention, and notwithstanding popular tradition from the earliest times, the Church of Rome long maintained that Mary Magdalene, the sinner, was not the same person as the Mary who performed the anointing. They insisted that Jesus would never have been anointed by a sinner. There were, however, two different anointings. These will be referenced in due course but, to counter that particular clerical opinion for the time being, the first anointing (Luke 7:37–38) is clearly stated to have been performed by the 'sinner' at the house of Simon the Pharisee.

When dealing with the second anointing of Jesus at the house of Simon the leper, John 11:2 stipulates just as emphatically that it was done by the same woman as before. Simon the Pharisee and Simon the leper were one and the same, but, more importantly, so were Mary the sinner and Mary of Bethany. Pope Gregory I (590–604) had argued this; artists and chroniclers were always convinced of it and, finally, *The Catholic Encyclopedia*[9] acknowledged the fact in 1910.

In artwork, therefore, the alabaster ointment jar has been Mary's constant symbol of recognition, and it has been used by artists in whatever circumstances of her portrayal. It appears with her at the cross and at the tomb, sometimes in her penitent solitude, generally in paintings of Mary with Martha of Bethany, and always in representations of the Messianic anointings.

The key artistic genre classifications for Mary Magdalene are, therefore: 'At the foot of the Cross' (including the 'Deposition' scene), 'At the Tomb' (including the 'Lamentation' and 'Resurrection' sequences along with *'Noli me tangere'*), and the earlier anointing rituals which are generally grouped as 'At the House of Simon'. There are also many straightforward portraits, which fall into a category known as 'The Alabaster Jar', while another favourite is 'Jesus at the House of Martha'. In addition, and equally prolific, are the non-biblical Penitent and Repentant depictions. But there are others, which similarly have nothing to do with the canonical Gospels. Among these groupings are 'Mary Magdalene in Provence' and 'Magdalene carried by the Angels', along with various imaginary scenes of 'Mary Magdalene and Jesus'. There are some alternative classifications (often allegorical) but in essence we are looking at around a dozen or so subject themes for thousands of individual representations.

Mary Magdalene eventually made her saintly appearance in the Church Calendar as recently as 1969, with a feast day on 22 July. This feast day had actually been acknowledged in the West since the 8th century, and there are 187 ancient church dedications to her in England alone.[10] Yet it was not until the late 20th century that her canonical status was formalized, although the Roman Missal (which determines Latin Rite liturgy) still rejects the fact that Mary Magdalene and Mary of Bethany are synonymous.

The 1969 amendment to Mary's canonical status was based on the presumption of her repentance – a penitence that was deemed to have prevailed for long enough. Apparently, she repented for having been a prostitute, but nowhere in any scriptural text did it ever say that Mary was a prostitute. So we come back to the question posed earlier: Why did the Church elect to demean Mary Magdalene in the first place? Something about her presence in the life of Jesus obviously bothered the bishops greatly. As we shall discover, this was indeed the case, but it was only bothersome because the Church had been designed as a celibacy-based, male prerogative institution. This, in turn, was specifically because of a Magdalene influence that somehow threatened to undermine a hybrid Christianity.

Seven Devils

To substantiate their maligning of Mary, and to place her in an apparent state of repentance for wantonness, the clerics associated her with another Gospel character with whom she had no relationship whatever. It was felt necessary to have an explainable transition of some sort from Mary the sinner to Mary the companion of Jesus' mother. The only acceptable way for this to have occurred was if Jesus had forgiven Mary Magdalene for her shameful sin. In this regard, there was a conveniently unnamed woman whom Jesus did forgive for loose behaviour, and so Mary was identified with her. She was the woman who, in John 8:1–11, was 'taken in adultery', and whom Jesus did not condemn, but bade her 'go, and sin no more'. There was not the slightest connection between Mary Magdalene and this woman, but the strategy was considered good enough and Mary, the supposed adulteress, was said to have repented.

A further association between this woman and Mary Magdalene was made by virtue of the sequence in Luke 7:37–49 when a sinful woman anointed Jesus' feet at the house of Simon the Pharisee. The Gospel relates that Jesus said to her, 'Thy sins are forgiven'. But, as we have seen, the Gospel of John states that Mary of Bethany and the woman who performed this first anointing were one and the same. Hence, in setting up the fabricated 'penitent' state for Mary

Magdalene, the Church did indeed acknowledge that Mary Magdalene was Mary of Bethany. What makes no sense at all is that, in every other respect, the bishops denied this association, notwithstanding its positive clarification in John.

Now things have taken an even stranger turn and, since April 1969 when Mary Magdalene's sainthood was formalized, the Missal determines that there were three separate Marys: Mary the sinner, Mary of Bethany and Mary Magdalene. So the woman they canonized was not, in practice, the 'penitent' Mary after all! This, of course, begs the question: Why then is Mary Magdalene listed as the patron saint of repentant sinners?

The 1969 action now brings the Western Church of Rome into line with the Eastern (Byzantine) Orthodox Church, which has long maintained that there were three Marys. But, if that were the case, it is curious that just about every Magdalene icon of the Eastern Church depicts Mary holding the alabaster ointment jar. This is, in fact, contrary to Eastern doctrine since it clearly implies that Mary Magdalene and Mary of Bethany were identical.

What do Protestant Christians think in this regard? It all depends on which of the many Protestant branches one asks. In fact, the whole thing has got into a dreadful tangle, with Catholics and Protestants alike now more confused than ever. This is all because Mary Magdalene poses such a problem that, whatever doctrinal strategies are imposed to manipulate her position, they all self-destruct because she cannot be fitted into a box where she does not belong. Neither can she be ignored because the Gospels make her involvement with Jesus and his family perfectly clear.

Despite all the attempts to dub Mary with a whoredom that has no foundation, there is only one comment in the Gospels concerning her supposed sin. It is given at her introduction in Luke 8:2, and is repeated in the Resurrection sequence of Mark 16:9. All that is said is: a) Mary was a 'woman out of whom went seven devils', and b) she was a woman 'out of whom he [Jesus] had cast seven devils'. That is the extent of it. There is nothing related to adultery or prostitution. So, what did it mean? Who or what were the seven devils?

In the year 591, Pope Gregory I gave an historic sermon which included references to Mary Magdalene. It was in this address that he confirmed Mary the sinner and Mary of Bethany to be one and the same, as detailed in John 11:2. But in the course of this, he also tackled the subject of the 'seven devils', coming to the conclusion that they represented the seven Capital Sins (the 'deadly vices' as they are more commonly called). Mary was guilty, he intimated, of pride, envy, gluttony, lust, anger, greed and sloth – all seven! It is a wonder that she ever recovered, and just as well that Gregory did not accuse her of the Mortal Sins as well!

In taking a clear look at the subject of the seven devils, the first thing to consider is the community relevance of the Greek name 'Mary' (from the Egyptian, Mery, meaning 'beloved', and seemingly equivalent to the Hebrew, Miriam). Similar Egyptian names include Meryamon (Beloved of Amon) and Merytaten (Beloved of Aten). Other European variations of Mary are Marie and Maria.

In the Gospel era, as in the Greco-Egyptian culture, 'Mary' was not so much a name as a distinction. This is why there were a number of Marys associated with Jesus. Although nominally apparent in the New Testament, the non-canonical *Gospel of Philip* makes particular mention of this: 'There were three who always walked with the Lord … his sister and his mother and his consort were each a Mary'.[11] The name was a conventual style of the era, and is still used by many nuns in convents today, placed before their baptismal names to become Sister Mary Louise, Sister Mary Theresa and the like. Mark 6:3, for example, is generally presented with Jesus as the 'son of Mary', but when correctly translated it reads, 'son of the Mary'.

Marys were raised in a chaste monastic environment within specific holy orders, and they were subject to strict regulations that applied until they were chosen to be betrothed. Prior to this, Marys were under the authority of the Chief Scribe, who was classified as the Demon Priest Number 7. Ranking in seniority from Number 1 upwards, the seven demon priests were established as a symbolic opposition group to those priests who were considered to represent the seven lights of the Menorah (the seven-branched candlestick of Jewish tradition). It was the duty of the seven demon priests to supervise and keep watch on the female celibates – just like the Devil's Advocate, who probes the background of potential candidates for canonization in the Roman Catholic Church today. Upon marriage, however, the women were released from the charge of the seven demons (or devils), which meant in effect that the rules of celibacy no longer applied.[12] What we glean from this is that, when the seven devils 'went out' of Mary Magdalene, she was being released from conventual ties in order to marry.

Magdalene Heritage

While on the subject of names, we should also look at the name Magdalene. It is sometimes spelt Magdalen, and has the European variants Maddalena and Madeleine. It is commonly suggested that Magdalene derives from the place name Magdala, and they do indeed have the same root in *migdal*, meaning 'tower'. But this is not reason enough to determine that Mary came from Magdala. We are told only that she joined the ministry of Jesus in Galilee (roughly speaking, the region north of modern Haifa).

Magdala was a fishing town on the Sea of Galilee, just north of Tiberius. Noted also for its flax weaving and dyeing, Magdala was a wealthy, bustling trade centre in Gospel times. It is mentioned in Matthew 15:39, although it is rendered in some Bible editions as Magadan. But in the older Gospel of Mark 8:10, the place name Dalmanutha is used in this context.[13] There are no ruins of any real significance there today, just scraps of a paved road, the remains of some Roman baths, and a building foundation. The impoverished site is now known as el-Medjel.

Magdala was a centre for processing fish as well as for fishing, and the Jewish *Talmud* uses the longer, more correct name, Magdal Nunaiya, meaning 'Fish Tower'. The historian Flavius Josephus was Commander of Galilee during the unsuccessful Jewish Revolt against the Romans in AD 66, and he wrote of Magdala using the alternative Greek name Taricheae. In his 1st-century *Wars of the Jews*, Josephus recorded that around 40,000 people lived there at that time.[14]

Subsequently, he related, about 6,500 of them were slaughtered in the great land and sea battles that ensued against the Roman troops of General Flavius Titus.[15]

As with Magdal Nunaiya, many other Gospel locations are cited with different names. This can lead to confusion at times, but arose by virtue of a multicultural linguistic tradition with places named in Hebrew, Greek, Syrian, Latin, or even by way of descriptive local custom. In Matthew, Mark and John, for example, the Crucifixion site is named as Golgotha, whereas in Luke it is given as Calvary. Both names (Hebrew, *Gulgoleth;* Aramaic, *Gulgolta;* Latin, *Calvaria*) derive from words that mean 'skull', and the meaning of the place name, as given in all the Gospels, is straightforward: 'a place of a skull'.

The Sea of Galilee was originally called Chinneroth (Hebrew: 'lyre shaped') as in Joshua 11:2. It was also called the Lake of Gennesaret (Luke 5:1), and the Sea of Tiberius (John 2:1) from which its modern name, Bahr Tubarîya, derives.[16]

Although the Palestinian regions of Galilee, Samaria and Judaea were under Roman occupation in Gospel times, previously they had been subject to controls from Egypt, where the Greek pharaohs of the Ptolemaic dynasties, down to Queen Cleopatra VII, had reigned from 305 to 30 BC. Greek was, therefore, very much a language used in Jesus' time, along with a version of old Mesopotamian Aramaic and, of course, Hebrew. Flavius Josephus was a Hasmonaean Jew, trained for the Pharisee priesthood, but he often used Greek terminology, and Greek was the language of the original Gospel texts. There is little doubt, however, that the Magdalene name had its origin (as did Magdala) in the Hebrew word *migdal* (meaning tower or castle).

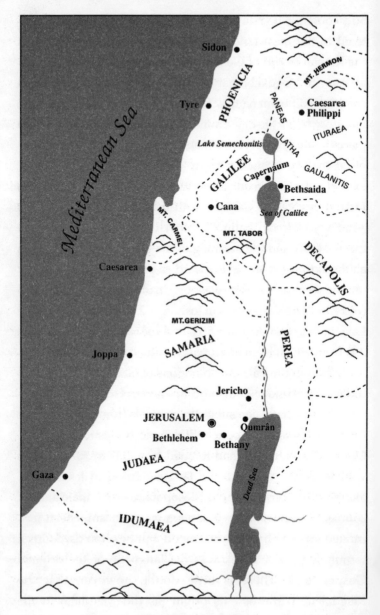

The Gospel Lands

When Jacapo di Voragine,[17] 13th-century Archbishop of Genoa, wrote up the *Life of Mary Magdalene* from Church records,[18] he stated that Mary 'possessed the heritage of the castle of Bethany' – or the tower (*migdal*) of Bethany as it should be more correctly translated. But there never was any significant castle or tower at Bethany, and, in any event, titular Marys were not allowed to own property.[19] The heritage described by Jacapo actually related to personal status – a high community station (castle/tower) of community guardianship, as in Micah 4:8, the *Magdal-eder* (Watchtower of the flock) – and it is to this social position that the Magdalene distinction refers.[20] Thus it is significant that, at Mary's introduction in Luke 8:2, she is described as 'Mary, called Magdalene' – that is, 'Mary, called the Watchtower'.

Rather than coming from Magdala, the more likely Galilean home of Mary Magdalene was the nearby coastal town of Capernaum, where Jesus began his early ministry.[21] The great marble synagogue at Capernaum (which still exits as an impressive ruin) was the province of the Jairus priests in dynastic descent from Ira the Jairite, a chief priest of King David.[22] This priestly line originated with the Old Testament sons of Jair[23] in the time of Moses.

According to Jacapo (1229–1298), Mary Magdalene's father was called Syro (or Syrus). As Syro the Jairus, he was the Chief Priest (subordinate to the Jerusalem High Priest), and Mary makes her first biblical appearance as the daughter of the Jairus, whom Jesus raised from death in Matthew 9:18–25.[24] This form of initiatory raising from figurative 'death' (darkness) into the degree of community 'life' (light)

15

was part of an ongoing instructional process called The Way, and was performed at the age of twelve. In the Jairus' daughter sequence, Mark 5:42 confirms this, stating: 'And straightway the damsel arose, and walked; for she was of the age of twelve years'.

Jacapo further explains that Syro was a Syrian nobleman, whose wife Eucharia (Mary's mother) was of royal kindred. He further states that the Magdalene 'was born of right noble lineage, and parents which were descended of the lineage of kings'. In a much earlier manuscript of Archbishop Rabanus Maurus, Eucharia is more fully detailed as a descendant of the Royal House of Israel.[25] That was not the Davidic House of Judah, but the priestly Hasmonaean House of the Maccabees,[26] who reigned in Jerusalem from 166 BC until the Roman occupation from 63 BC under General Pompeii.

Academia

The work of Jacapo di Voragine, entitled *La Légende de Sainte Marie Madeleine*, exists within his greater compilation, the famous *Légenda Aurea* (Golden Legend). Two centuries after the author's death, this was one of the earliest books printed at Westminster, London, by William Caxton in 1483. Previously published in French and Latin, Caxton was persuaded by William, Earl of Arundel, to produce an English version translated from the European manuscripts. It is a collection of archival chronicles detailing the lives of selected saintly figures, and was highly venerated in religious society. Notwithstanding the more general undermining of

Mary Magdalene's community status by the bishops, the work was given public readings on a regular basis in medieval monasteries and in some churches.

The Benedictine scholar, Rabanus Maurus (776–856), was Archbishop of Mayence (Mainz) and Abbé of Fulda, the greatest seat of learning in the Frankish Empire in the days of Charlemagne. Rabanus was renowned as the most learned sage of the era, and it was said that, in matters of scriptural knowledge, canon law and liturgy, he had no equal.[27] His great work, *The Life of Saint Mary Magdalene*, was composed as fifty chapters, bound into six volumes of richly illuminated manuscript. It incorporated much that was held on record about Mary back in the 4th century when the Church of Rome was founded by Emperor Constantine to supersede the earlier form of Nazarene Christianity. The book begins:

> The contemplative life of the most blessed
> Mary Magdalene, named with the highest
> reverence as the sweetest chosen of
> Christ, and by Christ greatly beloved.

In the early 1400s, a monastic copy of the Rabanus manuscript was discovered in England at Oxford University. A few years later, in 1448, Magdalen Hall – now Magdalen College – was founded at the University by William of Waynflete, Bishop of Winchester and Chancellor of England for King Henry VI. Dedicated to Mary, the College was among the first to teach science, and the *Magdalene* manuscript is still held there today.

Earlier, the Rabanus work had been referenced in the *Chronica Majora* of Matthew Paris (*Matthaei Parisiensis*).[28] He was a monk at the Abbey of St Albans who collated the writings of his Abbot, John de Celia, from around 1190. The Rabanus manuscript is also listed in the *Scriptorum Ecclesiasticorum Historia literaria Basilae*[29] at Oxford.

In the 1470s, shortly after the Magdalen foundation at Oxford, an educational hostel for Benedictine monks at Cambridge was rebuilt under the patronage of Henry Stafford, Duke of Buckingham, to become Buckingham College. Subsequently, lay students were admitted as well as monks. Then, in Tudor times, the College came into the possession of Thomas, Lord Audley, as a result of Henry VIII's Dissolution of the Monasteries. He dedicated the College to Mary as The College of Saint Mary Magdalene in 1542. At that stage, Lord Audley contrived a way to differentiate, in audible terms, between his College and that of its sister institution at Oxford. By introducing his own name into the equation, he decided that the Magdalene College at Cambridge should be pronounced 'Maudleyn', and the tradition prevails to this day.[30]

In phonetic terms, there was an earlier precedent for the nominal corruption in that Mary had previously appeared as Mary Mawdelyn in *The Book of Margery Kempe* (1438) – 'Have mend, dowter, what Mary Mawdelyn was, Mary Eypcyan, Seynt Powyl, and many other seynts that arn now in hevyn'. Well known to Lord Audley, this spiritual diary of a Norfolk visionary is reputed to be the first published autobiography in English. Despite the author's illiteracy, for which the book subsequently attracted much criticism, it is a fascinating record of life in turbulent 15th-century England.[31]

And so, quite apart from England's numerous Mary Magdalene churches, the nation also boasts colleges dedicated to her at both Oxford and Cambridge universities. There is no doubt that, while the Church of Rome was doing its best to sideline Mary Magdalene, if not to blacken her name entirely, she was greatly revered in England's monastic circles – from the Benedictines of Oxford to their brothers in St Albans.

It was much the same in France, where Rabanus Maurus was a Benedictine abbot, while in Italy Jacapo di Voragine was a Dominican. Even earlier, when the French Cistercian abbot, Bernard de Clairvaux, formalized the Order of the Knights Templars at the Council of Troyes in 1129, he instituted their Oath of Allegiance to Mary Magdalene. The French King Louis XI (1461–83) was insistent about Mary Magdalene's dynastic position in the royal lineage of France, and a particularly informative work entitled *Sainte Marie Madeleine* was produced by the Dominican friar, Père Lacordaire, soon after the French Revolution.[32]

It is against this background that we need to ask why the monastic scholars were at odds with the ecclesiastical clerics in their enthusiasm over Mary Magdalene. The answer is straightforward: the monks were academics and, although dealing with an ostensibly religious subject, their concerns were about documented record. The bishops, on the other hand, were concerned only with religious doctrine and, since they determined the doctrine, historical record was not a matter of importance for them. In fact, they endeavoured to force their doctrine on people by way of compulsory dogma when the *Congregatio Propaganda Fide* (Congregation for the Propagation of the Faith) was introduced by Pope Gregory XV in 1662. He established the College of the Propaganda of Cardinals, whose job it was to compel compliance with Church teaching. In this regard, the Church not only used propaganda, but also invented the word from a Church Latin root (*propagare:* to multiply) as in the propagation of plants – 'breeding cloned or like specimens from a parent stock'.

Fear and Trepidation

Where then does Mary Magdalene stand personally in all this? Was she truly important to the life and mission of Jesus, or was she just an incidental character?

From the Gospels, we gather that Mary was a constant companion and sponsor of Jesus. She anointed him with spikenard oil on two separate occasions, and had a close relationship with his mother and sisters. She supported them at the Crucifixion and went with them to Jesus' tomb, where she was the first to speak with Jesus after his Resurrection.

There is nothing remotely untoward or controversial in any of this. Indeed Mary's loyalty to Jesus and his family far outweighed that of the unpredictable Peter and other seemingly erratic apostles. She was a woman, of course, but that was not sufficient in itself to warrant the posthumous assaults on her by the Church. Jesus' mother was also a woman, and yet she became venerated. Apparently, there was far more to Mary Magdalene than is immediately obvious – something which left the bishops in fear and trepidation of her legacy.

Readers of Dan Brown's bestselling novel, *The Da Vinci Code*, will know that his plot reveals Mary Magdalene not just as a beloved companion of Jesus, but as his wife. Also that they had a child and descendants – a secret that was said to have been guarded for centuries, to the present day, by an underground society of trusted initiates.

Some years ago, I introduced and discussed the subject of Jesus' marriage and offspring in *Bloodline of the Holy Grail*,[33] but not to the extent of there being any secrets that were unknown to the Church. Logically, that aspect of the *Da Vinci Code* does not hold up if considered as fact rather than novelistic fiction. If the bishops had not known about Mary Magdalene's nuptial relationship with Jesus and her resultant motherhood, they would have had no reason whatever to vilify her memory. Like so many others, she would have remained an important, but incidental, character in the Christian story.

Yes, there were indeed historically supportive groups who championed the legacy of the Magdalene, but little of this was ever secret. Mary Magdalene posed a considerable threat to the Church. The bishops knew it, the monks knew it, organizations such as the Templars knew it, and many people at large knew it. The fact is that one does not need to access conspiratorial records or secret society archives to discover the truth of Mary Magdalene. Her story has long been in the public domain, and we can learn a great deal more about her by taking a closer look at the New Testament Gospels themselves.

Persecution

Towards Oblivion

In 1964, Pope Paul VI released an eminent Vatican professor from his vows of poverty and obedience in the Jesuit Order. Prior to that, the priest had been instrumental at the Pontifical Biblical Institute, also at the Pontifical Council for Promoting Christian Unity under the presidency of Cardinal Augustin Bea. He had previously studied at Oxford University and at the Hebrew University in Jerusalem, with doctorates in Semitic languages, archaeology and oriental history. From 1958, he had served the Holy See at the Vatican alongside Pope John XXIII. He was established, respected, and had some thirty years of loyal Church service behind him. But, in 1964, he resigned from a top position in Rome and went to live in New York, where he died in 1999. His name was Father Malachi Martin, and his resignation was prompted by a schism that had taken more than 1,600 years to surface.

From that day in AD 312 when Emperor Constantine saw the sign of a cross in the sky and decided to remodel Christianity as a Roman hybrid religion, his Church has lived with a constant dilemma: to what extent should it serve people's spiritual needs and to what extent should it be involved with the power and politics of secular life? Was the institution concerned with serving souls, or was it intent on ruling the Western world? From the very outset, there were those in Church ranks who would have answered either way, and so an internal conflict existed from the moment of its inauguration.

In 1958, when Father Martin took his position at the Vatican, Angelo Roncalli, Cardinal and Patriarch of Venice, became the Bishop of Rome as Pope John XXIII. Following the death of Pius XII, John was expected to be a transitional Pope, but he made his mark very quickly as a social reformer. He expanded and internationalized the College of Cardinals, called the first diocesan Synod of Rome in history, revised the code of Canon Law, and called the Second Vatican Council to revitalize the Church. Pope John was a liberal and a liberator, and the sweeping changes that he made were as profound as Constantine's act of creating the Church in the first place. In taking such measures, however, John set the old schism on its head – right from the top. As the Pope, he *was* the Church, and his message rang out loud and clear. He was interested in spiritual service, not in secular power.

This was welcome and refreshing news for many but, while granting greater freedoms to the people, Pope John's measures had the effect of demolishing the supreme authority of the Church and many of its long-held doctrines. Catholics at large, including numerous priests, abandoned their beliefs in such concepts as Original Sin and the Devil. Priests wanted to be married; women wanted to become priests; bishops wanted to become regional popes; people claimed the acceptable rights of birth control and divorce. Meanwhile, as the Bishop of Rome, John was unremitting in the attendance of his diocese, visiting hospitals, prisons and schools – acting as no other Pope had ever done before. He was certainly popular with the people, but he was equally unpopular with elements of a Church hierarchy that was fast losing its power base under his command.

Pope John XXIII died in 1963. Many were desperately sad at this, while others breathed a sigh of relief – but for them it was too late. The damage (as it appeared to them) had been done and the Church of Rome would never be the same again. Its dogmatic authority was now in severe decline. When Giovanni Montini, Archbishop of Milan, succeeded in 1964 as Pope Paul VI, he said, 'The Devil has entered the Church; there is smoke around the altar'. He tried, but could do nothing to stem the onslaught of public and clerical pressure for continued reform.

It was at this stage that Father Malachi Martin, having witnessed such a major turn of events from within the Vatican, elected to sever his ties. The period of his Vatican service, from 1958 to 1964, saw one of the greatest turning points in all religious history. Martin had been in a unique position throughout this, having been party to the transitional debates. He knew that someone had to write about this monumental era for posterity, and he was the very man to do it – but he could not do so from a perspective of objectivity while in continued employment within the Vatican.

And so, in 1964, he retired to become a writer. His resultant works are brilliant expositions of the Church and its leaders from the earliest times, and he announced that, in weighing all the probabilities and consequences, the Church as we know it has now begun its downward slide towards eventual obscurity.

Heirs of the Lord

In relating the history of the Church from the inside out, Martin made it very clear that the hierarchy has long maintained a privileged position in terms of knowledge acquisition by way of an intelligence network. Because of this, nothing relevant to the Church has ever been a secret to the Church. Alternatively, many of its own secrets were not broadcast unless this became a doctrinal requirement. In this regard, Father Martin let loose a Greek word which had been logged in Imperial records before the Roman Church ever came into being. The word was *Desposyni*.

As has since been discovered, the word was always in the public domain, but not in a way that most people could understand it, even if they did happen to study the appropriate documents. *Desposyni* was the most hallowed of distinctions in early Christian times, and for a good while thereafter. It meant 'Heirs of the Lord' and, as Father Martin explained, 'it was reserved uniquely for Jesus' blood relatives'. He further qualified this by saying that 'only those persons in the bloodline with Jesus through his mother qualified as *Desposyni*'.[1]

Jesus, we are told in the Gospels, was of the House of Judah, and of the royal lineage of King David, who reigned in Jerusalem around 1000 BC. Both Matthew and Luke give Jesus' generational descent in the male line, down to his father Joseph.[2] Matthew opens with: 'The book of the generations of Jesus Christ, the son of David, the Son of Abraham', and follows through each ancestor to conclude with 'And Jacob begat Joseph the husband of Mary, to whom was born Jesus, who is called Christ'. The corresponding genealogical item in Luke traces the ancestry in reverse, going way back beyond Abraham, to finish with '… Enos, which was the son of Seth, which was the son of Adam, which was the son of God'.

It is essentially from the Luke listing that Jesus became personally defined as the 'son of God'. Matthew states that Jesus was the 'son of David', which he was not in the literal sense. It was a symbolic definition to determine his House of lineage. However, tracing further back, Luke maintains that the ultimate ancestor of Jesus and David was Adam, who was the 'son of God'. With due genealogical licence therefore, and based on the symbolic concept of Matthew, it is fair to say that, in the same manner, Jesus could be called the 'son of God'.

In the book, *Lost Secrets of the Sacred Ark*, I discussed the various biblical references with regard to the 'Son of God' entries in respect of Jesus. I have included this item again as Appendix I of this work for the benefit of new readers. More relevant at this particular stage, however, is our pursuance of the *Desposyni* inheritors.

The *Desposyni* definition, as we have seen, is specifically confined to those in Jesus' lineage via his mother, Mary. In tracing the earliest use of this word, we find that it was not used until after the Crucifixion, Resurrection and Ascension of Jesus. This makes sense given that the word relates to the 'heirs of' or those 'belonging to' the Lord.

If, as according to the Matthew and Luke lists, Jesus was the royal heir to the House of David, then the senior dynastic succession of that House would terminate with Jesus, unless of course he had a son. But, in AD 70, when the Romans finally crushed the four-year Israelite uprising against them, it appears that Emperor Vespasian still had a problem with the House of David. This was close to forty years after the crucifixion of Jesus. In the writings of the 2nd-century Palestinian chronicler Hegesippus, we read that Vespasian commanded 'the family of David to be sought, that no one might be left among the Jews who was of the royal stock'.[3] In one way or another, therefore, the family of David was known to be extant at that time in AD 70. The edict does not refer, however, to every living descendant of David (even if it had been possible to tell who they were). It specifically defines 'the family' and 'the royal stock', which narrows the field considerably.

The first definable use of the word *Desposyni* seems to come from a contemporary of Hegesippus – the historian, Julius Africanus of Edessa. He is generally regarded as the father of Christian chronography, and made his reputation by translating into Latin a series of works by the 1st-century disciple Abdias, the Nazarene Bishop of Babylon, installed by Jesus' brother Jude. The *Books of Abdias* amounted to ten volumes of first-hand apostolic history, entitled *Historia Certaminis Apostolici*. However, like so many other important eyewitness accounts of the era, his books were rejected out-right for inclusion in Emperor Constantine's New Testament in the 4th century. Abdias is recorded as one of the seventy-two disciples of Jesus referred to in Luke 9:57–10:1.[4]

Africanus related that, even before Vespasian, during the lifetime of Jesus, Herod-Antipas (son of Herod the Great) had ordered the destruction of all aristocratic genealogies. But, Africanus continues, 'A few careful people had private records of their own ... and took a pride in preserving the memory of their aristocratic origin. These include the people ... known as *Desposyni* because of their relationship to the Saviour's family'.[5]

Succeeding Vespasian was his son Titus, whose brother Domitian followed in AD 81. Domitian detested the Christians even more than his father had done, and his regime of persecution was as cruel as it had been in the days of Emperor Nero, who had executed Peter and Paul. According to the Roman annals, a favoured torture of Nero was to tie Christians to stakes in his palace gardens, and to fire them as human torches at night.[6] It was in Domitian's reign that St John the Divine, author of *The Revelation*, was sentenced to confinement on the Greek island of Patmos.[7]

Hegesippus reported in his *Hypomnenata* (Memoirs) that Domitian ordered the execution of all the *Desposyni* inheritors of Jesus. But, although many were seized, some were released and 'on their release they became leaders of the churches, both because they had borne testimony and because they were of the Lord's family'.[8] From Patmos, John wrote about this in his *Apocalypse*. In relating the persecution of the *Desposyni*, he explained how a woman who bore the crown of Sophia had fled into the wilderness to escape the Imperial dragon that 'went to make war with the remnant of her seed, which keep the commandments of God, and have the testimony of Jesus Christ'.[9]

In the Christian tradition of the era, Sophia (the Greek goddess of wisdom), who wore the crown of twelve stars described in *The Revelation*, was represented by Mary Magdalene, who had fled into exile in AD 44 (*see* page 222). This exile followed the seizure of Peter and the execution of the apostle James Boanerges by King Herod-Agrippa I of Jerusalem (Acts 12:1–2). The king's advisers had decreed that the Christian movement was subversive and would lead to the overthrow of secular and Temple authority – but soon afterwards Herod-Agrippa was murdered by poisoning.[10]

In fear of retribution (having been implicated in the assassination), other apostles fled from Judaea at that time. Peter and Simon Zelotes escaped, but Thaddaeus was not so fortunate. He was caught by Herod, King of Chalcis (in Syria), at the River Jordan and was summarily executed. Mary Magdalene appealed for protection from young Herod-Agrippa II (then aged 17 and a one-time student of St Paul). He duly arranged her passage to the Herodian estate in Gaul (France), where Herod-Archelaus (brother of Herod-Antipas) had been exiled in AD 39. The Herodian land was at Vienne, near Lyon, to the north of Marseilles. Writing very soon after the event, Flavius Josephus recorded that the Romans had retired Herod-Archelaus to this place following the kingly accession of his nephew Herod-Agrippa I.[11]

As we shall see, these historical events tie in precisely with the Rabanus Maurus account of Mary Magdalene's life.

For now, however, we should consider more of what John wrote in his *Apocalypse* while on Patmos. The word *apocalypse* is Greek and means 'revelation'. Hence, the New Testament book in this regard is known in English as *The Revelation*.

The Revelation

Given that so many books were excluded from the New Testament when the selection was made at the Council of Carthage in AD 397, it is quite remarkable that, of all books, St John's *Apocalypse* escaped close scrutiny at that time. The Church has done its best to put people off this book ever since by portraying it as a sinister work of foreboding and doom. By way of propaganda from the 1662 Congregation for the Propagation of the Faith, even the very word *apocalypse* has become emblematic of disaster. The fact is, however, that John's writing (esoteric as it is in some respects) is precisely what its title conveys. It is a 'revelation'.

In considering John's account of the Magdalene flight into exile, it is appropriate to recognize that prior to discussing the Imperial persecution of 'her seed, which keep the commandments of God, and have the testimony of Jesus Christ', he relates that she was pregnant when she fled: 'And she being with child cried, travailing in birth, and pained to be delivered'.[12]

From time to time, theologians have suggested that this Revelation account perhaps refers to Jesus' mother Mary (rather than the Magdalene). The official Church response, however, is that it could not possibly apply to Jesus' mother because she never 'travailed in birth'. Genesis 3:16 relates that the pains of pregnancy and childbirth were a punishment by God for the fact that Eve had sinned. Consequently, the bishops maintain that the woman of The Revelation 'must have been a sinner'! The wilderness flight of the expectant Magdalene has been allegorically portrayed by artists such as the 17th-century Italian painter Giovanni Lanfranco (*see* plate 11).

In the medieval tradition of France and Flanders, Mary Magdalene was traditionally known as *Notre Dame de Lumière* (Our Lady of Light). In this regard, she was associated with the ultimate wisdom of Sophia, and was sometimes portrayed in early and medieval times wearing Sophia's halo of twelve stars, as referred to by John in the book of The Revelation. A good example is the famous Black Madonna statue at Verviers, near Liège.

Jesus' mother Mary was customarily referred to as the White Madonna, but a particular category of Magdalene portrayal was dubbed 'black'. In some cases these sculpted figures are black all over, but many have only black faces, hands and feet. It is not a question of discolouration, as some clerics have suggested. Neither are the features of the mother and child in any way negroid; they are quite simply black in colour. Some are modestly garbed, but others are displayed with varying degrees of prestige and sovereignty. A statue at Neuilly-sur-Seine is stunning in this regard (*see* plate 6). With a golden crown and sceptre, she wears red and black, along with ermine and *fleur-de-lis* to denote her attachment to the royal line of France.

Black Madonna veneration emanated in AD 44 from Ferrières in the Languedoc region of Provence. There were nearly 200 of these ornamental representations in France by the 16th century, and more than 450 have now been discovered worldwide.

Images of the Black Madonna and her child have presented a constant dilemma for the Church – especially those on display at notable churches and shrines in Europe. A few have been overpainted in pale flesh tones, while a number have simply been removed from the public gaze. She is, nevertheless, black because Wisdom (*Sophia*) is black, having existed in the darkness of Chaos before the Creation. This is explained in a 3rd-century Christian tractate entitled *On the Origin of the World*.[13] Sophia was considered to represent the Holy Spirit which, according to Genesis 1:1, 'moved on the face of the waters' and brought light to the world when 'darkness was upon the face of the deep'.

The early Christian Father, Origen of Alexandria (AD c185–254), equated Mary Magdalene figuratively with the royal bride of the Old Testament *Song of Solomon*, otherwise known as the *Canticle of Canticles*.[14] She states, 'I am black, but comely, O ye daughters of Jerusalem' (*Song* 1:5). This character association was widely upheld as late as the Middle Ages, and was referred to by the 12th-century Bernard de Clairvaux in his *Sermons on the Canticles*. In his Sermon 57, he alluded to Mary Magdalene as the 'Bride of Christ'.[15]

The *Song of Solomon* is a series of love poems concerning a forlorn bride and her husband, the king. In the course of their back-and-forth dialogue, the queen is referred to as a

Shulamite, which provides another Magdalene similarity. The Shulamites were from the Syrian border town of Sölam,[16] and we have seen that Mary's father Syro was from Syria.

The *Song of Solomon* recounts the love contest between King Solomon and his brother Adonijah over the Shulamite noblewoman Abishag, as related in 1 Kings 2:13–25 – a contest which cost Adonijah his life. The details in this Old Testament account are expressly important in understanding the nuptial ceremony of Jesus and Mary Magdalene (*see* page 198).

It was from the Sophia connection that the bishops first identified Mary Magdalene as a whore – not from anything written about her in the Bible. To the Romans, anything connected with the Greeks was lewd. The Roman Empire had taken over from Alexander's, and they maligned the Greek wisdom culture in particular. In this context, they had a constant nickname for goddesses such as Sophia and Aphrodite. The name was *Porne*, which meant whore, harlot or prostitute. If Mary Magdalene was a manifestation of Sophia, then Mary Magdalene was Porne![17]

In referring to Imperial Rome, John's allegorical *Apocalypse* uses the literary device of 'a great red dragon with seven heads ... and seven crowns'.[18] Not only did the Romans display a crimson dragon on their standard, but Rome was itself known as the City of the Seven Kings – the number of crowned heads before the Republic was formed in 509 BC. From 753 BC, these kings were said to have been Romulus, Numa Pompilius, Tullius Hostilius, Ancus Marcius, Lucius Tarquinius Priscus, Servius Tullius and Tarquinius Superbus.[19]

1st-century Roman standard

As Father Malachi Martin made clear from Vatican records, only those in the bloodline of Jesus through his mother qualified as Desposyni. He tells of a particular occasion in ad 318 (also recorded by the contemporary historian, Eusebius of Caesarea) when a Desposyni delegation journeyed to Rome. The men were given audience by Bishop Sylvester at Constantine's newly commissioned Lateran Palace. Through their chief spokesman, Joses, the delegates argued that the Church should rightfully be centred in Jerusalem, not in Rome. They claimed that the Bishop of Jerusalem should be a true hereditary Desposynos, while the bishops of other major centres – such as Alexandria, Antioch and

Ephesus – should be related. After all, they declared, Bishop Clement of Alexandria had written that Jesus' brother James (as the appointed Nazarene Bishop of Jerusalem) was 'the Lord of the Holy Church and the bishop of bishops'. In that respect, their Israelite-Christian movement was of far higher authority than a contrived Roman offshoot centred upon St Peter, who was a mere apostle of the Lord and not a family member.

Not surprisingly, their demands were made in vain, for Sylvester (ostensibly, the first Pope) was hardly in a position to countermand the decrees of the emperor. The teachings of Jesus had been superseded, he said, by a doctrine more amenable to Imperial requirement, and he informed the men that the power of salvation no longer rested in Jesus, but in Emperor Constantine.[20]

For centuries since the first Roman emperor, Augustus in 44 BC, the emperors had been afforded a particular reverence as deities on Earth. They were treated like gods, and regarded themselves as such. In addition to this, Emperor Constantine had claimed a personal Messianic privilege.

After the meeting between Bishop Sylvester and the *Desposyni* delegation, Constantine decided that he needed a strategy to place himself above the blood relatives of Jesus in terms of Christian significance. In fact, more than that, he needed to become of greater relevance than Jesus.

By merging various attributes of early Christianity with aspects of *Sol Invictus* sun worship, Constantine had created a hybrid religion which became the Church of Rome. But the figure of Jesus posed a real problem since the original Nazarene following was still considerable within the

4th-century Empire. The Emperor knew that he had to do something about this, and he dealt with it very expediently at the Council of Nicaea in AD 325. The Christians had been expecting a Second Coming of their Messiah sooner or later, and so Constantine found a way to fulfil, even to surpass, this expectation.

The mission of Jesus against Roman dominion in Judaea had failed because of disunity among the sectarian Jews. Although the Nazarene and Essene communities had supported him, the Hebrew faction had not – especially those priests of the Jerusalem Temple and the Sanhedrin council of elders. They were content to hold high-status positions in a Roman environment. They also objected strongly to the fact that Jesus wanted to share access to the Jewish God with Gentiles. As a result, from the 1st century onwards, the Christians had received little support from the orthodox Jewish community, and had been treated very badly by the authorities in Rome. Constantine took due advantage of all this by making the point that Jesus had left the Christians in a weak and vulnerable position because he had handled things badly on their behalf. He then sowed the seed of a new idea: Perhaps Jesus was not the true Messiah after all.

In furtherance of this, since it was the Emperor (not Jesus) who had actually ensured freedom for the Christians within the Empire, then surely their true Saviour was not Jesus, but Constantine! He knew, of course, that Jesus had been venerated by Paul as the Son of God, but there was no room for such a concept to persist. Jesus and God had to be merged into one entity, so that the Son was identified with the

Father. It thus transpired at the Council of Nicaea (now Iznik in Turkey) that God was formally defined as Three Persons in One: a deity consisting of three coequal and coeternal parts – the Father, Son and Holy Spirit (or Holy Ghost).

There were some bishops at Nicaea who opposed this concept – theologians of the old school who averred that Jesus was indeed the Son, and furthermore that the Son had been created in the flesh by God, but that he was not himself God. Irrespective of this, their objections were overruled and the *Nicene Creed* of the Holy Trinity was established as the basis for the new, reformed Christian belief. And so it was that, with God designated as both the Father and the Son, Jesus was conveniently bypassed as a figure of any practical significance. From that moment, the Emperor was regarded as the Messianic godhead. He was not just the Second Coming of the Messiah; he was the First Coming – an inheritance that was deemed to have been reserved for him since the beginning of time.

Brothers and Sisters

Although Jesus' brothers and sisters are rarely discussed in modern scriptural teachings, nevertheless they are cited in the New Testament, especially James, the eldest of Jesus' brothers. The difficulty which has long confronted the Church with regard to Jesus' siblings has been the matter of the *Desposyni* and their definition in the Vatican records: 'Only those persons in the bloodline with Jesus through his mother qualified as *Desposyni'*.

This definition has long posed a significant problem for the Church because it can only mean one of two things:

1 If Jesus were the one and only son of Mary, the *Desposyni* could only be his personal descendants.
2 If there were some *Desposyni* in descent from Mary, but not from Jesus, then Mary must have had offspring other than Jesus.

Whichever one of these the Church authorities elect as probable, they end up with a dilemma. To admit that all the *Desposyni* inheritors were descendants of Jesus makes a nonsense of his perceived celibate status within the Catholic faith. However, the doctrine that Mary was a virgin was compounded by a resolution of the Council of Trullo, under Pope Justinian II, in AD 692. This was a decree that she remained a virgin for ever. The precise wording from the Council canons and commentaries is:

> The Catholic Church has always taught
> the Virgin birth, as well as the Virgin
> conception of our Blessed Lord, and has
> affirmed that Mary was ever-virgin, even
> after she had brought forth the incarnate
> Son.

If ever forced to make a choice, the bishops would necessarily have to dismiss the Trullo decision because the Gospels make it perfectly clear that Mary's family was larger than Jesus alone.

Some virgin-school apologists have suggested that perhaps the brothers and sisters of Jesus mentioned in the
Gospels were really his cousins, or maybe they were offspring of Joseph, born to a woman other than Mary. But the
New Testament makes it abundantly clear that neither was
the case. Both Matthew 1:25 and Luke 2:27 stipulate that
Jesus was Mary's 'firstborn' son. Nowhere does it state that
he was her only son.

Matthew 13:55 clarifies that Jesus had brothers, and
names them as James, Joses, Simon and Judas. Their names
are repeated again in Mark 6:3. In the New Testament
Epistles, St Paul specifically refers to his meeting in
Jerusalem with 'James, the Lord's brother' (Galatians 1:19).
Other entries refer to James presiding over the famous cir-
cumcision debate in Jerusalem as a leader of the Nazarene
Church (Galatians 2:1–10 and Acts 15:4–34). Also, the chroni-
cles of the 1st-century historian Flavius Josephus relate to
'James, the brother of Jesus, who was called Christ'.[21]

This last entry also provides a good example of a contemporary mention of Jesus outside the Bible. Elsewhere in
The Antiquities of the Jews, Josephus refers to Jesus again as
'the Christ',[22] while his sentence by Pontius Pilate (the
Governor of Judaea) is logged in the *Annals of Imperial Rome*.
The Roman entry describes Jesus' mission as a 'shameful
practice'.[23]

In addition to Jesus' brothers, Matthew 13:56 and Mark
6:3 both state that he also had sisters. They are named in
the *Panarion* and *Ancoratus* of Epiphanius[24] as being Mary,
Salome and Joanna. Sisters of Jesus are also mentioned in the
Protevangelion of James,[25] in the *Gospel of Philip*,[26] and in the

Church's own *Apostolic Constitutions*. In the New Testament Gospels, these sisters appear at the cross and at the tomb of Jesus, along with Mary Magdalene. Mary and Salome appear, for example, in Mark 15:47, while Joanna and Mary appear in Luke 24:10, and Mary features again in Matthew 28:1. (Salome was also known as Sarah or Sarah-Salome – *Sarah* being a distinction which meant 'princess'.)

Theologians who suggest that Jesus' brothers and sisters may have been offspring of Joseph by another woman, prove only that they have not read what the Gospels actually state – or maybe they suppose that most other people have not read them. The fact is that the Gospels are explicit enough in clarifying that Mary was also the mother of James, Joses and Salome. These brothers and sisters are used strategically in the biblical text to define the physical state of Jesus during the Passion sequence. Prior to the Crucifixion, Mary is referred to as the 'mother of Jesus' (for instance, John 2:1). But from the point at which Jesus is considered to be dead, she is defined in a different manner. At the cross she is referred to as the 'mother of James and Joses' (Matthew 27:56 and Mark 15:40), while at the tomb she is given as the 'mother of James and Salome' (Mark 16:1). Subsequently, however, once Jesus is on the scene again after the Resurrection, there is a reversion to Mary's previous style as the 'mother of Jesus' (Acts 1:14).

It was during the middle of the 2nd century that a new style of theological Christianity began to emerge with scholars such as Irenaeus of Lyons, Clement of Alexandria and others now classified as the Church Fathers. During this era, the concept of Mary's virginity evolved, to become firmly established by AD 383 when St Jerome wrote *The Perpetual Virginity of Blessed Mary* for the newly devised Church of Rome. Prior to that, Mary was not classified as a virgin in any original Gospel. The earlier Greek and Aramaic texts (from which the modern New Testament was translated) refer to Mary simply as a 'young woman', using the Semitic term *almah*. The corresponding Semitic word denoting a physical virgin was *bethulah*, a term that was never applied to Mary.[27] In Latin translation, *almah* became *virgo*, which means 'damsel'. To imply the modern connotation of 'virgin', the Latin word had to be qualified by the adjective *intacta – virgo intacta*; 'damsel intact'.[28] Mary's virgin status was a spurious notion invented by the early Church, but not found in the primary Gospel texts of the *Codex Vaticanus* in the Vatican Archive.

The Forbidden Tomb

In the past couple of years, there has been much discussion and written about an inscribed Jerusalem ossuary (bone casket) attributed to Jesus' brother James. It was brought to light in the *Biblical Archaeological Review* for November–December 2002. The ossuary is inscribed in Aramaic with the name *'Ya'akov bar Yohosef akhui di Yeshua'* (that is, 'Jacob, son of Joseph, brother of Joshua' – or, in English, 'James, son of Joseph, brother of Jesus'.

Whether this is truly the ossuary of Jesus' brother James is a matter of debate and will probably never be known. However, an error which has been perpetuated throughout the discussions is the notion that this is the first and only artefact from the 1st century that mentions the name 'Jesus'.

In 1980, a 1st-century family tomb was unearthed during excavations at East Talpiot, Jerusalem. Archaeologists then moved the tomb's ossuaries into museum storage at Romemma, and the Curator of Archaeology and Anthropology for the Israel Antiquities Authority later commented that this find was 'really impressive'.

The ossuaries were individually inscribed:

> *Jesus son of Joseph*
> *Mary*
> *Joseph*
> *Jude*
> [the name of one of Jesus' brothers]
> *Mary*
> [the name of one of Jesus' sisters]

This intriguing family tomb was hailed as the greatest Christian-related discovery of all time. News hit the British press on 31 March, 1996, with front-page headlines and a lengthy feature article in the *Sunday Times*, entitled 'The Tomb that dare not speak its Name'.

On Easter Sunday, 7 April 1996, excitement heightened when Joan Bakewell, CBE, hosted the much-publicized BBC television feature documentary *The Body in Question*. Filming from the crypt where the ossuaries were held, Joan Bakewell announced, 'Our find will renew the debate of the Resurrection' – but, in the event, it did not. The Church lambasted the BBC for drawing attention to the matter of Jesus' brothers and sisters. The bishops also objected to the fact that the 'Jesus' inscription referred to 'son of Joseph' (not 'son of Mary' or 'son of God'). In view of the Ascension dogma, they were also concerned that Jesus might even have been thought to have had an ossuary.

It does not matter whether or not this was the authentic ossuary tomb of the biblical Jesus and his family. Most likely it was not, and such things can never be proved or disproved. The relevant aspect of what happened in 1996 is that the Inquisition against any discussion of Jesus' brothers and sisters was still operative. Meanwhile, that Easter week's *Radio Times* TV guide is now among the rarest of collectors' editions since the magazine's first publication in 1923.

Apocalypse

Fruit of the Vine

Allegorical artwork concerning Mary Magdalene is a subject of heightened public fascination at this time, having been brought to the fore by Dan Brown in *The Da Vinci Code*. We shall go on to consider some of the paintings mentioned in the novel, but at this stage it is worth looking at allegorical art in general terms, and with regard to Mary Magdalene in particular.

According to etymological dictionaries, the word 'allegory' comes from two Greek words – *allos* (other) and *agoria* (speaking aloud). It is a figurative description that relates to the broadcast of an underlying significance or meaning – something in addition to the literal sense that is superficially conveyed, and which is not always readily apparent. Allegory can be expressed in both written language and art. Fables and parables are allegories – simple stories on the surface, but having moralistic or social implications within.

In Psalm 80, the sovereignty of Israel is expressed as a growing vine. This is pure allegory which appeals immediately to the visual imagination. For this reason, running vines have often been used in artwork to demonstrate life, growth and generational progression. Ezekiel 19:10 states, for example, 'Thy mother is like a vine in thy blood, planted by the waters; she was fruitful and full of branches'.

Onwards from the Old Testament book of Genesis, there are constant references to vineyards and lineal descent, with the repeated assertion, 'Be fruitful, and multiply'. Exodus 1:7 states: 'And the children of Israel were fruitful, and increased abundantly'. In discussing Jesse, the father of King David, Isaiah 11:1 decrees: 'There shall come forth a rod out of the stem of Jesse, and a branch shall grow out of his roots'. Prior to that, in Isaiah 5:7, Israel and the Davidic House of Judah are described as the Lord's 'cherished plant'. And ultimately, in John 15:1, Jesus makes his claim: 'I am the true vine'.

Vine terminology is also used in the adventurous lore of the Holy Grail. In the romance of *Parzival*, by the 13th-century Bavarian knight Wolfram von Eschenbach, it is said of the Grail Queen that she 'bore the perfection of earthly paradise, both roots and branches. It was a thing men call the Grail'.

The fruit of the vine is the grape, and from the grape comes wine. The red wine of the Eucharist is the eternal Christian symbol of Messianic blood, and it is in this context that the Grail's representations as both a chalice and a vine coincide. The age-old ceremony of the Grail is precisely that which is still performed as a communion ritual in churches today. The Holy Sacrament is fully synonymous with the ancient Mass of the Holy Grail. It is for this reason that, in terms of allegorical fine art, Jesus has often been painted in conjunction with a wine-press.[1] It is of particular relevance to us, however, that certain Grail emblems and watermarks from Provence in the Middle Ages depict a chalice or vase with clusters of grapes – the fruit and seeds of the vine – and some carry the Magdalene initials '*MM*'.[2] In accordance with this imagery, Mary Magdalene became the mother protectress of winegrowers.[3]

According to historical accounts of the paper-making industry, Provence was the capital of worldwide paper manufacturing for many centuries.[4] From a base concept of Egyptian papyrus, paper made from cotton had been developed by Israelites who expanded their trade in Provence following their 1st-century exile after the fall of their Judaean homeland. The world's first ever watermarks appeared in Provence from 1282. Harold Bayley, a leading authority of the paper trade, wrote in 1912 that these Provençal watermarks are like 'thought fossils in which lie enshrined aspirations and traditions … They are historical documents of high importance, throwing light not only on the evolution of European thought, but also upon many obscure problems of the past … They are explicable by a code of interpretation'.[5]

In this context, the Grail-related and *MM* watermarks come from the earliest of sources, and are relics of an underground Church fraternity. The marks were discovered just 100 years ago in the pages of medieval French Bibles, and they constitute their own allegory. On the surface, the Bibles are like any others produced for use in churches at that time. But hidden beneath the surface, embedded secretly into the paper sheets and quite unknown to the bishops or the friars of the Inquisition, was the heretical watermarked legacy of Mary Magdalene and the Holy Grail.

Grail watermark from 13th-century Provence

Fertile Allegory

Notwithstanding Jesus' comment about the wine at the Last Supper: 'This is my blood of the new testament ...' (Mark 14:24), the opinion of early Christian fathers had a more precise emphasis. Teachers such as Valentinus and Marcus (AD c150) considered that the wine was symbolic of Jesus' maternal inheritance, not of the man's own blood in particular. They insisted that wine has unique female qualities because of its association with wisdom (*sophia*), grace (*charis*) and intelligence (*epinoia*) which, in Greek, are female gender words.[6] In this regard, the chalice (Holy Grail) which contains the wine (Messianic blood) is representative of the womb – the *vas spirituale* (spiritual vessel), as determined in the 1587 Marian *Litany of Loreto*.[7] Hence, the original chalice and wine ceremony, prior to Catholic eucharistic intervention, was an emblematic communion of motherhood and generation.

The eternal chalice emblem of the female was devised as a V-glyph (a receptacle), and shrines dating from 3500 BC associate this symbol with the womb of the Mother Goddess.[8] The Holy Grail was likened to a vessel because it was said to carry the sacred 'blood royal' – the *Sangréal*. Just as the kraters and cauldrons of ancient mythology contained their various treasures, the Messianic inheritance was reckoned to be contained figuratively within a cup. It was, however, the chalice of Mary Magdalene which carried the *Desposynic* blood *in utero*. It was she who inspired the *Dompna* (Great Lady) of the troubadours who were so callously treated by the Inquisition – and who called her the Grail of the World.[9]

The reverse male symbol (an upturned V) represented a blade or horn. It was generally depicted as a sword, although its most powerful representation was in the fabulous mythology of the unicorn. In Psalm 92:10 we read: 'My horn shalt thou exalt like the horn of an unicorn'.

When brought together, point to point, with the female symbol above the male, an X mark is formed. This glyph of conjoined gender opposites was used from early times to identify the sacred unity of the bridal chamber. It was the original holy sign of the cross, and was used as a mark of baptism long before the time of Jesus. As confirmed in the Dead Sea Scrolls, it was placed on the foreheads of those who cried for Jerusalem (Ezekiel 9:4), and was granted at the highest degree of initiation into the community sanctuary.

By way of later Roman influence, a new cross was devised – the upright Latin cross of St Peter's Church, with its high crossbar. At that time, the original device became a sign of heresy in the eyes of Rome. As a result, this heretical connotation has been perpetuated to this day as being associated with flesh and the devil – as in X-rated movies. Indeed, its anti-establishment significance has been indoctrinated in schools through the simple process of using X to mean 'wrong'.

Even though the cross of St Peter's crucifixion in AD 64 was Latinized to resemble the standard design for the cross of Jesus, the tradition of Peter's brother Andrew was maintained by the original X, which became known as St Andrew's cross. Andrew was executed at Patras near the Black Sea, where he had worked among the Scythians before they began their westward movement to Ireland and the far north of Britain. Consequently, Andrew became the patron saint of Scotland, and his cross became the national *Saltire.* Since Scotland (unlike England) was not a Papal State, the bishops were unhappy about the reappearance of this ancient esoteric device, and the explanation was invented that Andrew must have perished on an X-shaped cross.

In this connection, it is worth studying works of religious art from the Inquisitional era – especially from 1252 when torture, secret trials and death by burning were authorized by the Pope. Even though X was deemed an heretical device, it was cleverly used in many paintings. In Sandro Botticelli's *Madonna of the Pomegranate*, an angel wears a red-ribboned X on his chest; in his *Madonna of the Book*, the Madonna wears a red X on her bodice; and in Fra Angelico's *Noli me tangere* Resurrection scene, there are three intricately made red X-marks on the grass in front of Mary Magdalene (*see* plate 5).

An extended variation of the V symbolism emerged in the heraldic arts of 'indenting' and 'engrailing'. These Grail representations were aligned V or cup shapes in a running series to form scalloped edge designs. Engrailing was indicative of dynastic generation, and artists made use of the device to denote lineal descent. One of the most telling of all paintings in respect of Mary Magdalene's motherhood and Grail association is Caravaggio's stunning *Mary Magdalene* portrait from the Italian collection of Prince Pamphili. In this seated portrayal from 1595, the contemplative Magdalene, with her customary long reddish hair, makes her gravidity very apparent in a simulated nursing pose. The scene is completed by a shell-designed chalice on the very front of her skirt (*see* plate 9). The engrailed scalloping on this device is the most forthright of Grail-related generational allegory.

Scallop engrailing was at all times connected with love goddesses and fertility cult females associated with the sea – from Mary Magdalene to Aphrodite. Botticelli's painting, *The Birth of Venus*, is a supreme icon of this tradition.[10] In the Middle Ages, knights of Grail Orders bore engrailing within their arms. This is exemplified by the Scottish shield of the Saint-Clairs (Sinclairs) of Rosslyn, with its engrailed (scalloped) black cross upon silver. Examples of this can be seen today in the carved stonework of Rosslyn Chapel near Edinburgh. The name Saint-Clair derives from the Latin *Sanctus Clarus,* meaning Holy Light.

The engrailed black and silver shield of Saint-Clair

These days, the Midlothian town of the Saint-Clairs is spelled 'Roslin', although the chapel retains the traditional 'Rosslyn' spelling. Originally, in Celtic times, the place was called 'Ross Lynn', relating to the rock promontory (*ross*) of a waterfall (*lynn*) – but it has nothing to do with a north-south Rose Line that runs through Glastonbury as cited in *The Da Vinci Code*. Rosslyn and Glastonbury are not on the same meridian and have no longitudinal connection.

Magdalene Emblems

In *The Da Vinci Code*, it is suggested that Leonardo da Vinci painted Mary Magdalene in his mural of *The Last Supper*, substituting her for one of the apostles. Although this notion works well for the conspiratorial plot, we shall see later that it was not actually the case. Allegory in art is never crude or unduly surreptitious – especially not from masters like Leonardo. As in the example of Caravaggio's engrailed chalice, it is generally blatant, although often esoteric. To comprehend it, one has to recognize the symbols and understand their meaning. Symbols and emblems have often been used in art to convey things that could be written as descriptive explanations in a book. The skull, book, mirror, jewellery and candle of the 'Penitent Magdalene' depictions are all allegories – a type of artistic shorthand by way of consistently identifiable representations.

Another example of Magdalene allegory is found in the 'red egg' portrayals in numerous icons and other works. In the Russian Church of Saint Mary Magdalene in Jerusalem, there is a painting of Mary holding a red egg in the presence of Emperor Tiberius (*see* plate 14). In this work, Mary wears a white nun's habit – a familiar Magdalene attribute in artwork, especially in paintings emanating from Dominican and Franciscan sources. The egg presentation is the original Easter scene of the Christian movement. Again, like the grapes (and sometimes pomegranates), the egg is symbolic of birth and new life.

At the 664 Synod of Whitby in England, the Roman bishops achieved their first doctrinal victory over the traditional Celtic Church. The main debate concerned the festival of Eostre, the ancient goddess of spring – and it was decided to subsume the Eostre (Easter) custom into the mainstream Christian framework. The purpose of this was to separate

the Crucifixion and Resurrection of Jesus from their historical association with the Jewish Passover. It just so happened
that Eostre's feast day coincided, and so was the perfect candidate for the substitution.

According to the Old Testament book of Leviticus 23:4–6,
the Passover (which celebrates the Israelites' exodus from
Egypt) falls on the 14th day of the month of Nisan
(March–April), being the first full moon after the equinox. It
is followed from 15th Nisan by the seven days of unleav-
ened bread.[11]

As established at Whitby in the 7th century, the annual
date for the Christian Easter is rather more complicated,
having a number of variable days between 22 March and
25 April. In essence, it is the first Sunday after the first full
moon after the vernal equinox. The Chief Pontiff's requirement in 664 was that Easter should always fall on a
Sunday. This meant that a specific date could not be set
to apply every year. From the earliest times, it had been
Jewish custom to recognize what became known as
Saturday as their holy Sabbath. But Roman Christianity
was founded upon many principles of the *Sol Invictus*
sun cult, and (as another contrived separation from its
Nazarene Judaic base) the bishops elected for their sacred
day to be the Sun Day.

Despite the spring placement of Eostre's date in the
northern hemisphere, the Celtic festival was not a Passover
celebration in the Jewish style – nor was it anything to do
with Jesus. It was, in practice, a *fertility* celebration. Against
all prevailing custom, however, the Catholic Church succeeded in its ambition. The Passover was disassociated from

the Resurrection and, at the same time, an ancient Celtic tradition was demolished.

In doing this, certain of Eostre's familiar goddess symbols were embraced within the new structure, which became in effect a Christian–pagan hybrid. A long-standing custom of Eostre's festival was the presentation to friends and family of brightly coloured eggs – Eostre eggs. In terms of springtime activity, these were wholly representative of female fertility, and it is from this that we derive the modern name for the female hormone 'estrogen' (or 'oestrogen').[12]

Mary Magdalene's association with red egg evolved directly from the old Eostre tradition and, like her ointment jar, it became well used in icons and other pictorial artwork. The New Testament book of The Revelation describes the persecution by Rome of 'the remnant of her seed' and, in this connection, Mary's presentation of a red egg before Emperor Tiberius is an allegorical reminder that, as with the Resurrection of Jesus, life will prevail and the seed is eternal.

In essence, because Mary Magdalene was the first to discover Jesus' resurrection from the tomb (John 20:1–17), she became the Christian equivalent of Eostre. But because Eostre was a rural (pagan) goddess of the West, a new story was concocted by the Eastern Church so as to relate Easter to the Gospel tradition. It was said that Mary went from Judaea to Rome for an audience with Emperor Tiberius. Presenting an egg as a gift to the Emperor, she told him of how Jesus had come back to life, whereupon Tiberius remarked that it was as impossible as it would be for the egg turning red. On saying this, the egg in Mary's hand turned red – and that is why Easter eggs became a popular tradition. A fascinating and romantic tale, but it does not explain why Mary would travel 1,500 miles across the Mediterranean Sea to give the Emperor an egg.

In Mary Magdalene portraits, it is common for her to be given red or red-tinged hair. Victorian artists of the Pre-Raphaelite school, such as Dante Gabriel Rossetti and Frederick Sandys, made a feature of this with their flame-haired Magdalenes. The tradition began in Renaissance times when the writings of Rabanus Maurus and Jacapo di Voragine moved centre stage. Red hair was an allegorical representation of Mary's birthright – a visual pointer to her royal status, even though a 1st-century Syro-Galilean woman would more likely have been dark-haired.

Red hair was an attribute of certain prominent noble strains, and it was known that European dynastic royalty had begun with the Royal Syths of the Caucasian regions, extending from Carpathia to the Caspian Sea. As recent unearthings of their ancient mummies have confirmed, they were indeed red or auburn haired.[13] When Renaissance artists portrayed kings, queens and royalty in general, it was easy enough to convey noble status by way of regalia, insignia and courtly trappings, but with Mary Magdalene it was more problematic. Red hair was, therefore, a way of introducing a recognizable aristocratic element to her image.

In addition to red hair, Mary Magdalene is usually depicted with long hair. Frequently (in paintings, sculptures and carvings), she is seen with extremely long hair that completely, or partially, envelops her otherwise naked form. In February 2001, an article by a professor of theology addressed this matter in the *National Catholic Reporter*.[14] The best reasoning she could give, however, was that the nakedness and long hair resulted from an erotic preoccupation of Renaissance artists – 'a way of exploiting an artistic type'. This, of course, means absolutely nothing except that the writer did not have a clue about why Mary Magdalene is commonly featured in this way.

In a more authoritative vein, however, the professor discussed why the Magdalene legacy is now claimed as being emblematic of a growing trend in women's ministry. The point is correctly made that Mary was indeed venerated during the early years of Christianity, and that the 2nd-century Church father, Hippolytus, had referred to her as 'the apostle to the apostles'.

With regard to Mary Magdalene's hair, an apocryphal story entitled '*Vita eremitica beatae Mariae Magdalenae*' emerged from Italy in the 9th century. It explains that for thirty years she lived as a hermit in the desert of Arabia after the Ascension of Jesus[15], and in this account she was attributed with especially long hair. The story was a medieval standard, however, and was similarly told in respect of Martha, Mary the Egyptian and other supposed female penitents, whose clothes apparently rotted away and had to be substituted by hair.

In reality, the extraordinarily long hair attributed to the Magdalene image stemmed from the same culture that gave rise to the romantic Carolingian fairy-tale tradition of those such as Rapunzel. The feature was attributed to Mary expressly to counter the Church propaganda about her supposed wanton behaviour.

In the tale of Rapunzel, her golden locks are presented as being plaited into a lengthy braid, by means of which the prince scales the tower to effect her rescue. Before being freed, however, her hair is cut off by the enchantress, thereby implying the release of the maiden's chastity. The importance of very long hair was that it afforded an appropriate veil of modesty even when in a naked state. Although perhaps physically or metaphorically divested of clothes (as symbolized by the subordination – or, in Mary's case, oppression by the Church), the maiden with tresses was never vulnerable. Her dignity was preserved, and neither her body nor soul was fully bared until the appropriate time. This theme evolved from the 4th-century martyrdom of St Agnes of Rome. Stripped and tormented for refusing to marry at the age of thirteen, she escaped the gaze of her captors by concealing herself within the wrap of her flowing hair. This scene was exquisitely depicted by the 17th-century baroque painter, Jusepe de Ribera.

It is for this reason that Mary Magdalene was so often depicted with long, enveloping hair – as painted on occasions by Giotto and Botticelli, or in the Sforza *Book of Hours* interpretation of her arrival in Provence.[16] The Church's official Magdalene image was that of a flighty harlot, but enlightened artists were often quick to establish the reality of her modest estate. A wonderful portrayal in this genre is at the Magdalene Basilica in Tiefenbronn, Germany, by the 15th-century Burgundian artist Lukas Moser. Here, the hair-clad Magdalene is seen in communion with Bishop Lazarus of Marseilles (*see* plate 10). This painting is part of a fabulous screen called *Der Magdalenaltar*, which also includes Mary's anointing of Jesus at Bethany and her subsequent sea voyage to Provence.

There are a number of such narrative art depictions of Mary's life in a sequence of pictures at various churches in Europe. Among the best known are the 1320s frescoes of Giotto di Bondone in the Magdalene Chapel of the Church of San Francesco in Assisi. Similar scenes are displayed from even earlier (c1210) in the magnificent Magdalene window at Chartres Cathedral in France.

A further item of Magdalene association in art is a white dove, which is similarly included in many Holy Grail representations. The Magdalene-related painting, *The Holy Grail* by Dante Gabriel Rossetti, is a good illustration in this regard. (*see* plate 12). In ancient times, the dove was associated with the goddesses Ishtar, Astarte and Aphrodite. The white dove especially signifies feminine purity and, with a laurel sprig in its beak, is a symbol of peace. In particular though, it is a eucharistic emblem which has long been used in Christian art to exemplify the Holy Spirit.[17] In this it is not unique to Mary Magdalene, and is often found in representations of Jesus' mother Mary and other female saints.

Armageddon

As we have seen, allegorical inclusions in artwork were a very effective form of artistic shorthand – an abbreviated, symbolic mode of expression. Sometimes they were meant for the world at large to comprehend. On other occasions they were directed towards a particular enlightened audience, and were not meant to be understood by all and sundry. As Jesus was reputed to have said: 'Unto you it is given to know the mystery of the kingdom of God; but unto them that are without, all these things are done in parables' (Mark 4:11).

It is not by chance that Sandro Botticelli's painting *The Madonna of the Pomegranate*, and his *The Madonna of the Magnificat*, both show the infant Jesus clutching the ripe, open pomegranate of fertility. Nor is it the result of a pointless whim that, in Botticelli's *Madonna of the Book*, Jesus holds three miniature golden arrows – the esoteric symbol of the Three Shafts of Enlightenment, a motif of Hermetic alchemists. Such things are wholly non-biblical, but they did not appear in Botticelli's art by accident. Everything painted by intelligent artists such as Botticelli had a purpose and a meaning, whether or not the reasonings were immediately apparent to everyone.

There are a good many paintings entitled *The Allegory* ... of this or that. A majority of these, however, are simply paintings without known titles that have been dubbed 'allegorical' subsequent to the artists' deaths because their subject contexts are not understood. True allegory is always apparent in its context, even if the message is sometimes hard to understand by virtue of our educational conditioning in some alternative direction.

In the world of fine art, the master of allegory is generally reckoned to be the Nuremberg artist Albrecht Dürer (1471–1528). One of his most ambitious and best-known projects was a series of fifteen woodcuts and two title pages for printings in 1498 and 1511 of *The Apocalypse of Saint John the Divine* – the New Testament book of The Revelation. As previously mentioned, the Greek word *Apocalypse* translates to Revelation, or even more precisely to an Unveiling.

The Revelation is quite unlike any other book in the Bible since it is not recounted as a straightforward chronicle. Its stage is set in a seemingly visionary fashion, almost as if John were sitting in a theatre watching events being played out before him. In essence, that is more or less what it was, for The Revelation is really a chronological continuation of the Gospels and the Acts of the Apostles. Its status has been obscured by means of a series of epistles by St Paul, St Peter and some other ancillary works – twenty-one books in all – being placed in between. In practice, The Revelation should follow The Acts, with the other books and letters forming no more than appendices to the New Testament. The reason for the predominance of Peter's and Paul's expositions is that the Roman Church of Constantine was founded on the teachings of Peter and Paul, with the emperor as its figure-head. It was not founded on the teachings of Jesus as original Christianity had been. It is, in fact, rather more 'churchianity' than Christianity.

At first glance it appears baffling that The Revelation was included in the New Testament at all, since it follows the post-Resurrection lives of Jesus, Mary Magdalene and their offspring through a balance of the 1st century.[18] However, the inclusion of The Revelation proved to be a remarkable strategy in that its very esoteric nature enabled Rome to turn it to considerable advantage by misrepresenting its text from the pulpits; this, of course, was at a time when the general populace did not have Bibles to read for themselves.

The Dead Sea Scrolls, discovered at Qumrân in 1947, have given us much information concerning the beliefs, customs, rituals, politics, philosophies and traditions of the pre-Gospel and Gospel eras in Judaea. A fundamental belief was that the universe contained the two cardinal spirits of Light and Darkness. In their respective contexts, Light represented truth and righteousness, whereas Darkness depicted perversion and evil. The balance of one against the other in the cosmos was settled by celestial movement, and people were individually apportioned with degrees of each spirit as defined by their planetary circumstances of birth. The cosmic battle between Light and Darkness was thus perpetuated within humankind, and between one person and another.

God was held to be the supreme ruler over the two cardinal spirits, but for a person to find the way to the Light required following a long and arduous path of conflict. Such a path culminated in a final weighing of one force against the other at a Time of Justification – later called the Day of Judgement. It was thought that as the time drew near, the forces of Darkness would gather in strength during a Period of Temptation. People would naturally be subject to this testing process. Those who followed the Way of Light thus sought to avoid the impending evaluation with the plea, 'Lead us not into temptation, but deliver us from evil'.

In the book of The Revelation 16:16, the great final war between Light and Darkness (between good and evil) is forecast to take place at Armageddon (*Har Megiddo*) – that is at the Height of Megiddo, an historically important Palestinian battlefield where a military fortress guarded the plains of Jezreel, south of the Galilean hills.

The *War Scroll* describes in detail the foreseen struggle between the Children of Light and the Sons of Darkness at the great battle of Har Megiddo. The tribes of Israel were to be on one side, with the Romans and various heathen factions on the other. It was to be a violent mortal combat between the Light that was Israel and the Darkness of Imperial Rome.

In later times, the basic notion behind this ancient concept was adopted and adapted by the emergent Church of Rome. The perceived battle of Har Megiddo was removed from its specific location and reapplied on a world scale, with Rome (the hitherto Darkness) usurping the Light in its own favour from the day when Emperor Constantine placed himself at the head of Christianity.

In order that the rule of the Catholic bishops should prevail, it was decreed that the Day of Judgement had not yet come. Those who thereafter obeyed the revised principles of the Roman Catholic Church were promised the right of entry to the Kingdom of Heaven, as sanctified by the bishops. The one-time Palestinian hill-fort of Har Megiddo was thereby invested with a supernatural dimension, so that the very word Armageddon took on a hideous ring of terror. It implied the fearsome ending of all things, from which the only sure route to salvation was absolute compliance with the rule of Rome. This proved to be one of the most ingenious political manoeuvres of all time – or, at least, until the Dead Sea Scrolls were discovered and the historical truth of Armageddon became known.

Agony and Torment

We have seen that the story of Mary Magdalene's exile and flight is given in Revelation 12, and various artists have portrayed the historical event of her AD 44 sea voyage to Provence. But where is the pictorial agony of her torment? Where is the painting that somehow depicts the ruthless dragon of Rome that 'went to make war with the remnant of her seed'? Who has painted the allegory of the persecution of the *Desposyni* heirs of the Lord?

In 1961, the most expensive book in the world was produced by the French publisher, Joseph Foret. It was a one-off edition that sold to a collectors' consortium for $1,000,000, and which has resided subsequently in a Swiss bank vault. Prior to this, however, the book was displayed in a plastic bubble and exhibited around the world. It was entitled *L'Apocalypse de Saint Jean*.

Everything about the book was special, from its handmade parchment leaves to its sculpted bronze cover, encrusted with precious stones. Hand calligraphed throughout, and weighing 463 lbs (210 kg), it included specially commissioned original artwork by a number of the world's most prominent artists. Joseph Foret was a foremost publisher for Livres d'Artistes, presenting works by Picasso, Utrillo, Cocteau and others. He is perhaps best known for his publication of Dante's *La Divine Comedie*, with 100 woodblock prints by the surrealist Salvador Dali.

Dali was selected again by Foret as one of the artists for *L'Apocalypse de Saint Jean*, and he produced a series of works in watercolour, collage, etching and multimedia. As a theme for torture and persecution within these portrayals, Dali used depictions of nails – so perpetuating the Crucifixion symbol into other areas of The Revelation story.

In the course of this unique commission, Salvador Dali painted an extraordinary picture of the assault against Mary Magdalene's posterity. He produced this work in 1960 and entitled it *The Life of Mary Magdalene* (*see* plate 8). In true Apocalypse style, it is unmistakably blatant and forthright in its implication – a bare torso section of Mary Magdalene, with fierce Roman nails driving viciously into her abdomen.

4

The Other Mary

Heritage of the Nazarene

To appreciate the political and social ramifications of Mary Magdalene's nuptial relationship with Jesus, it is first necessary to understand the nature of their social, religious and political environment. We need to ascertain the particular marital regulations that would have applied in order to move from circumstantial evidence to proof of their wedlock. At present, our investigative situation is rather like stepping out in the morning to find that the grass is sodden, the paths are in puddles, the trees are dripping, and the gullies are flowing – we know that it has rained during the night, but we have no documentary evidence to confirm the fact.

Writing in the AD 70s, shortly after the Gospel era and directly after the Judaean Revolt, Flavius Josephus (born AD 37) recounted that there were a number of sects and subsects among the Jews of his homeland. The three main philosophical groups were the Pharisees, the Sadducees and the Essenes.[1] Their community cultures were distinctly different in many respects, and Josephus explains that the Essenes had 'a greater affection for one another than the other sects have'. The Pharisees and Sadducees were strictly regulated in the Hebrew tradition, whereas the Essenes were rather more liberal and Hellenized.

The Pharisees observed ancient Jewish laws, and Luke 19:39 tells us that the Pharisees ordered the disciples of Jesus to be rebuked for creating a disturbance when they came in to Jerusalem. The Sadducees had a more modern outlook, but were largely non-spiritual, while the Essenes were inclined towards mysticism. Influenced by Hellenist culture, they were advocates of the Greek philosopher Pythagoras (c570–500 BC). Josephus relates that the Essenes were practised in the art of healing and received their therapeutic knowledge of roots and stones from the ancients.[2] Indeed, the term *Essene* refers to this expertise, for the Aramaic word *asayya* meant physician and corresponded to the Greek word *essenoi*.

In Matthew 16:1–12 (and elsewhere) Jesus seems constantly to have challenged the regimes of the Pharisees and Sadducees. His behaviour in all respects was far more akin to the Essene lifestyle of healing, esoteric philosophy and liberal attitude. Indeed, as documented in *The Antiquities of the Jews*, the Essenes were 'excluded from the common court of the Temple'.[3] It was immediately after the affront of being rebuked by the Pharisees that Jesus retaliated by entering the Temple court and overturning the tables of the traders and money changers.

Josephus, although essentially a Pharisee, was nonetheless very complimentary towards the Essenes, and wrote:

> Their course of life is better than that of
> other men, and they entirely addict
> themselves to husbandry. It also deserves
> our admiration how much they exceed all
> other men that addict themselves to
> virtue ... This is demonstrated by that
> institution of theirs which will not suffer
> anything to hinder them from having all
> things in common; so that a rich man
> enjoys no more of his own wealth than he
> who hath nothing at all.[4]

The main residential hub of the Essenes was at Qumrân on the north-west coast of the Dead Sea, to the east of Jerusalem. Other nearby settlements were at Murabba'at, Ain Féshkha and Mird. Overall, the region was known as the wilderness of Judaea, and it was in the local caves that the Dead Sea Scrolls of Essene records were discovered from 1947.[5] These numerous parchment scrolls are now the most valuable aids to understanding the Essene structure during the Gospel era.

Having been hidden in earthenware jars for nearly 2,000 years, the records were found accidentally by a Bedouin shepherd boy when searching for a lost goat. Almost prophetically, the Old Testament book of Jeremiah 32:14 had stated: 'Thus saith the Lord of Hosts ... Take these evidences ... and put them in an earthen vessel, that they may continue many days'.[6] Altogether, the jars contained around 500 Hebrew and Aramaic manuscripts – among them Old Testament writings and numerous documents of community record. With some of their traditions dating back to c250 BC, they were secreted during the Jewish uprising against the Romans (AD 66–70) and had never been retrieved. Unfortunately, many of the scrolls became fragmented after their discovery – their importance was not immediately apparent – and, being very brittle, they fell apart when badly handled, so a good deal was lost.

The Essene community was referred to as the *Nazrie ha Brit* (Keepers of the Covenant),[7] and it was from this name that the term *Nazarene* derived. The Islamic Koran refers to Christians as *Nazara*, and a general Arabic expression for them is *Nasrani*.[8]

One of the most misleading errors of the New Testament occurs in the translation of this Palestinian terminology. At the outset of Jesus' story, Matthew 2:23 makes it clear that Jesus was a 'Nazarene', but it is suggested that this was because his parents came from Nazareth.[9] There is, in fact, no record of Nazareth's existence at that time. It is not mentioned in the Hebrew *Talmud*, nor in any of the letters of St Paul. The name is absent from the Roman archive and from all the historical writings of Josephus. Indeed, Nazareth is not to be found in any book, map, chronicle or military record of the period so far discovered.

In practice, Nazarenes of the Gospel era had nothing whatever to do with a town called Nazareth that was to be settled and named in later times. The Nazarenes were a sub-sect of the Essenes, and their sectarian status is described in Acts 24:5 when St Paul is brought on a charge of sedition before the Governor of Caesarea: 'For we have found this man a pestilent fellow, and a mover of sedition among all the Jews throughout the world, and a ringleader of the sect of the Nazarenes'. Outside of the translatory error in the New Testament scriptures, there never was a Jesus of Nazareth. He was Jesus the Nazarene.

Gabriel

Another major clue to Jesus' sectarian position in Jewish society is provided by the angel Gabriel. This character's name appears only four times in the whole Bible, with his second mention being related to the first.

Gabriel makes his entrance in the Old Testament book of Daniel 8:16, with a continuation of the sequence in Daniel 9:21. In this context, Gabriel is referred to simply as a man who explained a vision to Daniel. Then, in the New Testament, Gabriel appears to Zacharias (Luke 1:9) with the news that a son (the eventual John the Baptist) would be born to his wife Elizabeth. Subsequently, Gabriel visits Joseph's wife Mary (Luke 1:26) with the announcement that she too will bear a son, to be named Jesus. In Matthew, Gabriel is not named; he is simply called 'the angel of the Lord' (Matthew 1:20), and makes his visit to Joseph rather than to Mary.

With a gap of over 400 years between the Old and New Testaments, a couple of possibilities emerge: 1) The man, Gabriel, as in the book of Daniel, was a different character to the angel Gabriel in the book of Luke; 2) Alternatively, he was the same figure with some transcendent quality of extreme longevity. In orthodox Christian thought, the second viewpoint is favoured although there is no evidence to support this notion. Far more likely is a third scenario whereby *Gabriel* was a titular distinction rather than a personal name as such. We need to discover, therefore, whether there was perhaps a dynastic tradition of some sort in the angelic structure.

In the Christian doctrine, Gabriel is referred to as *Fortitudo Dei* (Strength of God). He is an angel of incarnation and consolation, while Michael is rather more the angel of judgement.[10] In contrast, in the apocryphal Book of Enoch, Gabriel (meaning Man of God) appears as an intercessor and punisher of the wicked.[11] This compilation work (now only extant in Ethiopian, with some retrieved Greek fragments) was put together from component parts written by Palestinian Jews of the orthodox Hasidic school between c200 BC and the Gospel era.[12]

The Annunciation, from a relief carving by Luca della Robbia
(1400–83)

The Book of Enoch ties in very well with certain aspects of the Dead Sea Scrolls, and seems to have provided a base source of various angelic names which are not mentioned in the Bible. The British Museum possesses some magic bowls inscribed with Hebrew, Aramaic and Syriac incantations in which the angelic distinctions of Michael, Raphael and Gabriel occur. These bowls, dating from around 550 BC, were found at the Babylonian site of Hillah in Iraq, and constitute an interesting relic of the Israelite captivity under Nebuchadnezzar as described in the Old Testament.

The importance of this is that, although Gabriel appears in the Old Testament book of Daniel (written in Babylon during the 70 years of the Captivity from c586 BC), he did not feature elsewhere in religious texts until the Gospels were compiled in the 1st century AD. In the interim, it was Jews of the Hasidic school (the originators of the Enoch material) who had founded the settlement at Qumrân.

Excavations at Qumrân have produced relics dating from about 3500 BC, at which time the settlement was a Bedouin encampment. The period of stabilized formal occupation seems to have commenced in about 130 BC. From subsequent times, Jewish chronicles describe a violent Judaean earthquake in 31 BC,[13] and this is confirmed at Qumrân by a break between two distinct periods of habitation.[14] According to the *Copper Scroll*, old Qumrân was called Sekhakha.

The second residential period began during the reign of Herod the Great (37–4 BC). Herod was an Idumaean Arab, installed as King of Judaea by the Roman authorities who had first taken control of the region under Julius Caesar. Apart from the evidence of the scrolls, a collection of coins has also been amassed from the Qumrân settlement relating to a time-span from the Hasmonaean ruler John Hyrcanus (135–104 BC) to the Jewish Revolt of AD 66–70.[15]

The uprising in 168 BC, when the priestly caste of Hasmonaean Maccabees (Mary Magdalene's ancestors) came to prominence, was prompted largely by the action of King Antiochus IV of Syria, who had foisted a system of Greek worship upon the Jewish community. The Maccabaean army defeated the Syrians and later reconsecrated the Jerusalem Temple but, successful as they were against Antiochus, some internal social damage was done because the campaign had necessitated fighting on the Sabbath. A core of ultra-strict Jewish devotees known as the *Hasidim* (Pious Ones) strongly objected to this and, when the triumphant House of Hasmon established their own king and high priest in Jerusalem, the Hasidim voiced their opposition and marched out of the city. Subsequently, they established their own 'pure' community in the nearby wilderness of Qumrân. Their building work started in around 130 BC.

About a century later the earthquake struck. Qumrân was vacated, then rebuilt. This was the era of Queen Cleopatra VII of Egypt, whose Greek dynasty of Ptolemaic pharaohs had been reigning throughout the period of Qumrân settlement. Prior to the Roman intervention in 44 BC, the Greco-Egyptian influence had been strong in Judaea, and it was during this time that the Essenes evolved from their Hasidic base to become a monastic, Egyptian-style healing community known as the Therapeutate (cognate with the English word 'therapeutic'). As we have seen, the Greek word *essenoi* related to physicians (*see* page 66).

In the course of this, Qumrân had become the figurative home of the angels, who played no part in the Hebrew traditions of the Pharisees and Sadducees in Jerusalem. In his exposition on the Essenes, Josephus is adamant that it was they who 'preserved the names of the angels'.[16] The angelic appearance of Gabriel in the annunciations to Mary and Joseph (also previously in the account of Mary's cousin Elizabeth and her husband Zacharias) make it abundantly clear that these Gospel stories emanate from the Essene culture and that, within that environment, these families were of the sect of the Nazarenes. Jesus the Nazarene was, therefore, an Essene and the product of a liberal therapeutic community.

Marriage Regulations

This now makes it entirely possible to piece together the marital regulations that would have applied to Joseph and Mary, and to Jesus and Mary Magdalene, for the Nazarene customs were quite different to the Jewish norm in this regard. To enter this realm it is necessary, for the benefit of new readers, that we cover some ground that was trodden in a previous work. It will be useful for others of us, however, to delve rather more extensively into the subject on this occasion.

Jesus' father, Joseph, is given in the Matthew and Luke genealogical lists as a descendant of the royal House of David. More expansive details in this respect are given in Appendix I, but it is worth noting that Luke 1:27 specifically cites Joseph as being 'of the house of David'. Many Christian apologists, in an effort to justify the Virgin Birth dogma, have suggested that since Jesus is said on so many occasions to have been 'made of the seed of David according to the flesh' (for instance, Romans 1:3), then it must have been Mary who was a descendant in this royal line. Maybe she was, but the Gospels do not at any point state this as a fact. They claim only that Joseph was a Davidic dynast, and that Jesus gained his royal heritage as the Christ (Greek: *Christos*; King) from his father.

This being the case, why would the apparently high-born Joseph be classified in the Gospels as a 'carpenter'? In fact, he was never given as such – at least not in any original Gospel. As with the word *almah* in respect of Mary, it is the 17th-century translation into English (subsequently transcribed from English into other European languages) that is at fault.

The term that was translated into English as 'carpenter' was the ancient Greek *ho tekton*, a rendition of the Semitic word *naggar*.[17] As pointed out by the Semitic scholar and Scrolls translator Dr Geza Vermes, this descriptive word could perhaps be applied to a trade craftsman, but would more likely define a notable scholar or teacher. It certainly did not identify Joseph as a woodworker. More precisely, it defined him as a man with skills – a learned man and a master of his occupation. Indeed, a better translation of *ho tekton* would be 'master of the craft'.

Matthew 1:18, Luke 1:27 and Luke 2:5 all claim that Mary the *almah* (young woman) was 'espoused' to Joseph, and she is referred to in these and other contexts as his 'wife'. It is stated in these passages that the angel Gabriel appeared to both Joseph (in Matthew) and Mary (in Luke), explaining that Mary would bear a son who 'shall be called the Son of the Highest; and the Lord God shall give unto him the throne of his father David'.

The translated wording of Luke 1:28 has led to other theological speculation in an effort to remove Joseph from the parental equation. The verse states: 'And the angel came in unto her, and said, Hail thou that art highly favoured, the Lord is with thee'. The suggestion in this regard is that perhaps the angel Gabriel was actually the physical father of Jesus by divine proxy. Once again, anything is possible, but if this were the case, then Mary would still not be a virgin, and Jesus would not be a descendant of the House of David via Joseph. There has to be a better explanation of the events which took place in this sequence, and knowing of the Essene connection it becomes far easier to understand.

The word 'espoused', as used in Gospel descriptions means that Joseph and Mary were married. In strict linguistic terms, it denotes a contractual arrangement (to have a spouse) as against the comparative informality of a betrothal. That being the case then, it is unclear why Mary's pregnancy was an embarrassment to Joseph as determined in the Gospel narrative. Matthew 1:18–25 relates: 'Then Joseph her husband, being a just man, and not willing to make her a public example, was minded to put her away privily'. Was there perhaps some feature of Essene wedlock that caused a wife's conception and gestation to be in some way humiliating?

In terms of the Jewish social norm, motherhood and family life were, and still are, paramount in the culture. Indeed, it is by way of birth from a Jewish mother that one is reckoned to gain a truly Jewish inheritance. In historical terms, the Jews were the regional residents of Judaea (which included Jerusalem and Qumrân), whereas Israelites were the wider inhabitants of Israel. Theoretically, Israelites were descendants of the Old Testament character Jacob-Israel,[18] grandson of Abraham. In practice, however, they were the Judaeans, Samaritans and Galileans, apart from Palestinian Arabs and various others which the Gospels loosely classify as Gentiles.

In the context of this framework, Jesus was from Judaea (previously called Judah before Roman times) and was therefore a Jew (a Judaean), but Mary Magdalene can only be termed Israelite since she was a Galilean (Galilee being the region to the north of Judaea and Samaria).[19] That would not prevent her, however, from being a Nazarene in sectarian terms, and in some paintings she is dignified with the black robe of a Nazarene priestess (Jan Provost's Renaissance work, *The Sacred Allegory*, for example).[20] This was another reason for her Black Madonna status (*see* page 31).

Josephus explains that the Essenes of Qumrân were monastic and conventual. The men and women lived in separate quarters and, for the most part, they maintained a celibate lifestyle. Marriage and procreation were condoned in some cases where heritable interests were important, but there were strictly applied regulations which bore no resemblance to the Jewish family norm.

In terms of Essene hierarchical structure, the names of the angels were preserved within specific dynasties of the high-ranking priesthood. There was always a Michael, a Gabriel, a Raphael, an Uriel and a Sariel within the establishment. These men, in the strict sense of the term 'angel' (meaning 'messenger'), were the top-ranking ambassadors of the community. They were, in essence, the regulators.

There was also a patriarchal structure maintained within the hierarchy based on the Abrahamic family (with titular names such as Isaac and Jacob), along with a prophetic council of elders designated Isaiah, Zechariah and suchlike. Additionally, there was a kingly branch in descent from the royal House of David – the House of Judah into which Joseph and Jesus were born.[21] St Paul made particular mention of this in his letter to the Hebrews, stating that although Jesus had a kingly inheritance, he had no birthright to the priesthood.[22] It is in respect of these hierarchical distinctions that Jesus (as the David) made his appearance on the mountain with Moses and Elias (Mark 9:2–4). The triarchy (corresponding to Priest, King and Prophet) held the symbolic titles of Power, Kingdom and Glory.

In the community patriarchy, the 'Father' (the Abraham) was supreme, and his two immediate deputies were designated his Son and his Spirit. In the parallel angelic structure, the Zadok high priest held the distinction of Michael, while the Abiathar priest (second in command) was distinguished as Gabriel. These priestly distinctions had been established at the time of King David (2 Samuel 20:25). The Zadok/Michael was known as the 'Lord' (like unto God), and the Abiathar/Gabriel was the designated 'angel of the

Lord'. This angelic system is detailed in the Book of 1 Enoch, and the Qumrân *War Scroll* 9:15–17 identifies the angels' order of priestly ranking during the Gospel era. Also in the Davidic line-up (as given in 2 Samuel 20:26) was the Jairus priest, whose eventual successor in later times was Mary Magdalene's father.

It can be seen from all this that, by virtue of the appropriate titular styles, the terms Lord and Father had a revered, but mundane, significance. Where they appear in New Testament narrative and dialogue, it is generally presumed (by way of Christian doctrine) that they refer always to God. To the Essenes, however, God was represented on Earth by aristocratic figures who bore these appellations, just as the Pope is the Father (Papa) of the Catholic community today.

Returning to the account of Gabriel's visits to Zacharias, Joseph and Mary, we can see that the angelically defined person who gave his consent for the births of their respective sons was the Abiathar priest. But why would these individual confinements require priestly approval and permission? The answer is that the sons of both Zacharias and Joseph were offspring of dynastic inheritance – Zacharias being in the Zadokite high-priestly succession, and Joseph in the Davidic kingly succession. Even though the Essenes prized their celibacy, and brought in abandoned or illegitimate children from outside to perpetuate their community, physical procreation was vital where dynastic succession was concerned. But it had to be approved, and there were strict guidelines governing the necessary relationships.

In the case of Zacharias and Elizabeth, we see in Luke 1:22 that, in preparation for his wife's confinement,

Zacharias was rendered speechless in the temple: 'And when he came out, he could not speak unto them … he beckoned unto them and remained speechless'. This refers to his being granted a period of procreational leave from his priestly duties – in other words, he was prevented from speaking in his usual ordained capacity. It is then stated in Luke 1:24 that, following conception, Elizabeth hid herself away. In the case of Joseph and Mary, Joseph similarly refers to the prospect of having Mary 'put away privily'.

In accordance with Essene custom, Josephus explains that within the dynastic order it was appropriate for men not to 'accompany their wives when they are with child, as a demonstration that they do not marry out of regard to pleasure, but for the sake of posterity'.[23] This makes it clear that, whether we are discussing Zacharias and Elizabeth, Joseph and Mary, or Jesus and Mary Magdalene, we are not necessarily in the realm of a romantic love match. Rather, this is the domain of contracted wedlock agreements and strategically selected couples in order to progress important lineal dynasties. It was therefore imperative that both Mary and Joseph should receive their instruction and consent in this regard from the Abiathar Gabriel.

The first three months of confinement were crucial in determining whether a dynastic husband would retain his selected wife or not, for there were others in the noble caste who may have been equally suitable. It was always possible that a wife might miscarry, in which event she was looked upon as inappropriate and another was elected in her stead. Miscarriages generally occurred, if they occurred, within the first three months of pregnancy, and so a wife was especially vulnerable during this period. There was also the prospect that a wife might prove wholly infertile and, to accommodate this, the 1st-century *Wars of the Jews* explains that the first three years of wedlock in the dynastic order were afforded as a trial period.[24]

There were, therefore, two stages to such marriages. Following a term of betrothal, a couple would be married on a trial basis, but the marital contract was not fully cemented at the outset. During this experimental period, even if the espoused wife conceived, she was still considered to be a 'damsel' (an *almah* or *virgo*) until three months of her confinement had elapsed. Only then was the second stage of the marriage ceremony conducted, at which time she gained the right to be called 'wife'. It was at this stage that the Abiathar priest (the Gabriel) would have intervened to sanction the gestation and fully legalize the wedlock.

On the eventual birth of her child, the wife became recognized as a 'mother'. Prior to that, at all stages of her *almah* status (as conferred by her convent of origin), she would be referred to as 'sister'.[25] In this light, the story of Mary and Joseph is correctly portrayed with Mary conceiving as an *almah* – albeit the term was mistranslated to become 'virgin'. She then duly received the consent of the Most High (the Zadok priest) from his angelic deputy, the Gabriel. There was, however, still an element of risk and a possible cause for embarrassment if Mary should have miscarried. And so, in preparation for this and in accordance with custom, Matthew 1:19 explains that 'Joseph her husband, being a just man, and not willing to make her a public example, was minded to put her away privily'. (There was also a further reason for Joseph's misgiving in this regard, and we shall return to this when dealing with the later marriage of Mary Magdalene – *see* page 192.)

Immaculate Conception

It is worth drawing a distinction between the Virgin Birth of Jesus, as defined in Church dogma, and the Immaculate Conception which relates specifically to the birth of Jesus' mother Mary.

Despite the tremendous veneration of the Blessed Mary in Christian theology, there is no information concerning her background in the New Testament Gospels. These canonical texts deal only with the lineage of Jesus' father Joseph. It was by way of much later clerical interpretation that Mary was moved into a primary position by the Catholic Church,[26] and it occurred as a result of the ongoing Trinity Dispute, which had begun at Emperor Constantine's Council of Nicaea.

Although it had been decreed by Constantine's bishops that God was 'three persons in one' – a deity consisting of three coequal and coeternal parts: the Father, Son and Holy Spirit – there were still Christians of the pre-Roman school who insisted that God was God and Jesus was a man, an hereditary Messiah of the Davidic succession. They were absolutely emphatic about this and repudiated any notion that the Blessed Mary was a virgin. Their view was similar to that which had been expressed by the Libyan priest Arius at Nicaea, but although he had been vilified and banished, his sentiments were still being expressed.

This made life very difficult for the later Emperor Theodosius, who convened a Council of Constantinople in AD 381 with the intention of ending the dispute. By AD 390, the *Apostles' Creed* had been developed as an alternative to the *Nicene Creed*. It began, 'I believe in God the Father Almighty and in Jesus Christ, his only begotten Son, our Lord'. This front-line reintroduction of Jesus (who had been sidelined by Constantine) was hardly conducive to the Messianic status of the Emperor but, within a few years, Rome was sacked by the Goths and the Western Empire moved into decline.[27]

From that point the Church fell to the supreme authority of the Popes and a new protagonist emerged in the Trinity Dispute; he was Nestorius, Patriarch of Constantinople. Nestorius maintained that the argument over whether Jesus was God or the Son of God was totally irrelevant, for it was plain to all that Jesus was a man, born quite naturally of a father and mother. From this platform, he stood against his Catholic colleagues, who were by then referring to Mary as the *Theotokas* (Greek: 'bearer of God') or *Dei Genitrix* (Latin: 'conceiver of God'). As a result, the Nestorian precept that Mary was a woman like any other was condemned by the Council of Ephesus in AD 431, and she was venerated thereafter as a mediator (or intercessor) between God and the mortal world.

Time moved on, but the Trinity arguments persisted with Mary stuck in the middle. She was not a part of the Holy Trinity, but her ecclesiastical position was governed by the perceived relationships between God, Jesus and the Holy Spirit. In this regard, the Roman Catholics of Western

Christendom decided to ratify what was called the *Filioque Article*, introduced at the Council of Toledo in 598. It declared that the Holy Spirit proceeded 'from the Father *and from the Son* (Latin: *filioque*)'. Without the emperors in control, however, an alternative Eastern Church was evolving from a Byzantine base. It claimed that the Spirit proceeded 'from the Father *through the Son* (Greek: *dia tou huiou*)'. It was an intangible and quite extraordinary point of theological dispute, but it split formal Christianity down the middle.

Either way, Mary was no longer considered to be the Mother of God. She was henceforth the Mother of the Son. She was the vehicle through whom, in one way or another, the Holy Spirit had passed. In reality, the *Filioque* debate was merely a trivial controversy in a wider-scale battle about whether the Church should be politically managed from Rome or from Constantinople. Neither side won, and the result was the formation of two quite distinct Churches from the same original. The Vatican's final separation from the Eastern Orthodox Church occurred in 867, when the latter announced that it upheld the true Apostolic Succession.[28] The Vatican Council disagreed, and so Photius, Patriarch of Constantinople, excommunicated Pope Nicholas I of Rome.

The main biographical sources concerning Mary are not the canonical Gospels but the apocryphal scriptures, the *Gospel of Mary* and *The Protevangelion*. Many of the great artistic depictions of Mary's life and family are based on these – paintings such as Albrecht Dürer's *The Meeting of Anna and Joachim* (Mary's parents). The most comprehensive work on the subject is customarily accepted to be *La Leggenda di Sant Anna Madre della Gloriosa Vergine Maria, e di*

San Gioacchino ('The Story of Saint Ann, Mother of the Blessed Virgin Mary, and of Saint Joachim'). This account of Mary's life was brought to Western Europe from Byzantium by the Crusaders, and its popularity spread throughout the Christian world. In France, a Feast of Saint Ann was established in the 14th century, and Pope Urban VI extended it to England at King Richard II's request in 1378. It was not until 1584 that the feast became universal, when Pope Gregory XIII prescribed it for the whole Church.

In the course of the Marian legend, it was determined that for Mary to be so special as to conceive and give birth as a virgin, then she must have been somehow unique. She could not have been an ordinary child, and must herself have emanated free of male intervention. Hence, it was construed that her father Joachim was not directly responsible, and that Mary was the product of her mother Ann's Immaculate Conception. This gave rise to some extraordinary artwork, not the least of which, *St Ann Immaculately Conceiving* by Jean Bellagambe (c1500), depicts a clothed, adult Mary forming within her mother.[29]

Surprising as it might seem, it was not until comparatively recent times that certain aspects of the Catholic creed (hitherto only implied) were determined as explicit items of faith. The doctrine of the Immaculate Conception was not formally expressed until 1854, when Pope Pius IX decreed that Mary, the mother of Jesus, was herself conceived free from Original Sin. Mary's Assumption into Heaven was not defined until November 1950 by Pope Pius XII, whilst Pope Paul VI did not proclaim her Mother of the Church until 1964. Such decrees were themselves rendered possible by the ultimate assertion of authority – that of Papal Infallibility. This dogma was proclaimed at the Vatican Council in 1870; it stated, 'The Pope is incapable of error when defining matters of Church teaching and morality from his throne'!

Irrespective of hitherto opinions, interpretations, dogma and decrees, the 1960s saw the beginning of a new enlightened era, when the Dead Sea Scrolls made their debut in published translation. Faith in doctrinal belief continues, but has now been separated fully from the documented history of Judaean life in the approach to the Gospel era. Even the duties of the Messiah of Israel and his Council of twelve delegate apostles are detailed in the Essene *Scroll of the Rule*, which also describes the ritual of observance for the annual Messianic Banquet. It was this event in AD 33 which became so famed in scriptural tradition as the Last Supper of Jesus.

Sepulchre of the Magdalene

The Holy Balm

Alongside the Emperors, who had professed a Messianic status from Constantine's era, the Bishops of Rome (or Popes, as they became better known)[1] were established at the magnificent Lateran Palace as second in command of the Church. They claimed their privilege by way of an Apostolic descent from St Peter, who had been executed by Emperor Nero in AD 64. The succession from one Pope to another was formalized as a handing down of episcopal authority through a laying-on of hands. However, the problem was that the premise on which this was based was wholly invalid. The apostle Peter (a 1st-century promoter of Christianity in Rome, along with St Paul) had never held any formal office. The first appointed leader of the Church movement in Rome was Britain's Prince Linus (a son of Caractacus the Pendragon) and, as recorded in the Church's own *Apostolic Constitutions*, Linus was installed by St Paul during Peter's lifetime in AD 58.[2]

Even if the people at large did not know this, then the leaders and missionaries of the *Desposyni* churches certainly did, as did others of the Celtic and Gnostic[3] movements. In a 4th-century treatise entitled *The Apocalypse of Peter*,[4] they referred to the Church of Rome's hierarchy as 'dry canals'. The document continues:

> They name themselves bishops and
> deacons as if they had received their
> authority directly from God ... Although
> they do not understand the mystery, they
> nonetheless boast that the secret of Truth
> is theirs alone.

In the early days from Prince Linus, it had been customary for the prevailing Christian Church leader to nominate his own successor before he died, but this tradition had been changed when Constantine proclaimed himself 'God's Apostle on Earth'. It then became the Emperor's right to nominate and ratify appointments, and the various candidates often came to blows, giving rise to bloodshed in the streets. Once installed, however, it was their duty to enforce the new dogma as widely as possible within the Empire.

The first Imperial Bishop (AD 314–335) had been Sylvester, who was crowned with great pomp and ceremony. This was a far cry from the shady back-room proceedings of earlier times. Christians were no longer fettered and sent to work in the quarries and mines; they could now move openly in society, with their hierarchy draped in gold, ermine and jewels. Many people were offended by this and saw it as a profanation of their ideals, but they had no choice in the matter. Their once persecuted religion had now become the official Church of Rome.

The main regional areas of difficulty for the popes were Britain and France. The Celtic Church in Britain had its own *Desposynic* tradition, and could not be intimidated. Eminent pre-Roman Church fathers, such as Eusebius of Caesaria (AD 260–340), who was at the Council of Nicaea, and St Hilary of Poitiers (AD 300–367), told of early apostolic visits to Britain. They correspond to a period shortly after the Crucifixion – prior to when Peter and Paul were in Rome, and before the original Gospel texts entered the public domain.

In his *De Demonstratione Evangelii*, Eusebius wrote: 'The apostles passed over the ocean to the islands known as Britain.'[5] Other historians subsequently confirmed this. The Welsh chronicler Gildas II Badonicus (516–570) stated in his *De Excidio Britanniae* that the precepts of Nazarene Christianity were carried to Britain in the last days of Emperor Tiberius, who died in AD 37. In later times, even the Vatican's own librarian, Cardinal Cesare Baronius, recorded in his 1601 *Annales Ecclesiastici* that Christian teaching first came to the West in AD 35. Hugh Cressy, a Benedictine monk who lived shortly after the Reformation, wrote in his *Church History of Brittany*:[6]

> In the one-and-fortieth year of Christ,
> St James, returning out of Spain, visited
> Gaul, Brittany and the towns of the
> Venetians, where he preached the Gospel,
> and so came back to Jerusalem to consult

> the Blessed Virgin and St Peter about
> matters of great weight and importance.

The weighty matters referred to by Cressy concerned the necessity for a decision on whether to receive uncircumcised Gentiles into the Nazarene Church. As head of the *Desposyni* delegation in Jerusalem, Jesus' brother James presided at the Council which handled the debate. (This meeting is referenced in the New Testament, Acts 15:4–34.)

In AD 303, the Phoenician historian Dorotheus of Tyre wrote in his *Synopsis de Apostole* that 'the apostle Simon Zelotes preached Christ through all Mauritania … At length he was crucified in Britannia'. This was confirmed by Nicephorus, Patriarch of Constantinople (758–829), who stated:

> Saint Simon, surnamed Zelotes …
> travelled through Egypt and Africa, then
> through Mauritania and all Libya,
> preaching the Gospel. And the same
> doctrine he taught to the peoples of the
> Occidental Sea and the islands called
> Britannia.

Much earlier writings by the Roman churchman Hippolytus (born AD c160) list Aristobulus as a bishop of the Britons. Cressy maintained that Aristobulus was ordained by St Paul himself. The Greek *Church Martyrology* claims that Aristobulus was martyred in Britain 'after he had built churches and ordained deacons and priests for the island'.

St Dorotheus wrote that Aristobulus was in Britain when St Paul sent greetings to his household in Rome: 'Salute them which are of Aristobulus' household' (Romans 16:10). Additionally, the *Jesuit Regia Fides* states: 'It is perfectly certain that before St Paul reached Rome, Aristobulus was away in Britain'. He was, in fact, executed by the Romans at Verulamium (St Albans)[7] in AD 59. This was further confirmed by St Ado (800–874), Archbishop of Vienne, in the *Adonis Martyrologia*.

Aristobulus was the brother of King Herod-Agrippa I (also of Herod of Chalcis and of Herodias, mother of the deadly dancer Salome). In collaboration with young Herod-Agrippa II, Aristobulus had been Mary Magdalene's ally when she was afforded protection by the Herodian establishment at Vienne.[8] In Britain he was referred to as Arwystli Hen (Aristobulus the Old) so as to distinguish him from a younger Aristobulus who was married to Salome.[9] The Welsh town of Arwystli in Powys was named after him.

In recounting the martyrdom of Simon Zelotes in Britain, the Vatican's *Annales Ecclesiastici* of Cesare Baronius confirms (in agreement with Dorotheus and Nicephorus) that he was crucified by the Romans under Catus Decianus at Caistor in Lincolnshire. The text adds that, at the saint's own request, his remains were shipped to be placed with those of Mary Magdalene in Provence.

The heritage of Mary Magdalene and the *Desposyni* heirs of the Lord in Southern France posed enormous problems for Imperial Rome. In an attempt to suppress the Nazarene believers, Emperor Septimius Severus concentrated his assaults on Lyon and the region of the Vienne estate. In a short period from 28 June AD 208, he had 19,000 Christians put to death in the area. In a similar manner, matters were no less difficult for Constantine and his successors, even though they had taken charge of the Church. There were shrines set up all over France to Ste Marie de Madeleine, including her burial place at the Abbey of St Maximus la Sainte-Baume,[10] where her sepulchre and alabaster tomb were guarded, day and night, by Cassianite monks. The place was named after the Holy Balm (*la Sainte Baume*) with which Mary had anointed Jesus at Bethany.

The Cassianite Order was founded by John Cassian in about AD 410, and was the earliest monastery to maintain independence from the episcopal Church. In commenting on the Church of Rome, Cassian denounced the taking of holy orders as 'a dangerous practice' and declared that his monks should 'at all costs avoid bishops'. Initially an ascetic hermit in Bethlehem, John Cassian established two conventual schools at Marseilles – one for men and another for women.

Marseilles subsequently became a recognized monastic centre, and was the birthplace of the Candlemas ritual which succeeded the earlier torchlight procession of Persephone of the Underworld. Culminating at the harbour, near the fortress-style Abbey of St Victor, the event (with its long green fertility candles) still takes place on 2 February each year. It coincides with the Imbolc spring festival of the pagan calendar and, in recognition of Mary Magdalene's sea voyage, the Abbey bakery produces orange-flavoured, boat-shaped biscuits called *navettes*. St Victor's contains John Cassian's sarcophagus, a medieval Black Madonna (*Notre*

Dame de Confession), and an ancient altar in the crypt inscribed with Mary Magdalene's name.

A New Emphasis

In the 5th century, the Church of Rome was placed under the management of a city administration, the members of which were referred to as the Cardinals (a title derived from the Latin *cardo*: pivot), and there were twenty-eight appointees stationed at the Vatican. Meanwhile, there was strong competition from the fast-growing Byzantine Church, with its key centres in Constantinople, Alexandria, Antioch and Jerusalem.

During the years of conflict between the Eastern and Western factions of Christendom, before the Churches eventually separated, each vied for supremacy. After the fall of the Roman Empire, the Bishops of Rome were dominant in the West, with the Patriarch of Constantinople heading up the Church in Byzantium. The unresolved debate over the Trinity had driven a permanent wedge between the factions, and each claimed to represent the true faith.

While the Church of Rome was being restructured, the Western Empire collapsed – demolished by the Visigoths and Vandals. The last Emperor, Romulus Augustulus, was deposed by the German chieftain Odoacer, who became King of Italy in AD 476. In the East, however, the Byzantine Empire was destined to flourish for another 1,000 years. In the absence of a Roman Emperor, the prevailing High Bishop, Leo, gained the title of *Pontifex Maximus* (Chief

Pontiff, or Head Bridge-builder), becoming Pope Leo I.

In AD 452, along with an unarmed body of monks, Leo confronted the fearsome Attila the Hun and his army by the River Po in northern Italy. At that time, Attila's empire stretched from the Rhine across into Central Asia. His well-equipped hordes were ready with chariots, ladders, catapults and every martial device to sweep on towards Rome. The conversation lasted no more than a few minutes, but the outcome was that Attila ordered his men to vacate their encampments and retreat northwards. What actually transpired between the men was never revealed, but afterwards Leo the Great was destined to wield supreme power.[11]

Some time earlier, in AD 434, an envoy sent by the Byzantine Emperor Theodosius II had met the dreaded Hun in similar circumstances by the Morava River (south of modern Belgrade). He had given Attila the contemporary equivalent of millions of dollars as a ransom for peace in the East. Bishop Leo's arrangement was probably much the same.

Notwithstanding this, in the West, as the might of Imperial Rome crumbled, so too did Roman Christianity subside. The Emperors had been identified with the Christian God, but the Emperors had failed. Their religious supremacy had been switched to the Chief Pontiff, but his was now a minority religion in a Christian environment of Gnostics, Arians, Nazarenes, and the fast-growing Celtic Church.[12]

Following the Synod of Whitby and the hijacking of Easter in 664 (*see* page 53), the Catholic Church increased its strength to a degree, but when the new papal supremacy was tested on Dianothus, Abbot of Bangor in North Wales, he responded that neither he nor his colleagues recognized

Emperor Constantine gains Messianic approval for *The Donation*
(from a 12th-century Roman manuscript)

any such authority. They were prepared, he said, to acknowledge the Church of God, 'but as for other obedience, we know of none that he whom you term the Pope, or Bishop of Bishops, can demand'. An earlier letter, written to the Abbot of Iona in 634, referred unequivocally to St Patrick of Ireland as 'Our Pope'.

In an effort to heighten the profile of the Church, the bishops decided to link Jesus even more closely to their institution. The medieval clerics produced manuscript illuminations of past Emperors and Popes in the company of Christ – even of Constantine being granted his privilege as the personally designated Saviour of mankind. Preceding this, and to give such imagery its necessary impetus, a great masterstroke was performed in 751 by Pope Zachary.

Zachary's Deceit

Without revealing his source, Zachary produced a previously unknown document that was seemingly 400 years old and carried the signature of Emperor Constantine. It proclaimed that the Pope was Christ's personally elected representative on Earth, with a palace that ranked above all the palaces in the world. His divinely granted dignity was above that of any earthly ruler and only he, the Pope, had the power and authority to create kings and queens as his subordinates. The charter made it forcefully clear that the Pope held a vicarious office as Christ's chosen deputy, granting him the style *Vicarius Filii Dei* (Vicar of the Son of God).

The document became known as the *Donation of Constantine*,[13] and its provisions were put into force by the Vatican in 751. By virtue of this, the whole nature and structure of monarchy changed from being an office of community guardianship to one of absolute rule. Henceforth, European monarchs were crowned by the Pope, becoming servants of the Church instead of being servants to the people.

Pope Zachary's first initiative, under the terms of this apparent Imperial charter, was to depose the long-standing Royal House of France – the Merovingians of Gaul. Boasting a genealogical descent from King David of Israel, this enigmatic dynasty had been Lords of the Franks for 300 years. In accordance with the Old Testament, they wore their hair long in the Nazarite tradition of Numbers 6:5, and they modelled their establishment on the court of King Solomon. Letters patent of Louis XI, dated 1482, refer to a visit by the Merovingian King Clovis to Mary Magdalene's tomb in AD 480, and Clovis had married the Burgundian Princess Clotilde at the Black Madonna centre of Ferrières.[14]

From the days of King Clovis, the Merovingians had formed a peaceful alliance with the Church of Rome, but now this was to no avail. In the old style of princely guardianship, they were representative Kings of the Franks, not territorial Kings of France. Zachary's plan was to change this tradition by granting territorial dominion to future kings, who would rule (rather than reign) under his supreme authority. The defunct Roman Empire was a relic of history, but Zachary had a new concept – a Holy Roman Empire controlled from the Vatican.

There was no place for the Merovingians[15] in this since they were *Desposyni* inheritors and, despite their prominence as founders of the French monarchy, they posed a severe threat to the papal regime. In his effort to maintain good relations, Clovis had been baptized by St Remy, Bishop of Reims, but his descendants still sported the Judaic trefoil of the *fleur-de-lis* (the lily flower, as depicted on the ancient coins of Jerusalem) to denote their bloodline,[16] and they carried the Lion of Judah on their shields. In line with the 1st-century edict of Emperor Vespasian, which had ordered 'the family of David to be sought, that no one might be left among the Jews who was of the royal stock',[17] the Merovingians should never have existed as far as Zachary was concerned, let alone become a reigning dynasty.

The Merovingians were, therefore, deposed by papal command on the authority of the *Donation of Constantine*,[18] with their last king being Childeric III. Papal troopers seized Childeric and incarcerated him in a monastery dungeon, where he died four years later. Installed in their stead was a family of hitherto regional mayors. Descendants of the renowned Carolus Martel, who had turned back a Moorish invasion near Poitiers in 732, they were subsequently styled Carolingians. In all the 236 years of Carolingian monarchy, their only king of any significance was Martel's grandson, the legendary Charlemagne. Nevertheless, a new tradition had been born, and the Holy Empire was begun. Henceforth, European kings were crowned by the Pope – and in England by his appointed Archbishop of Canterbury. Scotland stood alone in resisting the Catholic invasion, and her monarchs remained forever Kings of Scots, never Kings of Scotland.

Over 500 years ago in the Renaissance era, proof emerged that in fact the *Donation of Constantine* was an outright forgery. Its New Testament references relate to the Latin Vulgate Bible[19] – an edition translated and compiled by St Jerome, who was not born until AD 340, some 26 years after Constantine supposedly signed and dated the document. Apart from this, the language of the *Donation*, with its numerous anachronisms, both in form and content, is that of the 8th century and bears no relation to the writing style of Constantine's day.[20] It is as different as modern English is to that of William Shakespeare (with a similar amount of time in between).

The *Donation* was first declared to be fraudulent by the Saxon Emperor Otto III in 1001. Intrigued by the fact that Constantine had moved his personal capital from Rome to Constantinople, Otto recognized that this was a ruse to pre-empt any Merovingian ambition to centre their own kingly operation in Rome in opposition to the Imperial bishops. Although Otto was a German, his mother was an East Roman who was well aware that this same fear had existed in the late Merovingian era, at which time the *Donation of Constantine* was implemented.

Otto's pronouncement came as unwelcome news to the prevailing Pope Sylvester II, but the matter was ignored and did not come to the fore again until the German theologian and philosopher Nicholas of Cusa (1401–64) announced that Constantine had never written the *Donation*.[21] But although a doctor of canon law who decreed that the Pope was actually subordinate to the members of the Church movement, Nicholas was somehow overawed by the bishops and took up a Cardinalate position in 1448, becoming a staunch supporter of the papacy!

The *Donation* was not publicly mentioned again until its authenticity was fiercely attacked by the Italian linguist Lorenzo Valla in the 15th century.[22] Valla (c1407–57) was chosen by Pope Nicholas V to translate the works of Herodotus and Thucydides from Greek into Latin. But Valla was not just an eminent scholar, he was an ardent spokesman for the reform of education and firmly believed that the spirit of Greco-Roman antiquity had been lost during the Middle Ages. Angered by the fact that the elegance of classical Latin had given way to a clumsy medieval language (as exemplified by the corrupted and largely incomprehensible style of Church Latin), he was highly critical of the Church's Vulgate Bible and its strategic errors in translation from the earlier Greek texts. This led other scholars of the Renaissance, such as the Dutch humanist Desiderius Erasmus (c1466–1536), to revert their Bible studies to the more original texts. As a result, in 1516 Erasmus issued his own Latin translation of the Greek New Testament, thereby exposing the Vulgate as a cleverly mistranslated document, which he called a 'second-hand account'.

The outcome of Lorenzo Valla's investigation into the *Donation of Constantine* was that he denounced it as an 8th-century hoax. In his report, he wrote: 'I know that for a long time now men's ears are waiting to hear the offence with which I charge the Roman pontiffs. It is, indeed, an enormous one'.[23] Yet it was this very document which facilitated a whole new style of papal kingship. It was the device by which the Roman Church reverted political power to itself and eclipsed the *Desposyni* inheritors of Jesus and Mary Magdalene after the collapse of the Empire.

Notwithstanding the debates that ensued from Valla's findings in 1450, the Church managed to survive the Renaissance period of enlightenment, branding many of the great thinkers of the time as heretics. And so Valla's report (known as the *Declamatio*) was conveniently lost within the

Vatican Archive. It was not discovered for more than 100 years until once more revealed by the 17th-century priest Murator, who worked in the Vatican Library.

Subsequently, the spurious nature of the *Donation* was discussed anew by the Anglican minister Henry Edward Manning (1808–92),[24] but he was swayed from the Church of England and, in the footsteps of Nicholas of Cusa, become a Vatican Council member and Cardinal Archbishop of Westminster. Later, he published his book *The Temporal Power of the Vicar of Jesus Christ* in 1862.

The task of exposing the fraud was then taken up in the USA by Christopher B Coleman, a director of the Historical Commission and Historic Bureau at Indiana State Library from 1924. He produced an updated commentary entitled *The Treatise of Lorenzo Valla on the Donation of Constantine*,[25] which is now the foremost authoritative work on the subject.

Pope Zachary's milestone deception (in Latin, the *Constitutum Constantini*) was designed specifically to strengthen the power of the Church and, in particular, the Roman See after the fall of the Western Empire. Although the charter purported to be an Imperial grant by Emperor Constantine of temporal power in the West to the papacy, it thoroughly misrepresented the territorial status of the Popes by vesting them with a great, but false, antiquity. It was said to be the document presented by Constantine to Pope Sylvester I but, in historical terms, the key documentation of that era relates only to the Emperor's bequest of the Lateran Palace and other benefits and buildings to the newly styled Church of Rome.

From its implementation in 751, there is no further official reference to the *Donation* until it was mentioned in a letter written by Pope Leo IX to Michael Cerularis, the Patriarch of Constantinople, in 1054. By the 12th century, however, it had become the primary document of papal lordship over the whole of Christendom and its monarchs.

Living Waters

In spite of all this Vatican skulduggery, the public reverence for Mary Magdalene was impossible to contain. The whole concept of *Desposynic* heritage was very important to some noble families, and Mary's legacy was similarly upheld in monastic circles.

For more than 1,000 years, from AD 411 until the Renaissance era, the Cassianites guarded the sacred relics of La Sainte-Baume.[26] They even referred to the rock-spring of their hermitage as the 'fountain of living waters' in reference to the Old Testament *Song of Solomon* (4:15) with which the Magdalene had become so closely associated. It had been prophesied in Zecharia 14:8 that the 'living waters shall go out from Jerusalem, half of them toward the former sea, and half of them toward the hinder sea'. The monks considered this to be manifest in the two aspects of Christianity, with Mary's sea voyage representing the fount of the *Desposyni*. Because of this, she was called *la Dompna del Aquae*: the Mistress of the Waters.

In the early 8th century, Arabs and Berbers from northwest Africa made extensive incursions into Provence and

Northern Spain. The Spanish called them Moors, while in France they were known as Saracens.[27] These dark-skinned Muslims of the Baghdad Caliphate soon took control of the whole Iberian peninsula, and were dominant for around 300 years.[28] With the Saracen capital at Narbonne, along the coast from Marseilles, and a strong foothold at Nimes in Languedoc, the monks at La Sainte-Baume became very fearful. Consequently, they moved Mary's remains from her alabaster tomb to another in the same crypt: the marble sepulchre of St Sidonia, Bishop of Aix. In doing this, as a pre-cautionary measure, they also placed an inscribed notice of what they had done in the tomb.

Just 40 years later came the *Donation of Constantine*, by which time southern France and Spain were largely under Saracen Islamic control. Charlemagne's father, Pepin, was the newly installed Carolingian King of France, and he decided to take some action by soliciting help from the Jews of Narbonne. There was a strong *Desposynic* base in the city, headed by Guilhelm de Toulouse, who was the rec-ognized potentate of the Royal House of David. Pepin agreed, therefore, to establish a Jewish kingdom in the south of France if Guilhelm would help him drive the Saracens down into Spain. Guilhelm duly complied, and in 768 the Kingdom of Septimania was established with Guilhelm at its head.[29]

Pepin's son Charles became King Charlemagne of the Franks from 771 and Holy Roman Emperor from 800. He ratified Guilhelm's entitlement to dynastic sovereignty in Septimania, and gained acceptance of this from the Caliph of Baghdad and Pope Stephen in Rome. All acknowledged

Guilhelm of the House of Judah to be a true bloodline descendant of King David in the *Desposynic* succession.

More than 300 years later, the Davidic house was still extant in Septimania and the Spanish Midi, although the kingdom had ceased to function as an autonomous state. In 1144, the English monk, Theobald of Cambridge, wrote:

> The chief men and rabbis of the Jews who
> dwell in Spain assemble together at
> Narbonne, where the Royal Seed resides,
> and where they are held in the highest
> esteem.

In 1166, the chronicler, Benjamin of Tudela, reported that there were still significant estates held by the prevailing Davidic heirs:

> Narbonne is an ancient city of the Torah[30]
> … Therein are sages, magnates and
> princes, at the head of whom is
> Kalonymos, son of the great Prince Todros
> of blessed memory, a descendant of the
> House of David, as stated in his family
> tree. He holds hereditaments and other
> landed properties from the rulers of the
> country, and no one may dispossess him.

Meanwhile, the Cassianite monks continued their vigil at St Maximus la Sainte-Baume, but when, in the 11th century, word leaked out of Mary's tomb being empty, a spurious rumour was instigated. It was said that Gerard de Roussillon, Governor of Provence, had taken Mary's bones to a new home at the Abbey of Vézelay, where they were kept in the chancel beneath the high altar.

The diocesan bishop of Autun and Vézelay became worried that, in the light of this false story, his beloved 9th-century abbey might become an unwarranted tourist attraction. He therefore applied to the Holy See in Rome for an edict to prevent this. Much to his surprise, however, Pope Paschal II became personally enthused by the prospect of a new pilgrimage centre. He even arranged for the old abbey-church to be transformed into a magnificent basilica from 1096. Then he issued a Bull in 1103 to proclaim the new site, inviting all Catholics to congregate at Vézelay.[31] The place acquired such a reputation that King Louis VII, Queen Eleanor and St Bernard de Clairvaux went there in 1147 to preach the Second Crusade at the basilica, with the French and Flemish nobility and around 100,000 people in attendance. From that date, the veneration of Mary Magdalene was intimately allied to the crusaders' campaign, and, in 1190, Philippe Augustus and Richard Coeur de Lion of England announced their Third Crusade at Vézelay, where it met with similar enthusiasm.

It was not until 1254 that King Louis IX began to wonder what proof there was of Mary's relics being at Vézelay. After all, the Bishop of Autun (who was in charge at the time), had strongly denied that such a receipt had ever taken place. Louis discovered, of course, that there was no truth in the rumour and, along with the Sire de Joinville, he set out at once for St Maximus la Sainte-Baume, where the monks were still in residence. The Lord of Joinville wrote in his memoir:

> We came to the city of Aix in Provence to
> honour the Blessed Magdalene who lay
> about a day's journey away. We went to
> the place called Baume, on a very steep
> and craggy rock, in which it was said that
> the Holy Magdalene long resided at a
> hermitage.

A Gothic Bequest

King Louis was outraged that his royal predecessors, along with the Holy Land crusaders and St Bernard, Abbot of Clairvaux – Patron and Protector of the Knights of the Temple of Solomon – should have been so unwittingly deluded. The Dominican records tell of how Louis decided to set matters straight, even at that late stage. He embarked on an enterprise with his nephew Charles, Prince of Salerno and Count of Provence, who later became King Charles II of Naples and Count of Anjou. Of the initial investigation by Charles, it is related:

> He accordingly came to St Maximus
> without any parade, accompanied by a
> few gentlemen of his suite, and after
> having interrogated the monks and old
> men, he had a trench opened in the old

> basilica of Cassian, the 9th
> December 1279.[32]

It is subsequently recorded that, on advice from the monks, Charles entered the tomb of St Sidonia nine days later on 18 December. In the presence of King Louis, the bishops of Arles and Aix, together with several prelates and others, the prince broke the seals of the sarcophagus and opened it. In front of all the attesting witnesses, he removed a roll of fragmenting cork, from which he produced the skin of parchment that was placed in the tomb so long before by the Cassianites. He read the document:

> The year of our Lord 710, the 6th day of
> the month of December, in the reign of
> Eudes the most pious of France.[33] When
> the Saracens ravaged that nation, the
> body of our very dear and venerable
> Mary Magdalene was very secretly, and
> during the night, removed from its own
> alabaster tomb and placed in this one,
> which is of marble, whence the body of
> St Sidonia had been previously taken, in
> order that the relics of our holy saint
> should be more secure against the
> sacrilegious outrage of the perfidious
> mussulmen.

An authorized copy of the inscription and its discovery was drawn up by Prince Charles and signed by the archbishops and bishops present. On 5 May in the following year, an assembly was held of prelates, counts, barons, knights and magistrates from Provence and the neighbouring areas. The details of the Vézelay hoax were made known at this convention and, on 12 May 1280, the delegates were taken to see the Magdalene relics at La Sainte-Baume. It was reported that 'the head of the saint was perfect, while the other parts of the body were only a few bones'. There was just one small fragment of flesh on her right forehead, and a deputation from the Tribunal of the Cassation of Aix (including the President, the Solicitor General and two councillors) signed an account of their witness to this. They referred to it as the *Noli me tangere* spot – a romantic allusion to where Jesus might have touched Mary when he asked her not to cling to him after his resurrection.

Prince Charles then separated Mary's bones into three shares. He had her skull encased in a magnificent gold bust, with a moulded glass covering for the face. His father, Charles I of Anjou, sent his own crown from Naples, so that its gold and jewels might be used in the holy enterprise. Mary's other bones were laid to rest in a silver casket, and in later times her upper arm bone, the humerus, was placed in a reliquary of silver gilt upon a pedestal supported by four lions.

It was then determined that, since the Church of Rome had been responsible for perpetuating the Vézelay myth, the prevailing Pope should consecrate the relics to set the record straight. At that stage, however, Charles was called to other duties after the death of his father, and it was nearly five years before he gained his audience with Boniface VIII in the chair of St Peter. Prior to this, the sworn declarations of all the noble and ecclesiastical Sainte-Baume witnesses were presented to the Pope, along with the original parchment of the 8th-century Cassianite monks.

On 6 April 1295, Pope Boniface issued a Bull declaring the relics to be the true and authentic remains of Ste Mary Magdalene. He authorized Charles (then King of Naples and Count of Provence) to transfer the monastery of St Maximus to the recently constituted Dominican Order of the Friars Preachers. Funding was made available to build a great basilica on the site of the old Cassianite oratory – a worthy place for the relics to be displayed.

It took far longer than Charles's lifetime to design and construct the majestic Gothic edifice, and the work was not fully completed for nearly 200 years.[34] Meanwhile, there was the question of what to do with the gold and silver encased treasures. At that time, the Capetian King of France was Philippe IV (1285–1314), and he duly staked his royal claim. Pope Boniface, however, was no friend of this wayward monarch, who was levying illegal taxes against the clergy. This led to Boniface's papal Bull, *Clerics laicos*, on 24 February 1296, in which he forbade the clergy to give up ecclesiastical revenues or property without permission from the Apostolic See; also that princes imposing such levies – essentially King Philippe – were declared excommunicated.

In such an environment of conflict, Pope Boniface refused Philippe's application for the Magdalene relics. Instead, he made alternative arrangements. They seemed logical and appropriate at the time, but led directly to one of the most brutal and tragic episodes in Middle Ages European history.

Guardians of the Relic

Daughter of France

The records we have been studying in respect of Mary Magdalene's remains are those of the Dominican Order of the Friars Preachers. From 1295, one of their primary constitutional objectives was the basilica project at St Maximus la Sainte-Baume, as instigated by Pope Boniface VIII. Mary was designated as the patron saint of the Order, which was also responsible for the convent of the Sisters of Saint Magdalen in Germany.[1]

It is fairly common in modern academic theological works for the Dominicans to take the blame for many of the atrocities of the Catholic Inquisitions. In recent times, (along with the Franciscans in particular) they have provided a convenient scapegoat for the popes, cardinals and bishops who were truly responsible for the hideous persecutions. From the earliest monastic days of Saints Cassian, Martin, Benedict, Columba and Patrick, there had been a continuing rivalry – often an enmity – between the monks and the orthodox clergy. As John Cassian had said, 'Monks should at all costs avoid bishops'.

The monastic regime was harsh and rigorous, as against the lavish lifestyles of the episcopal clerics. The monks were disciplined in the extreme and this was apparent in their undertakings, which included the collating and writing of historical records. Whether the churchmen liked it or not, the monks recorded events as far as they were able, and were not moved by politically motivated propaganda or ecclesiastical dogma. It was for this reason that Henry VIII Tudor dissolved and destroyed the monasteries in England. His ambition was to rid his realm of monastic libraries and artwork in an attempt to suppress historical education in favour of his self-styled notions and concepts. It was precisely the same tactic which had been employed by Emperor Theodosius in AD 391, when he authorized Bishop Theophilus to sack and burn the ancient Library of Alexandria.

In contrast, the monks had endeavoured to compile and relate historical facts, and they generally understood the differences between history and dogmatic delusion. It was the Benedictine scholar, Cressy, and the Celtic monk, Gildas, who had written about early apostolic visits to Britain, France and Spain. It was the Benedictine Abbé Rabanus who had recorded Mary Magdalene's flight to France, and it was the Dominican friar Père Lacordaire who published the Sainte-Baume records of the Friars Preachers. While the Church bishops were busy denouncing Mary as a harlot and veiling her legacy, the monks were upholding her virtue and championing her corner.

These are examples of how the monastic scholars differed in matters of educational practice from the orthodox clergy. Indeed, as mentioned in the Introduction to this book, it was a Dominican friar who put this into perspective on national television with me a few years ago (*see* page xviii).

Père Jean-Baptiste-Henri Dominique Lacordaire (1802–61) is described in *The Catholic Encyclopedia* as 'the greatest pulpit orator of the 19th century'.[2] Before becoming a Dominican friar, he was trained as a lawyer and practised as a successful Bar advocate for a number of years. Subsequently ordained by the Archbishop of Paris, he became a noted champion of religious freedoms and a free press. No one, whether layman or cleric, royalist or liberal, was safe from his assailing pen or his critical lectures if he saw they were in any way politically or religiously manipulative.

Notwithstanding, Lacordaire was greatly revered and, in 1835, was offered the cathedral pulpit of Notre Dame de Paris, where he hosted a series of astonishingly controversial conferences. Forsaking prayers, hymns and scriptural readings, he spoke on subjects never before heard in the confines of a church, and he was especially concerned with matters of religious history that were not generally discussed. He followed these with similar conferences at Metz and Toulouse, and his open style of oratory became renowned. But in the course of this, he entered the Dominican Order of the Friars Preachers, and was invited into the foremost literary arena of the Académie Française. For a while, after the 1848 revolution of the Second Republic, he was editor of the New Era journal *L'Ere Nouvelle*, but spent most of his latter years writing a series of works based on unfamiliar aspects of Church record. Among these was his book *Sainte Marie Madeleine*, wherein he recounted the 13th-century excavation of Mary's tomb at St Maximus la Sainte-Baume.

Medieval France

The Dominican annals tell of many notable people who made pilgrimages to La Sainte-Baume. King Louis XI (1461–83) claimed Mary as 'a daughter of France belonging to the monarchy'.[3] His successors, Charles VIII and Louis XII, followed his example. Anne of Brittany (successively the wife of both monarchs) had a small gold figurine of herself, praying, set within the shrine. François I (1515–47) made extensive additions to the Sainte-Baume Hospital for Strangers, and his successor Charles IX made further bequests to the foundation. In 1622, Louis XIII paid his respects at the holy site and, on 4 February 1660, Louis XIV arrived with his mother Anne of Austria. They presided over the placement of Mary's silver casket of small relics into a porphyry crystal urn, which had been specially made and sent from Rome by the General of the Friars Preachers.

Never before had a saintly shrine attracted so much auspicious attention. In one single day during the basilica's construction, five kings[4] arrived from different parts of Europe, and in the course of just a century no less than eight popes[5] were recorded at the site.

A certain amount of damage was done at La Sainte-Baume during the French Revolution (1789–99), when unruly citizens were intent to demolish everything previously held sacred in their land. But the key relics were preserved in safe custody, except for the crystal urn that was lost.

By the Monday of Pentecost 1822, the necessary repairs had been accomplished and some 40,000 people congregated to watch the Archbishop of Aix return Mary's gold and silver clad relics to their rightful home. Soon afterwards, in 1842, the imposing church of La Madeleine was completed near the River Seine in Paris. Overlooking the Place de la Concorde, where 'Madame la Guillotine' had done her work in the Revolution, this Napoleonic monument, commissioned by Lucien Bonaparte, reflected the Magdalene fever that was sweeping through the nation. Built in the style of a classical Athenian temple, the church facade mirrors the National Assembly building opposite, across the square beyond the Luxor obelisk. Within this church is one small Magdalene relic – a piece of bone removed from the porphyry urn at the request of Louis XVI in 1785. It was originally a gift to the Duke of Parma but in view of the subsequent loss of the urn and Louis' execution in the Revolution, it was passed to the Archbishop of Paris in 1810.

Faith Wisdom

In Gnostic circles, Mary Magdalene was associated with the wisdom of the immortal Sophia (*see* page 32). A document which makes this especially clear is the *Pistis Sophia* (Faith Wisdom) acquired by the British Museum, London, in 1785. Purchased from the heirs of a Dr Anthony Askew, it is otherwise known as the *Askew Codex*.[6] This ancient tractate is an amalgam of six works, of which only the second is correctly styled *Pistis Sophia*, although this title is commonly applied to the whole. The more correct title for the entire compilation is *Books of the Saviour*.

The bound codex consists of 178 leaves (356 pages) of parchment, and is presented in two columns averaging thirty-two lines per column. It was written in the Coptic language of Upper Egypt during early Christian times, but was not selected for New Testament inclusion. Coptic was a vernacular form of Egyptian which was no longer written in hieroglyphics, but by means of the Greek alphabet supplemented by symbols that represented certain vocal sounds.[7] The Coptic text of *Pistis Sophia* preserves many aspects of antiquity, with words and terminology which make it plain that it was originally composed in Greek – as were the New Testament Gospels.

In essence, *Pistis Sophia* is a dialogue between Jesus and his apostles, along with his mother, his sister Salome, Mary Magdalene and Martha. The scene is set in AD 44, eleven years after Jesus' crucifixion and resurrection. This is a particularly important date because it is the same year that Mary Magdalene sailed to her exile in Provence. The text begins:

> But it happened that after Jesus had risen
> from the dead he spent eleven years
> speaking with his disciples. And he
> taught them only as far as the places of
> the first ordinance and as far as the places
> of the first mystery.[8]

In order to progress his companions' understanding of the higher mysteries of salvation, Jesus brings them together on the Mount of Olives, where they take their turns in a question-and-answer session. Mary Magdalene features prominently in this, with her name mentioned over one hundred and fifty times as against Peter, for example, who is referred to only fourteen times. Jesus refers to Mary Magdalene as 'thou pure of the light'.

In fact, Peter becomes annoyed that Mary is hogging the proceedings, and he challenges Jesus, stating, 'My Lord, we are not able to suffer this woman who takes the opportunity from us, and does not allow anyone of us to speak, but she speaks many times'.[9] Jesus rebukes Peter for this but, in her own later response, Mary adds, 'I am afraid of Peter, for he threatens me and he hates our race'.[10]

The series of back-and-forth conversations all concern 'the words which Pistis Sophia said', and Jesus asks each of them in turn to give their interpretation of the mysterious wisdom. One by one, they comply, but when Mary Magdalene gives her initial response, Jesus tells her, 'Thou art she whose heart is more directed to the Kingdom of Heaven than all thy brothers'.[11] Mary emerges as the one with the greatest empathy for the immortal Sophia, and was forever after associated with her.

Breath of the Universe

Irrespective of the Church and its variously created monarchies (crowned in accordance with the *Donation of Constantine*), the most powerful and prestigious fraternity in the Middle Ages was the Order of the Poor Knights of Christ and the Temple of Solomon.[12] Established during the First Crusade, these French and Flemish Knights were a Christ-dedicated unit of warrior monks, as against the Baptist-centred Order of the Knights of the Hospital of St John of Jerusalem. In abbreviated form, the two became commonly styled the Templars and the Hospitallers. Under the direction of Hugues de Payens (a cousin of the Count of Champagne), the Templars excavated the Jerusalem Temple site to bring back a wealth of manuscripts and precious items of treasure in 1127. On their return to France, their Patron and Protector, St Bernard de Clairvaux, wrote:

> The work has been accomplished with
> our help, and the Knights have been sent
> on a journey through France and
> Burgundy, under the protection of the
> Count of Champagne, where all
> precautions can be taken against all
> interference by public or ecclesiastical
> authority.[13]

Subsequently, at the Templars' historic Council of Troyes in January 1129, Hugues became the formally appointed Grand Master, and St Bernard established the Constitution and Rules of the Order. In doing this, he specified a requirement for the 'Obedience of Bethany, the castle of Mary and Martha'.[14] St Bernard is depicted welcoming Mary to Provence in the symbolic painting, *St Mary Magdalene with St Dominic and St Bernard*, by the 16th-century Spanish artist Nicolás Borras (*see* plate 18).

Some of the Jerusalem treasure had been secreted prior to the invasion by Nebuchadnezzar of Babylon in 586 BC, and some during the 1st-century Jewish Revolt against the dominion of Imperial Rome. With this resurrected hoard to form a collateral base, the Templars became the most successful financial organization the world has ever known. Indeed, within a short space of time, they were advisers and bankers to monarchies and parliaments throughout Europe and the Levant.

In the 1860s, the British explorer Sir Charles Warren conducted extensive excavations beneath Jerusalem's Temple Mount for the Palestine Exploration Fund,[15] and the Fund's records of the project are very revealing. The team dug a number of vertical shafts down to the bedrock, and then opened lateral tunnels between them to identify the lower walls and foundations of the Temple. They then progressed even deeper into the limestone rock, where they discovered an astonishing subterranean labyrinth of winding corridors and passages. Branching off these were large storage facilities and a series of cleverly engineered caves and water cisterns.[16]

During the course of this, the square foundation of King Solomon's original Temple was found. Its lower retaining walls were still intact, and their masonry techniques were quite distinct from those of the Second Temple and its later Hasmonaean and Herodian extensions.

Shortly after, in 1894, the underground complex was fully mapped by British military engineers, and a particularly interesting reward from this enterprise in the tunnelling was the discovery of a Templar cross, a broken Templar sword, and other related 12th-century items.[17]

The documentation concerning the Magdalene relics (*see* page 108) explains that, when the basilica of St Maximus la Sainte-Baume was consecrated and opened in the late 1400s, the Magdalene relics were installed, and have remained there to this day (*see* plate 53). But where had they been in the meantime, and to whom had Pope Boniface VIII entrusted them while the building work was in progress from 1295?

By virtue of the Templars' paramount status and their banking security facilities, in 1295 Boniface had passed the relics to the Order for safe keeping. His other reason for doing so was his outrage at what had happened during the

Vézelay hoax.[18] Along with King Louis VII and a good many others, St Bernard, the Cistercian Abbot of Clairvaux, had been fully duped by the false rumour, and it was only right that the Templars should be honoured with custody of the relics as a form of redress.

This, of course, infuriated King Philippe IV, whose own application had been declined. He already owed a fortune in loans to the Order and, being practically bankrupt, he viewed them with great trepidation. He also feared their political and esoteric might, which he knew to be far greater than his own. Philippe was convinced that they had brought the Ark of the Covenant back from Jerusalem, and now they had the Magdalene relics as well – including the greatest prize, the golden bust which contained her skull from St Maximus la Sainte-Baume. Consequently, he embarked on a campaign of hatred against the Templars, and against Pope Boniface.

As featured in *Lost Secrets of the Sacred Ark*,[19] the Templars appear to have been especially interested in the production of quintessential gold after their Jerusalem expedition. It seems that the anti-gravitational properties of this exotic material were of significant value in their construction of the great *Notre Dame* Gothic cathedrals of France, and Philippe was in awe of the Templar's scientific expertise. This mono-atomic powder – referred to by Nicolas Flamel and other chemists as the Philosophers' Stone – was undoubtedly used in the manufacture of the brilliant Gothic stained-glass windows. They were designed by Persian philosophers of the school of Omar Khayyām, who explained that their method of glass production incorporated the *Spiritus Mundi*

– the cosmic breath of the universe. When discussing Cistercian–Templar glass in the 16th century, the hermeticist Sancelrien Tourangeau wrote:

> Our Stone has two more very surprising
> qualities. The first, with regard to the
> glass, to which it imparts all sorts of
> interior colours, as in the windows of
> Sainte-Chapelle at Paris and those in thy
> churches of Saint-Gatien and Saint-Martin
> in the city of Tours.[20]

It is not insignificant to note that the Templar fraternity of the era referred to this branch of their activities as *Ormus*.[21] Today (since the rediscovery of this occult science just a couple of decades ago), the mysterious substance is classified by physicists as *ORMEs* – Orbitally Rearranged Monatomic Elements.[22] We shall return to this subject later in our investigation (*see* page 245).

To manufacture the exotic *Ormus* material, the Templars required a supply of easily accessible alluvial gold, and they found this at Bézu in the region of Languedoc. The land around Bézu was rich in near-surface gold from old mine workings – precisely what they needed for the transmutation process. To facilitate access to the estate, the landowner Bertrand de Blanchefort was brought into the Order, and was later rewarded with the Grand Mastership in 1153.

Inquisition

Associated with the Templars' hermetic activities in the early 1200s was the Cistercian advisory clerk Vilars Dehoncort of Picardy.[23] He was a geometrician, architect and alchemist, whose *Album de croquis* (sketchbook) – parchment sheets in a pigskin wallet – was lodged with the Bibliothèque Nationale[24] in 1795 by the Paris monastery of St Germain. It had been held there since the Middle Ages. This prized artefact contains many of the architectural drawings for the finer points of the Gothic cathedrals, including the design for the famous labyrinth at Chartres.[25] The pattern was obtained from a 2nd-century Greek alchemical manuscript, and was dedicated to the patron goddess of France, *Notre Dame de Lumière* (Our Lady of Light). It is reckoned to be one of the most sacred designs on Earth.

The 17th-century Catholic clergy were so fearful of the Templar labyrinths that they destroyed many of them – at Auxerre in 1690, Sens in 1768, Reims in 1778 and Arras in 1795. But Jean-Baptiste Souchet, Canon of Chartres who died in 1654, never dared attempt any desecration at Chartres. It remains today the largest, best preserved, and traditionally the most magical of all labyrinths from medieval times.

Hailed as the 'Gothic Leonardo', Dehoncourt referred to Mary Magdalene's gold-encased skull as the *Caput Mortuum* – not because it was a 'death head' (as the Latin implies), but because of the alchemical technique used in its preservation. *Caput Mortuum* was the term for a deep purple substance encountered in the process of making the *Ormus* powder. It also represents the purple–red ferric oxide pigment Cold Haematite, which was used from early Renaissance times, and can still be obtained as *Caput Mortuum* from specialist art suppliers today.

Also associated with the Templars in the Bézu period was the noted theologian, hermetic philosopher and experimental chemist, Albertus Magnus (Albert the Great 1206–80).[26] Albertus provides yet another link with the Dominican Friars Preachers. A member of the Order from 1223, along with his colleague St Thomas Aquinas (also a natural philosopher), he was Master of the Sacred Palace in Rome, taught at the General Chapter in Valenciennes, and also at the College of St James in Paris where he was Master of Students at the University.[27] Albertus wrote much about the nature of the *Ormus* Philosophers' Stone, confirming yet again that alchemical pursuits were paramount within the interconnected fraternities at that time.

By 1296, the previously scattered Templar activities at Bézu had become centred on one major preceptory. This became the key workshop at nearby Campagne-sur-Aude, and knights were brought in from Aragon to provide a permanent guard with lookout sentries. Philippe suspected that the Ark and the Magdalene relics were kept at this place, but since the Templars had been granted their own State autonomy, with no superior but the Pope, there was not much that he could do in terms of making a direct assault on Bézu. What he needed was a Pope who could be manipulated to grant him the freedom he required.

He therefore arranged for the assassination of Boniface VIII, whose successor, Benedict XI, was subsequently poisoned by Philippe's lawyer William de Nogaret.[28] Benedict was then replaced, in 1305, by Philippe's own candidate, Bertrand de Got, Archbishop of Bordeaux, who duly became Pope Clement V. With a new Pope under his control through personal indebtedness, Philippe's plan was to isolate totally the Bézu fraternity, leaving them with no support to call on.

Consequently, on Friday 13 October 1307, Philippe's henchmen struck,[29] but he had not anticipated the extent of the Templars' intelligence network. Word of his intention had reached the Lord Chaplain of La Buzadière, who was duly alerted to the impending Inquisition. Seven knights were commissioned to convey the news to key positions, including Paris, St Malo and Bézu. They were Gaston de la Pièrre Phoebus, Guidon de Montanor, Gentilis de Foligno, Henri de Montfort, Louis de Grimoard, Pièrre Yorick de Rivault and Cesare Minvielle.[30]

At that time, the overall Grand Master of the Order was Jacques de Molay. Most of the Templar treasure was in the vaults of their Paris Chapter House – the setting for the famous painting of the Templars with the Ark of the Covenant in 1147, which now hangs in the Château de Versailles.

Jacques duly arranged for the Paris hoard to be removed in a fleet of galleys from La Rochelle. Most of these ships sailed to Scotland, and others to Portugal. He and some key officers then remained in France to continue their work – a primary aspect of which was to get word to those knights who were not aware of Philippe's onslaught. Couriers sped far and wide with their message of warning, but in many cases they were too late. However, it was also too late for

King Philippe. By the time his men reached the preceptory and alchemical workshops at Bézu, the place was deserted. In practice, the French king had no right to be there anyway since Bézu, at that time, came under the authority of the Spanish Court of Aragon.

In the course of this, Philippe drew up a list of accusations against the Order, with the primary charge being that of heresy. Templars were seized throughout France, to be imprisoned, interrogated, tortured and burned. Witnesses were paid to give evidence against them, and some truly bizarre statements were obtained. But once they had given their evidence, under whatever circumstances of bribery or duress, many of the witnesses disappeared without trace.

In his attempt to find the Magdalene skull, one of the charges laid by Philippe was that the knights had in their possession a head which they ceremonially venerated. William de Nogaret instituted torturous interrogation procedures to try and establish where it was kept, but he met with little success. One by one, the Paris Templars came up with different stories, but none was what Philippe wanted to hear, while outside the 'witnesses' and those who had attempted infiltration did not have a clue what it was all about. Some said it was the head of a cat; others said it was a cockerel, a goat or a demon too terrible to describe.[31]

Rainier de Larchant confessed that there was indeed a head. Guillaume d'Arbley said it was a bearded male. Hugues de Piraud said that the head also had four legs. Then Guillaume changed his mind, and said it was the beautiful head of a woman. The idol had one face, two faces, three faces. It was bearded; it was bald; it was silver;

it was wood; it was John the Baptist; it was St Ursula; it was Hugues de Payens; it was a preserved virgin; it was very large; it was small; it had smooth skin; it had carbuncles; it was Veronica's veil; it was a painting – it was everything one could imagine! But this was all useless to Philippe. He knew precisely what it was. What he wanted to know was *where* it was.

A constant factor throughout, however, was that the Knights who were truly aware of what was being discussed were in common agreement. When questioned about the mysterious head, they each called it the 'Baphomet'.

The Baphomet Cipher

The Dead Sea Scrolls are now the most useful aids to understanding the Judaean culture of the pre-Gospel era.[32] Among the more important manuscript texts, the *Copper Scroll* gives an inventory and the locations for the treasures of Jerusalem and the Kedron Valley cemetery. The *War Scroll* contains a full account of military tactics and strategy. The *Manual of Discipline* details law and legal practice along with customary ritual, and describes the importance of a designated Council of Twelve to preserve the faith of the land. The fascinating *Habakkuk Pesher* gives a commentary on the contemporary personalities and important developments of the era. Also in the collection is a complete draft of the book of Isaiah which, at more than 30 feet (9 m) in length, is the longest scroll and is centuries older than any other known copy of that Old Testament work.

In addition to these discoveries, another significant find from the post-Gospel era was made in Egypt two years earlier. In December 1945, two peasant brothers were digging for fertilizer in a cemetery near the town of Nag Hammadi when they came upon a large sealed jar containing thirteen leatherbound books. The papyrus leaves contained an assortment of scriptures, written in Coptic in the Gnostic Christian tradition. They became known as the 'Nag Hammadi Library'.

The Coptic Museum in Cairo ascertained that the codices were, in fact, copies of much older works originally composed in Greek. Indeed, some of the texts were found to have very early origins, incorporating traditions from Gospel times. Included in the fifty-two separate tractates are various religious texts and a number of previously unknown Gospels. They tend to portray an environment very different from that described in the Bible. The cities of Sodom and Gomorrah, for example, are not presented as centres of wickedness and debauchery, but as cities of great wisdom and learning. More to our purpose, they describe a world in which Jesus gives his own account of the Crucifixion, and in which the true nature of his relationship with Mary Magdalene is stunningly revealed.

During the 1950s, more than 1,000 graves were unearthed at Qumrân, where the Dead Sea Scrolls were found. A vast monastery complex from the second habitation was also revealed, with meeting rooms, plaster benches, a huge water cistern and a maze of water conduits. In the scribes' room were ink-wells and the remains of the tables on which the Scrolls had been laid out – some more than 17 feet (5 m) in length.[33]

Many Old Testament biblical manuscripts have been found at Qumrân. As well as Isaiah, they relate to such books as Genesis, Exodus, Deuteronomy and Job. There are also commentaries on selected texts and documents of law and record. Among these ancient books are some of the oldest scriptural writings ever discovered, predating anything from which the traditional Bible was translated.

Of particular interest are biblical commentaries compiled by the scribes in such a way as to relate the Old Testament texts to the historical events of their own time.[34] Such a correlation is especially manifest in the scribes' commentary on the Psalms and on prophetical books such as Nahum, Habakkuk and Hosea. The technique applied to link such Old Testament writings with the New Testament era was based on the use of Eschatological Knowledge – a form of coded representation that used traditional words and phrases to which were attributed special meanings relevant to contemporary understanding.[35] These meanings were designed to be understood only by those who knew the code.

The Essenes were trained in the use of this allegorical code, which occurs in the Gospel texts particularly in relation to those parables heralded by the words 'for those with ears to hear'. In order that the Gospels should be beyond Roman understanding, they were largely constructed with dual layers of meaning (evangelical scripture on the surface and political information beneath), and the carefully directed messages were generally based on the substitution codes laid down by the Qumrân scribes. However, a working knowledge of the code was not available until some of the

Dead Sea Scrolls were published. Only since then has an appreciation of the cryptic technique facilitated a much greater awareness of the political intelligence that was veiled within the Gospel texts.

One of the scholars who worked on deciphering the Dead Sea Scrolls was Dr Hugh Schonfield. A specialist in Middle Eastern studies and Past President of the Commonwealth of World Citizens and the International Arbitration League, Dr Schonfield was nominated for the Nobel Peace Prize in 1959. He was the first Jew to make an objective and historical translation of the New Testament from the Greek into English – a work which received the highest praise for its accuracy.

In studying the scribal codes of the Scrolls in relation to aspects of the Old Testament, Hugh Schonfield came across one particular cipher that was well used, but very simplistic. The Hebrew alphabet has 22 letters, and the cipher exchanged the first 11 letters for the last 11 in reverse order. With the English alphabet this would mean that Z was substituted for A; Y for B; X for C, and so on. In Hebrew this would be *Aleph* = *Tau*, and *Bet* = *Shin*. Thus (as ATBSh), it was called the *Atbash*.[36]

This cipher was subsequently used to glean a good amount of information hidden within scriptural texts, but the big surprise came when Dr Schonfield applied it to the strangely used Templar word 'Baphomet'. The reason that he did this was because the word had first appeared in the records of the 14th-century Templar Inquisition, and he knew that the Templars had brought back many old manuscripts from Jerusalem in 1127. Just as the Dead Sea Scrolls had brought the *Atbash* code to light in modern times, he

Templar effigy of the Baphomet–Sophia

figured that maybe the Templars had also acquired an Essene document of explanation. Transcribing the word 'Baphomet' into Hebrew, he then applied the *Atbash* cipher, and it converted immediately into 'Sophia'.[37]

Although some of the Templar victims had admitted that their relic was the beautiful gilded head of a woman, others had said that it was a bearded male, so Dr Schonfield tried another approach. In the medieval Jewish culture of Kabbalah, with which the Templars were well acquainted, the bearded male symbol represented Cosmic Man, who was defined in Hebrew as *Chokmah*. In straightforward translation, *Chokmah* means Wisdom – the very same as *Sophia* means in Greek. It appears that in giving their evidence to the Inquisitors, the Templars were not telling untruths. Neither were they disagreeing with each other when relating their individual descriptions of the relic, for Baphomet = Sophia = Wisdom = Magdalene.

Dr Schonfield concluded his report with the comment: 'There would seem to be little doubt that the beautiful woman's head of the Templars represents Sophia in her female and Isis aspect, and she was linked with Mary Magdalene in the Christian interpretation'.

At this stage, it is apparent that the Magdalene relics had been with the Knights Templars from the time that Pope Boniface VIII instituted the building of the St Maximus basilica in 1295. But since the Templars were disbanded in France in 1307, the question then arises: Who held the relics from 1307 until the new basilica opened in the late 1400s? The answer to this will be revealed later in our story.

Remarkable Texts

Martha

In the Gospel of John there is an account of Jesus raising a certain Lazarus of Bethany from his grave.[1] It is reckoned to be one of his primary miracles, and is stated to have been the reason why High Priest Joseph Caiaphas and the Pharisees became fearful of Jesus and 'took counsel together for to put him to death' (John 11:47–53). Yet, for all its seeming importance as a precursor to Jesus' trial and crucifixion, the story does not appear in Matthew, Mark or Luke.

Whereas the Gospel of John stands alone in many respects, the other three are generally referred to as the Synoptic Gospels. This comes from the Greek *syn-optikos*: '[seeing] with the same eye'. In this context, Mark is the primary Gospel from which the writers of Matthew and Luke took their respective leads. The original Gospel of Mark was written in Rome by St Paul's colleague Johannis Marcus, referred to in Acts 12:25 and 15:37 as John Mark.[2] The 2nd-century churchman, Clement of Alexandria, confirmed that it was promulgated in AD c66, when the Jews of Judaea were in revolt against their Roman overlords. It was during the course of this revolution that the historical chronicler Flavius Josephus became the military commander of Galilee.

The Jewish Revolt was the main reason why the Mark Gospel was released into the public domain within the Roman Empire – to bring an element of hope in troubled times. Apart from the conflict in Judaea, Peter and Paul had recently been executed by Emperor Nero, and Christians were being treated brutally in Rome. The aim of the Gospels was to convey an evangelical message (Greek: *eu-aggelos* – 'bringing good news'). The English word *gospel* is an Anglo-Saxon translation from the Greek, meaning precisely the same thing.

If the story of the raising of Lazarus had been in Mark, there is a good chance that it would also be in Matthew and Luke, which appeared a little later that century. The Gospel of John differs from the others in content, style and concept, being strongly influenced by Essene traditions of the Herodian era. Consequently, it has its own adherents who preserve its distinction from the Synoptic Gospels. Although openly published after the other three, its Dead Sea Scrolls characteristics indicate that it was composed around AD 37.[3] John includes countless small details which do not appear elsewhere – a factor which has led many scholars to conclude that it is a rather more accurate testimony.

There are certain items in Matthew and Luke which do not appear in Mark. The Nativity for example, which is totally ignored in Mark and John. However, whilst Matthew and Luke contain elements which Mark does not, there is not much in Mark that does not also appear in the other Synoptic Gospels. Why then did the writer of Mark not include something so important as the raising of Lazarus? Why is John the only Gospel to carry this story?

In John's account, Mary Magdalene and Martha are given as being sisters of Lazarus. The women are also seen as sisters in the Luke account of Jesus' visit to the house of Martha. In this short story, Martha becomes annoyed because she has to do all the serving, whilst Mary sits at Jesus' feet, talking. There are only five verses of this briefly recorded episode (Luke 10:38–42), but it has inspired numerous paintings from prominent artists such as Vermeer, Brueghel, Reubens, Tintoretto and Velasquez.

This and the tale of Lazarus are the only occasions when Martha is apparent in the New Testament. She is not given anywhere as a regular disciple of Jesus, and she does not appear at the cross or at the tomb with Jesus' mother and her companions. She does feature, however, in the *Pistis Sophia* document along with Mary Magdalene, Mother Mary and Salome. In this regard, she is equally involved in the Wisdom discussions with Jesus eleven years after his resurrection, and was subsequently recorded as being with the Magdalene in Provence.

Martha's remains lie buried in a church dedicated to her at Tarascon in the French province of Vienne. Built in the form of an inverted boat, the church pillars simulate masts, and artwork portraying the Magdalene voyage adorns the nave. Also, there is an inset wall tablet commemorating a visit to the site's earlier chapel by King Clovis in AD 500.[4]

According to the will of St Caesarius of Arles (AD 470–542),[5] the Collegiate Church of St Martha was originally

The Raising of Lazarus – woodcut by
Julius Schnoor von Carolsfeld (1794–1872)

called *Sancta Mariae de Ratis* (St Mary of the Boat), and even today the vespers of the church include the words, '*Veni, Sponsa Christi, accipe coronam, quam tibi Dominus præparavit in æternum*' (Come, thou bride of Christ, receive the crown which the Lord hath prepared for thee for ever). In respect of Martha, it is added in the lesson:

> This is one of those wise virgins, whom
> the Lord found watching, for when she
> took her lamp, she took oil with her …
> And at midnight there was a cry made,
> Behold, the Bridegroom cometh, go ye out

> to meet him. And when the Lord came,
> she went in with him to the marriage.[6]

Like the noble distinction 'Mary', the 'Martha' designation was also titular. Martha meant 'Lady', and the difference between Marthas and Marys was that Marthas were allowed to own property, whereas Marys were not. Hence, the Bethany house in Luke 10:38 is specifically cited as being Martha's house. Martha was not a sibling sister of Mary Magdalene; she was the sister of the priest Simon-Lazarus. Mary Magdalene was their devotional sister, carrying the rank of *almah* (damsel) as discussed in chapter 4. Martha and Lazarus were, in fact, Mary's maternal aunt and uncle (*see* chart 'Bloodline of the Holy Grail', page 427).

Suppressing the Evidence

Bearing in mind that Mark was, to a great extent, the lead Gospel for the Synoptic threesome, it is significant that there are two blatantly apparent anomalies in its structure. The first is that the familiar version includes items which are not in the earliest available Greek manuscripts. The second is that it does not include a section that *was* in the original version.

In the 4th century, when the New Testament was collated, the Gospel of Mark ended at the present chapter 16, verse 8, before the narration of the post-Resurrection events.[7] These shorter manuscripts are part of the *Codex Vaticanus* and the *Codex Sinaiticus* in the Vatican Archive.[8] It is now generally accepted that the final twelve verses of Mark 16, with their different literary style, were appended as newly written additions by the bishops of the New Testament selection council sometime after AD 397.

As it originally stood, Mark 16:8 concluded the Gospel with Mary Magdalene and the other women departing from Jesus' empty tomb. The extra verses were added to perform two specific functions. The spurious Mark 16:9 is a strategic reminder of Mary's 'seven devils' as referenced in Luke 8:2. In fact, it is the only other biblical reference in this connection, but has the effect of diminishing Mary's status at this crucial stage of the proceedings. Against this, in the equally spurious Mark 16:15, the resurrected Jesus instructs his male apostles: 'Go ye into all the world, and preach the gospel to every creature'. Once again, this manoeuvres Mary Magdalene and the women successfully out of the evangelical picture so as to claim back the male prerogative of the movement.[9]

In direct contrast to this additional narrative, it was revealed quite recently that a substantial portion concerning Mary Magdalene, Martha and the raising of Lazarus had been removed from the Gospel of Mark before its inclusion in the New Testament. In 1958 Morton Smith, later Professor of Ancient History at Columbia University, found an intriguing manuscript of the Ecumenical Patriarch of Constantinople in the Tower Library of the monastery at Mar Saba, near Qumrân. This monastery, with terraces running down a cliff to the Kedron Valley, is one of the most spectacular buildings in Judaea.

Smith had been commissioned to catalogue the library's collection, and in the course of this he made an extraordinary discovery. Within a book of the 1st-century works of St Ignatius of Antioch was the transcript of a letter written by the churchman Clement of Alexandria (AD c150–215).[10] It was addressed to his colleague, Theodore, and included a little unknown section from the Gospel of Mark. Clement's letter discussed an unorthodox group called the Carpocrations, who were inspired by the teachings of Martha and Salome (that is Helena-Salome, the wife of Simon-Lazarus, not Jesus' sister Sarah-Salome).[11] It decreed that some of the original content of Mark was to be suppressed because it did not conform with orthodox requirement. In explaining his reason for the deletion, Clement wrote:

> For even if they [the Carpocrations]
> should say something true, one who loves
> the Truth should not, even so, agree with
> them. For not all true things are the Truth;
> nor should that truth which seems true
> according to human opinions be preferred
> to the true Truth – that according to the
> faith. To them one must never give way;
> nor, when they put forward their
> falsifications, should one concede that the
> secret Gospel is by Mark, but should deny
> it on oath. For not all true things are to be
> said to all men.[12]

The removed section of Mark has Lazarus calling to Jesus from within his tomb even before the stone was rolled back.[13]

This makes it quite clear that the man was not dead in the physical sense, and that Jesus' act of 'raising' him was not a supernatural miracle in the way it is customarily portrayed.

With the Lazarus raising having been deleted from Mark by St Clement, it does not therefore appear in Matthew or Luke – only now in John. The main difference between John and the secret Mark account, however, relates to the behaviour of Mary Magdalene in the context of this event. John 11:20–29 describes:

> Then Martha, as soon as she heard that
> Jesus was coming, went and met him: but
> Mary sat still in the house … [Martha]
> called Mary her sister secretly, saying, The
> Master is come, and calleth for thee. As
> soon as she heard that, she arose quickly
> and came unto him.

No reason is ventured for Mary's hesitant behaviour but, apart from that, the passage seems straightforward enough – Martha left the house, but Mary stayed indoors until summoned by Jesus. The incident was described in much greater detail, however, in the suppressed portion of Mark. It explains that Mary did indeed come out of the house with Martha on the first occasion, but was then chastised by the disciples and sent back indoors to await Jesus' instruction.

The fact is that, as Jesus' wife, Mary was bound by a strict code of bridal practice. She was not permitted to leave the house and greet her husband until she had received his express consent to do so.[14] John's account leaves Mary in her rightful place without explanation, but the more detailed Mark text was expressly withheld because it made the marital reality too apparent. In Clement's own words, it exposed the Truth rather than conveying the alternative 'truth according to the faith'.

The suppression of the Lazarus story is why the accounts of Mary Magdalene's subsequent Bethany anointing of Jesus are located at the house of Simon the leper in the Gospels of Mark and Matthew (the man called Simon the Pharisee in Luke), instead of at the house of Lazarus as in John.[15] To comprehend the relevance of this, we need to look at the bigger picture of this episode. It is also necessary to understand the biblical use of the word 'death' in this context, as determined by the scribal codes of the Dead Sea Scrolls.

The man referred to as Lazarus was Jesus' friend and apostle, Simon, a one-time Pharisee. In the apostolic lists of Matthew 10:4 and Mark 3:18 we are introduced to him as Simon the Canaanite, while in Luke 6:15 and Acts 1:13 he is called Simon Zelotes (Simon the Zealot). The Zealots were militant freedom fighters and advocates of war with Rome – sometimes called *Kananites* (Greek: 'fanatics').

In AD 32, Simon fell foul of the authorities, having been party to an unsuccessful revolt against the Roman Governor, Pontius Pilate. The reason for the uprising, as related by Josephus in *The Antiquities of the Jews*, was that Pilate had been using public funds to have his personal water supply improved.[16] A formal complaint was lodged against him in court, whereupon Pilate's soldiers murdered the known complainants. Armed insurrection immediately ensued, led by Simon Zelotes. Perhaps inevitably, the revolt failed and

Simon was outlawed by edict of King Herod-Agrippa I.

Under Jewish law, outlawry was a form of death by decree – the spiritual execution of a social outcast (akin to excommunication), and was figuratively referred to as 'death'. However, it took four days for complete implementation. In the meantime, the excommunicatee was stripped, wrapped in a shroud,[17] shut away, and held to be 'sick unto death'. In the case of Lazarus, Martha and Mary knew that his soul would be forever condemned if he was not reprieved (raised) by the third day, and so they sent word to Jesus that Simon was 'sick' (John 11:3).

At first Jesus was powerless to act, for only the High Priest or the Father of the Community could perform such a raising (resurrection) and Jesus held no priestly office. It happened, however, that Herod-Agrippa fell into an argument with the Roman authorities, losing his jurisdiction to the short-term benefit of his uncle, Herod-Antipas, who had supported the Zealot action against Pilate. Seizing his opportunity, Antipas countermanded the order of outlawry and instructed that Simon should be resurrected from death.

Although the time of spiritual death (the fourth day following excommunication) for Simon had arrived, Jesus decided to presume a priestly entitlement and perform the release in any event. In doing this, he confirmed the spiritually dead Simon's rank as that of Abraham's Steward, Eliezer (Lazarus), and summoned him, under that distinguished name, to come forth from the bosom of Abraham. And so it was that Lazarus (Simon Zelotes) was raised from the dead without official sanction from the High Priest, the Father or the Sanhedrin Council of Elders.

Jesus had blatantly flouted the rules of Temple society, but Herod-Antipas then obliged the hierarchy to acquiesce in the *fait accompli* – and to the people at large this politically unprecedented event was indeed a miracle. It was then that (as given in John 11:47–53) High Priest Caiaphas and the Pharisees 'took counsel together for to put him to death'.

The description 'Simon the leper' applies because he was classified in the community as a leper, being rendered hideously unclean by his excommunication. This, in turn, explains the subsequently anomalous account of a leper entertaining prestigious friends at his fine house (Matthew 26:6 and Mark 14:3).

The Great Heresy

In 1959 a controversial tract concerning Jesus and Mary Magdalene was issued by the Dominican friar Antoine Dondaine.[18] Entitled *Durand de Huesca et la polémique anti-cathare* (Durando d'Osca and the anti-Cathar polemic), the report was compiled for the journal *Archivum Fratrum Praedicatorun* – the annual review of the Dominican Historical Institute in Rome.[19] In discussing the Middle Ages historical records of the sect of Cathars in Southern France, Dondaine related that they believed 'Mary Magdalene was in reality the wife of Christ'.[20]

A century before the Templar Inquisition, the Cathars of Languedoc (west-north-west of Marseilles, on the Golfe du Lion) were the most victimized of heterodox Christians – 'heretics' as they were called. In line with their Magdalene beliefs, they were supporters of the *Desposyni* inheritance, and referred to the Messianic bloodline as the *Albi-gens*. In the language of old Provence, a female elf was an *albi* (*elbe* or *ylbi*), and Albi was the name given to the main Cathar centre in Languedoc. This was in deference to the matrilineal heritage of the Grail dynasty of the Davidic blood royal known as the *Sangréal*. (Notwithstanding the Anglo-Saxon mythological use of the word 'elf' [Semitic: *elef*], in Old Testament terminology it related to the head of a king-tribe.)[21]

In 1208, the Cathars were severely admonished by Pope Innocent III for unchristian behaviour. Then, in the following year, a papal army of 30,000 soldiers descended upon the region under the command of Simon de Montfort. They were deceitfully adorned with the red cross of the Holy Land Crusaders, but their purpose was immeasurably different. They had been sent to exterminate the ascetic Cathari sect (the Pure Ones) who, according to the Pope and King Philippe II of France, were abominable heretics. The slaughter went on for thirty-five years, claiming tens of thousands of lives and culminating in a hideous massacre at the seminary of Montségur, where, in 1244, more than 200 hostages were set upon stakes and burned alive.[22]

In religious terms, the doctrine of the Cathars was essentially Gnostic; they were notably spiritual people, who believed that the spirit was pure but that physical matter was defiled. Although their convictions were unorthodox in comparison with the avaricious pursuits of Rome, in reality the Pope's dread of the Cathars was caused by something far more threatening. They were said to be the guardians of a great and sacred treasure associated with a fantastic and ancient knowledge – a uniquely esoteric wisdom, called *Sapientia*, that transcended Christianity. The Languedoc region was substantially that which had formed the 8th-century Jewish kingdom of Septimania, and was steeped in the traditions of Lazarus and Mary Magdalene, whom they regarded as the Grail Mother of Christendom.[23]

Like the Templars, the Cathars were expressly tolerant of the Jewish and Muslim cultures. Indeed, the Counts of Toulouse were censured by the papacy for affording Jews positions of public office. The Cathars also upheld the equality of the sexes[24] but, for all that, they were condemned and violently suppressed by the Catholic Inquisition (formally instituted in 1233) and were charged with numerous offences of blasphemy and sexual deviance. Contrary to the charges, the witnesses brought to give evidence spoke only of the Cathars' 'church of love' and of their unyielding devotion to the ministry of Jesus. They believed in God and the Holy Spirit, recited *The Lord's Prayer* and ran an exemplary society with its own welfare system of charity schools and hospitals. They even had the Bible translated into their own tongue, the *langue d'oc* (hence the regional name), and the non-Cathar population benefited equally from their altruistic efforts.

In practical terms, the Cathars were simply nonconformists, preaching without licence and having no requirement for appointed priests or the richly adorned churches of their Catholic neighbours. St Bernard de Clairvaux had said, 'No sermons are more Christian than theirs, and their morals are pure'. Yet still the papal armies came, in the outward guise of a holy mission, to eradicate their community from the landscape.

The edict of annihilation referred not only to the mystical Cathars themselves, but to all who supported them – which included most of the people of Languedoc. At that time, although geographically a part of France, the region was a semi-independent State. Politically, it was rather more associated with the northern Spanish frontier, having the Count of Toulouse as its overlord. In contrast to the prevalent subjugative climate in Western Europe, Languedoc society was markedly more tolerant and cosmopolitan.[25] The region was, in fact, the prominent centre of Troubadour lyric poetry and Courtly Love, which flourished under the patronage of the Counts of Béziers, Foix, Toulouse and Provence. Classical languages were taught, along with literature, philosophy and mathematics. The area was relatively wealthy and commercially stable, but all this was to change in 1209 when the papal troops arrived in the foothills of the Pyrenees. In allusion to the Cathar support of the dynastic *Albi-gens* (the Kingly bloodline) the savage campaign was called the Albigensian Crusade.[26]

Of all the religious cults that flourished in medieval times, Catharism was the least menacing, and the fact that the Cathars were associated with a particular ancient knowledge was no new revelation. Guilhelm de Toulouse de Gellone, King of Septimania, had established his Judaic Academy in Languedoc more than four centuries earlier. The Roman bishops feared, however, that the Cathars were in a position to overturn the orthodox Church doctrines, and there was only one solution for a desperate and fanatical regime. Consequently, the word went out to 'Kill them all'.

The Magdalene Archive

Earlier, we looked at the *Pistis Sophia* tractate of the Askew Codex, which featured Mary Magdalene and the apostles at a lesson with Jesus in AD 44 (*see* page 115). As with the secret Gospel of Mark, however, there are other ancient texts which distinguish Mary in a less common light. This is the Magdalene whom Hippolytus and the pre-Roman Christians referred to as the *Apostola Apostolorum* (Apostle of the Apostles).

In 1969, Mary was formally sainted by the Catholic Church (feast day 22 July), but it is interesting to note that in the 17th century a request for this, made by the Dominican convent at La Sainte-Baume, had been turned down.[27] This move on the part of the French Dominicans was instigated by Fra Michaelis of Provence, an active reformer at the time of his election as Prior of St Maximus la Sainte-Baume. Previously, in 1691, the historian Thomas Souéges, who composed the saintly entries for each day in *The Dominican Year*, wrote (when he got to 22 July): 'Mary Magdalene, the Mother Protectress of the Order of Preachers'. He then added, as a personal aside to Mary: 'You were kind enough to do us the honour of treating us as children and brothers ... It pleased you that you wished the precious remains of your body to be guarded, and the place of your penance honoured'.

The first Dominican prior, Guillaume de Tonneins, had taken possession of the Sainte-Baume shrine from the Cassianites on 20 June 1295 and, apart from a short lapse during the French Revolution, the monks remained in residence until 1957. The monastery was then handed over to nuns, who had established their convent there in 1872. Subsequent to the work at St Maximus la Sainte-Baume by King Charles II of Naples, Sicily and Provence, along with his Dominican adviser and confessor Pierre de Lamanon, Mary Magdalene's feast day was first celebrated throughout the Dominican Order in 1297, as recommended by the General Chapter of Bologna.[28] Jesus' mother Mary has always been a Mother Protectress of the Dominican Order, but Mary Magdalene was established as its parallel Mother Protectress, giving the two Marys equal status from the outset. As Fra Mortier, author of *The Dominican Liturgy*, has so aptly put it: 'The body of the Magdalene is guarded by the Preachers; the Order of Preachers is guarded by the Magdalene'.[29]

Testimony to this is found in the general iconography for Mary Magdalene, who has been artistically portrayed with St Dominic; also with the 14th-century Dominican affiliate St Catherine of Siena, who visited La Sainte-Baume in 1376. In around 1320, the Dominican Bishop of Savona commissioned a representation of himself with Mary Magdalene by the Italian artist Simone Martini. Also in the 1320s, the Franciscan, Teobaldo Pontano, commissioned an extraordinary depiction of himself and Mary Magdalene by Giotto di Bondone. This fresco, in the Magdalene Chapel of the Church of San Francesco in Assisi, portrays a very subordinate Pontano in the company of a proportionately gigantic, red-clad Magdalene (*see* plate 17).

Père Lacordaire's Dominican mentor, St Thomas Aquinas, gave a milestone sermon concerning Magdalene portrayals in 1787, stating that 'red is the colour of faith'.[30] This was to some extent in accord with orthodox Church opinion since red was the colour of the cardinals. The difference, however, was that the Vatican did not recognize this as far as women were concerned. For a female to wear a red mantle was not only blasphemous, it signified the lust and wantonness of the Scarlet Women. In conventual circles, it was also common for Mary Magdalene to be painted wearing a white habit, as we saw in the red egg portrait (plate 14). This again was unacceptable to the Roman Church since white was the colour of purity, and should not be attributed to a sinner. (We shall return to the subject of fine art regulations in due course.)

The important detail to bear in mind regarding the persistent monastic involvement with Mary Magdalene is that it all started back in AD 410 with the Cassianite monks of Marseilles. Their founder, John Cassian, had previously been a resident of Bethlehem when Emperor Constantine's Catholic bishops were compiling their New Testament at the Council of Carthage in AD 397. At that time, gospels, epistles and other texts not selected for canonical inclusion were sentenced to be destroyed, as a result of which copies were buried and hidden in various parts of the Empire.

Cassian knew precisely what was contained in these manuscripts concerning Mary Magdalene, but it was not until the 18th-century *Pistis Sophia* revelation, and the more recent 1945 discoveries of 52 texts at Nag Hammadi, that some of these secreted documents came to light. Indeed, the latter books were not published in translation until the 1970s and, for well over 1,500 years, the Church's canonical New

Testament was the single available source of Christian scripture. Only in very recent times have we become aware of what John Cassian once knew, and what the Dominican Friars Preachers had always taken on trust.

Forgotten Gospels

In view of latter-day discoveries such as the Dead Sea and Nag Hammadi collections, along with tens of thousands of other documents now unearthed from Old Testament times, it is impossible for established Church dogma to carry the weight that has been its long-standing tradition. People are, of course, entitled to believe whatever they choose, but the lately-found documentation casts a whole new light on many aspects of religious history. In some instances it serves to underpin what has long been believed, but in other cases different scenarios are presented.

Blind faith is no longer a viable option for now there are new balances to be weighed. Either we take full account of the evidence to hand, or we ignore it to follow the old courses regardless. What we now have are alternative accounts – options on which to base considered judgement. One cannot challenge dogma on the one hand, and then introduce a new dogma to override it with the other. Dogma is an obligatory system of acceptance, but it cannot function in an environment of free will and choice.

The word 'heresy' derives from the Greek *hairesis*, meaning 'choice'. Thus, a charge of heresy was a denial of choice. In Inquisitional times, it was an offence to disobey the rule of Rome and the dogmatic opinions of the bishops. Today matters are different; choice must prevail, but it should be an informed choice. To facilitate that process it is as necessary to study non-canonical material as it is to study those documents that were selected (on our behalf but without our consent) by those with particular vested interests many centuries ago.

Shortly, we shall take a look at just how the New Testament Gospel selection was made. But first let us consider some of the books that were not chosen for the canon – works that were, in effect, selected against for one reason or another.

One of the texts which, along with *Pistis Sophia*, would have been familiar to John Cassian, is that known as *The Dialogue of the Saviour*. This is another question-and-answer session, but in a more limited environment it centres on Jesus, Matthew, Thaddaeus and Mary Magdalene. The discussion is in some respects mildly kabbalistic and akin to Grail lore in that its message concentrates on salvation and personal attainment of the Light. It is based on a wide collection of the sayings of Jesus known as 'Q' (from *quelle*, meaning 'source'). Many of these sayings appear in John and the Synoptic Gospels, but others do not, even though they are recorded elsewhere in the 'Q' context. The important aspect of *The Dialogue of the Saviour* as far as we are concerned is that the text portrays Mary Magdalene as an insightful visionary; the apostle who excels above the others, and 'the woman who knew the All'.[31]

Apart from the fact that Jesus was said to love Mary Magdalene, there is an apparent veiling of their intimate closeness in the New Testament. This is not the case, however, in the *Gospel of Philip*, where the relationship between Jesus and Mary is openly discussed:

> And the consort of the Saviour is Mary
> Magdalene.[32] But Christ loved her more
> than all the disciples, and used to kiss her
> often on the mouth. The rest of the
> disciples were offended by it and
> expressed disapproval. They said unto
> him, Why do you love her more than all
> of us? The Saviour answered and said to
> them, Why do I not love you like her? ...
> Great is the mystery of marriage, for
> without it the world would not have
> existed. Now the existence of the world
> depends on man, and the existence of
> man on marriage.

Notwithstanding the particular references to 'consort' (royal spouse) and the importance of marriage in this passage, the mention of kissing on the mouth is especially relevant. It relates specifically to the sacred offices of the bride and bridegroom, and was not the mark of extramarital love or friendship in Judaean society. As a part of the royal bridal refrain, such kissing is the subject of the first entry in the Old Testament *Song of Solomon*, which opens, 'Let him kiss me with the kisses of his mouth; for thy love is better than wine'.

Another intriguing text is the *Gospel of Peter*. This was found in 1886 by the French Archaeological Mission of Cairo in a monk's grave within an ancient cemetery at Akhmîm (Panopolis) in Upper Egypt.[33] Like so many of these old parchment books, the leaves are quite fragmented and much has been lost. That apart, some fascinating content has been preserved from a tradition that dates back to the 2nd century Anatolian Christians of Rhossus.

The *Gospel of Peter* follows similar lines to the New Testament Gospels in telling the story of Jesus' crucifixion, burial and resurrection. It does, however, have different emphases in many respects, and gives a particular prominence to the role of Mary Magdalene. In relating the initial account of the women at Jesus' tomb, the gospel makes no mention of his mother, nor of anyone else by name – stating simply that Mary Magdalene 'took her friends with her and came to the sepulchre where he was laid'. Then, in another verse, the text refers only to 'Mary Magdalene and the other Mary'.

Perhaps the most important book of all is the *Gospel of Mary Magdalene*. This text was a part of the Nag Hammadi find, but an earlier copy had been previously discovered in Cairo by the German scholar, Dr Carl Reinhardt, in 1896. By virtue of two World Wars, it was not translated and published until 1955, by which time the second copy had also been found. These were both Coptic texts, but subsequently two older Greek fragments have been discovered. Although it has been possible to piece much of the text together from the remnants, there is still a good deal missing – ten pages in all. The Gospel, as it stands, begins at chapter 4 of the original. It relates to the period immediately after Jesus' resurrection, stating that for a short time some of the apostles knew nothing about the event.

Fragment of the *Gospel of Mary Magdalene*

The account tells that the apostles 'wept copiously, saying, How can we possibly go to the gentiles and preach the gospel of the kingdom of the Son of Man? If they were ruthless to him, won't they be ruthless to us?' Having already spoken with Jesus at the tomb, Mary Magdalene was able to reply: 'Stop weeping. There is no need for grief. Take courage instead, for his grace will be with you and around you, and will protect you'.

Peter then said to Mary, 'Sister, we know that the Saviour loved you more than other women. Tell us all that you can remember of what the Saviour said to you alone – every-thing that you know of him but we do not.'

Mary recounted that Jesus had said to her: 'Blessed are you for not faltering at the sight of me: for where the mind is, there is the treasure'. Then Andrew responded, and said to the brethren, 'Say whatever you like about what has been said. I for one do not believe the Saviour said that'. Peter, agreeing with Andrew, added, 'Would he really have spoken privately to a woman, and not freely to us?' At this:

> Mary wept and said to Peter … Do you
> think that I thought this all up myself, or
> that I am not telling the truth about the
> Saviour? Levi answered, and said unto
> Peter … You have always been hot-
> tempered. Now I see you arguing with
> the woman as if you were enemies. But if
> the Saviour found her worthy, who are
> you, indeed, to reject her? The Saviour
> surely knows her well enough.

Taking these commentaries into account, it is not in any way surprising that Emperor Constantine's bishops elected to sideline these and other similarly worded Gospels. Not only was Mary Magdalene far more significant historically than was acceptable to their male-dominated establishment, but she appears to have been severely at odds with Peter in whose name the Roman Church had been founded. The *Desposyni* inheritors of Jesus and Mary Magdalene were the greatest of all threats to the Imperial machine and, despite continued decrees of persecution and assassination from the Emperors, the family heirs and their Nazarene Church still wielded considerable influence within the Empire.

When faced with dozens of Gospels and texts to consider at the Council of Carthage, these documents and others like them were in the same melting pot. In this textual selection we have seen references to Mary Magdalene being the consort of Jesus; items which explain that he kissed her often, and loved her more than all the others. She was called the Apostle of the Apostles; an insightful visionary who excels above the others, the woman who knew the All, and the one whose heart was more directed to the Kingdom of Heaven than all her brothers. Over and above all that, when questioned about her favoured position in the scheme of things by jealous male apostles, Jesus responded with a lecture about the importance of marriage!

There was only one way for the Imperial Church to suppress such manuscripts. The bishops had to contrive a new document for public consumption – a strategically organized, official and compulsory book of the Faith which did not include them. And so the New Testament was born.

8

Women and the Church

A Matter of Dates

A curious fact about the New Testament Gospels is that, although they each tell essentially the same story, they are not always in such accord as one might imagine. There are some individually unique features, such as the wedding at Cana and the raising of Lazarus, but once these are removed from the equation, the basic story of Jesus' life and ill-fated mission is common to all. There are many discrepancies, however, in the way in which that biographical account is conveyed.

A good example of how the Gospels differ in their telling occurs at the very beginning with the Nativity, which is common to two of them. Mark makes no reference to this event, while John alludes to it briefly in passing. The subject is only fully covered in Matthew and Luke, but their time-frames are completely different.

In Matthew 2:3 the Nativity is set during the reign of King Herod of Judaea. Matthew 2:22 details this king's son as Archelaus, so we know that the Herod in question was Herod I, the Great, who died in the year we now classify as 4 BC.

Luke 2:1–2 gives an alternative chronology, claiming that Jesus was born in the year of the Judaean census of Emperor Augustus, when Cyrenius was Governor of Syria. It is chronicled in the 1st-century *Antiquities of the Jews* that there was indeed a taxing census in Judaea conducted by the Roman senator Cyrenius at the behest of Caesar Augustus.[1] It is the only recorded census for the region, and it took place in the last regnal year of Herod the Great's son, Herod-Archelaus, who was deposed in AD 6.[2]

The Gospels refer to Herod the Great and Herod-Archelaus simply as 'Herod', as if they were the same person. Subsequently, Herod-Antipas of Galilee, Herod-Agrippa I of Judaea, Herod-Agrippa II and Herod of Chalcis are each similarly called 'King Herod'. It is therefore essential to get the Gospel chronology into perspective so as to know which Herod is being discussed at any given time.

Regarding the birth of Jesus, we are provided with the knowledge that it occurred before 4 BC (Matthew) and in AD 6 (Luke). This constitutes a nine-year minimum time difference and, without access to the community records of the Dead Sea Scrolls, it would be quite impossible to understand why there is an apparent discrepancy in this regard. It transpires, however, that 'birth' was a twofold event. First there was physical birth; then there was birth into the community. The second was a symbolic ritual of rebirth, when the child was ceremonially wrapped in linen cloths (swaddling) and figuratively brought into society. This is the event which is recorded in Luke, whereas Matthew deals with Jesus' earlier physical birth.

Historically, in the Essene tradition, these birthing events were twelve years apart.[3] Community Birth was the precursor to the *Bar Mitzvah* (Son of the Covenant) tradition which, from the Middle Ages, has signified membership of the Jewish congregation from the onset of age thirteen. Luke explains that the second event took place in AD 6 (the year of Cyrenius and the Imperial census), so we can ascertain from this that Jesus was actually born in 7 BC, which was indeed during the latter reign of Herod the Great.

The misunderstanding of this twelve-year custom led to a subsequent error in the translation of Luke when dealing with Jesus' initiatory raising to manhood. The story is told in Luke 2:41–50 of how Jesus was delayed at the Temple when in Jerusalem with his parents. The event is reported as occurring when Jesus was twelve years old, but it should actually relate to his designated 'twelfth year'. That is not twelve years after his birth into the world, but twelve years after his birth into the community. At the Passover of that year, Jesus would actually have been twenty-four – the age of social majority. Instead of accompanying his parents to the related celebrations, he stayed at the Temple to discuss his degree status with the teachers,[4] stating, 'Did you not know I was bound to be occupied with my Father's affairs?' His spiritual father, the Father of the Community, was at that time the priest Eleazer Annas.

In biblical chronologies, the Nativity is generally given as being in the year 5 BC (in the *Oxford Concordance Bible* for example). This is only two years adrift from the reality – but what has any of this got to do with our conventional Before and After Christ (BC and AD) dating structure?

The first published sequence of biblical dates appeared in 526, as calculated by the monk Dionysius Exiguus. By his reckoning, Jesus was born in the Roman year 754 AUC (*Anno Urbis Conditae*, meaning 'Years after the founding of the City [of Rome]'). In this context, 754 AUC was equivalent to the restyled calendar date of AD 1, which makes sense of the *Anno Domini* (Year of Our Lord) classification. The first Christian ruler to employ the Dionysus calendar was Emperor Charlemagne in the 8th century, and its use spread gradually throughout Europe, thereby determining the millennium years that we apply today.

It was subsequently decided however that, since Jesus was born in the reign of King Herod the Great, then he must have been born before Herod's death in 750 AUC, which had already been designated as 4 BC. Consequently, the monk's calendar was adjusted by the English publisher William Eusebius Andrews of Norwich (1773–1837) along with his New York counterparts George Pardow and William Denman. They re-established the date of Jesus' birth more accurately as being 5 BC (749 AUC), a year before Herod's death. This is the date which is now generally given in modern reference books, but it makes a complete nonsense of the previously cemented BC and AD classifications.[5]

By virtue of the confusion in this sequence of dating and redating, the recent Millennium festivities might well have celebrated 2,000 years of an arbitrarily introduced Roman calendar, but they were seven years too late to have any relevance to the actual birth of Jesus.

From this we can see that, while neither Matthew nor Luke is inaccurate, they appear to differ on the surface until we understand the customs and terminology of the Gospel era. Without knowledge of these, a good deal of New Testament narrative can easily be misread. In our investigation of the life of Mary Magdalene, it is imperative that we acknowledge the nature of certain contemporary traditions in order to ascertain the precise details of Mary's marriage to Jesus as they are described in the New Testament.

Jesus' Birthday

The Jerusalem degree event on Jesus' 24th birthday is of express significance because it determines the precise month, and it is stated in Luke to have been at the time of the Passover.

The Old Testament book of Leviticus 23:5 sets up the law in this regard, stating that the Lord's Passover is on the evening of the '14th day of the first month'. The Jewish New Year is celebrated in September, with Passover being in March. There is a difference, however, between the terms New Year and First Month, although neither conform to the January–December cycle of the Gregorian calendar.

The Jewish New Year, known as *Rosh Hashanah* (Head of the Year), occurs on the 1st and 2nd days of Tishri (September–October), whereas Leviticus refers to the Day of Remembrance, *Yom Ha-Zikkaron*, in the month of Nisan (March–April). In practice, the festivals fall in the equinox months of March and September. Somewhat confusingly though, the 'first month' of the Jewish calendar is not Tishri, but Nisan – the month used historically for counting the reigns of the kings.

In any event, since Jesus entered his 'twelfth year' (age 24) in 759 AUC [AD 6] and took his appropriate degree with the Temple doctors at the Passover, we can ascertain from this that his birthday was early in Nisan (March), on a date prior to the 14th as given in the Leviticus Passover ruling.

In calculating the precise date, we can turn to the dating phraseology of the New Testament as established in the Essene dating terms of the Dead Sea Scrolls. These begin by determining the equinoxes and solstices. In New Testament Greek, the phrase *en ekenais tais hemerais* (in those the days) refers to the equinox month of Tishri (September), whereas the phrase *en tais hemerais ekenais* (in the days those) refers to the equinox month of Nisan (March). The phrase *en tais hemerais tautais* (in the days these) means Tamuz (June), and *en tautais tais hemerais* (in these the days) is Tebeth (December). The important factor is the positioning of the noun *hemerais* (days).[6]

Continuing, more specifically, *treis hemerais* (three days) refers to Day-3 (Tuesday), with Sunday being Day-1, and so on. When a definition such as *hemerai okto* (Day-8) is used, it is positioned relative to Day-1 – that is to say the 8th day after a particular Sunday event (ie, the following Sunday), as against it being cited as Day-1 in another weekly cycle. This is important when considering the Luke account of Jesus' circumcision.

The covenant of circumcision is laid down in Genesis 17:11–12, which states that it shall be performed when a boy is 8 days old. This is corroborated in Leviticus 12:3. In respect of Jesus, Luke 2:21 relates, 'And when eight days were accomplished for the circumcising …' But the original Greek does not state *okto hemerais* (8 days), it states *hemerai okto* (Day-8), denoting a Sunday following a particular Day-1 Sunday. We know from Leviticus, however, that this was also 8 days after Jesus' birth, which must similarly have been on a Sunday. Additionally, we know that this was a Sunday before the Passover on the 14th Nisan (March), which narrows the field to it being just one of two Sundays.

Reverting now to days of the month, we find that there were specific definitions for key dates, with terminology such as 'this day', 'that day', 'next day' and 'last day'. The 1st of a month was identified by 'this day', a term which also identified the date of the Roman New Year in accordance with the Julian calendar introduced in 46 BC. For Jesus' birthday, the term is very specifically used: 'For unto you is born this day …' (Luke 2:11), and the Roman calendar began on 1 March.

In conclusion, the birth date of Jesus appears to have been Sunday, 1 March 7 BC by the Julian calendar. And according to *Finigan's Handbook of Biblical Chronology*, this date was indeed a Sunday.[7]

To conform with Messianic convention, Jesus would subsequently have been allotted an official dynastic birthday of 15 September to regularize his status. In some strictly orthodox traditions, Jesus' birth date is still reckoned to have been in September (Tishri), the month of Atonement (*Yom Kippur*). This was the officially designated birth month of dynastic heirs, irrespective of when they were actually born.[8] It was not until AD 314 that Emperor Constantine arbitrarily changed the date of Jesus' birthday to 25 December. His reason for this was twofold. Firstly, it separated the Christian celebration from any Jewish association, thereby suggesting that Jesus was himself a Christian and not a Jew. Secondly, it was designed to coincide with the pagan sun festival after the winter solstice – a date with which the citizens of Rome were familiar.

Consort of the Saviour

In some cases, where the Gospels deal unanimously with a particular event, there are significant differences in the presentation. One of these, which involves Mary Magdalene in particular, is the scene at Jesus' tomb after the Crucifixion – the scene that defines the Resurrection.

In the course of Jesus' crucifixion on the Passover Friday of AD 33, Joseph of Arimathea negotiated with the Roman Governor, Pontius Pilate, to have Jesus' body removed from the cross after just a few hours of hanging. This was to facilitate a change of executional procedure in accordance with an ancient law as laid down in the Old Testament book of Deuteronomy 21:22–23 and confirmed in the Qumrân *Temple Scroll*:

> And if a man have committed a sin
> worthy of death, and he be put to death,
> and thou hang him on a tree, his body
> shall not remain all night upon the tree,
> but thou shalt in any wise bury him that
> day.[9]

Pilate therefore sanctioned the change of procedure from hanging (as manifest in Roman crucifixion) to the alternative Jewish custom of burial alive. Jesus was then placed in a tomb belonging to Joseph, and Mark 15:47 confirms that 'Mary Magdalene and Mary the mother of Joses [Jesus' younger brother] beheld where he was laid'.

The next day was the Sabbath, about which the Gospels have little to tell. Only Matthew 27:62–66 makes any mention of this Saturday, but refers simply to a conversation between Pilate and the Jewish elders in Jerusalem, following which Pilate arranged for two guards to watch Jesus' tomb. Apart from that, all four Gospels continue their story from the Sunday morning thereafter.

When the women arrived at daybreak they were amazed to find the tomb's entrance stone rolled from its position. In practical terms, there was nothing startling about this – anyone could have moved it. Indeed, the women would have rolled it away themselves, for they had no reason to anticipate a prevention of access. What was so unthinkable was that the stone had been moved on the Sabbath, a sacred day on which it was utterly forbidden to shift a burden. The mystery was not in the act of the stone's removal, but in the day of its removal.

The bigger mystery lies, however, in who was present with Mary Magdalene on that occasion. The Gospels are in a general disagreement about this, and the overall picture is very confusing.

Matthew 28:1 tells that Jesus' mother Mary and Mary Magdalene made their way to the tomb, while Mark 16:1 includes Jesus' sister Salome as well. Luke 24:10 introduces

The Three Marys at the Empty Tomb – woodcut by
Julius Schnoor von Carolsfeld (1794–1872)

his other sister, Joanna, but omits Salome, whereas John 20:1
has Mary Magdalene arriving entirely alone. Mark, Luke and
John claim that when the woman/women arrived, the stone
had already been displaced. In Matthew, however, the two
sentries were on guard and the stone was still in position.

Then, to the astonishment of the women and the sentries, 'the angel of the Lord descended ... and rolled back the stone'.

It subsequently became apparent that Jesus was not in the tomb where he had been laid. According to Matthew 28:5–6, the angel led the women into the sepulchre. In Mark 16:4–5, they went in by themselves and were confronted by a young man in a white robe. Luke 24:3–4, however, describes two men standing inside. John 20:2–12 relates that Mary Magdalene went to fetch Peter and another disciple before entering the cave with them. Then, after her companions had departed, Mary found two angels sitting within the sepulchre.

In the final analysis, it is not clear whether the guards existed or not. The number of women was either one, two, or three. Perhaps Peter was there, or maybe he was not. There was either an angel outside or a young man inside; conversely, there were two angels inside, who might have been sitting, or might have been standing. As for the stone, it was possibly still in position at daybreak, or perhaps it had already been moved.

There is only one potential common denominator in all of this: Jesus was no longer there – but even that is not certain. According to John 20:14–15, Mary Magdalene turned away from the angels to find Jesus standing in the garden. She moved towards him, but Jesus prevented her embrace, saying, 'Do not cling to me' (John 20:17).[10]

These are the four accounts on which the entire tradition of the Resurrection is based, and yet they conflict in almost every detail. Because of this, centuries of argument have ensued over whether it was Mary Magdalene or Peter who first saw the risen Christ. There is no way of knowing which of the accounts is correct, if indeed any is in its entirety. In real terms, it does not really matter, but since the non-canonical Gospels of *Peter* and *Mary Magdalene* both grant the privilege to Mary, the odds are certainly in her favour.

The *Gospel of Philip* maintains that 'There were three who always walked with the Lord ... his sister and his mother and his consort were each a Mary'. These three were at the cross, and were probably at the tomb. Elsewhere in the same Gospel it is stated, 'And the consort of the Saviour is Mary Magdalene'. (In strict terms, each of Jesus' sisters would have been a designated *Mary*.)

The key to Mary Magdalene's status is in the original Greek word from which these translations were made. A 'consort' is, in dictionary terms, 'a royal spouse: one who holds title in common',[11] and the word used in the *Gospel of Philip* in this regard is *koinonôs* (consort). This word is absolutely explicit in meaning; it has positive conjugal connotations and relates expressly to a wedded sexual partner.[12]

Whether there was one woman, two or three at the tomb, the scenario caused a significant problem for the Church of Rome, which was founded as the Apostolic Church of St Peter. It was for this reason that a spurious twelve verses were added to the Gospel of Mark in the 4th century, with similar additions made to the Synoptic Gospels of Matthew and Luke.

By this strategy, Mary Magdalene's status was diminished, along with the relevance of her *Desposyni* heirs and their Nazarene movement. All that remained was for the bishops to draw up a blueprint that would belittle the status of women in general. This was done by way of the *Apostolic Constitutions* and the *Precepts of Ecclesiastical Discipline*.

Selecting the Gospels

The New Testament, as we know it, began to take shape in AD 367 when a library of writings was sifted and collated ready for selection. This initial part of the process was carried out by Bishop Athanasius of Alexandria, who invented the term 'canon' (approved law) and subsequently became known as the Father of Orthodoxy.[13] Prior to this there had been no formally compiled book of the faith, just a series of individual Christian texts which had their greater or lesser popularities in various parts of the Roman Empire.

From the Athanasius shortlist, certain works were approved and ratified by the Council of Hippo in AD 393, and by the Council of Carthage in AD 397. There were, nevertheless, various criteria which governed the selection – the first being that the Gospels chosen for the New Testament must be written in the names of (or attributed to) Jesus' own apostles. But this ruling appears to have been disregarded from the outset, and the four Gospels that emerged for approved canonical use were those of Matthew, Mark, Luke and John.

According to the apostolic lists given in the New Testament, Matthew and John were indeed apostles of Jesus. But Mark and Luke were not. They are presented in The Acts as being later colleagues of St Paul. On the other hand, Thomas, Philip and Peter were all listed among the original

The bishops submit their Gospel selections to Emperor
Constantine (from a 12th-century Roman manuscript)

twelve, and yet the Gospels in their names were excluded. Not
only that, but they were sentenced to be destroyed and,
throughout the Mediterranean world, people buried and otherwise secreted their copies of these works, along with the
Gospel of Mary and numerous other texts which had, quite sud-
denly, been declared heretical.

Following this, the strategically compiled New Testament
was subjected to any number of edits and amendments,
until the version with which we are now familiar was
approved by the Council of Trento, in Northern Italy, as late
as 1547.

Only in recent times have some of the early manuscripts
been unearthed, but the existence of these books had been
no secret to religious historians. Certain of them, including

the *Gospel of Thomas*, the *Gospel of the Egyptians* and the *Gospel of Truth*, had been cited in the writings of early churchmen such as Clement of Alexandria, Irenaeus of Lyon and Origen of Alexandria.

What then was the criterion by which the Gospel selection was truly made? It was a wholly sexist regulation which precluded anything that upheld the status of women in Church or community society. The Church of Rome was the Apostolic Church of St Peter, and Peter's views were made abundantly clear in the *Gospel of Thomas*, which claims that Peter objected strongly to Mary Magdalene's presence in Jesus' entourage. The text states that, addressing the other apostles, 'Simon Peter said unto them, Let Mary leave us, for women are not worthy of life'.[14]

In addition to this, we have already witnessed Peter's apparent dislike of Mary's involvement on other occasions. In the *Gospel of Mary*, Peter challenges her relationship with Jesus, saying, 'Would he really have spoken privately to a woman, and not freely to us? Why should we change our minds and listen to her?' Again, in the Coptic tractate of *Pistis Sophia* Peter complains about Mary's participation, and asks Jesus to restrain her from undermining his supremacy.

From the earliest days of 1st-century Christian society, two distinct factions emerged. In primary position was the Nazarene movement of Jesus' brother James, with which Simon Zelotes, Philip, Thomas and Thaddaeus, along with Jude, Salome, Mary Magdalene and the *Desposynic* family in general were associated. Then there was the evangelical school of Peter and Paul (generally called the Pauline movement), which was centred in Rome. In time, this became 'churchianity' rather than Christianity in its original form, and eventually overwhelmed the Nazarene fraternity after becoming the official state religion of the Emperors.

Although Constantine manipulated Christianity into a 4th-century hybrid with the sun cult and other pagan beliefs, he cannot be held responsible for the full extent of the corruption. Early protagonists of what became the orthodox Church had been moulding the religion to suit their own ambitions long before Constantine's day. Clement of Alexandria had removed the Lazarus story from Mark's Gospel in about AD 195, and Quintus Tertullian had already set the scene against female involvement at much the same time, stating from the *Precepts of Ecclesiastical Discipline*,

> It is not permitted for a woman to speak
> in church, nor is it permitted for her to
> baptise, nor to offer the Eucharist, nor to
> claim for herself a share in any masculine
> function, least of all in priestly office.

In this regard, Tertullian (a Church father from Carthage) was expressing a general sentiment of the Pauline movement – reiterating and highlighting the documented opinions of his predecessors, notably Peter and Paul.

In the *Gospel of Philip*, Mary Magdalene is regarded as being emblematic of divine wisdom, but all such texts were excised by the bishops of the evolving Church because they weakened the dominance of the male-only priesthood. In accordance with the epistles of St Paul, his teaching was expounded instead:

> Let the woman learn in silence with all
> subjection. But I suffer not a woman to
> teach, nor to usurp authority over the
> man, but to be in silence.
> (1 Timothy 2:11–12)

Such directives, along with other similar pronouncements, are found in the *Apostolic Constitutions* – a lengthy and comprehensive set of Catholic Church regulations begun by St Clement and concluded by the Constantinian bishops. They have been called 'the most sacred of canonical books and Christian laws'.[15]

Authoritative edicts such as those cited were successful in suppressing the legacy of Mary Magdalene. Just to make sure, however, the *Apostolic Constitutions* actually went so far as to specify her by name, adding, 'Our Master and Lord, Jesus himself, when he sent us the twelve to make disciples of the people and of the nations, did nowhere send out women to preach'. Then, quoting St Paul again (from 1 Corinthians 11:3), it continued: 'For if the head of the woman is the man, it is not reasonable that the rest of the body should govern the head'!

It is plain from the text of the *Constitutions* that, within the Nazarene community, women were closely involved in the ministry. The document therefore goes to great lengths in warning against the practice, claiming that 'there is no small peril to those who undertake it'. Discussing baptism in particular, the *Apostolic Constitutions* claim that it is 'wicked and impious' for a woman to perform this or any other priestly function. In justifying this, it is explained that 'if baptism were to be administered by women, certainly our Lord would have been baptised by his own mother, and not by John.' 'These heretical women,' wrote Tertullian, 'how audacious they are! They have no modesty. They are bold enough to teach; to engage in argument'.[16]

To get all this into perspective, it should be remembered that this form of pre-Roman Church Christianity was very much a Jewish-style institution. The followers were, in practice, Judaeo-Christians and clung to many traditional notions. In Hebrew society, women were never counted in the minimum number of ten required for a synagogue service to take place.[17] The *Palestinian Talmud* states, 'The words of the Torah will be destroyed in the fire sooner than be taught to women'.[18] And women were, in general terms, treated as lesser mortals with few of the privileges of men. Deuteronomy 22:23–27 states, for example, that a virgin who is raped in a city should be sentenced to death because she could easily have cried out for help!

It was with regard to such matters as these that the more liberal, tolerant and socially balanced views of Jesus' Nazarene fraternity so differed. There was a marked degree of equality not found in strict Jewish or later Judaeo-Christian society but, unfortunately, Roman Christianity inherited the intolerant perspective of those such as Tertullian.

Many of the women, who led Nazarene-style groups that were formally pronounced heretical, promoted a teaching based on instruction from the ascetic Therapeutate at Qumrân. Such teaching was inclined to be spiritually based, whereas the Roman form of Christianity was very materialistic, and mystical teaching was perceived as an enormous threat. Rome's strategy against the women teachers was that they were to be considered sinners and subordinates on the authority of St Paul, who wrote (in 1 Timothy 2:13–14): 'For Adam was first formed, then Eve. And Adam was not deceived, but the woman being deceived was in the transgression.'

By the 2nd century AD, a process of segregation had commenced in Christian churches: the men performed the rite, the women worshipped in silence. At the end of the century, even this level of involvement had gone, and women's participation in religious worship was forbidden altogether. Any female known to take part in religious practice was denounced as a strumpet and a sorceress.

At this time the Nazarenes were unpopular not only with the Roman authorities, but were also being severely harassed by the Pauline Christians – particularly by Irenaeus, Bishop of Lyon (born AD c120). He condemned them as heretics for claiming that Jesus was a man and not of divine origin as ruled by the new Faith. In fact, he even declared that Jesus had himself been practising the wrong religion, and that he was personally mistaken in his beliefs! Irenaeus wrote of the Nazarenes, whom he called *Ebionites* (Poor):

> They, like Jesus himself, as well as the
> Essenes and Zadokites of two centuries
> before, expound upon the prophetic
> books of the Old Testament. They reject
> the Pauline epistles, and they reject the
> apostle Paul, calling him an apostate of
> the Law.

In retaliation, the Nazarenes of the *Desposynic* movement denounced Paul as a 'renegade and a false apostle', claiming that his idolatrous writings should be rejected altogether.

In view of the Church's particular dread of Mary Magdalene, an extraordinary document was produced for the orthodox market. It set down what the bishops reckoned to be Mary's position within the scheme of things. Entitled the *Apostolic Church Order*, it was the transcript of a presumed discussion between the apostles, and it claimed (which the Gospels do not) that both Mary and Martha had been present at the Last Supper. In this respect, it rather defeated part of its own objective by affording the women such a prerogative – but it had a distinctly destructive purpose. An extract from the supposed debate reads:

> John said: When the Master blessed the
> bread and the cup, and assigned them
> with the words, This is my body and
> blood, he did not offer them to the
> women who are with us. Martha said: 'He
> did not offer them to Mary because he
> saw her laugh'.[19]

On the basis of this imaginary dialogue, the Church decreed that the first apostles had decided that women were not allowed to become priests because they were not serious! The essence of this fabricated conversation was then adopted as formal Church doctrine and Mary Magdalene was thereafter pronounced a disbelieving recusant. Over 1,600 years later, nothing much had changed and, in 1977, Pope

Paul VI decreed that a woman could not become a priest 'because our Lord was a man'!

Throughout the setting-up of the *Apostolic Constitutions*, the apparent dislike of women by Peter and Paul was tactically used to establish a male-dominated environment, but the quoted statements from these men were chosen very carefully, if not sometimes out of context. Despite St Paul's apparent desire for male dominance, his letters made particular mention of his own female helpers: Phebe, for example, whom he called a 'servant of the church' (Romans 16:1–2), along with Julia (16:15), and Priscilla the martyr (16:3–4). In fact, the New Testament (even in its strategically edited form) is alive with women disciples, but the Roman Church bishops elected to ignore them all.

The Church hierarchy was so frightened of women that a rule of celibacy was implemented for its priests – a rule which became a law in 1138, a rule which persists even today. What really bothered the bishops however was not women as such, nor even sexual activity in general terms; it was the prospect of priestly intimacy with women. Why? Because women can become mothers, and the very nature of motherhood is a perpetuation of bloodlines. This was a taboo subject which, at all costs, had to be separated from the necessary image of Jesus.

But, it was not as if the Bible suggested any such thing. In fact, quite the reverse was the case. St Paul had actually said in his second epistle to Timothy 3:2–5 that a bishop should be the husband of one wife and that he should have children. He explained that a man with experience in his own household is better qualified to take care of the Church.

Even though the bishops elected to uphold the opinions of Paul rather than the teachings of Jesus, they chose to disregard completely this particular directive so that Jesus' own marital status could be ignored.

9

The Sacred Marriage

Aspects of Translation

Throughout the period from AD 397 to the 17th century, the Church was in a strong position as far as its literature was concerned. The Library at Alexandria had been destroyed, a majority of non-canonical works were forgotten from one generation to the next, and the New Testament prevailed. From a working base of Greek manuscripts, transcribed from their originals by Clement and others in the 2nd century, New Testament editions such as the *Codex Sinaiticus* and the *Codex Vaticanus* were completed soon after the Council of Carthage.

Just prior to this, in AD 383, Pope Damasus I had commissioned the Roman Church scholar, St Jerome, to translate the various texts into Latin. Jerome separated out a number of works which he regarded as being apocryphal (denoting 'hidden things'), and from the balance constructed the *Vulgate Editio* – a scriptural edition for common (vulgar) use. But it was not as if everyone had a copy of the Vulgate.[1] Its 'common' usage was that it became the pulpit standard, so in many ways the priests were left to their own devices as to how they interpreted the text and taught from it. In essence, they could preach whatever they wanted.

Given that there were numerous differences in the four Gospels, a new Gospel was invented – an altogether smoothed-over tale that extracted the most entertaining features from each, and merged them into a single romantic story that was never authentically written by anyone. A version of this continuous narrative had been compiled AD c175 by Taitan, a Syrian theologian. It became known as *The Diatessaron* – from the Greek: 'According to Four'.[2] The Gospel story is still taught in very much the same way in schools and churches today.

There were a few vernacular renditions of selected New Testament extracts prepared in medieval times, but they were not widespread.[3] In England, the Oxford master John Wycliffe, along with John Purvey and Nicholas of Hereford, produced an English translation of the Vulgate in 1382 – but their work was condemned by the Vatican. At the same time Wycliffe openly criticized ecclesiastical practice such as priestly absolution, confession and indulgences, with the result that he was branded a heretic and his books were burned.

The university cleric William Tyndale produced an English New Testament from the Greek texts in 1526. His work made its way into many churches, only to be banned soon afterwards by the Catholic Queen, Mary Tudor. Swiss Protestants produced the famous Geneva Bible in 1560, and an English work called the Great Bible (edited by Tyndale's disciple Miles Coverdale) was approved by Queen Elizabeth I for her new Anglican Church. As a result, she was excommunicated by Rome. Meanwhile a new, more accessible version of the Vulgate, called the Douai Bible, appeared in stages between 1582 and 1610 for Catholics in France.

It was at the height of the 16th-century Protestant Reformation that Latin biblical supremacy was successfully challenged by the German reformer, Martin Luther. He made a comprehensive translation from the Greek texts, producing an edition that people could obtain and read for themselves. Subsequently, in 1611 came England's parallel version with the King James Authorized Edition. It was this newly printed text that England's Pilgrim Fathers and their eventual followers sailed with to America from 1620. Once there, having landed and settled in a variety of places on the eastern American seaboard, their differing local interpretations of the scripture gave rise to numerous small (and often competitive) church movements, as against the larger Christian denominations of Britain and Europe. In Massachusetts, the Protestant missionary John Elliot was not content with his English Bible, so in 1663 he produced a regional idiom version in the now extinct local language of the era.

How accurate then was the King James translation which remains the standard model today? It was, for the most part, transcribed from the Great Bible which, in turn, had been translated from the Greek texts. It does not suffer therefore from the considerable inaccuracies of the Latin Vulgate, but there are many instances where old Greek, Aramaic and Semitic words and phrases had no counterparts in Jacobean English. Consequently, certain errors were made. We have looked at two of these,[4] whereby *almah* (young woman) became 'virgin', and *ho tekton* (master of the craft) became 'carpenter'.

A particularly relevant inaccuracy of this sort is found in Luke 7:37, where Mary Magdalene is identified as a 'sinner' when she first anoints the feet of Jesus. (Before the second anointing by Mary in Bethany, John 11:2 explains that it was she who had anointed Jesus on the previous occasion.) The Luke entry is the only time when Mary is classified as a sinner, but it is in fact a poor translation. The original Greek word, *harmartölos*, was a sporting term which meant 'one who misses the mark'. Used in archery and similar pursuits, it related to being 'off-target'. In everyday use it pertained to one who perhaps did not observe certain doctrines, one who deviated from conventional practice – but it had nothing whatever to do with sin. Like *ho tekton* ('carpenter') in the case of Joseph, the term 'sinner' resulted in translation because there was no single word that corresponded to *harmartölos* in the English language. In Luke 5:8, the apostle Peter refers to himself as an *anër* [married man] *harmartölos*, which is similarly translated as 'I am a sinner'.

A translatory error which relates to Jesus' parents and the Nativity is that which led to the now common, but erroneous, belief that Jesus was born in a stable. There is actually no basis whatever for this image. No stable is mentioned in any original Gospel, neither is the word or anything like it used in the King James Bible. In fact, Matthew 2:11 states quite clearly that the baby Jesus lay within a house: 'And when they were come into the house, they saw the young child with Mary his mother, and fell down, and worshipped him.'

As we have seen, Luke is the only other Gospel which deals with the Nativity, and it is here that the translatory

Mary Magdalene anoints the feet of Jesus

confusion arises – not from any mention of a stable, but because Luke 2:7 states that Jesus was laid in a manger 'because there was no room for them in the inn'. Actually, there were no inns in 1st-century Judaea. Travellers were invited into people's homes, and it was regarded as a pious duty to provide hospitable lodgings.[5] The original Greek (from which the translation was made) actually states that there was 'no *topos* in the *kataluma*', which denotes that there was 'no *place* (or provision) in the *room*'.[6] In short, Jesus was laid in a manger because there was no cradle provided in the room. A manger was (as it still is) an animal feeding-box,[7] and it was not at all uncommon for mangers to be used as emergency or substitute cradles.

The Scarlet Woman

Other similar translatory misunderstandings occur with scriptural identifications where the use of language has changed over the years. A good example is found in Matthew 21:31, which states, 'Jesus saith unto them, Verily I say unto you, that the publicans and the harlots go into the kingdom of God before you'. In today's English language, a publican is 'the keeper of a public house (a pub)' – an innkeeper. In biblical times, a publican was a tax collector. More important to our investigation, however, is the word 'harlot', which is so often wrongly ascribed in translations from ancient texts.

Earlier, we considered the 'whore' definition as applied to those such as Sophia and Mary Magdalene. This word entered the English language from the Old Middle German *höre*, which related to adultery rather than to prostitution as we have lately come to understand the term.

The word 'harlot' has nothing to do with any of this, and was in fact a strictly masculine gender word until the

15th century.[8] It achieved a female connotation when used as a corruption of 'whorelet'[9] (little whore – slang for gypsy flower girls). Before that, however, the word meant 'vagabond' or 'rover'.

Once the term had achieved a feminine status, as related to 'whorelet', it became used as a means to translate the ancient and obscure word *hierodule*. This word appears as far back as the Sumerian *Song of Inanna* from around 2500 BC (before the Old Testament era of Abraham).[10] This erotic *Song* was related to the sacred marriage of the goddess who took as her bridegroom the shepherd Dumuzi (or Tammuz, for whom the women of Israel wept in Ezekiel 8:14).

Kings were referred to as 'Shepherds' in those days; they were guardians of their flocks, and the goddess (Inanna or Ishtar) was the *Magdal-eder*, the Watchtower of the flock. She presided from the Great House of the *E-gal*. As we have seen, it is from this distinction that the *Magdalene* title derives. It is of particular relevance that when Mary is introduced in Luke 8:2 (her earliest chronological reference), she is given as 'Mary *called* Magdalene', and she is commonly identified as *the* Magdalene. These citations of her *Magdal-eder* status are of express importance; *Magdalene* was a distinction, not a surname, nor anything to do with a place.

In Mesopotamian Sumer (the land of Abraham: Genesis 11:28–31)[11] the priest-king was called a *Sanga-lugal* – whence emerged the French *sang* (blood) as in *Sangréal*, the Blood Royal[12] – and his rod of assembly was a shepherd's staff (a crook or crosier). It was not until much later that the eventual Christian Church misappropriated the royal crosier as an instrument of authority for its bishops. Inanna, the goddess-queen was held to be the 'cup-bearer', whose sacred essence – the 'nectar of supreme excellence – was called the *Gra-al* (in later English, 'the Grail'). From Victorian times, the Holy Grail has become associated with the cup used by Jesus at the Last Supper, but it was never that in any original story. The concept of the Grail existed long before the days of Jesus.[13]

In the context of all this, the *hierodule* (as represented by Inanna) was the most holy aspect of the bridal ritual. Inanna, the goddess of light and fire, was later identified with Diana of the Nine Fires (*an-na* being an Akkadian word meaning 'fire-stone'). Her symbol, as shown on coins of the era, was the *Rosi-crucis* – the Dew Cup – a cross within a circle, the original emblem of the Holy Grail.[14]

In conventual terms, the *hierodulai* (plural) were 'sacred women', associated in New Testament times with the high priestesses of the Order of Diana of Ephesus. The robes of the *hierodulai* were red. They represented the *ritu* (truth), from which comes the word 'ritual'. In her priestly capacity as an emblematic *hierodule*, artists very often portrayed Mary Magdalene wearing red (*see* plates 17 and 18). By virtue of the linguistic perversion from *hierodule* to 'harlot' shortly before the Bible was translated into English, Inanna the Great became associated with the Whore of Babylon in the book of The Revelation 17:1–5, and red became directly associated with prostitution. Indeed, prostitutes still use the perverted Church imagery by perhaps wearing red, or by displaying themselves in red light.

Notwithstanding this, *hierodule* was the root of the Sacred Marriage, referred to as the *Hieros Gamos*. The *Song of Inanna* was an earlier version of the Old Testament *Song of Solomon*, and it is here that the bridal ceremony of the *Hieros Gamos* is explained – a sacred ritual that is repeated in the New Testament marriage scenes of Jesus and Mary Magdalene.

Female Ministry

When considering the comments made by St Paul concerning women and the ministry, there appears to be a persistent anomaly. At times, he draws individual attention to his female helpers, praising them for their work, while on other occasions he forbids women to take any active part in worship, let alone ministerial duties.

It seems to be the case that those such as Clement, Tertullian and others who later compiled the *Apostolic Constitutions* selected the passages from Paul's writings that most suited their particular vested interests, while ignoring the rest. But that still does not account for Paul's contrary standards in this connection which have led many theologians to suspect that maybe the epistles of St Paul were tampered with before publication, so as to make them suitable to requirements. Others have suggested that perhaps he did not personally write the epistles as they are presented. There is really no way to prove this either way since the original letters no longer exist, but it is apparent that there was a considerable time-span between Paul and those who used his work to support a newly emergent branch of the Christian faith.

Paul makes his New Testament appearance in AD 40, and was martyred in AD 64. Tertullian was born AD c160; Clement was a contemporary who died AD c215, and Constantine's first Council of Nicaea was in AD 325. Notwithstanding the 261 years between St Paul and the establishment of the Roman Church, there was over 100 years from Paul's death to the activities of the Church fathers. In the meantime, Christians were being persecuted within the Empire, especially in Rome where Peter and Paul were executed.

There is no doubt that Paul had a tough job to do. Whereas Jesus' own apostles had been operating in familiar homeland territory, Paul's mission was rather different. His allotted task was to progress the Christian message in the Greek-speaking countries of the Mediterranean coastal lands. In this environment, he had to compete with a variety of pagan beliefs. There were many religions whose gods and prophets were supposedly born of virgins and defied death in one way or another. They were all of supernatural origin and had astounding powers over ordinary mortals. To be fair to Paul, he certainly encountered problems that the original apostles never faced in their native environment. But his route to success against such odds was to present Jesus in a way that would transcend even these paranormal idols. In the event, however, it was the transcendent Jesus of Paul's invention who later became the divine Jesus of orthodox Christianity.

Originally, Paul (Saul of Tarsus) was a devout Hebrew and tutor to the son of King Herod-Agrippa I. His conversion to the more liberal Nazarene way occurred when he visited Damascus to arrest the disciples of Jesus whose Hellenic doctrines were contrary to the Hebrew law. Acts 9:1–2 states that this commission was enacted by a mandate from the High Priest in Jerusalem, but that cannot have been the case.

The Jewish Sanhedrin Council of Temple elders had no jurisdiction whatever in Syria.[15] It is far more likely that, since
Paul was attached to the Herodian administration, he would
have been acting for the Romans as part of their attempt to
suppress the Nazarenes.[16]

That apart, the important aspect of Paul's story lies in his
conversion and the fact that, when he was later brought on
a charge of incitement before the Governor of Caesarea, his
accuser stated, 'We have found this man, a pestilent fellow
and a mover of sedition among all the Jews throughout the
world, and a ringleader of the sect of the Nazarenes.'(Acts
24:5)

Following his experience with the apostles in Damascus,
Paul had become a Nazarene, and it is in this context that we
subsequently find him working with women in the ministry
of Jesus. If we now look again at the epistle references to his
female helpers, we discover that there is a repetitive error in
translation from the Greek copies of his letters.[17]

When Paul discusses those such as Phebe, for example,
we read that she was a 'servant of the church' (Romans 16:1).
When correctly translated, however, the word is found not
to be 'servant', but 'deacon'.[18] Having ascertained this, it
becomes clear that there was a distinct difference between
Nazarene practice and the 'new Church' ideals of those such
as Tertullian more than a century later. We are told that from
the outset of Jesus' ministry he had female helpers apart
from his mother and sisters. There was Mary Magdalene
and Martha of course, but Luke 8:3 also mentions 'Joanna,
the wife of Chuza … and Susanna, and many others which
ministered to him of their substance'.

The Nazarene Christian movement of Jesus, the apostles, St Paul and other New Testament founders was not the later Christianity of Clement or Tertullian; it was nothing like it. Nor indeed was it the eventual 'churchianity' of the Bishops of Rome. It was, as we have seen, the most threatening competitor of these institutions – the fraternity which Eusebius confirmed was run by the *Desposyni* heirs in a 'strict dynastic progression'. Inasmuch as St Paul might have exaggerated the image of Jesus for the benefit of his pagan audience, there is no doubt that the later fathers of the new Church manipulated Paul's writings to suit their endeavours, just as St Clement brazenly corrupted the Gospel of Mark.

Even during his lifetime, Paul had occasion to warn people about fictitious letters purporting to be from him,[19] and it was not uncommon for epistles to be fabricated for propagandist purposes.[20] Paul's letters to Timothy, Titus and Philemon have been the subjects of particular linguistic scrutiny, and it is doubtful that they represent authentic missives from his own hand.[21] These individually addressed correspondences (known as the Pastoral Letters) are very different in style and vocabulary from those addressed to community congregations such as the Corinthians, Galatians and Thessalonians. It is in the epistle of 1 Timothy that Paul's supposed comments about the repression of women are found,[22] but scholars now believe they were spuriously written some considerable time after Paul's death.

In consideration of this, we should look at some other early documentation in this regard to see what the generally unpromoted writings have to say about women in the ministry. Surprisingly, we find that Clement of Alexandria, in his *Commentary on 1 Corinthians*, wrote that the apostles worked in the company of women, who were 'sisters' and 'co-ministers'. Origen of Alexandria (AD 185–255), when writing about Paul's assistant, Phebe, stated that women were 'instituted as deacons in the church'. The Roman senator, Pliny the younger, wrote in AD 112 about female deacons. A Council of Nicaea transcript discusses the ecclesiastical role of a deaconess, as did Epiphanius of Salamis (AD 315–403), St Basil of Caesarea (AD 329–379) and numerous others. Perhaps most astoundingly, despite all the anti-feminine content mentioned in the previous chapter (*see* page 170), and in contrast to the general tone of the document, even the *Apostolic Constitutions* set out the differences in office between male and female deacons.[23]

It is therefore illogical and wholly misrepresentative for the Church hierarchy to claim that 'Our Master and Lord, Jesus himself, when he sent us the twelve to make disciples of the people and of the nations, did nowhere send out women to preach'. The documentary evidence proves beyond doubt that this is untrue. The practice of ordaining women for clerical office was extant long after New Testament times. Perhaps the most renowned of these women was the 4th-century St Olympias of Constantinople.

Having been left an immense fortune by her parents, Olympias married Nebridius the Prefect of Constantinople. He died shortly afterwards and Olympias, a young and wealthy childless widow, built the *Hagia Sophia* – the principal church of the city, where she was consecrated as deaconess by High Bishop Nectarius. Subsequently, she worked with his successor, the famous St John Chrysostom. The

Byzantine Church owes much of its historical success and prestige to Olympias, as did the Eastern Empire in general, which benefited greatly from her philanthropy to the poor of the realm.[24]

Dynastic Wedlock

The biblical *almahs* of the New Testament (including Jesus' mother Mary and Mary Magdalene) were the equivalent of conventual nuns, raised and educated for the prospect of dynastic marriage. They were high-bred priestesses in their own right, assigned to various tribal Orders such as those of Dan, Asher and Manasseh, and were attached to the ascetic Therapeutate community at Qumrân.[25]

The Essenes of Qumrân and the wilderness of Judaea are often said to have been celibates, and for the most part they were. They prevailed for many generations, however, and were necessarily procreative, although self-regulated by very strict rules. Sexual activity was not a leisure or pleasure pursuit, nor even particularly related to affection. The guidelines were rigid and tightly controlled by angelic priests such as the Gabriel whom we have already discussed. Josephus has much to say from his first-hand knowledge of the Essene sect in his *Antiquities and Wars of the Jews*.

In respect of Jesus' mother Mary, both Matthew 1:18 and Luke 2:5 state that she was 'espoused' to Joseph and she is thereafter referred to as his 'wife'. Here, the word 'espoused' does not mean betrothed or engaged; it refers to contractual wedlock. Matthew 1:1–17 and Luke 3:23–38 also give generational lists of the male ancestral descent to Jesus, via his father Joseph in the line of the Royal House of David.[26] The Davidic ancestry is confirmed in Hebrews 7:14, which makes the point that Jesus was of the kingly descent of Judah.

As the wife of a dynastic husband, Joseph's wife Mary would have been governed by the regulations applicable to Messianic (anointed) lines such as those of King David and Zadok the Priest. These dynastic rules were no ordinary matter and were quite unlike the Jewish marital norm.[27] Parameters of operation were explicitly defined, dictating a celibate lifestyle except for the procreation of children and, only then, at set intervals. Three months after a betrothal ceremony, a First Marriage was formalized to begin the espousal in the month equivalent to September. Physical relations were allowed after that, but only in the December. This was to ensure (as effectively as possible) that any resultant dynastic birth occurred in the following Atonement month of September. If the bride did not conceive, intimate relations were suspended until the next December, and so on.[28]

Once a probationary wife had conceived, a Second Marriage was performed to legalize the wedlock. However, the bride was still regarded as an *almah* until completion of the Second Marriage which, as qualified by Flavius Josephus, was celebrated when she was three months pregnant.[29] The purpose of this delay was to allow for the possibility of a miscarriage. Second Marriages thus took place in the month of March. The reason that full wedlock was not achieved until pregnancy had been firmly established was to accommodate the dynastic husband's legal change of wife if the first should prove barren.

In the case of Joseph and Mary, it is apparent that the rules of dynastic wedlock were infringed, since Mary gave birth to Jesus at the wrong time of year (Sunday 1 March, 7 BC).[30] Sexual union must therefore have taken place six months before the designated December, in June, 8 BC – at about the time of their initial betrothal – some three months before their First Marriage in the September. Mary not only conceived as an *almah* (damsel/sister), but also gave birth as an *almah* ('virgin' in the translated text) before her Second Marriage.

Once Mary's unauthorized pregnancy had been confirmed, Joseph would have been granted the option of not going through with the Second Marriage ceremony. To save embarrassment he could have placed Mary in monastic custody ('put her away privily', as in Matthew 1:19), where the eventual child would be raised by the priests. But if the child were a boy, he would be Joseph's firstborn descendant in the Davidic succession. It would have made little sense to bring him up as an unidentified orphan, leaving a possible younger brother to become his substitute in the kingly line. Joseph and Mary's unborn child was plainly a significant prospect and demanded special treatment as an exception to the rule. The angelic Gabriel (the Abiathar priest) would have advised that, since a sacred legacy was at stake, Joseph should go ahead with the Second Marriage ceremony, 'for that which is conceived in her is of the Holy Ghost' (Matthew 1:20).

Following this dispensation, the normal rules would have been applied once more – the first being that no physical contact was allowed between man and wife until some while after the child had been born – 'Then Joseph being raised from his sleep did as the angel of the Lord had bidden him, and took unto him his wife: And knew her not till she had brought forth her firstborn son: and he called his name Jesus.' (Matthew 1:24–25)

The Betrothal

A cursory glance through the New Testament Gospels reveals one wedding in particular where Jesus was an active participant. This is the wedding at Cana, where he performed the water and wine transformation. Like the raising of Lazarus, however, it is strange that such a seemingly important event is only mentioned in the Gospel of John. The raising of Lazarus was Jesus' last miracle; the water and wine miracle was his first, but it is similarly confined to just one Gospel account.

Jesus had little patience with the rigorous creeds of Jewish groups like the Pharisees, and he knew the people of Judaea could not be freed from Roman oppression until they had forsaken their own uncompromising sectarianism. He was also aware that a Saviour Messiah had long been anticipated – a prophesied redeemer who was expected to introduce a new era of deliverance. As the heir to the Davidic royal house, he knew that he was qualified to be that Messiah and that, if he should emerge as such, few would be unduly surprised. With this in mind, he was revolutionary in outlook and made a point of setting himself apart from customary practice.

What Jesus did not have, though, was any designated social authority; he was neither a reigning king nor a high priest. But he paid little heed to such technicalities, and proceeded to implement ritualistic changes, flouting many Hebrew traditions regardless of his titular deficiency. Miracles are not necessarily supernatural events, but they are by their very nature extraordinary and unprecedented. In fact, the word used in the Gospels (as translated to 'miracle') was *dunameis*, which relates to an action 'of power', sometimes accompanied by *teras* (an 'astonishment') and *semeion* (a 'sign').[31]

On his first opportunity to break openly with convention at the Cana wedding, Jesus hesitated, claiming, 'Mine hour is not yet come'. But his mother waved aside his lack of entitlement and directed the servants, saying, 'Whatsoever he saith unto you, do it' (John 2:4–5).

In describing the wedding feast, the Gospel explains: 'And when they wanted wine, the mother of Jesus saith unto him, They have no wine'. It then continues with an account of Jesus seemingly turning pots of water into pots of wine. The Qumrân *Scroll of the Rule* defines that, at such community tables, the service of wine was the prerogative of the presiding priest.[32] As identified in Hebrews 7:14, Jesus had no priestly authority, so any intervention on his part concerning the wine before it was poured would be a breach of the *Rule*, and yet he clearly intervened.

The relevance of the sequence is that only fully initiated Levites were allowed to drink ceremonial wine. All others present were regarded as unsanctified and were restricted to a purifying ritual with water.[33] These included married men, novices, Gentiles and all lay Jews. This is confirmed in John 2:6, which states: 'There were set there six water-pots of stone, after the manner of the purifying of the Jews'.

The significance of Jesus' action is that he took it upon himself to break with tradition when he abandoned the purification water and allowed the uninitiated guests to take the sacred wine. The Ruler of the Feast (Greek: *Architriclinos*) 'knew not whence it was (but the servants which drew the water knew)'. He did not comment on any marvellous transformation, but simply remarked that he was surprised the good wine had made its appearance at that stage. As Mother Mary declared, having instructed the servants to obey Jesus, the episode 'manifested forth his glory and his disciples believed on him'.

There is no talk in John's Gospel of any marriage service at Cana, only of a wedding feast and of the water and wine. Some of the disciples were there, as were various guests including Gentiles and others who were technically unclean. This, then, was not a ceremony of marriage but the wedding meal of a betrothal. The custom was for there to be a formal host (as appears in the account); he would be in charge of proceedings as the Ruler of the Feast. Secondary authority rested only in the bridegroom and his mother, and this is entirely relevant for, when the matter of the communion wine arose, Jesus' mother said to the servants, 'Whatsoever he saith unto you, do it'. No invited guest would have had any such right of command and, as many theologians have commented, Jesus and the bridegroom would appear to have been one and the same. Not least in this regard is Bishop John Shelby Spong of Newark, whose treatise on

Mary Magdalene is very revealing as far as some modern Church thinking is concerned.[34]

As well as discussing the wedding at Cana, Bishop Spong makes some interesting observations about other New Testament entries. He draws particular attention to 1 Corinthians 1:5 regarding the apostles' wives and sisters who accompanied Jesus, and asks:

> How does Mary Magdalene become the senior of this group of wives (the Apostle of Apostles), her name always first in the lists, if she is not the consort of Jesus?

> How would she have the right to claim the body of Jesus for taking away (as in John 20:15) if she were not his next of kin?

> Why would she presume the wifely duty of anointing Jesus for burial if not his wife?

In the light of these and other similarly intriguing instances, Bishop Spong suggests that the cumulative argument is indeed in favour of Jesus and Mary being man and wife. He writes: 'The record was suppressed, but not annihilated, by the Christian Church ... Yet so real was this relationship that hints of it are scattered all over the Gospels'.

Many apologists for the Church's dehumanization of Jesus make the point that nowhere in the Gospels does it say that he was married. The same could, of course, be said of his apostles – but why limit the New Testament to the Gospels which account for less than 50 per cent of the whole? Elsewhere in the New Testament, the apostles' wives are indeed discussed. In response to the apologists' claim, many others have remarked that nowhere in the Gospels does it say that Jesus was unmarried. But there is little point in countering a negative with a negative when there are positives to consider. As we shall discover, the Gospels (all four of them) certainly do state that Jesus was married.

In terms of Gospel chronology, the wedding feast at Cana in Galilee took place in June AD 30, which is absolutely right for a dynastic betrothal three months before a September First Marriage. Following that same chronology, we find that in September AD 30 Mary Magdalene anointed Jesus at Simon's house (Luke 7:37–38).[35] At that stage, she would also have wept for her husband (as indeed Luke 7:38 relates that she did) before they were parted for their statutory October–November separation. Subsequently, as an *almah* in betrothal, she would have been ranked as a *crippled woman* until the couple were permitted to come together for physical union in the December.[36]

In the world of fine art, it was often taken for granted that Mary Magdalene was present at the Cana wedding feast, and when portrayed she occupies the table position to the left of Jesus. In the 15th-century fresco by Giotto, for example, she sits between Jesus and his father, while in the 15th-century painting by Gerard David, Mary is placed between Jesus and his mother (*see* plate 13).

The Inheritors

Marriage of the Magdalene

The term *Messiah*, as applied to Jesus, derives from the Hebrew *māsach* ('anoint'). A Messiah was an 'Anointed One'.[1] The Greek equivalent was *Christos*, whence the kingly designation of 'Christ'. In this respect, therefore, Jesus was not unique. He was a Messiah, but there had been other Anointed Ones in the kingly line before him. Among the Dead Sea Scrolls, the text known as the *War Rule* (written long before Jesus' time) sets out a battle strategy for war against dark oppressors, and names the Messiah as the supreme military commander of Israel.[2] Another Qumrân scroll, entitled the *Messianic Rule*, deals with the Messianic office and the community Council of the Congregation.[3]

In ancient Egypt, kings were anointed with crocodile oil because it was associated with sexual prowess. The sacred crocodile of the Egyptians was the *Messeh*, which corresponds to the Israelite *Messiah*. Before that, in Mesopotamia the intrepid royal beast (a four-legged monitor) was called the *Mûs-hûs*. From these traditions, royal anointing came into Israel when the realm was established by King Saul

(1 Samuel 10:1). King David was then anointed (2 Samuel 5:3), as was his son Solomon (1 Kings 1:39) with whom the rite was granted to Zadok the priest. Thereafter, the Zadokites held the high-priestly prerogative throughout the Davidic succession – much as later European monarchs have been installed by the Pope or the Archbishop of Canterbury.

Such regal anointing determined the status of a Messiah. Hence, David, Solomon and their reigning dynasty were Messiahs (Anointed Ones). But Jesus never had a regnal position, and did not achieve his Messiah status until Mary Magdalene performed the anointing at Bethany in the week before his crucifixion. In this instance, however, there were differences in practice. This was no anointing for the throne, nor did it involve the Zadok priest. It was more akin to traditional marriage anointings by the sister-brides of the pharaohs, or the queens of Syria and other lands outside the Hebrew domain.[4] Also, instead of olive oil mixed with cinnamon, myrrh, calamus and cassia (as laid down for holy anointing oil in Exodus 30:23–25), Mary used the 'ointment of spikenard', a costly root extract from the Himalayas (John 12:3).[5]

The account of this anointing, which followed the raising of Lazarus and took place in his house, is given in the Gospels of Matthew, Mark and John.[6] When recounting the Lazarus event, John 11:1–2 explains that Mary had anointed Jesus on a previous occasion. This relates to the earlier anointing as given in the Gospel of Luke.[7]

The first anointing (Luke) was in September AD 30, when Mary anointed Jesus' feet and wiped them with her hair. The translation of this passage, in respect of 'her hair' has made its context a little unclear. The word was *thrix* (a type of veil described as 'a hair') and related to a headcloth worn by women of the era.[8] The second anointing was in March AD 33. On this occasion, John confirms that this same ritual was repeated, while Matthew and Mark add that Mary also took her 'alabaster box of ointment of spikenard, very precious ... and poured it on his head'.

As we have seen, the rules of dynastic wedlock were no ordinary affair. Explicitly defined parameters dictated a celibate lifestyle except for the procreation of children at regulated intervals. A lengthy period of betrothal was followed by a First Marriage in September, after which physical relationship was allowed in December. If conception took place, a Second Marriage ceremony was then celebrated in March to legalize the wedlock. During that trial period and until the Second Marriage, whether pregnant or not, the bride was regarded in law as an *almah*. What we have here, with Jesus and Mary Magdalene, is a precise adherence to this ruling – a September first anointing following the June betrothal feast at Cana, and a March second anointing. Since the second stage (the cementing of the contract) was not conducted until three months into pregnancy, this means that Mary must have conceived in December AD 32 and would therefore give birth in the Atonement month of September AD 33.

But why on this occasion was oil of spikenard used instead of the customary blend? Judas Iscariot apparently complained that it was far too costly to be used for such a purpose (John 12:4–5). In fact it is the spikenard which specifically sets this Messianic anointing apart as a bridal event, as distinct from a kingly installation as would have

Mary Magdalene anoints the head of Jesus. *At the House of Simon*
– woodcut by Julius Schnoor von Carolsfeld (1794–1872)

been performed by the Zadok priest. The Gospels all make
the point that the balm was precious and expensive, with
John 12:3 adding that 'the house was filled with the odour of
the ointment'. The key to this whole affair, and the reason for

the spikenard, is made clear by the fact that Mary Magdalene was of Syrian heritage, as explained in the Rabanus and Jacapo accounts of her family.

Among the more romantic books of the Old Testament is the Song of Solomon – a series of love canticles between a sovereign bride and her bridegroom. The Song identifies the potion symbolic of royal espousal as the aromatic ointment of spikenard: 'While the king sitteth at his table, my spike-nard sendeth forth the smell thereof' (Song 1:12).[9] This scene is replicated at Bethany where the office was also performed by Mary whilst Jesus sat at the table.[10] It alludes to an ancient rite by which a royal bride sanctified her bridegroom's meal. This was directly inherited from the Inanna–Dumuzi tradition of the *Hieros Gamos* (Holy Matrimony) of the Shepherd-king. The imagery is also apparent in the Old Testament Psalm 23, 'The Lord is my shepherd …', where it is said of the female aspect of the deity, 'Thou preparest a table before me … thou anointest my head with oil; my cup runneth over'.[11] To perform the nuptial anointing rite was the express privilege of a Messianic bride and was performed solely at the First and Second Marriage ceremonies.

Only as the wife of Jesus and a priestess in her own right could Mary have anointed both his head and his feet with the sacred ointment. The rite was prevalent in the most ancient princely culture of Mesopotamian Sumer as a repre-sentation of the Goddess bestowing favour and kingship on her chosen bridegroom.[12] In early times, there was no rule of primogeniture; kings were not automatically succeeded by their sons. Kingship depended on the choices of princesses, and their continued sexual acceptance of the Shepherd-kings depended on the fertility of the land.[13] Not only could a man not be a king without a queen, but that queen had to be of the royal blood.[14] Their personal relationships and the land were deemed to be inextricably linked; when one failed, the other failed.

In Arthurian romance, the land of Camelot fell into ruin when King Arthur lost Guinevere's affection to Lancelot. His knights subsequently quested to restore the matrilineal *Sangréal* (Holy Grail), and it was said that the barren wasteland would not return to fertility until the wound of the king was healed.

In chapter 2 (*see* page 33), we saw that the royal bride of the Song of Solomon, referred to as the 'Shulamite', was the noblewoman Abishag (Abigail) from the Syrian border town of Sölam (Shulam). The Song recounts the love contest over Abishag between King Solomon and his brother Adonijah, as related in 1 Kings 2:13–25. In this respect, it was the Syrian heritage of Mary Magdalene's ancestral family, which gave rise to the spikenard used at Bethany in the same context as the Canticles of the Song of Solomon. In his commentary on this subject, Samuel Noah Kramer of the Institute of Assyriology and Ancient Near Eastern Studies (affiliated to Bar-Ilan University, Tel Aviv) correctly identified that 'it is not concerned in any way with the history of the Hebrew people'.[15]

The Song of Solomon (*Shirath Shiram*) with its erotic essence of spikenard, and its parallel Magdalene anointings at Bethany are both of the same Syrian tradition. They stem from an ancient fertility rite based on the *Hieros Gamos* of Inanna and Dumuzi, and were part of the Threshing Floor rituals of the King's Week marriage festival of Sölam.[16] This tradition was recorded as being still extant as a rural festivity re-enactment as late as 1873.[17] A table and throne were prepared for the king from the threshing planks of the field and, while friends and family paid homage, the bride performed her queenly ritual. In doing this, she sang a wedding-night song that corresponded precisely with canticle sections of the Song of Solomon and, in reference to the same, was referred to as Abigail of Shulam.

St Bernard de Clairvaux, 12th-century patron of the Knights Templars was well aware of this symbolic association between Solomon and Jesus, Abishag and Magdalene. It was the reason why he claimed the Order's obedience to the Magdalene watchtower. It was why the Templars' *Notre Dame* cathedrals of France were originally consecrated to Mary Magdalene, the Lady of Light. It is why the foremost of these cathedrals, Notre Dame de Chartres, depicts the Bethany anointing in its magnificent Magdalene window. And it was why, in Sermon 57 of his *Sermons on the Canticles*, Bernard alluded to Mary Magdalene as the 'Bride of Christ'.[18]

Despite all that has been written in fiction and non-fiction works about the secret of Mary's nuptial relationship with Jesus, it has never been a secret as such. Knowledge of the Messianic bridal institution does not rely on access to conspiratorial archives, covert societies, or an understanding of enigmatic codes. The details of the ritual ceremony are set down in every New Testament Gospel. They have simply been veiled by a persistent Church assault on the Magdalene legacy – an attempt by the bishops to insinuate that, whilst marriage is an honourable estate for the rest of us, it was somehow beneath the dignity of Jesus. Hence, by way of arrogant association, it remains beneath the dignity of a priestly establishment that appears to care little for its reputation in other respects.

From the outset of Jesus' mission, Mary Magdalene is seen as a constant in his life. She sponsored him, travelled with him, anointed him, confided in him, and was companion to his mother and sisters. She was there at the foot of the cross; she went to attend Jesus with spices at the tomb, and was the first to speak with him in the garden. She is documented as Jesus' consort and the Apostle of Apostles, the woman whom Jesus kissed and called his blessed one – the woman who knew the All, and the woman that Jesus loved. In short, Mary Magdalene was closer to Jesus than anyone else, and this begs an intriguing question: For the sake of accepting that Jesus was married (like the apostles whose wives also travelled with them), would we really prefer to believe that Jesus opted for a noncommittal relationship with a prostitute instead of having a wife?

Mary Magdalene's reputation was decimated by a campaign of propaganda that had no biblical foundation whatever. In the course of this, Jesus' own humanity was substantially violated, while his mother became a thoroughly sexless wonder who represented nobody. Demeaned in such a way, she has never been a model for everyday womanhood, which is why so many now look to Mary Magdalene.

One cannot find anything of female consequence in a virgin mother image, but there is a romance of the sacred feminine in the Sophia inheritance of Mary Magdalene. From her feistiness to her weeping, from her wisdom to her uncertainty, she has all the attributes of reality and her loyalty is never once seen to waver. Of course Jesus loved her. Why would he not? She has been called the Goddess in the Gospels,[19] she has sexual presence, and her story embodies a wealth of adventurous experience. But she was the mother of the *Desposyni* heirs and, because of that, her character was brutally assassinated by a fearful and jealous establishment. And as for Jesus – his persona was left historically high and dry, with his mother a virgin and his loved-one a whore!

Kingdom of Heaven

Through application of the dynastic rules of the community, Mary Magdalene was three months into pregnancy at the time of the Crucifixion. She and Jesus had cemented their Second Marriage at the Bethany ritual in March AD 33, at which time Jesus' head was anointed and he gained his Messianic status. Apart from being able to glean this information directly from the Gospels, it is also a matter of straightforward calculation.

A male heir to the kingly succession was required ideally to have his first son at or close to his own 40th birthday. Forty years was the recognized period of royal generation.[20] This was based on Genesis 25:20 – 'And Isaac was forty years old when he took Rebekah to wife'. The royal bloodline of Israel had been promised to Abraham's son Isaac in Genesis 17:19 – 'I will establish my covenant with him for an everlasting covenant, and with his seed after him'. Thus, once the kingdom began, the 40-year standard was used in all records, irrespective of what might have been the case in reality – 'David reigned over Israel forty years' (1 Kings 2:11); 'Solomon reigned in Jerusalem over all Israel forty years' (1 Kings 11:42); and 'Jehoash began to reign; and forty years reigned he in Jerusalem' (2 Kings 12:1).

In detailing the Messianic line, the 40-year generation is apparent in the genealogical list of Matthew 1:6–16. It spans 1,080 years from King David to Jesus, and contains 27 generations of 40 years each. The significance of this as far as Jesus being the awaited Saviour (prophesied in Zechariah 9:9)[21] is that 1,080 was regarded as the magic lunar number of the eternal feminine – the spiritual energy of springs and streams.[22] Its polar opposite in the solar force was the male number 666. As given in Revelation 13:8, 'It is the number of a man'. Together the male and female numbers total 1,746, which Plato called 'fusion',[23] and in the numerical system of Greek Gematria this was the number of the Sacred Marriage – the *Hieros Gamos*.[24]

Dynastic First Marriages took place in the Atonement month of September, and would, theoretically be scheduled for the man's 39th September. With sexual activity allowed in the December, a child might well result in the following September. In practice, however, there was always the chance that the first child might be a daughter, so a contingency provision was made by bringing the First Marriage ceremony forward to the bridegroom's 36th September. The first chance of a child then fell in his 37th September. If there was no conception in the first December, the couple would try again a year later – and so on. For a son to be born in or around the husband's 40th year was fully acceptable within the generation standard.

During pregnancy, the couple were allowed no close physical contact. If a son was born, this constraint was perpetuated for six years.[25] Alternatively, if the child was a daughter the ensuing period of celibacy was limited to three years. Their eventual returns to the married state were called the Times of Restitution.

In accordance with these regulations, Jesus' First Marriage took place in September AD 30 (his 36th September) when Mary Magdalene first anointed his feet and wept (Luke 7:37–38). The symbolic weeping signified the bride's temporary downgrading from the status of 'sister' to that of 'crippled woman' (the same as 'widow')[26] until her Second Marriage. There was apparently no conception in that December, nor in the December of the following year. But, in December AD 32, Mary did conceive and duly anointed Jesus' head and feet at Bethany, formally sanctifying their Second Marriage, in March AD 33.[27] At that stage they were legally bound, and she would be raised again to the rank of 'sister', although still regarded as an *almah* (damsel) until she became a 'mother'.

Jesus' 39th September was in AD 33, six months after the Resurrection. The sequence of events concerning Jesus' trial, sentence, crucifixion and its aftermath, is fully discussed in *Bloodline of the Holy Grail*, but is partially included as Appendix II in this book for the benefit of new readers.

A point worth mentioning at this stage is the way in which the Gospels refer to Jesus' mother Mary either side of the Crucifixion and Resurrection. The entries related to her make the situation concerning Jesus' state of being abundantly clear. Prior to the Crucifixion, Mary is referred to as the 'mother of Jesus'. From the point when Jesus is considered to be dead on the cross, Mary is referred to (at the execution site and at the tomb) as the 'mother of James and Joses' (Matthew 27:56 and Mark 15:40), and as the 'mother of James and Salome' (Mark 16:1). Subsequently, however, once Jesus is on the scene again, there is a reversion to Mary's old style as the 'mother of Jesus' (Acts 1:14).

In September AD 33, a daughter was born to Mary Magdalene. She was named Tamar (Palm Tree), assimilated in Greek to the name Damaris.[28] In *The Da Vinci Code*, this daughter's name is given as Sarah, but *Sarah* was not her name, it was her distinction. In Hebrew, *Sarah* meant 'princess'. She was 'Tamar the Sarah'. Tamar was the original matriarch of the Royal House of Judah (Genesis 37–38) and the name of King David's sister (2 Samuel 13:1). Jesus was then required to enter a fully celibate state for three years until the Times of Restitution, as detailed in Acts 3:20–21:

> And he shall send Jesus Christ, which
> before was preached unto you: Whom the
> heaven must receive until the times of
> restitution of all things, which God hath
> spoken by the mouth of all his holy
> prophets since the world began.

The month of September AD 33 coincided with Simon Zelotes (Lazarus) being formally installed as the Father of the Essene Community, at which juncture Jesus was admitted to the priesthood – a ritual in which he figuratively 'ascended into heaven'.

Although recognized by many as the Davidic Messiah, Jesus had long sought entry into the inner sanctum of the senior Qumrân priests – the high monastery at Mird, known as the Kingdom of Heaven. With Simon in office, Jesus' wish was granted. He was ordained and conveyed to heaven by the Leader of the Pilgrims who was, by way of Old Testament imagery, designated as the Cloud.[29] A cloud had led the ancient Israelites into the Promised Land (Exodus 13:21–22), and the appearance of God to Moses on Mount Sinai had been accompanied by a cloud (Exodus 19:16). Consequently, in respect of priestly communication with God, the term Cloud was retained as a symbolic designation within the fraternity of Qumrân.

Jesus' elevation to the priesthood is recorded in the New Testament by the event generally known as the Ascension. Not only did Jesus speak himself in parables, the Gospel writers did the same, applying allegories and parallels that were meaningful to 'those with ears to hear' – those who knew the scribal codes. Thus, passages of the Gospel texts which seem to be straightforward narrative (no matter how apparently supernatural their contexts) are also parables. As Jesus said to the disciples (Mark 4:11–12):

> Unto you it is given to know the mystery
> of the kingdom of God: but unto them
> that are without, all these things are done
> in parables: That seeing they may see, and
> not perceive; and hearing they may hear,
> and not understand.

Although it has become a commonly used description for Jesus' priestly elevation, the term Ascension is not used in The Acts. It is simply stated: 'And when he had spoken these things, while they beheld, he was taken up, and a cloud received him out of their sight' (Acts 1:9).

As Jesus departed into the holy realm of Heaven, two angelic priests announced that he would eventually return to the earthly state: 'Behold, two men stood by them, in white apparel, which also said, Ye men of Galilee, Why stand ye gazing up into heaven? This same Jesus which is taken up ... shall so come in like manner as ye have seen him go' (Acts 1:10–11). And so it was that six months after his Resurrection, Jesus left the everyday world for three years, during which period Mary Magdalene, the mother of his child, would have no physical contact with him.

The Order of Melchizedek

According to Hebrews 3:1 and 5:6, Jesus was initiated at that time (September AD 33) into the priestly Order of Melchizedek. Bearing in mind that this was six months after his resurrection, it is wholly apparent that Jesus was still alive, and indeed remained so throughout the period of The Acts of the Apostles wherein his travels and meetings are recorded.

We have already encountered the fact that, as detailed in the Dead Sea Scrolls and the works of Josephus, the angelic structure was maintained within the priestly hierarchy of Qumrân. The Abiathar priest was the designated Gabriel, and his immediate senior, the Zadok high priest, was designated Michael – the Michael-Zadok (Melchizedek).

The original Melchizedek, priest-king of Salem, appears in Genesis 14:18–20, when he presented Abraham with the bread and wine of the Grail communion. In Hebrew terms, the name derives from *Melek* (King) and *Tsedeq* (Righteousness) – sometimes *Melchi-zaddiq* – King of Righteousness. Alternatively, as King of Salem,[30] he was (as described in Genesis) King of Peace. His statue is at the northern doorway of Chartres Cathedral – the Gate of the Initiates – where he is portrayed with his chalice and the daily bread of spiritual nourishment.

Fragments of the *Prince Melchizedek Document* found among the Dead Sea Scrolls indicate that Melchizedek and the Archangel Michael were one and the same. In these ancient parchments, Melchizedek is called the Heavenly One and the Prince of Light.[31]

Similarly, the Qumrân *Damascus Document* confirms that the styles of Zadok and Melchizedek were equivalent and mutually supportive. In essence, since Zadok was the ultimate high-priestly distinction, and since *Melchi* (or *Malchus*) related to kingship, it is apparent that Melchizedek was indicative of priest-kingship. This was of particular significance to Jesus because he had previously held no priestly entitlement. But at that stage in AD 33 he became an ordained priest-king on entry to the Kingdom of Heaven: 'Whither the forerunner is for us entered, even Jesus, made an high priest for ever after the order of Melchizedek' (Hebrews 6:20).

To explain the historical significance of this, Hebrews 7:14 totally dismisses the Gospel-interpreted notion of the

Virgin Birth in order to confirm that Jesus' real father was Joseph, in descent from Judah and Tamar. It states: 'It is evident that our Lord sprang out of Judah, of which tribe Moses spake nothing concerning priesthood'. It is also explained that the law concerning priesthood had to be changed to accommodate Jesus' new archangelic distinction (Hebrews 7:12).

The reason why this Zadokite priesthood was so important for the law to be amended was that there was a void to fill at the highest level of the community. The Zadok line, which had prevailed for more than 1,000 years, had expired. Being the closest relative to that dynasty, it was deemed that Jesus could take the responsibility.

In political terms, the apostolic party of Jesus and Simon Zelotes had been set up in parallel to that of Jesus' elder cousin John the Baptist. Through long prevailing custom, the Davidic kings were allied to the Zadokite priests, and the prevailing Zadok was John the Baptist, the son of Zacharias and Elisabeth (Jesus' maternal aunt).[32] John had risen to prominence in AD 26 upon the arrival of the Roman governor, Pontius Pilate, but he was very much of the narrow-minded Eastern persuasion, whereas Jesus was a Hellenist with more liberal Western views. Jesus' ambition for Israel and Judaea was one of harmonious, integrated society, but he was more than a little frustrated by the unbending Jews of rigid Hebrew principle, which included John the Baptist.

Jesus' vision was straightforward, and was based on the logic that a split Jewish nation could never defeat the might of Rome. But he also perceived that the Jews could not accomplish their mission if they continued to hold themselves separate from the native non-Jews. Even though John recognized Jesus as the legitimate kingly heir, and baptized him in the Jordan,[33] John's social persuasion was one of non-integration with the Gentiles.

Jesus knew that tradition had prophesied a Messiah who would lead the people to salvation, and he knew how desperately that Messiah was craved. John the Baptist was too much of a social recluse to fulfil that role, but there was a good deal of speculation over whether Jesus or John was the awaited Messiah. John was, after all, the prevailing Zadok, but when asked directly if he was the Saviour Messiah, he 'confessed, and denied not; but confessed, I am not the Christ' (John 1:20).

The Qumrân Scrolls indicate, however, that the community lived in expectation of two important Messiahs. One was to be of the priestly caste, whom they called the Teacher of Righteousness; the other would be a prince of the line of David – a warrior who would restore the kingdom of his people.[34] John made it quite clear that he was not the kingly Messiah: 'I said, I am not the Christ, but that I am sent before him' (John 3:28).

From a hitherto reserved position, Jesus then stepped into the public domain. In a short while, he gathered his disciples, appointed his twelve apostles, and began his ministry. Luke 3:1 states that this was in AD 29, the 15th year of Tiberius Caesar. A year later, however, John the Baptist was arrested and imprisoned by Herod-Antipas, Tetrarch of Galilee.[35] Antipas had married Herodias, the divorced wife of his half-brother, Herod-Philip, and the Baptist repeatedly condemned the marriage, declaring that it was sinful.

Subsequently, a daughter of Herodias demanded that John should be executed, and Herod-Antipas complied in September AD 31 (Matthew 14:10). The Gospel accounts do not identify this daughter by name, but *The Antiquities of the Jews* relate that Herodias had a daughter called Salome, so popular tradition has presumed that it was her.[36]

Apparently, this daughter requested that John should be stripped of his rank, and that his Zadokite *kephalë* (head-band) should be given to her.[37] (Because of the poor translation in this respect, this is often presumed to have been the actual head of the Baptist.) Since John died unmarried and childless, that was the end of the Zadok dynasty, which left the Messianic field free and clear for Jesus and his heirs. John had recognized the importance of this prospect, and had told the disciples, 'He must increase, but I must decrease' (John 3:30).

On his ignoble demise, John the Baptist was discredited and many of his followers turned their allegiance to Jesus. Some had thought that John was the expected Saviour Messiah, but a number of his prophecies had not been fulfilled and so he was discounted in any event. Some of the Temple Hebrews supported Jesus' younger brother James, who was at that time a member of the Sanhedrin Council, but James was not remotely interested in the Messianic contest.

Time of Restitution

Dynastic children were brought up and educated at a monastic centre, in which their mothers also lived. It was because Jesus had himself been brought up in such enclosed conventual surroundings that so little is told about his childhood in the Gospels. This residential complex, on the outskirts of Qumrân, was referred to as 'Bethlehem of Judaea' (as opposed to the separate Bethlehem settlement south of Jerusalem). Matthew 2:4–5 states that Jesus was born 'in Bethlehem of Judaea'.[38] Originally a palace for Hasmonaean royalty, the Qumrân *Copper Scroll* identifies it as the Queen's House.

Jesus' three-year period of monastic separation expired in September AD 36, following which physical relations with his wife were permitted once more in the December at the Time of Restitution. One very clear property of the language used in the New Testament is that words, names and titles which have a cryptic meaning are used with that same meaning throughout. Not only do they have the same meaning every time they are used, but they are used every time that same meaning is required. Undoubtedly the most thorough studies to date in this field of research have been conducted by Dr Barbara Thiering, a member of the University of Sydney Board of Studies in Divinity 1973–1991. Her research is based on information contained in the Dead Sea Scrolls commentaries that define the scribal codes of the Essene community. These Scrolls commentaries hold the secrets of the *Pesharim* (the routes to vital clues) and were produced in the pre-Gospel era by the learned scribes of Qumrân.

In some cases, individual derivations of coded names or titles might be complex or obscure, but more often they are straightforward, though rarely obvious. Frequently, cryptic information in the Gospels is heralded by the statement that it is intended 'for those with ears to hear' – the phrase being an inevitable precursor to a passage with a hidden meaning for those who know the code. The governing rules of the code are fixed and the symbolism remains constant, as in the case of Jesus himself.

By way of the inherent biblical *pesher* (singular of *pesharim* and meaning 'explanation' or 'solution'), Jesus is defined as the Word of God. This is established from the very outset in the Gospel of John:

> In the beginning was the Word, and the
> Word was with God … And the Word was
> made flesh, and dwelt among us, and we
> beheld his glory
> (John 1:1, 14).

There are no variables in the Gospel texts. Whenever the phrase 'word of God' is used, it means that Jesus either was present or is the subject of the narrative, as in Luke 5:1 when the word of God stood by the lake. The phrase was also used in The Acts to identify Jesus' whereabouts after the Ascension. So when we read that 'the apostles which were at Jerusalem heard that Samaria had received the word of God' (Acts 8:14), we may immediately understand that Jesus was in Samaria.

It follows, therefore, that when we read 'the word of God increased' (Acts 6:7) we should comprehend that 'Jesus increased',[39] as symbolized by the related *pesher* in the parable of the Sower and the Seed (Mark 4:8): 'And other [seed] fell on good ground, and did yield fruit that sprang up and increased'. As John the Baptist had said of Jesus, when pulling out of the dynastic contest, 'He must increase, but I must decrease'.[40] In short, the Acts reference means that Jesus yielded fruit and increased – that is to say, he had a son. Perhaps not surprisingly, this first son was also named Jesus (Yeshua).

As required by the Messianic rules, the birth took place in AD 37 – the year after Jesus returned to his marriage at the Time of Restitution. Following the birth of a son, however, Jesus was now destined for six more years of monastic celibacy.

THE LEARNING CENTRE
TOWER HAMLETS COLLEGE
POPLAR CENTRE
POPLAR HIGH STREET
LONDON E14 0AF

1 *In the House of Simon the Pharisee*
Philippe de Champaigne, c1656

2 *Penitent Magdalene*
Giovanni Gioseffo dal Sole (1654–1719)

3 & 4 *Mary Magdalene Renouncing Vanities* – before and after restoration
School of Franceschini Marcantonio (18th century)

5 *Noli me tangere*
Fra Angelico, 1441

6 Black Madonna of Paris at
Neuilly-sur-Seine

7 *Christ Falls under the Cross*
Francesco Bonsignori (1455–1519)

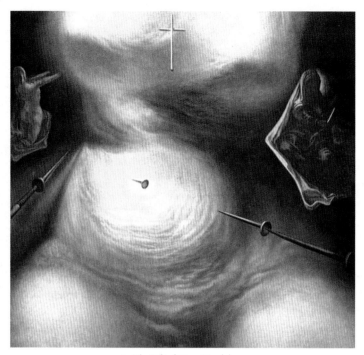

8 *The Life of Mary Magdalene*
Salvador Dali, 1960

9 *Mary Magdalene*
Caravaggio, 1595

10 *Mary and the Bishop of Marseilles*
Lukas Moser, 1432

11 *Mary Magdalene Carried by the Angels*
Giovanni Lanfranco, 1613

12 *The Holy Grail*
Dante Gabriel Rossetti, 1857

13 *The Wedding Feast at Cana*
(with Mary Magdalene) Gerard David, 1503

14 *Mary and the Red Egg*
Church of Saint Mary Magdalene, Jerusalem

15 *Mary Magdalene Ashore in Provence*
Pera Matas, 1526

16 *The Magdalene Voyage to Marseilles*
Giotto di Bondone, c1320 – San Francesco chapel of Mary Magdalene, Assisi

17 *Magdalene and Fra Pontano*
Giotto di Bondone, c1322

18 *Mary with Saints Dominic and Bernard*
Nicolás Borras, c1580

19 & 20 Studies for Mary Magdalene
Leonardo da Vinci (1452–1519) – The Courtauld Institute and Galleria degli Uffizi

21 *Allegory of Leonardo*
Sir Peter Robson, 1995. Detail from *Project Genisys*

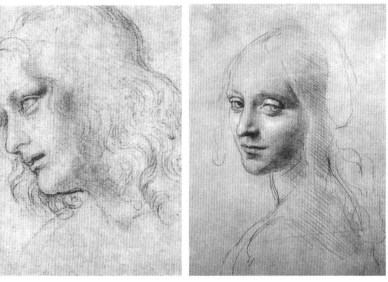

22 *Philip the Apostle* study drawing
Leonardo da Vinci, 1495

23 *Head of a Girl* for *Virgin of the Rocks*
Leonardo da Vinci, 1483

The Last Supper (Details showing the conversation between Peter and John)

24 Leonardo da Vinci, 1495   25 Hans Holbein the Younger, 1525

26 *The Redeemer* – Study of Jesus
Leonardo da Vinci, c1490

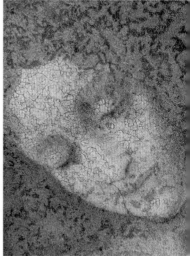

27 John (restored) – from *The Last Supper*
Leonardo da Vinci, 1495

28 *The Last Supper* (Restored detail showing figure relationships of John and Jesus)
Leonardo da Vinci, 1495

29 *The Last Supper* (Detail) – A variant of the Leonardo M-shape design
Philippe de Champaigne, c1648

30 & 31 *The Last Supper* (Details showing John's traditional youthful portrayal – as also below)
Domenico Ghirlandaio, 1480 and c1470

The Last Supper (Jesus and John details)
32 Paolo Veronese (1528–88)   33 James J. Tissot, c1890

34 *La Gioconda (Mona Lisa)*
Leonardo da Vinci, c1515

35 Gouache and ink study for *La Giaconda*
Leonardo da Vinci

36 *A Visit by Raphael* (Leonardo's studio with Lady Lisa Gioconda)
Aimée Pagès – later engraved copy 1845 by Lemoine

37 *Rest on the Flight into Egypt*
Gerard David, 1510 (Mother Mary in blue)

38 *Mary Magdalene Reading,* 1435
Rogier van der Weyden (Magdalene in green)

39 *Mary Magdalene*
Carlo Dolci, c1665 (Magdalene in red)

40 *Jesus and Mary Magdalene*
Federico Barocci, c1570 (Magdalene in gold)

41 *The Three Marys at the Tomb* Giovanni Battista Gaulli, c1685
(Mother Mary in blue; Magdalene in green, red and gold)

42 *Tempi Madonna*
Raphael, 1508

43 *Cowper Madonna*
Raphael, 1505

44 The Louvre version   45 National Gallery version

Leonardo da Vinci's *Virgin (Madonna) of the Rocks* – from 1483 (top arches cropped)

46 Beaux-Arts Caen version

47 The *Arnolfini* double portrait
Jan van Eyck, 1434

48 Magdalene window
Kilmore Church, Dervaig

49 *Sacred Allegory*
Giovanni Bellini, c1487

50 *Eucharist of the Last Supper*
(with Mary Magdalene) Fra Angelico, 1442

51 *Mary Magdalene Preaching in Provence*
Master of the Magdalene, c1510

52 *Jesus Maria* Stone at Glastonbury
53 Magdalene relics at La Sainte-Baume

The Grail Child

Separation

During the early AD 40s, the apostle Peter joined forces with the newly converted Paul in Antioch, Syria, while Jesus' brother James and his Nazarenes remained operative in Jerusalem. A further division in the ranks then became apparent when Simon Zelotes set up a separate base for his sect in Cyprus.[1]

Up to that point, Peter had been Jesus' right-hand man and, as such, he should have become Mary Magdalene's guardian during the years of her marital separation. But although Peter had been married himself, he had a low opinion of women and was not prepared to be at the beck and call of a priestess who threatened his authority. He therefore excluded Mary from any standing in the Antioch movement. The term 'Christian' was first used in Antioch in AD 44, and it was here that the new religion began to develop before moving onwards to Rome.

In the course of this, Jesus and Mary once more resumed their married state in December AD 43, six years after the birth of their son. Jesus does not appear to have been too concerned about Peter's attitude towards Mary, and seems to have been content that she had good friends in Simon Zelotes and his consort Helena-Salome. It was at that time, in December AD 43, that Mary conceived for the third time. But, by the spring of AD 44, Jesus had embarked on a mission to Galatia, in Central Asia Minor, with the Chief Proselyte,[2] John Mark.

During this period, James and his Nazarenes had become an increasing threat to Roman authority in Jerusalem. As a direct result, the apostle James Boanerges was executed by Herod of Chalcis in AD 44 (Acts 12:1–2). Simon Zelotes took immediate retaliatory action and had King Herod-Agrippa poisoned,[3] but was then obliged to flee. The apostle Thaddaeus was seized in his attempt to escape, and was executed by Herod of Chalcis. This placed the expectant Mary in a very precarious situation, for Chalcis knew that she was associated with Simon. She therefore appealed for protection from Paul's one-time student, young Herod-Agrippa II, who duly arranged her passage to the Herodian estate in Gaul.

We have seen that a couple of decades earlier, in AD 32, Simon was responsible for leading a Zealot revolt against Pontius Pilate in Jerusalem (*see* page 139). As a result, he was outlawed by Herod-Agrippa I, whose assassination he had now masterminded. Simon Zelotes, although an apostle of Jesus, was renowned as a *kananite* (fanatic). His associates were viewed with great suspicion by the Sanhedrin elders and Roman authorities, both of whom were instrumental in the trial and sentencing of Jesus. Mary Magdalene was a devotional sister and relative of Simon (Lazarus), and was constantly distrusted as a Zealot affiliate – she would have been classified as a law-defiant *harmartölos*: the word that was wrongly translated in Luke 7:37 to 'sinner'.

Inasmuch as Jesus had been said to love Mary, she also had a twofold professional role to play in the *Desposynic* campaign. Her first duty, in order to preserve the Davidic line, was to bear a son and heir for Jesus – a duty which she had successfully fulfilled. She was also a key player in the apostolic network, which was now widening its scope of operation into other lands. Irrespective of Jesus' personal relationship with Mary, the time had come for them to work apart from each other, and since Simon and Mary had to leave Judaea in any event, Mary was entrusted to Simon's guardianship.

The Magdalene Voyage

The wonderfully illuminated manuscript of *The Life of Mary Magdalene*, by Archbishop Rabanus Maurus, tells of how Mary, Martha, Simon-Lazarus and their companions left the shore of their homeland:

> And favoured by an easterly wind they
> travelled on across the Sea between
> Europe and Africa, leaving the city of
> Rome and all the land of Italy to the right.
> Then, happily changing course to the
> right, they came to the city of Marseilles
> in the Gaulish province of Vienne.

The libraries of Paris contain a number of manuscripts even older than that of Rabanus Maurus, which bear witness to Mary's mission in Provence. The story is mentioned in a hymn of the AD 600s that was republished in the records of the *Acta Sanctorum* by the Jesuit, Jean Bolland, in the 17th century.[4] Individual documents containing aspects of the story date back to the early 4th century, and a century before that the Cassianites were installed at La Sainte-Baume in the era of the Fisher Kings of Gaul, before Merovingian times. The 9th-century manuscript entitled *Vita emeritica beatae Maria Magdalenae* is reckoned to be copied from a Greek original from the 2nd century, possibly written by Hegesippus.[5]

In the world of religious fine art, there are numerous portrayals of Mary Magdalene in Provence. They show the landing of her ship, her meeting with the Queen of Marseilles (*see* plate 15), images of meditations in her grotto, paintings of her with Lazarus and Martha, and scenes of her preaching to the people of Languedoc (plate 51).

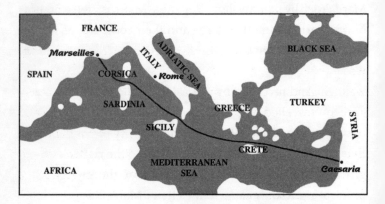

Course of the Magdalene Voyage

The accounts are unanimous in determining that the leader of the Provençal mission was Simon Zelotes, who became known as Lazarus the Great One (Maximus). He established his seat at Marseilles, where his statue was erected at St Victor's Church by the harbour. It was he who eventually laid the Magdalene to rest in her alabaster sepulchre at the Chapel of St Maximus in AD 63. Others in the original party were Martha's maid Marcella, accompanied by Philip the apostle and his companion Trophimus (later St Trophimus of Arles).

Philip was described by the historian Gildas I Albanicus (AD 425–512) as being the inspiration behind Joseph's subsequent mission in England. The *De Sancto Joseph ab Arimathea* states that 'Joseph came to Philip the apostle among the Gauls'. Freculphus, a 9th-century Bishop of Lisieux, wrote that St Philip then sent the mission from Gaul to England 'to bring thither the good news of the world of life and to preach the incarnation of Jesus Christ'.[6]

Also on the voyage were Jesus' sisters, Sarah-Salome and Mary Jacob Cleophas, along with Helena-Salome the consort of Simon-Lazarus. They are buried in the crypt of Les Saintes Maries de la Mer in the Camargue. Helena-Salome was a priestess of the Order of Ephesus, and was entitled to wear the red robe of the *hierodulai*.[7] Sarah-Salome, a black-garbed Nazarite priestess, became the revered patron saint of the gypsies, who call her *Sarah-la-Kali*, or Sarah the Black. Even now, from 24 May each year, the Roma attend in pilgrimage from all over the world to carry her reliquary in a procession to the sea.

Mary Jacob, the young widow of Cleophas (John 19:25),

had an extraordinary following in England, which was prevalent well into the Middle Ages. As a Nazarene priestess, she is recorded in *The Acts of Magdalen* and the ancient manuscript *History of England* in the Vatican Archive. Sometimes called Mary the Gypsy, her Oath of Wedlock was referred to as the *Merrie*, from which the verb 'to marry' derives, as does the medieval tag applied to Merrie Englande. Associated with the sea, Mary Jacob was an original merri-maid (mermaid)[8] and she was given the attributive name Marina in the Middle Ages. She is portrayed alongside Mary Magdalene in a window at the Church of St Marie in Paris, and her memory is preserved in Maid Marian and the Merrie Men of the Robin Hood legends. (The sisters, Mary Jacob and Sarah-Salome, were popularly dubbed 'gypsies' because of their visits from France to Egypt. It is from an old form of the word *Egyptian* that the term *gypsy* derives.)[9]

In the early days of Christianity, Emperor Constantine banned the veneration of Mary the Gypsy,[10] but her cult persisted and she was identified with the love goddess Aphrodite, who was said to have 'risen from the sea foam'.[11] Her most significant emblem was the scallop shell, depicted so effectively, along with her Aphrodite status, in the famous *Birth of Venus* paintings by Sandro Botticelli and Adolphe Bouguereau. Mary Jacob was ritually portrayed by the Anglo-Saxons as the May Queen, while in Cornwall they called her Merrow, and her dancers (Merrow's Men) still perform their rites under the corrupted name of 'Morris Men' in English rural festivities.

Mary Magdalene's sea voyage to Gaul has been depicted by numerous artists. An example, which has been exhibited at the church of Les Saintes Maries, is a painting by Henri de Guadermaris. It depicts the Marys' arrival in a boat off the coast of Provence and was shown at the Salon de Paris in 1886. Another famous picture along similar lines is *The Sea Voyage* by Lukas Moser, which forms part of the 15th-century altarpiece, *Der Magdalenenaltar*, at the Katholisches Pfarramt St Maria Magdalena, Tiefenbronn, in southern Germany. And from the 14th century comes *Voyage to Marseilles* by Giotto di Bondone, a fresco in the Chapel of Mary Magdalene at the Church of San Francesco in Assisi (*see* plate 16).

In Marseilles (Massilia) and the Provençal region, until the 5th century the official language was Greek.[12] A fact not generally understood, but which should perhaps be emphasized, is that the Aramaic-style language of Jesus and those concerned with Hellenic Judaism was heavily influenced by Greek. The Hebrews used their own specifically Semitic tongue, but having been under Roman occupation for so long, the Latin culture was to some degree incorporated. Language adjustments were also made in respect of the Gentiles (non-Jews) so that, within all the linguistic variables, there was a mutual understanding. The Romano-Greek language of Gaul would have been familiar enough to Mary and her colleagues.

In the West

In AD 44, Mary gave birth to her second son, and there is a specific reference to this in the New Testament: 'The word of God grew and multiplied' (Acts 12:24).[13] This son was the all-important Grail Child and, in recognition of his grandfather, he was called Josephes.

Having fulfilled his dynastic obligation to father two sons, Jesus was duly released from restrictions and was able to lead a normal life once more. From AD 46, his elder son, Jesus II (then aged nine), was schooled in Caesarea. Three years later, he underwent the ceremony of his community birth in Provence. In accordance with custom, he would have been symbolically born again from his mother's womb at the age of twelve.

In AD 53, Jesus junior was officially proclaimed Crown Prince at the synagogue in Corinth and duly received the Davidic Crown Prince's title of 'Justus' (the Righteous. Greek: *Dikaios*).[14] He thereby formally succeeded his uncle, James the Just, as the kingly heir. Having reached the sovereign majority age of 16, Jesus Justus also became the Chief Nazarite, gaining entitlement to the black robe of that office – as worn by the priests of Isis, the universal Mother Goddess.[15]

His father, Jesus the Christ, went via Crete to Malta in AD 61 with Luke and Paul (Acts 27:7–44, 28:1), subsequent to which Paul returned to Jerusalem. Once there, however, he was accused of conspiracy against the Sadducee high priest Jonathan Annas, who had been murdered by Felix the

Roman Governor of Jerusalem. Felix was sent for trial before Emperor Nero in Rome, and Paul was obliged to follow. After some time, Felix was acquitted, but Paul remained in custody because of his association with his ex-pupil Herod-Agrippa II, whom Nero detested.

At about the same time, but far from the perils of Rome, Jesus II's younger brother, Josephes, had finished his education at a druidic college and was settled in Provence with his mother, Mary Magdalene. They were later joined by young Josephes' uncle James, who came permanently to the West, having been hounded out of Jerusalem in AD 62. His Nazarenes had been subjected to brutal harassment by the Romans, and the Sanhedrin Council had charged James with illegal teaching.[16] He was, consequently, sentenced to a public stoning and was declared spiritually 'dead' (excommunicated) by the Jewish elders.[17] The once honourable counsellor of the Sanhedrin thus fell from the very pinnacle of civil and religious grace.

Having lost all spiritual credibility in the eyes of the law, James made his way westwards to join Mary Magdalene and her colleagues in Gaul. Back in Emperor Nero's Rome, Peter had arrived to assume responsibility for the Pauline sect, who were by then known as Christians. Then, in AD 64, Rome was engulfed by fire. The unbalanced Emperor was the suspected instigator, but he blamed the Christians and had both Peter and Paul put to death.

Nero's regime had caused a good deal of political nervousness, and temperatures were raised to dangerous heights in the Holy Land. Early in AD 66, sporadic fighting broke out in Caesarea between the Zealots and Romans. The hostility quickly moved to Jerusalem, where the Zealots gained a number of strategic positions. They held the city for four years until a massive Roman army led by General Flavius Titus arrived in AD 70, laying Jerusalem to waste. The Temple fell, and everything fell with it. Most of the inhabitants were slaughtered; the survivors were sold into slavery, and the Holy City was an empty ruin for the next six decades.

In the wake of this destruction, the Jewish nation was in a state of turmoil. Not only did Jerusalem fall, but so did Qumrân, and the famous last bastion was the mountain fortress of Masada, south-west of the Dead Sea. There, fewer than a thousand Jews withstood repeated sieges by a mighty Roman army, but they were gradually deprived of all supplies and provisions. By AD 74, their cause was hopeless and the garrison commander, Eleazar Ben Jair, organized a programme of mass suicide. Only two women and five children survived.[18]

Waves of Nazarene refugees fled the Holy Land to perpetuate their tradition in the northern reaches of Mesopotamia, Syria, Southern Turkey and parts of Europe. The later chronicler, Julius Africanus of Edessa,[19] recorded details of the exodus, stating (as we saw in chapter 2) that the Roman authorities caused all the public records in Jerusalem to be burned so as to prevent future access to the details of Jesus' family genealogy. He described these royal inheritors as the *Desposyni*.

Revelation of the Lamb

Apart from a couple of incidental references concerning Joseph as the father of Jesus,[20] he does not appear personally in the New Testament after Jesus' initiatory raising in Luke. Prior to that, Joseph was present when Simeon the Essene (the prevailing Gabriel) legitimized Jesus under the law in view of his unorthodox manner of birth (Luke 2:25–33). And that is the extent of the narrative as far as Joseph is concerned. We know from the Temple event of Jesus' community degree that Joseph was alive in AD 18, but he was not around for his son's crucifixion 15 years later. It is generally reckoned that he died before the start of Jesus' ministry in AD 29.

An unfortunate aspect of the way in which the New Testament was constructed is that Jesus' parents are more or less dismissed. We are told nothing of Mother Mary's daily life unless related directly to Jesus. Consequently, the date of her death is also unknown even though the feast of her Assumption is celebrated annually on 15 August. *The Catholic Encyclopedia* states that this date was an arbitrary dedication rather than a confirmed historical fact. Various years are presumed for her death, ranging from AD 36 to AD 48. What we do know from the Gospels, however, is that Jesus passed his mother into the care of his 'beloved disciple' at the Crucifixion: 'And from that hour the disciple took her unto his own' (John 19:27). In this regard, the word used to describe the disciple's obligation was *paranymphos*, which relates to a personal attendant or guardian.[21] Shortly, we shall consider the identity of the mysterious 'disciple whom Jesus loved'.

Following his visit to Malta (Melitia) in AD 61, it is difficult to trace Jesus' activities. It has been suggested by some that he followed Thomas the apostle's footsteps into India and that he died at Srinagar, Kashmir, where a tomb is attributed to him. But this resulted from a late Kashmiri proposal in 1894 that Jesus was synonymous with a prophet called Yuza Asaf, to whom the tomb was originally dedicated.[22] Although an intriguing concept, the evidence for this is far from conclusive (*see* Appendix III). Notwithstanding, it is clear that Jesus died in or before AD 73. In that year, his eldest son, Jesus II Justus, was bestowed with the Davidic title: 'I Jesus have sent mine angel to testify unto you these things in the churches. I am the root and the offspring of David, the bright and morning star' (Revelation 22:16).

Priests and clerics generally teach that the sequential weddings in the New Testament book of The Revelation are emblematic of Jesus Christ's marriage to the Christian Church. The fact is, however, that when John the Divine (the apostle John Boanerges) wrote his intriguing *Apocalypse* on the Greek island of Patmos, there was no Church. He knew absolutely nothing about an establishment that was to evolve after his own lifetime. The weddings discussed in his very esoteric style of writing were records of Messianic family history.

Jesus and Mary Magdalene's daughter, Tamar (Damaris), appears to have married St Paul in Athens in AD 53,[23] and the marriage of Jesus Justus is recounted as the Marriage of the Lamb in Revelation 19:7–9. As well as John referring to Jesus as the Word of God (John 1:1, 14), John the Baptist had called him the Lamb of God (John 1:29). These styles – Word and Lamb – became synonymous with Jesus' heirs in John's *Apocalypse*.

Jesus Justus (born AD 33) was aged 36 in AD 73, when his bride was said to have been 'arrayed in fine linen, clean and white' at the marriage supper. 'And he saith unto me … I am thy fellow servant, and of thy brethren that have the testimony of Jesus … And his name is called The Word of God' (Revelation 19:10–13).

His son, Jesus III, was born in AD 77, to become the *Alpha* and *Omega* (Revelation 21:16). This was a Sadducee distinction of the House of Herod, which was transferred to the House of David in AD 102 when the Herodian establishment terminated.[24] Jesus III was married in AD 113 (again aged 36 in accordance with dynastic custom) pronouncing, 'I am the root and the offspring of David, the bright and morning star' (Revelation 22:16).

Beloved Disciple

The 'disciple whom Jesus loved' is a character whose mysterious identity has been argued and debated for centuries. The hot favourite in this connection has long been the apostle John Boanerges, son of Zebedee and brother of James. Another contender is, of course, Mary Magdalene whom Jesus was said to love in the New Testament and in the Gospel of Philip. Third in the popular list of possibilities is John Mark, otherwise known as St Mark.

The only biblical mentions of this beloved disciple occur in the Gospel of John. One of these entries relates to the Crucifixion scene when Jesus appointed the beloved disciple as his mother's guardian – a reference which immediately rules out Mary Magdalene since the wording specifically denotes a male in this context:

> When Jesus therefore saw his mother, and
> the disciple standing by, whom he loved,
> he saith unto his mother, Madam, behold
> thy son … And from that hour the
> disciple took her unto his own.
> (John 19:26–27)

Apart from the 'beloved disciple', who is cited in John, only Jesus' female relatives are mentioned as being at the cross. This is the case in all the Gospels. There is no mention of Peter or any of the apostles at the scene. Prior to the event, Matthew 26:56 and Mark 14:50 both relate that, after Jesus' arrest, the disciples 'deserted him and fled'. Clearly, however, there was one who did not.

The anonymous disciple subsequently appears in the Resurrection sequence, which again rules out Mary Magdalene who talks to him in this scene. It also rules out Peter, since he is separately named:

> Then she runneth, and cometh to Simon
> Peter, and to the other disciple, whom
> Jesus loved, and saith unto them, They
> have taken away the Lord out of the

> sepulchre, and we know not where they
> have laid him (John 20:2).

Subsequently, in a conversation between Peter and Jesus, there are two further references to the 'disciple whom Jesus loved'[25] but his name is not given. John Mark can be ruled out of the equation, however, by virtue of the Gospel's very first mention of the mystery man, who is said to have been at the Last Supper: 'Now there was leaning on Jesus' bosom one of his disciples, whom Jesus loved' (John 13:23).

Although the Gospel of John does not specify precisely who was at the Last Supper, the other three Gospels do, and they are unanimous in stating that the party consisted only of Jesus and his twelve apostles:

> Now when the even was come, he sat
> down with the twelve. (Matthew 26:20)

> And in the evening he cometh with the
> twelve. (Mark 14:17)

> And … he sat down, and the twelve
> apostles with him. (Luke 22:14)

Since John Mark (who first appears in The Acts) is not listed in any Gospel as being among the twelve apostles, it necessarily follows that he was not at the supper, and could not have been the one leaning on Jesus' bosom. This appears to leave only John Boanerges, and it is for this reason that he has long been the favoured contender. The problem is that it is quite unlike the Gospel of John author to leave something as important as this so open-ended.

Of all the Gospels, John is the least ambiguous. It includes important items like the wedding at Cana and the raising of Lazarus, which other Gospels do not. It is the only Gospel to explain that Mary, who anointed Jesus at Bethany, was the same woman who had anointed him on the previous occasion. Discussing a particular disciple in a mysterious and surreptitious way is therefore quite contrary to the manner in which this seemingly meticulous author worked. In view of this, one would expect the enigmatic disciple to have been positively identified at some earlier stage. So, is there a previous entry in John which confirms Jesus' fondness for one male disciple in particular? Indeed there is. In fact, there are two such mentions related to the same individual.

The reason why the beloved disciple is not cited as such in the Synoptic Gospels was because his original reference in this context was lost to them. It was removed by St Clement in his bid to veil Jesus' relationship with Mary Magdalene in the account of the raising of Lazarus.[26] The author of John was not remiss concerning the beloved disciple's name after all; John 11:5 states: 'Now Jesus loved Martha, and her sister, and Lazarus'. A little later, in the sequence of Jesus raising his excommunicated friend Lazarus, John 11:36 confirms the relationship yet again: 'Then said the Jews, Behold how he loved him!'

Having stated this twice, the scene is set for the subsequent 'beloved' references at the Last Supper, the Crucifixion, and the Resurrection. The 'disciple whom Jesus loved' was

Lazarus, whose Abrahamic distinction of Eleazar had taken over in the text of John from his previously given name, Simon Zelotes. He was the most senior of Jesus' apostles; the man to whom Mary Magdalene had been a devotional sister, and he was married to Jesus' own aunt, Helena-Salome. Simon-Lazarus was not just an apostle and a patriarchal father of the Qumrân community, he was a member of Jesus' own family. Hence, there was good reason for Jesus to nominate him as the attendant of his mother.

Having established this, the question that remains is, who wrote the Gospel of John? Unlike The Revelation (*Apocalypse*), whose author (John Boanerges the Divine) actually gives his name as John,[27] the Gospel is anonymous. It was not written by the same hand, nor by the author of the New Testament tract John 1, or the epistles John 2 and John 3. The Gospel writer appears to have known many small details that are not in the Synoptic Gospels, and writes with a greater intellectual capability. The text also indicates a significant awareness of priestly practice and intimacy with Jesus.

Towards the end of John, we are advised that the source of the information contained in the Gospel was the beloved disciple, but that he was not the final author of the work. Following a conversation between Jesus and Peter about the beloved disciple, it states as a wrap-up to the narrative: 'This is the disciple which testifieth of these things, and wrote these things: and we know that his testimony is true' (John 21:24). Thus, 'his testimony' relates to the testimony of Simon-Lazarus, the beloved disciple, who provided some of the source material for the author of the Gospel. The narrative itself, however, gives the clues and the proof of who actually wrote the text.

We have seen how the four Gospels differ in their accounts of the women who went to the tomb of Jesus. They are each in agreement, however, that Mary Magdalene was present. In practice, she is the one who would need to have been there to anoint Jesus as his wife. The importance of John is that it is the only Gospel to have Mary Magdalene at the tomb alone.

John 20:2 relates that, having found the tomb empty, Mary went to fetch Peter and Lazarus. Having looked at the vacant tomb themselves, they then departed: 'Then the disciples went away again unto their own home. But Mary stood without at the sepulchre weeping ...' (John 20:10–11).

After a few brief words with two angels in the cave, Mary then met with Jesus out in the garden. This led to the *Noli me tangere* conversation, when Mary endeavoured to embrace Jesus, but was prevented by him from doing so. (The reason for this was that Mary was pregnant at the time, and physical contact was forbidden between them.)

John is the only Gospel to recount this episode – a private conversation, with recorded dialogue, between Jesus and Mary Magdalene. They were alone together. There are therefore only two people who could possibly have written the Gospel of John, and it was not written by Jesus. With supportive material and informative detail from Mary's close friend Simon-Lazarus (who accompanied her to Provence), the only Gospel to make it perfectly clear that the two anointings were conducted by the same woman must have been written by that woman herself. Only she would have known about an intimate conversation in the garden with Jesus. No one else was present to hear this. The author of John can only have been Mary Magdalene.

At the beginning of chapter 1, we saw that the female companions of Jesus are cited on seven occasions, and in six of these lists, Mary Magdalene is the first named. The seventh list gives Jesus' mother as first in the ranking. This is the group named as being at the cross in the Gospel of John. In all other cases, the Gospel writers afforded Mary Magdalene her right of seniority, but if she did indeed write the Gospel of John, it would have been a natural courtesy to place Jesus' mother in front of herself on that occasion.

Realm of the *Desposyni*

The Fisher Kings

Aix-en-Provence, where Mary Magdalene died in AD 63, was the old town of Acquae Sextiae.[1] It was the hot springs at Aix (Acqs) which gave the town its name – *acqs* being a medieval derivative of the old Latin word *aquae* (waters). In the Languedoc tradition, Mary is remembered as *la Dompna del Aquae*: the Mistress of the Waters. To the Gnostics (as indeed to the Celts), females who were afforded religious veneration were often associated with lakes, wells, fountains and springs.

The baptismal priests of the Gospel era were described as 'fishers' and, from the moment Jesus was admitted to the priesthood in the Order of Melchizedek, he too became a designated fisher. Just as Jesus has been incorrectly portrayed as the son of a jobbing carpenter through a misunderstanding of 1st-century terminology, we have also been seduced by images of salty workaday apostles with their nets and fishing boats. For example:

And Jesus, walking by the sea of Galilee,
saw two brethren, Simon called Peter, and
Andrew his brother, casting a net into the
sea: for they were fishers. And he saith
unto them, Follow me, and I will make
you fishers of men. (Matthew 4:18–19)

The Qumrân *Manual of Discipline* describes that, along with three Levitical priests, it was the brief of the twelve-man Council of the Community (the Messiah's delegate apostles) to 'preserve the faith in the land'.[2] Despite romantic pulpit imagery, it is plain that the apostles were no ragtag band of sheep-like devotees, who abandoned all family responsibility to follow a charismatic faith healer. They were prominent members of the community whose true functions have been lost to a misunderstanding of the jargon of the era. Symbolic fishing was a traditional part of the ritual of baptism.[3]

Mass baptisms took place in the water – the Dead Sea or the Sea of Galilee, while some individual or smaller-scale events might be conducted in the River Jordan. Gentiles who sought affiliation with the Jewish tribes could take part in baptism, but could not be baptized in the water. Although they joined the Jewish baptismal candidates in the inland seas, they were permitted only to receive priestly blessings after they had been hauled aboard ships in large nets. Hence, the priests who performed these baptisms were called 'fishers'. The baptismal candidates were the 'fishes'. The story in Luke 5:1–10 about catching the great draft of fishes after Jesus had 'taught the people out of the ship' is an account of a particularly successful conversion event. A similar gathering of fishes is recalled in John 21:1–11.

By way of a parallel transference of imagery, the Levite officials of the Sanctuary were called 'loaves'.[4] In the rite of ordination (the ceremony of admission to the ministry), the officiating Levite priests would serve seven loaves of bread to the priests, while to the celibate candidates they would administer five loaves and two fishes. There was some important legal symbolism in this, for whereas Gentiles might receive baptism as 'fishes', the law was very firm in that only Jews could become 'loaves'.

The relevance of this becomes clear in the miracle event known as the Feeding of the Five Thousand. As with the water and wine at Cana, Jesus resolved to flout convention and allow unclean Gentiles to partake of what was normally reserved for Jews who were candidates of the priesthood. In this regard, he made his concession to the representatives of the non-Jews of the Ham fraternity (known figuratively as the Five Thousand).[5] Thus, he granted their Multitude (their Governing Council) symbolic access to the ministry by serving them the five loaves and two fishes of the Jewish priestly candidates (Mark 6:34–44). In the separate episode known as the Feeding of the Four Thousand,[6] the seven loaves of the senior priests were proffered by Jesus to the uncircumcised Council of Shem (Mark 8:1–10).

By virtue of Jesus' acceptance into the Melchizedek priesthood, the dynastic line of the House of Judah was uniquely established as a dynasty of Priest Kings or, as Jesus' descendants became aptly known, Fisher Kings. The lines of descent from Jesus and Mary Magdalene, which emerged through the Fisher Kings, preserved the maternal Spirit of Aix to become the Family of the Waters: the House del Acqs. It is in this context of the Lost Bride imagery that Grail philosophy determines: 'Only by asking, "Whom does the Grail serve?" will the wound of the Fisher King be healed and the Wasteland returned to fertility'. This comes from *The High History of the Holy Grail*, a Franco-Belgian work dating from c1200 and also known as the *Perlesvaus*. This account, wherein the Messianic Fisher King is called Messios, is specific about the importance of Grail lineage, asserting that the *Sangréal* is the repository of royal heritage.[7]

The earliest written account of *le Seynt Graal* comes from the year 717, when a British hermit called Waleran saw a vision of Jesus and the Grail. Waleran's manuscript was referred to by Heliand, a French monk of the Abbey of

Angels of the Sangréal, from *Crucifixion* by Albrecht Dürer
(1471–1528)

Fromund, in around 1200; also by John of Glastonbury in the *Cronica sive Antiquitates Glastoniensis Ecclesie*, and later by Vincent of Beauvais in his 1604 *Speculum Historiale*. Each of these texts relates how Jesus placed a book in Waleran's hands. It began:

> Here is the Book of thy Descent.
> Here begins the Book of the *Sangréal*.

In Arthurian lore, the Davidic sovereign lineage was represented by the Fisher Kings of the Grail Family and the patriarchal line was denoted by the name Anfortas. This was a symbolic style corrupted from *In fortis* (Latin: 'In strength'). It was identified with the Hebrew name Boaz, the greatgrandfather of David (similarly meaning 'In strength'), whose legacy is celebrated in modern Freemasonry.

The name *Boaz* was given to the left-hand pillar of King Solomon's Temple (1 Kings 7:21 and 2 Chronicles 3:17). Its capitals, along with those of the right-hand pillar, *Jachin*, were decorated with brass pomegranates (1 Kings 7:41–42) – a symbol of male fertility, as identified in the Song of Solomon 4:13. It is not by chance that Sandro Botticelli's famous paintings, *The Madonna of the Pomegranate* and *The Madonna of the Magnificat*, both show the infant Jesus clutching a ripe, open pomegranate.

Mary Magdalene's descendant family of Acqs was prominent in Aquitaine – an area with a name that also has its roots in *acquae* ('waters') or *acqs*, as indeed does the town name of Dax, west of Toulouse, which stems from *d'Acqs*.[8] Merovingian princely branches that evolved here from the

Fisher Kings became Counts of Toulouse and Narbonne; also Kings of the Septimanian Midi between France and Spain.

Another family branch, related through the female line, was granted the Celtic Church heritage of Avallon in Burgundy, with Viviane del Acqs acknowledged as the hereditary High Queen in the early 6th century. Subsequently, in Brittany, a corresponding male branch of the Provençal House del Acqs became the Comtes (Counts) de Léon d'Acqs in descent from Viviane I's granddaughter Morgaine.

From the time that Chrétien de Troyes wrote his 12th-century romance of *Ywain and the Lady of the Fountain* (in which the Lady corresponds to *la Dompna del Aquae*), the heritage of Acqs has persisted in Arthurian literature. The *del Acqs* family legacy, which remained central to the Grail theme, was always directly related to the sacred waters and was always associated with Mary Magdalene. Alternatively, the name *du Lac* was used to signify relationship to the *Desposynic* bloodline (*lac*, or 'lake', being a red pigment from the Eastern dragontree – as in the paint colour Scarlet Lake). In 1484, Sir Thomas Malory's *Morte d'Arthur* used the latter distinction, with Viviane II (Lady of the Fountain and mother of Lancelot du Lac) duly classified as the Lady of the Lake.

House of Bread

Over and above the *Life* accounts of Mary Magdalene in Provence, a number of apocryphal legends also arose. One of these provided a good vehicle for nude figure painters such as Lefebvre, Etty and Dubois to display their talents, for it was claimed that Mary lived naked in a cave for a time. Others, like Titian, Guercino and Correggio, afforded her a little modesty with half-length portraits and various oddments of drapery.

Allied to this, however, is another aspect which is also apparent in the more academic Provençal accounts, and which led to what are generally classified as the *Ecstasy* portrayals. In these Mary is seen in the company of angels, who were said to have provided her nourishment with a mystical form of bread. Numerous artists have depicted this scene, including Lorenzo di Credi, Jusepe di Ribera, José Antolínez, Domenichino and Peter Strub. It is not, however, as strange as it might seem.

At the outset of the Messianic dynasty, King David had been born in Bethlehem, and the point is expressly made in the New Testament that so was Jesus: 'Hath not the scripture said, that Christ cometh of the seed of David, and out of the town of Bethlehem, where David was?' (John 7:42). It is also of note that John Cassian, who began the vigil at Mary Magdalene's tomb, had been a monk in Bethlehem before founding his cell at Marseilles. Bethlehem (*Beth-le-hem*) means 'House of Bread'.[9]

Tracing the 'house of bread' terminology back into ancient Egypt, we discover that the bread symbolism was prevalent in the culture of the pharaohs from the earliest dynasties of the Old Kingdom. There are references to a mystical bread in the temple reliefs of Karnak and Abydos, with numerous related inscriptions at the Horeb mountain temple of Moses in Sinai.[10] The fascinating thing about this 'bread' however was that it was said to be made from gold. It is listed in the golden treasures of Karnak,[11] and there are numerous depictions of enigmatic loaves being presented to the kings. This celestial food was said to heighten the pharaohs' powers of perception, awareness and intuition, and was responsible for an overall transcendence of personality to the angelic state. It was the root of the item in The Lord's Prayer, which, as defined in Matthew 6:9–13, relates to 'Give us this day our daily bread', and features in the Genesis communion ritual of Melchizedek.

Moreover, it is explained in the Old Testament book of Exodus 32:20 that Moses burned the golden calf in Sinai, and made from it a powder which he mixed with water and gave to the Israelites. The full story of this 'powder of projection' is related, from ancient to modern times, in *Lost Secrets of the Sacred Ark*. Its relevance in our present investigation, however, is that the Karnak priests in charge of its manufacture were the very people who eventually settled the Therapeutate within the Essene community at Qumrân.

There is a good deal of evidence to suggest that the Davidic dynasty was founded on the culture of this bread made from gold. The Greek *Septuagint* Bible calls it Bread of the Presence, and David required sanction from the priest in order to take it.[12] King Solomon's court was supplied with enormous quantities of gold from the Arabian mines, not least from those of Ophir and Sheba (Sāba). But, for all Solomon's apparent wealth, the Egyptian, Jordanian, Syrian and Phoenician kings supplied his shipping fleet, military protection, horses, chariots, and other expensive services, not to mention all the building supplies for his palace and temple. The Phoenician King Hiram of Tyre explained that his only requirement in return for all such favours was that Solomon should 'give bread to my household'.[13]

We saw in chapter 6 that the Knights Templars were active in the Bézu region of Languedoc, where they used the area's alluvial gold to manufacture their fabulous *Ormus* powder, which modern science now classifies as an Orbitally Rearranged Monatomic Element. Recent analysis tests at Qumrân reveal that the Dead Sea precipitate contains 70 per cent gold in the monatomic state. It is now also known that this exotic white-powder gold has precisely the qualities attributed to it by the Therapeutate priests, and it will resonate with human DNA to stimulate hormonal production and enhance the immune system.

In Gospel times, the Judaean and Egyptian practitioners of the gold processing art were called Master Craftsmen, and that is precisely what Jesus' father Joseph had been called – *ho tekton*: 'master of the craft' – the term that was wrongly translated to 'carpenter'. Another *ho tekton* of the era was Joseph of Arimathea, who was listed as being in Provence with the Magdalene party. Inasmuch as some people these days are once again using monatomic gold as a dietary supplement, there is no reason to suppose that the Magdalene missionaries were not doing the same.

Divine Highness

Given that there never was such a place as Arimathea, reference books generally suggest, very unsatisfactorily, that
Joseph of Arimathea perhaps came from Ramleh or
Ramathaim in the north of Judaea.[14] As well as being an *ho
tekton* like Jesus' father, Rabanus Maurus also referred to
Joseph as a *noblis decurion*. The 6th-century Welsh chronicler
Gildas II similarly described him as a 'noble decurio'. A *decu-
rion* was an overseer of mining estates and the term originat-
ed in Spain, where Jewish metalworkers had been operative
in the celebrated foundries of Toledo since the 6th century
BC.[15] So, who precisely was Joseph of Arimathea? And if
Arimathea was not a place, then to what did the word relate?

In the Gospels, Joseph is described as 'an honourable
counsellor [a member of the Sanhedrin], which also waited
for the kingdom of God' (Mark 15:43). He was also 'a disciple of Jesus, but secretly, for fear of the Jews' (John 19:38).
But although Joseph's political allegiance to Jesus was a
secret from the Jewish elders, his relationship came as no
surprise to the Roman Governor, Pontius Pilate, who accepted the man's involvement in Jesus' affairs without question.[16] When Joseph requested that Jesus should be removed
from the cross and placed in a garden sepulchre, Pilate complied unreservedly. Neither was Joseph's level of involvement a surprise to Jesus' mother Mary, Mary Magdalene,
Mary Jacob or Sarah-Salome. They all went along with
Joseph's arrangements, accepting his authority without
comment or demur.

Arimathea was, in fact, a descriptive title like Magdalene and a number of others in the New Testament. It represented a particularly high status. Just as the apostle Matthew Annas held the priestly distinction 'Levi of Alphaeus' (Levi of the Succession), so Joseph was 'of Arimathea'. However (as with Matthew's nominal style of Levi), Joseph was not his true baptismal name, and *Arimathea* derived from a combination of Hebrew and Greek elements. Its component parts were the Hebrew: *ha ram* or *ha rama* (of the height or top) and the Greek: *Theo* (relating to God) – together meaning 'of the Highest of God' (*ha Rama Theo*) and, as a personal distinction, Divine Highness.[17]

Jesus was the heir to the throne of David. Thus, he was 'the David', just as John the Baptist had been 'the Zadok'. In the kingly line, the patriarchal title of Joseph was applied to the next in succession.[18] When a dynastic son of the House of Judah (by whatever personal name) succeeded to become the David (the king), his eldest son (the crown prince) became the Joseph. But if there was no son at the time of a Davidic accession (or if the son was under sixteen years old), then the eldest brother of the David would hold the Joseph distinction. It would be relinquished to the senior line if and when a son was of age. In this respect, James (the eldest of Jesus' three younger brothers – born AD 1) was the designated Joseph (Hebrew: *Yosef*, meaning 'He shall add'). Hence, he was the Joseph *ha Rama Theo*, which became linguistically corrupted to Joseph of Arimathea.

Joseph of Arimathea emerges, then, as Jesus' own brother James. Consequently, it comes as no surprise that Jesus was entombed in a sepulchre that belonged to his own family. Neither is it surprising that Pilate should allow Jesus' brother to take charge of the post-crucifixion proceedings; nor that the women of Jesus' family should accept the arrangements made by Joseph (James) without question. Clearly, this meant that there were different Josephs of Arimathea at different times. But how is it that the Joseph of the Crucifixion sequence is generally depicted in artwork as an elderly man?

Apart from a few vague mentions of his wealthy councillor status, the New Testament gives no obvious clue as to what Joseph of Arimathea had to do with Jesus' family. Neither do the Gospels mention Joseph's age. Outside the scriptures, however, he is often presumed to have been Jesus' mother's uncle. As a result, paintings and picture-books portray him as somewhat aged in the AD 30s.

If Jesus' mother Mary was born in about 26 BC, as is generally reckoned, she would have been aged nineteen, or thereabouts, when Jesus was born. By the time of the Crucifixion she would have been in her middle fifties. So, if Joseph had been her uncle, he would have been, say, twenty years older than Mary – putting him somewhere in his middle seventies at that point in time. However, a number of written accounts, from a variety of sources, record Joseph as being in France and England thirty years later in AD 63. Furthermore, Hugh Cressy's *History* (which incorporates records of Glastonbury monastery) asserts that Joseph of Arimathea died on 27 July AD 82. By that reckoning, he would have died at around 125 years of age!

None of this makes any sense, and the hereditary aspect of the Joseph of Arimathea distinction has to be applied.

Hence, as established, the Joseph of the Crucifixion era was Jesus' brother, James the Just, born in AD 1. He died in AD 82, having been formally excommunicated in Jerusalem twenty years earlier.

It was by way of a 9th-century Byzantine concept that the Church first promoted Joseph as Mary's uncle. There is no mention of him in that role in any literature beforehand. The concept arose at a time when the cautiously fearful Church councils were debating the approved content of the New Testament. So long as Joseph of Arimathea could be contained as a sideline character, and so long as he was not associated with the key Messianic line, his royal descendants could not embarrass the self-styled Apostolic structure of the Roman bishops.

Inasmuch as the descendants of Jesus were *Desposyni* inheritors, so too were the descendants of James and Jesus' other siblings. By veiling James beneath his titular style of Joseph of Arimathea, his posterity was presumed to have been airbrushed from historical record. In practice, though, the plan failed and the documented royal lines from James/Joseph are of major significance in the founding royal genealogies of the Celtic realms.

The First Church

In his 1601 *Annales Ecclesiastici*, the Vatican librarian, Cesare Baronius, recorded that Joseph of Arimathea first came to Marseilles in AD 35, nine years before the Magdalene voyage. From there, he and his company crossed to Britain. This was confirmed long before by Gildas Badonicus in his *De Excidio Britanniae*, with earlier references by Eusebius of Caesaria (AD 260–340),[19] and Hilary of Poitiers (AD 300–367). The years AD 35–37, very shortly after the Crucifixion, are thus among the earliest recorded dates for Nazarene evangelism.

Another important character in 1st-century Gaul was St Philip, who was described in the *De Sancto Joseph ab Arimathea*, and in the monastic records, as a colleague of Joseph and Mary Magdalene in the West. The chances are that the Nag Hammadi *Gospel of Philip* was written by Philip himself during this period. He could also perhaps have authored the *Gospel of Mary Magdalene*. As confirmed by Freculphus, the 9th-century Bishop of Lisieux, Archbishop Isidore of Seville (AD 600–636) wrote:

> Philip of the city of Bethsaida, whence also
> came Peter, preached Christ to the Gauls,
> and brought barbarous nations and their
> neighbours … into the light of knowledge
> … Afterwards he was stoned and
> crucified, and died in Hierapolis, a city of
> Phrygia.

Upon their arrival in the West of England, Joseph and his twelve missionaries were apparently viewed with scepticism by the native Britons, but were greeted with some cordiality by King Arviragus of Siluria, brother of Caractacus the Pendragon. In consultation with other local chiefs, Arviragus granted Joseph twelve hides of Glastonbury land

– about 1,440 acres (about 582 hectares).[20] Here, in AD 63–64, they built a unique little church on a scale of the ancient Tabernacle of Moses.[21] These grants to Joseph remained holdings of free land for many centuries thereafter, and were confirmed in the *Domesday Book* of 1086: 'The Church of Glastonbury has its own ville twelve hides of land which have never paid tax'.

In that 1st-century era of Peter and Paul's executions, Christian chapels were hidden underground in the cata-combs of Rome, but when Joseph's wattle chapel of St Mary was built at Glastonbury, Britain could boast the first above-ground Christian church in the world.[22] Later called the *Vetusta Eccesia* (the Old Church) it was cited in royal charters of King Ina in 704 and King Cnut in 1032.

A monastery was subsequently added to the chapel, and the Saxons restructured the complex in the 8th century. Following a disastrous fire in 1184, Henry II of England granted the community a Charter of Renovation in which Glastonbury was referred to as: 'The mother and burying place of the saints, founded by the disciples of our Lord themselves.'[23] A stone-built Lady Chapel was constructed at that time, and the complex grew to become a vast Benedictine abbey, second in size and importance only to Westminster Abbey in London. Prestigious figures associ-ated with Glastonbury included St Patrick (the first Abbot in the 5th century) and St Dunstan (Abbot 940–946).

In addition to the accounts of Joseph of Arimathea at Glastonbury, others tell of his association with Gaul and the Mediterranean metal trade. Abbot John of Glastonbury (14th-century compiler of *Cronica sive Antiquitates Glastoniensis*

Ecclesie) and John Capgrave (Principal of the Augustinian Friars in England 1393–1464) both quoted from a book found by Emperor Theodosius (AD 375–395) at the Praetorium in Jerusalem. Entitled, *De Sancto Joseph ab Arimathea*, it tells how Joseph was imprisoned by the Jewish elders after the Crucifixion. This event is also described in the *Acts of Pilate* section of the *Gospel of Nicodemus*.[24] The historian, Gregory of Tours (AD 544–595), also mentioned the imprisonment of Joseph in his *History of the Franks*[25] and it was recounted yet again in *Joseph d'Arimathie* by the Burgundian Grail chronicler, Sire Robert de Boron, in the 12th century. The *Magna Glastoniensis Tabula*[26] and other manuscripts add that Joseph subsequently escaped and was pardoned. Some years later, he was in Gaul with his nephew Josephes, who was baptized by Philip the apostle.

It is likely that Joseph of Arimathea's mining interest was the primary reason for the generous land grant by King Arviragus.[27] He was, after all, a well-known metal merchant and artificer in metals: a 'master craftsman' (*ho-tekton*), as was his father, in the tradition of the Old Testament characters Tubal-cain and Bezaleel.[28]

The *De Sancto Joseph* states that Joseph of Arimathea's wattle church was dedicated 'in the thirty-first year after our Lord's Passion' – that is AD 64. This conforms with AD 63 as its date of commencement as given by the medieval historian William of Malmesbury. But, since the dedication was to St Mary (generally presumed to be Jesus' mother), it has long been a point of debate that a church should have been consecrated to her so many years after her death, yet long before there was any semblance of a Virgin Mother cult). As confirmed in the 12th-century *Chronica Majora* of Matthew Paris,[29] however, AD 63 was the very year in which the other Mary – Mary Magdalene – died at La Sainte-Baume.

The Bishops' Debate

Among the visits Joseph made to Britain, two were of great importance to the Church, and were later cited by a number of clerics and religious correspondents. The first (as described by Cardinal Baronius) followed Joseph's initial seizure by the Sanhedrin Council after the Crucifixion. This visit, in AD 35, ties in precisely with an account of Jesus' brother, St James the Just, in France and Spain. The Rev Lionel S Lewis (Vicar of Glastonbury in the 1920s) also related from his annals that St James was at Glastonbury in AD 35. The second of Joseph's visits followed the AD 62 stoning and denouncement of James the Just in Jerusalem.[30] This is not surprising since they were one and the same person.

There are many traditions of St James in Sardinia and Spain, but they mainly relate to the apostle James Boanerges (the brother of John). In 820, Bishop Theodosius forged an apostolic link when he announced that the remains of James Boanerges (known as James the Greater) had been unearthed at Compostela in Spain. In 899, the resultant shrine to Sant Iago (St James) became a great cathedral. It was destroyed by the Moors in 997, but rebuilt in 1078. During the period AD 33–44, it was said that James had visited Spain, but was executed on returning to Judaea by Herod of Chalcis (Acts 12:2), following which his disciples had brought his body back to Spain. There is nothing in the New Testament, however, to suggest that James Boanerges made such a visit before his execution. If the Spanish relics do indeed relate to a St James, they are more likely those of the other apostle, James of Alphaeus (known as James the Lesser), who could well have made the journey in post-crucifixion times. Santiago de Compostela is still the final destination of a medieval 713-mile pilgrims' way – the *Camino de Santiago* (Way of Saint James). Now a Unesco World Heritage Site, the majestic cathedral shrine attracts visitors from all over the world.

Misunderstandings, caused by the apparent anomalies and duplicated entries concerning Joseph of Arimathea and St James the Just, provoked a good deal of argument between the bishops at the Council of Basle in 1434. In Spain it was – and still is – difficult to separate the stories of James the apostle and James the Just but, one way or another, individual countries decided to follow their different traditions. It is St Joseph of Arimathea who is most remembered in connection with Church history in Britain, whereas it is as St James the Just that he is revered in Spain. Even so, the English authorities compromised when linking him with the monarchy, and the Royal Court in London is still operative as the Palace of St James.

The bishops' debate at Basle followed an earlier dispute at the Council of Pisa in 1409 on the subject of the seniority by age of national Churches in Europe. The main contenders were England, France and Spain. The case was finally ruled in favour of England because the church at Glastonbury had been founded by Joseph/James *'statim post passionem Christi'* (shortly after the Passion of Christ). Henceforth, the monarch of France was entitled His Most Christian Majesty, while in Spain the appellation was His Most Catholic Majesty. The bitterly contested title of His Most Sacred Majesty was reserved for the King of England.[31] Records of the debate – the *Disputatio super Dignitatem Angliae et Galliae in Concilio Constantiano* – state that England won her case because the saint was not only granted land in the West of England by King Arviragus, but he was actually buried at Glastonbury.

In apparent contrast to this, the Cistercian Grail romance, *l'Estoire del Saint Graal* (c1220),[32] claims that Joseph was buried at the Abbey of Glais in Scotland, but this is not as contradictory as it seems. At the time of Joseph's death, the Scots Gaels had not settled the Western Highlands (Dalriada) in the North of Britain, but constituted a tribal population of Northern Ireland (Ulster) who had infiltrated the South West of Britain. The West Country areas settled by the early Scots were referred to as Scotland (Land of the Scots), while the far North was called Caledonia.[33] The word *glais* (so common in old Scots names) comes from the Irish Goidelic, and means 'stream' or 'rivulet'. The name Douglas, for example, derives from *dubh glais* (dark stream). Early Glastonbury was set amid watery marshland, and was called the Isle of Glais.[34] Thus, Joseph's said burial place at the Abbey of Glais in *l'Estoire del Saint Graal* actually referred to the Abbey of Glastonbury.

Secret of the Lord

In the literary Grail tradition, Jesus II Justus (the first son of Jesus and Mary Magdalene) was referred to as Gais or Gésu. When he became the David in AD 73, his younger brother Josephes – then aged 29 – became the new Joseph ha Rama Theo (Josephes d'Arimathie). He was often portrayed as the nephew of the biblical Joseph of Arimathea, which of course he was. In fact, Joseph/James was his foster-father and legal guardian in the West, which is why some Grail legends classify Josephes as old Joseph's son.

Jesus Justus was married to a daughter of Nicodemus, the man who had assisted Joseph of Arimathea with Jesus' entombment (John 19:30). Their son, Jesus III, was referred to in France as Galains (or Alain).[35] The legacy of Davidic kingship (which was to become represented as Lordship of the Grail) was promised to Galains and was, in time, formally passed to him by his uncle and guardian, Josephes. But Galains, the *Alpha and Omega* prince of the *Apocalypse*, died without issue, and the Messianic heritage reverted to Josephes' junior line. It was inherited by his son Josue,[36] from whom the Fisher Kings of Gaul descended.

Back in AD 49, Joseph of Arimathea had been to England with the twelve-year-old Jesus Justus. This event is well remembered in West Country tradition and is evidenced in William Blake's famous song *Jerusalem*. The stories tell of how young Jesus walked upon the Exmoor coast and went to the Mendip village of Priddy. Because those royal feet did indeed 'walk upon England's mountains green' (albeit the

Josephes passes the Lordship of the Grail to Alain
(from a 13th-century French manuscript illumination)

son's feet rather than the father's), a stone in memory of his parents, Jesus and Mary Magdalene, was eventually set into the south wall of St Mary's Chapel at Glastonbury. This stone, on the site of Joseph's 1st-century wattle church, became one of the most venerated relics of the Abbey – a medieval prayer station that can still be seen today. It is inscribed *'Jesus Maria' (see* plate 52), and was called the *Secretum Domini* – the Secret of the Lord.

The original chapel was begun in AD 63, immediately after Mary Magdalene's death, and the annals state that young Jesus personally consecrated the chapel in honour of his mother.[37] It was, therefore, to Mary Magdalene (not to

Jesus Christ's mother Mary, as is customarily believed) that the Glastonbury chapel was dedicated by her eldest son, Jesus Justus, in AD 64.

The Holy Balm

Romance of the Grail

As well as being known as Joseph of Arimathea, St James the Just was called Ilid by the chroniclers of Wales. The name is thought to be a variant of the Hebrew *Eli* (meaning 'raised up') or the Mesopotamian *Ilu* (relating to a 'lord'), but the actual origin of Ilid is somewhat obscure. Joseph is referred to as Ilid in the bardic ode, *Cwydd to Saint Mary Magdalene*,[1] and is said to be the patron of Llan Ilid (now Llantwit) in Gwent, having founded the nearby mission-school of Caer Eurgain.

Additionally, the *Iolo Manuscripts*[2] recount that 'Ilid of the land of Israel' was summoned to Britain by Eurgain, the wife of King Caractacus of Camulod, and states, 'This same Ilid was called Joseph in the lections of his life'. Also the *Achan Saint Prydain* (Genealogies of the Saints of Britain) maintains, 'There came with Brân the Blessed from Rome to Britain, Arwystli Hen, Ilid, Cyndaf – men of Israel – and Maw or Mawan, son of Cyndaf'.[3] The 6th-century *Llandaff Charters* relate these events to AD 37, which ties in with the writings of Gildas Badonicus, who stated in his *De Excidio*

Britanniae that the precepts of Nazarene Christianity were carried to Britain in the last days of Emperor Tiberius.

We met earlier with Arwystli Hen (Aristobulus) in the writings of the 2nd-century chronicler Hippolytus, who told of the man's exploits in Britain.[4] So it is no surprise to find him recorded in the Welsh annals along with Joseph. The link with Brân the Blessed is of interest, however, since he is recorded in British Museum manuscripts as being married to Anna (Enygeus), the daughter of Joseph of Arimathea.[5] Anna is referred to as a *consabrina* (junior kinswoman) of Jesus' mother, Mary.

In AD 51, the Silurian[6] archdruid Brân was in Rome, along with Caractacus the Pendragon and Aristobulus. Whilst there, Gladys, a daughter of Caractacus (the King of Kings) married the Roman senator Rufus Pudens,[7] and thus became Claudia Rufina Britannica, as confirmed by the Roman poet, Martial, in about AD 68. At the same time, Prince Linus, the son of Caractacus, became the first appointed Bishop of Rome. This visit is confirmed in the New Testament writings of St Paul: 'Eubulus greeteth thee, and Pudens and Linus, and Claudia, and all the brethren' (2 Timothy 4:21). The name Eubulus (*eu-boulos*: 'well advised') was a variation of Aristobulus (*aristo-boulos*: 'best advised').

While in Britain, Joseph of Arimathea's enterprise was maintained in the apostolic tradition by a close circle of twelve anchorites (devotees). If one died, he would be replaced by another. These anchorite culdees were referred to as the 'Brethren of Alain', who was one of their number. As such, they were symbolic sons of Brân (the Father in the Old Church, as against the later-styled *Papa* in Rome).[8]

Following Joseph of Arimathea's death in AD 82, however, the group disintegrated – mainly because, by that time, Roman invasion and control had forever changed the character of England.

In the world of popular mythology, there are various levels of confusion regarding the descendants of Anna and Brân. Such works include the *Bruts*, the *Triads*, the *Mabinogion* and *Cycles of the Kings*. Historically, they are all important documents because they are not entirely fictitious, but these tales are purposefully romantic in construction and, as a result, many historians have attacked them mercilessly.

Grail romances are also constructed with degrees of literary licence – paying little heed to correct chronology, with the chivalric players scattered willy-nilly in the adventurous texts. The *High History of the Holy Grail* (c1220) provides a good example in claiming that Perceval (a 6th-century adherent of King Arthur) was the grandnephew of the 1st-century Joseph of Arimathea: 'Good knight was he of right, for he was of the lineage of Joseph of Arimathea, and this Joseph was his mother's uncle'. The significance of such items, nevertheless, is to make a succinct point about lineal descent without the constraint of interim detail. It works in much the same way as allegorical artwork in that it is the underlying message that matters, not the superficial image. Another example of how such legends were structured can be found in the Arthurian tale of the White Knight. This shows very clearly how historical fact was used to support a romantic storyline.

By the time of Mary Magdalene's death in AD 63, her son Josephes had become Bishop of Saraz. In Sir Thomas

Malory's *Morte d'Arthur*, Saraz features as the realm of King Evelake, and is mentioned in the story of Lancelot's son Galahad. The tale begins when Galahad inherits a supernatural shield and encounters a mysterious White Knight, who turns out to be Josephes' son Josue. Their ensuing conversation about the shield moves to a discussion concerning Joseph of Arimathea, and then to recollection of a conflict between King Evelake and a troublesome Saracen called Tolleme le Feintes.

Saraz was Sahr-Azzah on the Mediterranean coast[9] – the one-time Philistine centre where Samson met his fate (Judges 16). There is no record of a King Evelake as such, but the name is a literary variant of the governmental title *Avallach*. It was subject to many variations (such as Abalech, Arabach and Amalach), but all were ultimately corruptions of the Greco-Egyptian title *Alabarch* – a procurator or chief magistrate.

Tolleme le Feintes (Tholomy the false) was a real 1st-century character mentioned by Josephus in *The Antiquities of the Jews*. He was an arch-robber, and was indeed brought before Cuspius Fadus, the Avallach of Judaea, who had Tholomy executed in around AD 45.[10] There is some fact, therefore, in the root of the White Knight's story. Tolleme and Evelake were synonymous with Tholomy and the Avallach.

Additionally, the White Knight related that, on instruction from his father Josephes (Mary Magdalene's son), the shield had been placed with the holy hermit Nascien. This act was accompanied by a prophecy from Josephes that a knight of his descendant lineage would eventually carry the shield and 'do many marvellous deeds'. In the event, the shield fell to Sir Galahad.

In the *De Sancto Joseph* and elsewhere, Nascien is described not as a hermit, but as a Prince of the Medas, and it is with him that the historical line from Mary Magdalene and Josephes (the Grail Child) down to Galahad du Lac is cemented. Prince Nascien of the Septimanian Midi was a *Desposynic* ancestor of the Merovingian Kings of the Franks, from whose line sprang Viviane d'Avallon del Acqs (the Lady of the Lake) and her son Lancelot, the father of Galahad.

From this, it can be seen that the medieval Grail legends were, in many respects, no different from the parables told by Jesus, or the *pesher* codes of the Dead Sea Scrolls. They were written 'for those with ears to hear' in a manner that preserved the dynastic story of the *Desposyni* inheritors of the Messianic bloodline.

Mount of Witness

The names of characters in the Grail Quest stories are a particularly interesting feature of their composition. Retaining the heritage of *du Lac* (of the blood) and *del Acqs* (of the waters) along with Joseus and Josephes, the Magdalene legacy is constantly apparent. References to Joseph of Arimathea, the Lady of the Lake and the Fisher Kings also add to the *Desposynic* nature of the tales. But few people stop to wonder why there is such a proliferation of Jewish or Jewish-sounding names within what are generally considered to be

Christian stories. Even Galahad, the seemingly pure-bred French knight, was called Gilead or Galeed to begin. The original Gilead was a son of Michael, the great-great-grand-son of Nahor, brother of Abraham (1 Chronicles 5:14). The Hebrew term *Gilead* means a 'Heap of testimony'; the mountain called Gilead was the Mount of Witness (Genesis 31:21–25), and Galeed was Jacob's cairn, the Heap of the Witness (Genesis 31:46–48).

In the Cistercian footsteps of the Templar patron Bernard de Clairvaux, the Lincolnshire Abbot, Gilbert of Holland, equated Galahad directly with the family of Jesus in his *Sermons on the Canticles*,[11] and there is never any doubt as to the *Desposynic* nature of the romantic accounts. In the *Queste del Saint Graal*, when a venerable man in white addresses King Arthur on bringing Galahad to the Court of Camelot, he says, 'I bring thee the desired knight *(le chevalier désiré)*, who is descended from the high lineage of King David'.[12]

The reason for so many Jewish names is, of course, that Christianity grew out of Hellenist Judaism, and the Messianic family to whom the Grail legends pertain was originally Jewish. Apart from the names mentioned, there are others such as Lot, Elinant, Bron, Urien, Hebron, Pelles, Elyezer, Jonas and Ban, together with numerous references to King Solomon and the Davidic royal house. Even the priestly Judas Maccabaeus of Jerusalem (who died in 161 BC) is featured as 'the best knight of his faith that was ever … and the wisest'. Over the years, many have thought it strange that this well-born Hasmonaean hero of ancient Judaea is treated with such high esteem in a seemingly Christian story, but as an ancestor of Mary Magdalene his prominence was assured. (The Hasmonaeans had nothing whatever to do with the tribe of Benjamin, as was erroneously suggested for Mary Magdalene's heritage in *The Da Vinci Code*. They were descended from Aaron's son Elieazar and his wife Elisheba in the 4th female-line generation from Benjamin's brother Judah, the male-line ancestor of the House of David.)

In the Middle Ages, when the majority of Grail romances were written, there was little love for the Jews in Europe. Dispersed from Palestine, many had settled in parts of the West but, owning no land to cultivate, they turned to trade and banking. This was not welcomed by the bishops, and so moneylending was prohibited by the Church of Rome. In the light of this, King Edward I had all Jews expelled from England in 1209, except for skilled physicians. In such an atmosphere, writers (whether in Britain or continental Europe) would not have found it natural or politically correct to use a string of Jewish names for local heroes, knights and kings. Yet the names persist, from those of the early protagonists such as Josephes, to that of the later Galahad.

Christian authors would not have exalted men of Jewish heritage to high positions in a chivalric environment if they were simply writing fiction. They included them because Grail lore was not just about adventurous entertainment. It was about the preservation of a legacy within a Church-led environment that had suppressed the Grail family's history in academic terms.

Apart from the reminiscences of Waleran in AD 717, the literary Grail first appeared in the 1180s with *Le Conte del Graal – Roman de Perceval* by Chrétien de Troyes. This was at a high-point of Templar influence in Europe, and it is no coincidence that Chrétien dedicated his work to Philippe d'Alsace, Comte de Flandres. Nor was it by chance that Chrétien was sponsored and encouraged in his undertaking by Countess Marie and the Court of Champagne. Grail lore was born directly out of this early Templar establishment and the Order's affiliated Courts of Alsace, Champagne and Léon. The *High History of the Holy Grail* portrayed the Knights as wardens of a 'great and sacred secret'. In Robert de Boron's *Joseph d'Arimathie*, the Saint Graal is said to be 'a chalice of holy blood', while the 13th-century romance, *Parzival*, by the Bavarian knight, Wolfram von Eschenbach, describes the Knights of the Templeise as Guardians of the Grail Family.

Another Grail account to emerge from Templar circles at much the same time was the Cistercian *Vulgate Cycle*. Written by monks of St Bernard de Clairvaux' Order, this work contains the *Estoire del Graal*, the *Queste del Saint Graal* and the *Livres de Lancelot*. In the *Estoire*, the story of Joseph of Arimathea is told yet again, and Josephes is identified as the head of the Grail fraternity. In both the *Estoire* and the *Queste*, Grail Castle is symbolically called *Le Corbenic* – the Body Blessed (*Cors benicon*),[13] and once more the *Queste* identifies Galahad as being 'descended from the high lineage of King David'.

The Alabaster Jar

We have discussed how Mary Magdalene is so often depicted with an ointment jar (plates 15, 18, 38, 39). Whether plain
or ornate, it is her primary means of identification in artwork. Rather more of a pot with a lid than a jar as such, it
appears with her in countless paintings, icons, sculptures,
carvings and stained-glass windows, yet there appears to be
no textual basis for this specific image. In essence, the jar
relates to the Bethany anointing of Jesus by Mary but, apart
from the Gospel of John, which makes no reference to a container of any kind, the other three Gospels describe:

- An alabaster box of very precious ointment. (Matthew
  26:7)
- An alabaster box of ointment of spikenard very precious.
  (Mark 14:3)
- An alabaster box of ointment. (Luke 7:37)

Each of the Gospels details that Mary had an 'alabaster box'.
So why did so many artists appear to have got it wrong?

When considering the original language of these
Gospels, although the references are close to accurate in
translation, the word 'ointment', which denotes a greasy
preparation, is incorrect. The Greek translates to a liquid
'attar' (essential oil) or 'balsam' (balm) – hence the French *la
Sainte-Baume*: the Holy Balm.

During the 1900s, and especially since the Second World
War, a number of Bible revisions[14] have used the word 'jar'

instead of 'box', but this has resulted from an adherence to common perception rather than to accuracy in translation. They are interpretations, rather than translations, based on the premise that if people expect Mary to have a jar, then she shall have a jar. But even the word 'box' did not relate to the sort of container that would carry a liquid balm for pouring.

A direct translation of Mark 14:3 from the Greek text in the Vatican Archive[15] results in:

> And being in Bethany in the house of
> Simon the leper, as he [Jesus] reclined at
> table, a woman came having an
> alabastron of balsam of genuine nard,
> very valuable; and breaking it she poured
> down on his head.

When correctly translated, what Mary had was an '*alabastron*' (from the Greek *alabastros*). That is to say, she had a small vial or flask. Alabastrons were narrow containers for fragrant oils, and they did not have lids as might a pot or a box. They were either sealed and had to be broken (as appears to have been the case with Mary's), or they had small stopper-holes for use with a dipstick. They were not necessarily made of alabaster as the name seems to imply, but were often made of glass, porcelain or a type of pottery; sometimes even of precious metals. The prefix *ala* (as in 'ears') relates to small handling lugs that projected from their sides.

When anointing a dynastic husband on marriage, the wife was said to be anointing him for burial – as in a commitment unto death: 'For in that she hath poured this ointment on my body, she did it for my burial' (Matthew 26:12). She would then carry another small vial of the balm around her neck, with which (presuming she was still alive) she would anoint him again at his death.[16] It was for this reason that Mary would have gone to the sepulchre, as she did, following Jesus' entombment.[17]

The pot given to Mary Magdalene for centuries by artists is seemingly representative of the anointings at Bethany and the planned anointing at the tomb (*see* plate 41). But, if these were the only reasons, then why is she portrayed carrying it to France more than a decade later? (*see* plates 15 and 18). The pot, along with Jesus' crown of thorns, is as much a part of her *Arrival in Provence* depictions as it is in the Judaean scenes. It is shown in various sizes and made of different materials, appearing as a form of Christine relic rather than an object with a practical purpose.

In more recent times, it is likely that artists have simply been following a pictorial tradition, but that was not the case

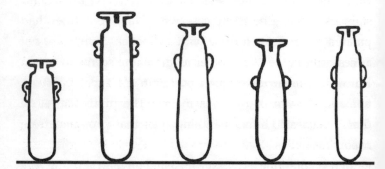

1st-century alabastron designs

in the early Renaissance era when the 'jar' tradition was begun. To the first artists of the genre, the pot served a dual purpose. It was indeed symbolic of the Bethany alabastron, but it also epitomized the Saint Graal (Holy Grail) that was said to contain the blood of Jesus.

The pot is, in effect, a wholly female symbol like the cups and cauldrons of old. In the style of a ciborium (an enclosed vessel containing the Eucharist) it is emblematic of the womb, and Mary Magdalene was said to have carried the blood royal of the *Sangréal* to Provence. In 1484, Sir Thomas Malory referred to the Holy Grail as 'The blessed blood of Christ' and, as related in The Revelation, the salvation of the *Desposyni* was in perpetuating their line irrespective of the persecutions that were levelled against them: 'For the accuser of our brethren is cast down, which accused them before our God day and night. And they overcame him by the blood of the Lamb, and by the word of their testimony' (Revelation 12:10–11).

In artistic terms, the Victorian Pre-Raphaelite Brotherhood and their followers were avid proponents of the Grail, committing its imagery to paper, canvas, tapestry and stained-glass. Well-known images of Mary Magdalene were painted by Frederick Sandys, Sir Edward Coley Burne-Jones and a number by the Brotherhood founder, Dante Gabriel Rossetti. Grail representation was of particular importance to Rossetti, whose *Seed of David* altarpiece graces the cathedral at Llandaff. His *Mary Nazarene* painting is of special significance, with a lone, green-clad Magdalene tending the garden of the Vine. And in Magdalene portraiture, he forsook the customary veiled symbolism of the balsam jar, resorting to the more forthright Grail image of a golden chalice as described in the *Lancelot* story of the *Vulgate Cycle* (*see* plate 12).

In the original tales of the Middle Ages, the Grail was symbolized by many things – a platter, a chalice, a stone, a casket, an aura, a jewel and a vine. However, the concept of the Grail being the cup used by Jesus at the Last Supper was not popularized until Victorian times. This was largely due to Alfred, Lord Tennyson's *Holy Grail*, published in 1859. Previously, the Grail had been likened to the *esceule* dish of the Eucharist, or was a cup said to have been used by Joseph of Arimathea to collect the blood of Jesus. In either sense (whether containing the body or the blood of Christ) it was recognized, above all things, as the 'Holy Vessel', the *vas uterus*, described by Sir Thomas Malory as the *Sankgreal*.

Rossetti's masterwork in Magdalene terms is undoubtedly the Fitzwilliam Museum drawing, *Mary Magdalene at the Door of Simon the Pharisee*. Indeed (along with Dali's *Life of Mary Magdalene*), it is one of the most telling Magdalene representations of all time. Produced in 1858, this extraordinary portrayal is fully reminiscent of a pagan Maytime marriage festival. It depicts the Magdalene's arrival for the anointing of Jesus, who is seen within the house – but Mary is surrounded by minstrels and young couples bedecked with flowers and garlands. There is no doubt whatever as to the nuptial symbolism of this scene and, to ensure that the message of impending marriage was fully conveyed, Rossetti even wrote a sonnet, referencing Jesus as the 'bridegroom', to accompany the artwork:

Why wilt thou cast the roses from thine
    hair?
Nay, be thou all a rose, wreath, lips, and
    cheek.
Nay, not this house, that banquet-house
    we seek;
See how they kiss and enter; come thou
    there.
This delicate day of love we two will
    share,
Till at our ear love's whispering night
    shall speak.
What, sweet one, hold'st thou still the
    foolish freak?
Nay, when I kiss thy feet they'll leave the
    stair.
Oh loose me! See'st thou not my
    Bridegroom's face
That draws me to Him? For His feet my
    kiss,
My hair, my tears He craves today – and
    oh!
What words can tell what other day and
    place
Shall see me clasp those blood-stain'd feet
    of His?
He needs me, calls me, loves me: let me
    go!

Mary Magdalene by Dante Gabriel Rossetti

Mary Magdalene at the door of Simon the Pharisee.
Ink drawing by Dante Gabriel Rossetti, 1859

Nascien and the Fish

King Nascien of the Medas (Nascien II of Septimania), as mentioned in the White Knight's story (*see* page 263), is an important character historically. A 5th-century *Desposynic* contemporary of Meroveus of the Franks, he was a direct descendant and senior successor of the Fisher Kings of Gaul. He was born into the famous House of Faramund from which many European royal families trace their ancestry. These include the Merovingians of France and the Stewart royalty of Scotland, along with the French nobility of Toulouse and Rousillon.[18]

Nascien's symbol, as detailed in related artwork, was a fish. This was in accordance with his heritage and denoted his priestly status. The Greek word for fish was *ichthys*, which had become emblematic in early Christian times for *Iesous Christos Theou Yios Soter* (Jesus Christ, Son of God, Saviour).[19] It was Nascien's granddaughter, Clotilde of Burgundy, who married King Clovis – and from them the Merovingian dynasty descended. The House was so named by virtue of Clovis' grandfather Meroveus of the Franks – another descendant of Fisher King Faramund, whose emblem was also a fish.

Despite the carefully listed genealogies of the era, the heritage of Meroveus was strangely obscured in the documentary annals. Although the rightful son of Clodion, son of Faramund, he was, nonetheless, said by the 5th-century historian, Priscus of Thrace, to have been sired by an arcane sea creature, the *Bistea Neptunis*.

The Sicambrians, from whose female line Meroveus emerged, were previously associated with Grecian Arcadia, originating before that in Scythia by the Black Sea. They took their name from Cambra, a tribal queen of about 380 BC, and were called the people of the *Newmage* (the New Covenant), precisely as the Essenes of Qumrân had once been known.[20] In view of their Arcadian heritage, the fish symbolism of the *Bistea Neptunis* was part of their tradition even before their association with the Fisher Kings in Gaul. Their navigational culture had been closely linked to Pallas, the Arcadian sea-lord, and variations of his name (such as King Pelles) were brought back into play in later Arthurian times.

Some generations before Nascien, his 3rd-century ancestor, Fisher King Aminadab (grandson of Mary Magdalene's son Josephes), had married Eurgen, the great-great-granddaughter of Brân the Blessed and Anna (*see* chart 'Bloodline of the Holy Grail'). This historically significant marriage had cemented the fraternal lines of Jesus and James, so that Meroveus, Nascien and the eventual Merovingian Kings were dually *Desposynic*. By the time of their 6th-century reign in France, the Magdalene legacy was individually realized by way of a separate matrilineal dynasty in Burgundy. This was the House del Acqs of the Viviane Queens of Avallon.

One of the best descriptions of the Holy Grail comes from Nascien in the *Queste del Saint Graal*. In accordance with the symbolism of eternal springs as represented by Viviane, Magdalene and the water mythos, he explains:

> The fountain is of such a kind that one
> cannot exhaust it, for never will one be
> able to take enough of it away. It is the
> Holy Grail, it is the grace of the Holy
> Spirit.

Despite a background that is both romantic and sacred, Grail lore remains an unproclaimed heresy because of its strong female associations, particularly with the ethos of Courtly Love (*Amour Courtois*) in the Middle Ages. The romantic notions of chivalry and the songs of the Troubadours were despised by the bishops because they placed womanhood on a pedestal of veneration, contrary to Catholic doctrine. Moreover, the Church has openly condemned the Grail as a pagan institution of blasphemy and unholy mysteries. To a greater extent though, the Church's reluctance to accept the *Sangréal* tradition derives from the Grail Family's specifical-ly defined Messianic lineage.

Eurgen, the wife and queen of Aminadab, was the aunt of King Coel II of Colchester, whose daughter Helena married Constantius of Rome to become the renowned mother of Emperor Constantine the Great. It was the Arimatheac her-itage of his mother on which Constantine had based his own claim to Messianic status as a female-line descendant of St James the Just. His problem was that alongside him was the line from his maternal grand-aunt Eurgen and Aminadab. This dynasty of Fisher Kings claimed descent from both Jesus and James, and therefore put Constantine in the shade as far as *Desposynic* inheritance was concerned. Consequently, since the Emperor could not compete on equal terms, he invented the concept of Apostolic Succession for his newly created branch of the Christian Church.

Helena's Colchester heritage was of tremendous significance however. Originally the seat of Caractacus the Pendragon, Colchester was the most impressive fortified city in Britain. It was called Camulod in those times (Romanized as Camulodunum) – from the Celtic *camu-lôt* meaning 'curved light'. Later, it became the model for the similarly named, and seemingly transient, Court of Camelot in Arthurian romance. (A biographical background concerning St Helena is given in Appendix IV.)

The father of Eurgen (matriarch of the Fisher Kings) was the most important king in the history of Christianity in Britain. Fourth in descent from James (Joseph of Arimathea), he was called Lucius, and it was he who built the first tower on Glastonbury Tor in the 2nd century.

The Great Luminary

King Lucius was the great-grandson of St James' benefactor Arviragus, whose son Marius had married Penardun, the daughter of James' daughter Anna and archdruid Brân the Blessed. Subsequent to the death of James/Joseph, the anchorites of the Brethren of Alain (Mary Magdalene's grandson) had ceased operations in England, but Lucius decided to revive the Nazarene movement. In doing this, he was said to have 'increased the light' of the first missionaries and, accordingly, became known as *Lleiffer Mawr* (the Great Luminary).

Lucius confirmed his Christianity at Winchester in AD 156, and his cause was heightened in AD 177 by a mass Roman persecution of Christians in Gaul. This was enforced especially in the old Herodian regions of Lyon and Vienne, where St Irenaeus and 19,000 Christians were put to death thirty years later. During the persecution, a good many Gaulish Christians fled to Britain, especially to Glastonbury, where they sought the protection of King Lucius.

This was a good while before Christianity had become the state religion of Rome, and Emperor Marcus Aurelius was hounding Christians in the tradition of his predecessors. Lucius decided, nevertheless, to contact Eleutherius, the Christian leader in Rome at that time. By virtue of his responsibility to the refugees, and indeed to the native people of his realm, Lucius wanted to know how a Christian kingdom might be perceived to function.

The letter in reply from Eleutherius is still extant in the *Sacrorum Conciliorum Collectio* in Rome. Eleutherius suggested that a good king was always at liberty to reject the laws of Rome, but not the law of God. The following is an extract in translation:

> The Christian believers, like all the people
> of the kingdom, must be considered sons
> of the king. They are under your
> protection … A king is known by his
> government, not by whether he retains his
> power over the land. While you govern
> well, you will be a king. Unless you do

> this, the name of the king endures not,
> and you will lose the name of king.[21]

John Capgrave (1393–1464), the most learned of Augustinian friars, and Archbishop Ussher of Armagh, in his 17th-century *De Brittanicarum Ecclesiarum Primordiis*, both recounted that Lucius sent the missionaries Medway and Elfan to carry his request for advice to Rome. They eventually returned with Eleutherius' agents Faganus and Duvanus (whom the Welsh annals name as Fagan and Dyfan). Their mission was referenced back in the 6th century by Gildas Badonicus, and the Venerable Bede of Jarrow (673–735) also wrote about the King's appeal, which is likewise mentioned in the *Anglo-Saxon Chronicle*.[22]

Fagan and Dyfan reinstated the old order of anchorites at Glastonbury and have since been credited with the second foundation of Christianity in Britain. Following this, the fame of Lucius spread far and wide. He was already celebrated as the builder of the Glastonbury tower on St Michael's Tor in AD 167, and now the church at Llandaff was dedicated to him as Lleurwgg the Great.[23] It is here that Rossetti's wonderful *Seed of David* altarpiece can be seen today.

Even more impressively, Lucius was responsible for founding the first Christian archbishopric in Britain. A Latin plaque above the vestry fireplace at St Peter's Church, Cornhill, in the old City of London, is a significant artefact. It records the time when the Catholic Church took over in England and moved the nation's archbishopric to where it remains today, at Canterbury:

In the year of our Lord 179, Lucius, the
first Christian king of this island now
called Britain, founded the first church in
London, well known as the Church of St
Peter in Cornhill; and founded there the
archiepiscopal seat, and made it the
metropolitan church and the primary
church of his kingdom. So it remained for
the space of four hundred years until the
coming of St Augustine … Then, indeed,
the seat and pallium of the archbishopric
was translated from the said church of St
Peter in Cornhill to Dorobernia, which is
now called Canterbury.

The advice given by Bishop Eleutherius in response to King
Lucius' plea is fascinating and fully in keeping with the
underlying principle of service that permeates the Messianic
Grail Code. This was established by Jesus when he washed
his apostles' feet at the Last Supper (John 13:5–15). Peter had
queried Jesus' action, expressing surprise that the Master
should wash his servants' feet, whereupon Jesus replied, 'I
have given you an example, that ye should do as I have done
to you'.

Kings of the original Grail dynasties in Britain and France
always operated on this basis. They were common fathers to
the people, never rulers of the lands. Territorial kingship
was a feudal and Imperial concept that completely under-
mined the Code, and was enforced in Europe after the fraudulent AD 751 *Donation of Constantine* (*see* page 95). The early

monarchs understood the difference in being Kings of the Franks as against being Kings of France, or in being Kings of Scots as against being Kings of Scotland. Grail Kings were defined as Guardians of the Realm and, in this regard, Bishop Eleutherius' advice to Lucius was both profound and enlightened: 'All the people of the kingdom must be considered sons of the king. They are under your protection'.

Kingdoms and Colours

The Holy Families

While the Fisher Kings of the *Desposynic* line from Jesus and Mary Magdalene prevailed in Gaul, and the strain of King Lucius reigned in England, the Avallachs of Arimatheac heritage took their seats in Wales. Descendants of Anna and Brân the Blessed, they continued the tradition of Brân's father King Llyr (Lear),[1] a son of the sovereign overlord Beli Mawr.

Another descendant of Beli Mawr was King Llud. He was the progenitor of the kingly houses of Colchester, Siluria and Strathclyde, and his family celebrated key marriages into the Arimatheac family. From among the Welsh princes in the *Desposynic* succession emerged the founders and local rulers of Brittany (Little Britain), a Frankish region that had previously been called Armorica.

King Llud's grandson, the mighty Cymbeline (father of Caractacus), was the Pendragon of mainland Britain during Jesus' lifetime.[2] The Pendragon, or Head Dragon of the Island (*Pen Draco Insularis*), was the King of Kings and Guardian of the Celtic Isle. The title was not dynastic;

Pendragons were appointed from Celtic royal stock by a Druid council of elders. Cymbeline governed the Belgic tribes of the Catuvellauni and Trinovantes from his seat at Colchester (Camulodunum).

North of Cymbeline's domain, in Norfolk, the Iceni tribes were ruled by King Prasutagus, whose wife was the famous Boudicca (or Boadicea). She led the great, but unsuccessful, revolt against Roman domination from AD 60, yelling her famous war-cry *Y gwir erbyn y Byd* (The Truth against the World). It was immediately after this (a little before the AD 66 Jewish Revolt against the Romans in Judaea) that Joseph of Arimathea came from Gaul to set up his Glastonbury chapel.

Following the Romans' withdrawal from Britain in AD 410, regional leadership reverted to tribal chieftains. One of these was Vortigern of Powys in Wales, whose wife was the daughter of the previous Roman governor, Magnus Maximus. Having assumed full control of Powys by AD 418, Vortigern was elected Pendragon of the Isle in AD 425.

By that time, one of the most prominent kings in descent from Anna and Brân was Cunedda, the ruler of Manau by the Firth of Forth. In a parallel family branch was the wise Coel Hen (Coel the Old), who led the 'Men of the North' (the *Gwyr-y-Gogledd*). Fondly remembered in nursery rhyme as Old King Cole, he governed the regions of Rheged from his Cumbrian seat at Carlisle. Another noted leader was Ceretic, a descendant of King Lucius.[3] From his base at Dumbarton, he governed the regions of Clydesdale. These kings were the most powerful British overlords of the 5th-century and, by virtue of their distant heritage, they were known as the Holy Families of Britain.

In the middle AD 400s, Cunedda and his sons led their armies into North Wales to expel unwanted Irish settlers at the request of Vortigern. In so doing, Cunedda founded the Royal House of Gwynedd in the Welsh coastal region west of Powys. The Picts of Caledonia in the far north of Britain then took advantage of Cunedda's absence and began a series of border raids across Hadrian's Wall. An army of Germanic Jute mercenaries, led by Hengest and Horsa, was swiftly imported to repel the invaders but, having succeeded, they turned their attentions to the far south and seized the kingdom of Kent for themselves. Other Germanic Saxon and Angle tribes subsequently invaded from Europe. The Saxons took the south, developing the kingdoms of Wessex, Essex, Middlesex and Sussex, while the Angles occupied the rest of the land from the Severn estuary to Hadrian's Wall, comprising Northumbria, Mercia and East Anglia. The whole became known as England (Angle-land) and the new occupants called the Celtic western peninsula Wales (*weallas* meaning 'foreigners').

Cunedda remained in North Wales and, after Vortigern's death in AD 464, he succeeded as Pendragon, also becoming the supreme military commander of the Britons. The holder of this latter post was called the *Guletic*. When Cunedda died, Vortigern's son-in-law, Brychan of Brecknock, became Pendragon, and Ceretic of Strathclyde became the Guletic. Meanwhile, Vortigern's grandson Aurelius – a man of considerable military experience – returned from Brittany to lend his weight against the Saxon incursion. In his capacity as a druidic priest, Aurelius was the designated Prince of the Sanctuary of the Ambrius – a holy chamber, symbolically modelled upon the ancient Hebrew Tabernacle (Exodus 25:8). The Guardians of the Ambrius were individually styled *Ambrosius* and wore scarlet mantles. From his fort in Snowdonia, Aurelius the Ambrosius maintained the military defence of the West and succeeded as the Guletic when Brychan died.

In the early AD 500s, Brychan's son (also Brychan) moved from Wales to the Firth of Forth as Prince of Manau. There he founded another region of Brecknock in Forfarshire, which the Welsh people referred to as Breichniog of the North. His father's seat had been at Brecon in Wales – and so the northern fortress was similarly called Brechin. Brychan II's daughter married Prince Gabràn[4] of Scots Dal-riada (the Western Highlands), as a result of which Gabràn became Lord of the Forth, inheriting a castle at Aberfoyle.

In that era, the Irish Gaels were in dispute with the house of Brychan and, under King Cairill of Antrim, they launched an assault against Scots Manau in 514. The invasion was successful and the Forth area was brought under Irish rule. Brychan duly called for assistance from his son-in-law, Prince Gabràn, and from the Guletic commander Aurelius. Rather than attempt to remove the Irish from Manau, the leaders decided to launch a direct sea offensive against Antrim in Northern Ireland.

In AD 516, Gabràn's Scots fleet sailed from the Sound of Jura with the Guletic troops of Aurelius. Their objective was the castle of King Cairill, the formidable hill-fort at Dun Baedàn (Badon Hill). The Guletic forces were victorious, and Dun Baedàn was overthrown.[5] In 560, the chronicler Gildas II wrote about this battle in his *De Excidio Conquestu*

Britanniae (The Fall and Conquest of Britain), and the great conflict featured in both the Scots and Irish chronicles.[6] Some years after the Battle of Dun Baedàn, Gabràn became King of Scots in 537, with his West Highland court at Dunadd near Loch Crinan.

At that time, the Pendragon was Cunedda's great-grandson, the Welsh king, Maelgwyn of Gwynedd. He was succeeded in this appointment by King Gabràn's son, Aedàn of

Aedàn the Pendragon

Dalriada, who became King of Scots in 574 and was the first British king to be installed by priestly ordination when anointed by St Columba.

Shortly before Aedàn's kingly ordination, King Rhydderch of Strathclyde had killed King Gwenddolau in battle near Carlisle. The battlefield sat between the River Esk and Liddel Water, above Hadrian's Wall. (It was here, at the Moat of Liddel, that the Arthurian tale of *Fergus and the Black Knight* was set.) Gwenddolau's chief adviser (the Merlin of Britain) was Emrys of Powys, the son of Aurelius. On Gwenddolau's death, however, the Merlin fled to Hart Fell Spa in the Caledonian Forest, and then sought refuge in King Aedàn's court at Dunadd.[7]

In those days, the most important urban centre in the north of Britain was Carlisle, which had taken over from Colchester as the primary Camu-lôt of the Sovereign Guletic. It had been a prominent Roman garrison town and, by AD 369, was one of the five provincial capitals. In his *Life of St Cuthbert*, the venerable Bede of Jarrow refers to a Christian community in Carlisle long before the Anglo-Saxons penetrated the area.

A little south of Carlisle, near Kirkby Stephen in Cumbria, stands the ruin of Pendragon Castle. Carlisle was also called Cardeol or Caruele in Arthurian times. *The High History of the Holy Grail* refers specifically to Arthur's court at Carlisle, which also features in the French *Suit de Merlin* and in the British tales, *Sir Gawain and the Carl of Carlisle*, and *The Avowing of King Arthur*.

Arthurian Descent

It is often claimed that the first quoted reference to King Arthur comes from the 9th-century Welsh monk, Nennius, whose *Historia Brittonum* cites him at numerous identifiable battles. But Arthur was recorded long before Nennius in the 7th-century *Life of St Columba*. He is also mentioned in the Celtic poem *Gododdin*, written in about AD 600.

When King Aedàn of Dalriada was installed by St Columba in 574, his eldest son and heir (born in 559) was Arthur. In the *Life of St Columba*, Abbot Adamnan of Iona (627–704) related how the Saint had prophesied that Arthur would die before he could succeed his father as King of Scots. Adamnan further confirmed that the prophecy was accurate, for Arthur was killed in battle a few years after Columba's own death in 597.[8]

In 858, Nennius listed various battles at which Arthur was victorious. The locations included the Caledonian Wood north of Carlisle (*Cat Coit Celidon*) and Mount Agned – the fort of Bremenium in the Cheviots, from which the Anglo-Saxons were repelled. Also featured was Arthur's battle by the River Glein in Northumbria, where the fortified enclosure was the centre of operations from the middle 500s. Other named Arthurian battlegrounds were the City of the Legion (Carlisle) and the district of Linnuis – the old region of the Novantae tribe, north of Dumbarton, where Ben Arthur stands above Arrochar at the head of Loch Long.

Arthur's father, King Aedàn mac Gabràn of Scots, became Pendragon by virtue of being Prince Brychan's grandson. Aedàn's mother, Lluan of Brecknock, was descended from Joseph of Arimathea. There never was an Uther Pendragon as featured in the Arthurian legends, even though he was spuriously grafted into English charts of the era in 16th-century Tudor times.[9] Historically, there was only ever one Arthur born to a Pendragon: he was Arthur mac Aedàn of Dalriada.[10]

On his sixteenth birthday in 575, Arthur became Sovereign Guletic, and the Celtic Church proclaimed his mother, Ygerna del Acqs, as High Queen of the Celtic kingdoms. Her own mother (in the hereditary lineage of Jesus and Mary Magdalene) was Queen Viviane I of Burgundian Avallon, Lady of the Lake. The priests, therefore, anointed Arthur as High King of the Britons following his father's ordination as King of Scots. At the time of her conception of Arthur by Aedàn, Ygerna (Igraine) was married to Gwyr-Llew, Dux of Carlisle. The ancient *Chronicle of the Scots* records the event as follows:

> Becaus at ye heire of Brytan was maryit
> wy tane Scottis man quen ye Kinrik wakit,
> and Arthure was XV yere ald, ye
> Brytannis maid him king be ye devilrie of
> Merlynge, and yis Arthure was gottyn
> onn ane oyir mannis wiffe, ye Dux of
> Caruele.[11]

On the death of Gwyr-Llew, however, Ygerna married Aedàn of Dalriada, thereby legitimizing Arthur before his titles were bestowed. By way of this union, the line of Jesus and Mary Magdalene was linked to the line of James/Joseph of Arimathea (*see* chart 'Bloodline of the Holy Grail', page 429). Arthur was the first product of such a *Desposynic* marital union in 350 years, which is why he became so important to the Grail tradition.

In the *Life of Saint Columba*, Abbot Adamnan relates that King Arthur mac Aedàn was killed in the Battle of the Miathi. The Miathi were a tribe of Britons who had been pushed northwards by the Angles in 574, and had settled by the Scottish border.[12] Their main stronghold was at Dunmyat in the district of Manau on the River Forth, where they had cast their lot with the Irish settlers. Despite the Irish King Cairill's 516 defeat at Badon Hill, the Irish were still being obstructive in Manau. Consequently, the Guletic forces made a second assault on Dun Baedàn.

This campaign was mentioned by Nennius, who rightly described Arthur's presence, whereas the Gildas account relates to the earlier 516 battle with Ambrosius Aurelius as the commander. Nennius gives Arthur rather more credit than his due, however, for on this second occasion the Scots were defeated and Arthur's father, King Aedàn, was obliged to submit to Prince Baedàn mac Cairill at Ros-na-Rig on Belfast Lough.[13]

Following King Baedàn mac Cairill's death in 581, Aedàn of Scots finally managed to expel the Irish from Manau and the Forth. Later, in 596, Arthur's cavalry drove the Irish out of Scots Brecknock. King Aedàn was present at the battles, but Arthur's younger brothers Brân and Domingart were killed at Brechin in 595, where Arthur and his third brother, Eochaid Find, were also recorded at the battle of Circinn.[14]

In confronting the Irish at Manau, the Guletic troops also had to face the Miathi Britons. They were successful in driving many of them back to their southern territory, but those who remained when the Scots departed had to contend with the Picts, who promptly moved into their domain. By the end of the century, the Picts and Miathi were united against Arthur's cavalry, whom they met at the battle of Camelyn, north of the Antonine Wall. Once again, the Scots were victorious and the Picts were driven northwards. Afterwards, a nearby ironworks foundry was dubbed *Furnus Arthuri* (Arthur's Fire) to mark the event. It was a long-standing attraction and was not demolished until the 18th-century Industrial Revolution.

In 603, just three years after Camelyn, the Scots faced the southern Miathi and the Northumbrian Angles. This confrontation was a protracted affair fought on two battlegrounds – the second conflict resulting from a short-term Scots retreat from the first. The forces initially met at Camlanna, an old Roman hill-fort by Hadrian's Wall. Unlike the previous Camelyn encounter, however, the battle of Camlanna was a complete fiasco for the Scots. Falling for a diversionary tactic by the Miathi, the Scots allowed the Angles to move behind them in a concerted north-westerly push towards Galloway and Strathclyde. The unlucky definition of a *Cath Camlanna* has been applied to many a lost battle thereafter.

Only a few months earlier, the Angle king, Aethelfrith of Bernicia, had defeated King Rhydderch at Carlisle, thereby acquiring new territory along the reaches of the Solway. The Dalriadan forces under Aedàn and Arthur were therefore under some pressure to intercept and halt the Angles' north-ward advance. They were said to have assembled immense forces, drawn from the ranks of the Welsh princes and they even gained assistance from Maeluma mac Baedàn of Antrim, the son of their erstwhile enemy. By that time, the Irish were themselves daunted by the prospect of an Anglo-Saxon inva-sion, and so the Irish had joined forces with the Scots.

The affray at Camlanna was short-lived and the Celtic troops were obliged to chase after the Angles, who had swept past them. They caught up again at Dawston-on-Solway (then called Degsastan in Liddesdale). The *Chronicles of Holyrood* and *Chronicles of Melrose* refer to the battle site as Dexa Stone. It was here, in 603, that Arthur, Prince and Sovereign Guletic of the Britons, fell (at the age of forty-four) alongside Maeluma mac Baedàn. Also killed at Dawston was Arthur's son Modred, archpriest of the Sacred Kindred of St Columba, described in the annals as *Modredus filius Regis Scotii* (Modred son of the King of Scots).

Queens of Avallon

The Battle of Dawston was one of the fiercest in all Celtic his-tory. The *Tigernach Annals* call it 'The day when half the men of Scotland fell'. Although Aethelfrith was victorious, he too sustained heavy losses. His brothers Theobald and Eanfrith were slain, while his opponent, King Aedàn, was forced to flee the field.

Aethelfrith never reached Strathclyde, but his success at Dawston enabled the Northumbrian territory to be extended northwards to the Firth of Forth, incorporating the Lothians. Ten years later, in 613, Aethelfrith besieged Chester and brought Cumbria fully under Angle control. This drove a permanent geographical wedge between the Welsh and the Strathclyde Britons. The Mercian Angles then pushed westwards, forcing the Welsh behind what was eventually to be the line of Offa's Dyke, while the Wessex Saxons encroached beyond Exeter, annexing the south-west peninsula.

In time, the once conjoined Celtic lands of Wales, Strathclyde and Dumnonia (Devon and Cornwall) were totally isolated from each other, and the Sacred Kindred of St Columba[15] held Arthur responsible. He had failed in his duties as Guletic and High King. His father, King Aedàn of Dalriada, died within five years of the Camlanna disaster, which was said to have opened the door to the final conquest of Britain by the Anglo-Saxons. The days of Celtic lordship were done and, after more than six centuries of tradition, Cadwaladr of Wales (26th in line from Joseph of Arimathea) was the last Pendragon.

In the wake of Arthur's defeats at Camlanna and Dawston (jointly called *di Bellum Miathorum*: the Battle of the Miathi), the old kingdoms of the North existed no more. The Scots, who were physically separated from their former allies in Wales, perceived that their only route towards saving the land of Alba (Scotland) was to become allied with the Picts of Caledonia. This was achieved in 844, when Aedàn's famed descendant, King Kenneth MacAlpin, united the Picts and Scots as one nation.[16] The records of Kenneth's installation support his truly important position in the family line by referring to him as a descendant of the Queens of Avallon.[17]

The Avallonian dynasty – a direct heritable estate of Mary Magdalene – was perpetuated in the female line, with the queens' daughters holding the senior positions, rather than their sons. The titular Queens of Burgundian Avallon emerged alongside the Merovingian Kings of the Franks, while another important offshoot was the Septimanian royal succession in the Franco-Spanish Midi.

Before marrying King Aedàn mac Gabràn of Dalriada, Ygerna d'Avallon del Acqs had a daughter by her former husband Gwyr-Llew of Carlisle. The daughter's name was Morgaine, and she subsequently became the half-sister of Arthur. In Grail romance she is known as Morganna or Morgan le Fay, but Morgaine is historically referenced in Royal Irish Academy texts as 'Muirgein, daughter of Aedàn in Belach Gabráin'.[18]

Morgaine's son Ywain (Eógain) founded the noble house of Léon d'Acqs in Brittany and the later arms of Léon bore the black Davidic Lion, without teeth or claws, on a gold shield (in heraldic terms: 'Or, a lion rampant, sable'). The province was so named because *léon* was Septimanian for 'lion'. Until the 14th century, Scotland's Lord Lyon, King of Arms, was still called the *Léon Héraud*. The Comité (County) of Léon was established in about 530 at the time of the Breton King Hoel I. He was of Welsh Arimatheac descent and his sister, Alienor (Elaine), was Ywain's wife.

At that time, there were two levels of authority in Brittany. In the course of a protracted immigration from Britain, Breton Dumnonia had been founded in 520, but it was not a kingdom in the true sense. There emerged a line of kings such as Hoel, but they were not Kings of Brittany, they

The Davidic lion of Léon d'Acqs

were Kings of the immigrant Bretons. Throughout this period, the region remained a Merovingian province and the local kings were subordinate to Frankish authority by appointed Counts styled *Comites non regis*. The supreme Frankish Lord of Brittany in 540–544 was Chonomore, a native of the Frankish State with Merovingian authority to oversee the development of Brittany by the settlers. Chonomore's forebears were Mayors of the Palace of Neustria and he was the hereditary Comte de Pohor. In time, the descendants of Ywain's aunt Viviane II del Acqs became overall Counts of Brittany.

Brittany features prominently in Arthurian romance. At Paimpont, about 30 miles (48 km) from Rennes, is the enchanted Forest of Broceliande, from which stretches the Valley of No Return, where Morganna confined her lovers. Also to be found are the magic Spring of Barenton and Merlin's Garden of Joy, although most of the Broceliande stories were actually transposed from far earlier accounts of the historical Merlin Emrys in the Caledonian Forest of Scotland.

The Magdalene Colours

The earliest examples of art used for Christian purposes are to be found in the catacombs of Rome. Laid in a single row, this network of passages and rooms would extend for about 550 miles (880 km). It was here beneath the city streets that the early Christians sheltered from Imperial persecution, and it is reckoned that around six million people are buried in the complex. Even the chambers used for interment in the 1st and 2nd centuries carry some decoration. Fish and doves were common symbols of the faith, and there are some crudely made biblical scenes, but there are none of the Crucifixion or of the Madonna, except perhaps in cryptic terms. *The Catholic Encyclopedia* confirms that the most common recurring theme is the Vine.[19]

Christian art began to evolve in the public domain from the Edict of Milan in AD 313, when Emperor Constantine proclaimed the new State religion of Rome. However, the earliest known Mary Magdalene portrayal comes from before that in about AD 240. She appears in a colourful wall-painting of her arrival at the tomb of Jesus, discovered in 1929 at Dura-Europos on the River Euphrates in Syria. Entitled *Myrrophore* (Myrrh bearer), the painting was removed from its chapel-house in the early 1930s, and is now at the Yale University Art Gallery in New Haven.[20]

By the 5th century, Christ and other characters had become more holy in appearance, and the halo was introduced for saintly figures. Although now a generalized term, the *halo* is correctly a ring (like the halo around the moon), whereas the saintly original was a bright aura called a *nimbus*, which might or might not have rays. The nimbus is usually of gold and may have a clearly defined outline, or the light may be diffused. A nimbus glow around the head is classified as an *aureole*, and if encompassing the body or having no specific outer shape, it is a *glory*. A nimbus can be a halo ring above or behind the head or a flat disc set above or behind the head. Discs set behind were more common in early art, when gold leaf was used to represent what actually would have been a surrounding aureole. Scientifically, a nimbus/halo is an illuminated aura – a high-energy field of radiated light. (Various *nimbus* styles are shown in the colour plates.)

The first ivory crucifix representations come from the 5th century, but it was not until the 6th century that the Crucifixion appeared in pictorial art. At about the same time, Madonna images began to emerge, but they were few. During the early centuries of Christianity, therefore, the birth and crucifixion of Jesus were of low priority. His portrayals were generally those of the 'good shepherd' – a clean-shaven young man, teaching, healing or with his apostles. It is therefore of some significance that, in Christian terms, one of the oldest known, above-ground pictorial relics is not of Jesus at all, but of Mary Magdalene.

From the 6th century, Christian art progressed in a multitude of directions, and a number of favourite themes were established. As the churches and cathedrals were built, pictorial and sculpted art became a widespread requirement, and the themes were consolidated into forms of doctrinal preference. Artists were generally instructed as to the content of their work, but there were differences in the Gospels which led to confusion in portrayal. Should there, for example, be one, two or three women at the tomb of Jesus? Should the Nativity be portrayed in a house as specified in Matthew, or in a stable as was presumed from the interpretation of Luke?

As the 'virgin mother' cult grew in significance, Jesus' father, Joseph, was deemed inconsequential in artwork, and the Church commissioners required that he be confined to inferior or background positions. The bishops would gladly have denied that Mary had ever married, but artists could not escape the directness of the Gospels. In an effort not to suggest any physical attachment between Joseph and Mary, the best they could do was to depict Joseph as being considerably older than his wife. The famous *Doni Tondo* by Michelangelo (1504) features a very bald and white-bearded Joseph, as does Caravaggio's *The Rest on the Flight into Egypt* (1597).

Joseph was also portrayed as taking little interest in his family, as in Ghirlandaio's *The Adoration of the Shepherds* (1485). His necessary presence at Jesus' birth was a particular cause of difficulty, but this was overcome in such paintings as Alessandro Moretto's *The Nativity* (c1520) by showing him as elderly with a supportive staff. Sometimes Joseph appears to be in his dotage, either asleep or reduced to a superfluous onlooker as in Hans Memling's *The Adoration of the Magi* (1470). He was seldom permitted to be a part of any relevant action and, in pictures such as Van Dyck's *Repose in Egypt* (1630), hardly seems capable of any action. Indeed, he was frequently shown as positively infirm, leaning uncomfortably on a crutch, while Mary remained young, beautiful and serene.[21]

Mary's father, Joachim, was similarly of little relevance because Mary was said to have been immaculately conceived. As early as the 14th-century frescoes of Taddeo Gaddi, it was preferred to sideline Joachim by showing him at his least dignified – being ejected from the Temple by the High Priest Issachar, having presumed to offer a feast-day lamb when he was not a father. His *Expulsion from the Temple* was a theme taken up by others such as Giotto and Ghirlandaio.

Mary's mother also came under strict regulation, and was seldom introduced into paintings with her daughter because her presence would detract from Mary's divine status. If Ann's visible attendance was essential, she was placed in a subordinate position. Francesco da San Gallo's *Saint Ann and the Madonna* (1526) provides a good example of how the mother is seated behind her daughter. Bartolommeo Cesi's *The Vision of Saint Ann* (1600) shows Ann kneeling before a vision of Mary. Leonardo da Vinci's *The Virgin and Child with Saint Ann* (1510) is cleverly contrived to position the adult Mary on her mother's knee, thereby keeping the Madonna to the fore. Similarly, Ann stands behind her daughter in Pietro Perugino's *The Family of the Virgin* (1502).

The main problem that occurred in all this was one of Mother Mary's personal identification when it came to female group portrayals such as the women at the cross or at the tomb of Jesus. Rules of colour coding were therefore introduced so that Mary and Mary Magdalene could be distinguished from one another.

Mother Mary's head, it was determined, should always be veiled, and her arms must always be covered. At the height of the Inquisition, it was not permitted to show Mary's feet or breasts. She could wear a close-fitting red tunic, so long as it was not overtly apparent, and she could wear some gold to signify her queenly status, but her outer gown should be blue, the colour of heaven. Some early paintings displayed Mary in a red robe, but this became expressly forbidden because it was the colour of the cardinals and a male ecclesiastical prerogative. When worn by a woman, a red outer garment was deemed sinful and heretical. Mary could wear the white of purity alone for her Immaculate Conception and Assumption, and could wear violet or grey at the Crucifixion and Entombment,[22] but predominantly her colour was to be blue – ultramarine in the early days, moving to royal blue and lighter shades in later times. From 1649, the Inquisition insisted that Mary must be rendered in blue and white.[23]

The one colour that was not afforded to Mary in any respect was green. This had strong pagan implications and was deemed to be the colour of nature, whereas Mary was above nature. Green also denoted sexual fertility, just as red on a woman defined lust and wantonness, being the colour of the *hierodulai* scarlet women. Green was, therefore, demoted in ecclesiastical terms to the colour of the earth state, whereas blue defined the heavenly condition. Hence, red and green became the colours associated with Mary Magdalene, who was also allowed to wear gold. In a Mother Mary context, gold represented her queenly rank, whereas for Mary Magdalene it was emblematic of avarice.

In overall terms, the colours that separated the two women pictorially were a predominance of blue, violet and grey for Mother Mary and a predominance of green, red and gold for Mary Magdalene. By this means, they became readily distinguishable one from the other (*see* plates 37, 38, 39, 40). In the conventual tradition of monastic Orders, Mary Magdalene could be portrayed wearing a habit as appropriate to the Order as a mark of piety and atonement.

The Three Marys at the Empty Sepulchre (plate 41) by Giovanni Battista Gaulli (Il Baciccio) exemplifies the colour schemes in operation – Mary is distinctive in blue, with Mary Magdalene in red, green and gold. The Magdalene scheme became the primary colouration for Grail-related artwork as in plate 12, whilst the bloodline significance of Jesus' own fertility had to be more surreptitiously conveyed by way of subtle iconography. A good example of this is the bunch of grapes introduced by Gerard David in his *The Rest on the Flight to Egypt* (plate 37).

In the High Renaissance era, Italian artists of the Florentine and Milanese schools achieved a recognized social status in their own right by virtue of patronage from the ducal families of Medici and Sforza. Not being necessarily reliant on the Church for commissions, they were thus afforded more freedom in their subjects sometimes almost to the extent of heresy. To that point in time, Magdalene artwork had mainly been a product of the monastic Orders, with artists such as Fra Angelico and Giotto di Bondone. There were also many Magdalene icons from the Byzantine school, while the Flemish and German masters were progressing the image of Mary in Provence.

It was during this period of Italian romanticism and the more enlightened Magdalene environment that numerous unconventional Madonna images emerged – paintings which seemingly flouted the ecclesiastical regulations. Not the least noticeable artist was the young 'prince of painters' Raffaello Sanzio, better known as Raphael. A master of allegory, as conveyed in *The Knight's Dream* (1504), Raphael's *Sposalizio* (The Marriage of Mary and Joseph) introduced a tall, vigorous young Joseph, quite contrary to anything that had gone before. He produced many Madonna paintings in a recognizable Marian format, but also strayed into a realm that was wholly unfamiliar.

It was not uncommon for artists to bend the rules here and there to provide a little individuality in their work. But if they had strayed too far, their characters would have been either unrecognizable or unacceptable. In general terms, they painted the familiar images. They would not, for example, have portrayed Jesus hanging from a tree (as described in Acts 5:30, 10:39 and 13:29) because the familiar image was of Jesus nailed to a cross. But Raphael was accused of bending the rules too far. From his studio emerged some very unusual Madonna and child paintings which totally disregarded the conventions of her sovereign countenance and dress colouration.

When challenged by the papal emissary, Count Baldassare Castiglione, who claimed that these Madonna and child portraits were not representative of the Virgin Mary, Raphael replied that they were not supposed to be portraits of her. When further pressed on the matter, he wrote to the Count stating that they were just imaginative portrayals (*'mi servo d'una certa idea che mi viene in mente'*).[24]

Two of these portraits are shown in plates 42 and 43. Although difficult to see in these small reproductions, both the mother and child in each painting have gold ring halos. The child's halo has a cross within it – a traditional Christian symbol. So if these paintings, in Raphael's own words, are not portraits of the Virgin Mary, then who do they represent? In artistic terms, Raphael – always accurate in his representations – did not break the Marian colour-code rules at all; he applied them precisely and unmistakably. This Madonna wears the traditional red and green colours of Mary Magdalene.

Leonardo da Vinci

Mona Lisa

In chapter 1 we learnt that many paintings are familiar today by names and titles that were unknown to their creators (*see* page 3), and the *Mona Lisa* portrait was cited as an example. Although popularly known by that name in the English-speaking world, she is known in France (where she hangs in The Louvre) as *La Joconde*, and in Italy – her place of origin – as *La Gioconda*.[1] *Mona Lisa* is a latter-day corruption of what was previously *M'onna Lisa*, and before that *Madonna Lisa* (My Lady Lisa).

Discussion of this painting is especially relevant because it sets the scene for some of the Magdalene-related art concepts in Dan Brown's novel, *The Da Vinci Code*. While it has to be remembered that this is a fictional work, and includes plot themes constructed with the usual novelistic licence, underpinning the story is a factual base which concerns the *Desposynic* legacy of Jesus and Mary Magdalene. Novelists do not generally expect their readers to believe made-up stories but, in these days of contrived-reality television characters, there is a tendency for something as compelling as *The*

Da Vinci Code to have that effect. Consequently, many people treat the words of the book's fictional cast as if they had just heard them as facts on a national news broadcast.

At one point, for example, the novel's Professor Robert Langdon (a Harvard symbologist) states that Mona Lisa's name derives from the ancient Egyptian deities Amon and Isis – corrupted to *Amon l'Isa*, and somehow from that comes *Mona Lisa*. This, he claims, proves that the portrait is androgynous, neither male nor female, but a divine union of both, and the reason for the lady's knowing smile.[2]

Given that Leonardo never knew his painting by the title of *Mona Lisa*, this scenario is clearly an impossibility. In fact, he probably never heard his portrait being called *La Joconde* or *La Gioconda* either. All early records of the painting entitle it *Courtisane au voile de gaze* (Courtesan of the gauze veil).[3]

Langdon further states that the background landscape, being lower on the left than on the right, is emblematic of the painting's dual-gender message. Such fanciful notions are fine in a novel, but in reality this is simply looking for allegory where there is none. It is well known that one's visual focus pulls downwards and to the right. Consequently, it was, and still is, common practice to compensate pictorially by weighting the left side of paintings – often with a tree, some solid object, or maybe with darker colour tones.

What Leonardo did was to drop the landscape a little on the left and, with water running from the right, there might easily be an unseen fall behind the woman's head. Had he not done this, the portrait would immediately have lost some of its masterful quality. This backdrop manipulation has the effect of what has been artistically dubbed

'Leonardo's trick'.[4] It causes the observer's eye to oscillate back and forth across the subject's eyes, creating an illusion of animation. Interestingly, the vertical centre-line of the painting falls through Lady Lisa's left eye, as against the right eye centre-points in Leonardo's other portraits, *Ginevra de' Benci*,[5] and *Cecilia Gallerani* (commonly known as *Lady with an Ermine*),[6] whose heads are turned in the opposite direction. Using the eye of the predominant cheek as an image centre was a common device of Renaissance portrait artists.

Making such calculated adjustments in a painting is not a random exercise. When done correctly, it follows specific architectural guidelines based on a mathematical principle called the Golden Mean. The same Euclidian formula is used when mounting prints and watercolours for framing, and again when decorating picture mats with plain or colour-filled wash lines at precise distances apart. To quote the author of a picture-framing manual: 'The Golden Mean is approximately 5 to 8 proportion. Numerically this ratio works out to 0.618 to 1. Any design I have ever done that was good used the Golden Mean'.[7]

When a framing mat is applied (even to a cleverly balanced work like the *Mona Lisa* when in print form), an adjustment has to be made in the mat so that it equalizes the compensation in the painting, otherwise the visual pulling-down factor will apply. If the artist was not as astute as Leonardo, and did not compensate within the picture, then an additional adjustment must be made in the mounting. It is for these reasons that correctly mounted pictures have mats that are deeper at the base than they are above the image – and to get this perfectly into balance, the Golden Mean ratio is used as a calculation.

A remarkable feature of the *Mona Lisa* portrait is that it is noted in the art world for its integral wealth of Golden Mean sectioning (sometimes called Sacred Geometry). Leonardo applied it in every aspect of the image, as if he were constructing a Gothic cathedral. There are more Golden Rectangles in the lady's face than in the whole of many far more complex paintings. Web sites have even been set up to demonstrate this in animation,[8] and it is another reason why this painting is reckoned to be among the greatest ever made. The keystone of these rectangles is that which encloses Lisa's facial area, from the top of her head down to the top of her bodice. It is identical to that used for *Ginevra de' Benci* and *Cecilia Gallerani*.[9] And within the top square of the larger section of this is another, from Lisa's hairline down to her chin.

In 1987, computer graphics pioneer Lillian Schwartz (a consultant for AT&T's Bell Labs and co-author of *The Computer Artist's Handbook*) conducted an on-screen experiment with the *Mona Lisa* image. She discovered that by positioning Leonardo's self-portrait alongside it, in a split-face fashion, the two could be morphed and matched. The individual male features were heavier of course, but the positioning of the features was close to identical. Working independently in England, a Dr Digby Quested came to the same conclusion. This has led, in *The Da Vinci Code*, to Professor Langdon's notion that not only was *Mona Lisa* contrived as an androgynous portrait, but that it is actually a female representation of Leonardo himself.[10] In consequence,

Langdon states that 'Da Vinci was a prankster', which is a necessary plot element to lead to other things later in the story. The fact is, however, that the morphing works because Leonardo applied the same Golden Rectangular structures to both portraits. The ratios and proportions of, and between, each facial feature (his own and Lady Lisa's) are the same.

Leonardo might not have been a prankster, but he was certainly an engineer, and he constructed his pictures to engineering standards as one might build bridges. His original letter to Duke Ludovicio Sforza of Milan requested employment not as an artist, but as a military and court engineer – a post which he took up when he moved from Florence in 1482.

An avid student and exponent of mathematics in art, Leonardo's base anatomical starting point was his famous Vitruvian Man. Like the Roman architect Vitruvius before him, Leonardo had made a close study of the human figure and of how geometric standards worked in its design. In his 1st-century treatise *De Architecture*, Vitruvius had stated,

> Now the navel is naturally the exact
> centre of the body. For if a man lies on his
> back with hands and feet outspread, and
> the centre of a circle is placed on his
> navel, his fingers and toes will be touched
> by the circumference. Also a square will
> be found within the figure ... For if we
> measure from the sole of the foot to the
> top of the head, and apply the measure to
> the outstretched hands, the breadth will

be found equal to the height, just like sites
which are squared by rule.[11]

With this as a starting base for his figures, Leonardo then applied the Golden Mean geometry of exact architectural proportion. In simplistic terms, the rule is: 'If a given line is marked into two unequal parts, the ratio of the short part to the long part is the same as the ratio of the long part to the whole'. In mathematical Greek, the Golden Ratio is referred to as (φ) *phi*, as against the Pythagorean (π) *pi*, which is achieved by way of Golden calculation (*see* Appendix V).

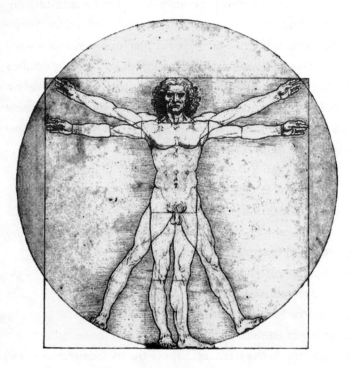

Leonardo's *Vitruvian Man*

So, who was Lady Lisa the *Courtisane*? She was first mentioned, while being painted, in the diary of Antonio de Beatis (half-brother of King Alfonso II of Naples). He visited Leonardo at Cloux manor house and saw the work in progress – subsequently referring to the sitter as 'the Florentine lady'.[12]

It can be seen from Leonardo's numerous study drawings that he preferred to position his figures in a nude state, so as to reconcile their anatomical composition before dressing them for his paintings. It was no different with Lady Lisa (*see* plate 35). His gouache and black chalk life sketch, now at the Musée Conde in Chantilly, is probably closer to her true likeness than the resultant painting with all its refinements and geometric accuracies (plate 34). Following such routes of exactitude will frequently lead to what one *thinks* a subject looks like, as against what they actually look like – in effect refining 'exact' geometry to become a form of 'preferred' geometry. Examples of this are often found in eye positioning. In a flat-on head portrayal (as in reality from crown to chin), eyes are at the equator of the head, but it is common for artists to portray them higher than centre because it seems to look better.[13] The same is often done in nude studies by lifting women's breasts into what would otherwise be a supported position.

In 1550, the Italian painter and biographer, Giorgio Vasari, wrote that Leonardo's Florentine sitter was Lady Lisa di Anton Maria di Noldo Gheradini. She was the daughter of Antonio Gheradini, and had been the third wife of wealthy silk merchant Francesco di Bartolommeo di Zanobi Giocondo since 1495. Hence derived the eventual portrait title, *La Gioconda*. This was later endorsed by Cassiano dal Pozzo, Minister of Culture and promoter of many great Renaissance artists.[14]

By the time of the commission, Lisa was already a mother (her son Andrea having been born in 1503). So why was she originally dubbed as the *Courtisane*, which denotes the 'mistress of a wealthy man', rather than a wife? It was because her husband was not part of the equation. Antonio de Beatis confirmed that the portrait was 'done from life at the request of the magnificent Giuliano Lorenzo di Medici'. Giuliano was a son of Lorenzo Medici the Magnificent, who had ruled Florence until his death in 1492.[15] Lorenzo had been Leonardo's primary patron before he went to Milan, and they were jointly involved with the University of Pisa. Giuliano, Duke de Nemours, was the younger of Lorenzo's sons and appears to have been Lady Lisa's lover.

The problem was that, while the work was in progress, Giuliano died unexpectedly at the age of 37,[16] and Leonardo was left with an unfinished painting. He was unable to pass it to the Giocondo household for fear that its provenance might be discovered. Neither could he submit it to the Medicis because, just a few months before his death in 1516, Giuliano had been contractually married to Philiberta of Savoy. The painting that was eventually to become the most famous in the world was left high and dry with no owner but the artist himself. Shortly afterwards, Leonardo moved to France, and took the painting with him.

A couple of years later, Leonardo died at Amboise, south of Paris, and he was still in possession of the portrait. When Vasari subsequently produced his famous book, *The Lives of the Most Eminent Italian Painters, Sculptors and Architects*, he wrote that Leonardo 'worked on this painting for four years, and then still left it unfinished'.[17] Indeed, the painting remains unfinished today. No other artist stepped in to complete the work because of its sensitive nature. Various final items and finishing touches are missing from the portrait – for example, Lisa's rings and jewellery were never added. The main peculiarity, however, is that the Lady has spent the past five centuries with no eyelashes or eyebrows, which is one of the reasons for her seemingly curious expression.

Thirty-six years after Leonardo's death, Vasari was the first to use the term *Madonna Lisa*. He recorded that 'while he [Leonardo] was painting M'lady Lisa, who was a very beautiful woman, he employed singers and musicians or jesters to keep her full of merriment'. A studio scene incorporating this aspect, in conjunction with a showing of the work to the artist Raphael, lives on in the painting by Aimée Pagès (*see* plate 36).

It was also Vasari who, in 1550, first coined the nominal description 'Leonardo da Vinci' (in English, Leonard from Vinci). During his lifetime, until 1519, Leonardo had been generally known as Il Fiorentino (The Florentine),[18] but his artwork was subsequently credited to 'Leonardo'. Vasari used the 'da Vinci' addition so as to distinguish him in literature from Leonardo da Pisa, whose mathematics Leonardo da Vinci had so liberally employed in his work. In this respect, therefore, 'da Vinci' was never a name as it is incorrectly used in the title and throughout *The Da Vinci Code* novel. His name was Leonardo, and to refer to him simply as 'Da Vinci' is like calling Jesus 'From Nazareth'.

In his own lifetime, Leonardo da Pisa (1170–1240) had called himself Fibonacci (abbreviated from *Filus bonacci*, meaning 'Son of the innocent').[19] It is as Fibonacci that he is now remembered, with his famous numerical sequence defined as the Fibonacci Series. Extensively used as a means of Divine Proportion, the series is based on a principle of adding each last two numbers in the sequence to produce the next – 1, 1, 2, 3, 5, 8, 13, 21, and so on (*see* Appendix V).

In the final event, despite all Sacred Geometry and pictorial manipulation, the true enigma of Lady Lisa lies in her mystic smile. There have been many attempts to reconcile this in artistic terms, leading to numerous suggestions. It is in this context that Leonardo is credited with the extensive use (even the invention) of the blurred image technique called *sfumato*.[20] This comes from *'s + fumare'* (to smoke), and is a veiled form of paintwork which cuts down the information presented, and thereby stimulates the mechanics of projection.

A part of Lisa's hypnotic quality is caused by the open-faced effect of her having no eyelashes or eyebrows. This is then enhanced by her eyes being turned to look directly at the viewer, instead of in the direction of her pose as in *Lady with an Ermine*. In Leonardo's other portrait, *Ginevra de' Benci*, the sitter's eyes have no particular point of focus, while the cleverly composed School of Leonardo portrait, *La Belle Ferronnière*, has the subject looking over the viewer's shoulder. Lisa's gaze, however, is direct and specific, demanding attention from the outset.

Her smile is not unlike those of many Greek statues on which a fashionable 15th-century Italian sculptural tradition was based – Antonio Rossellino's marble *Madonna* at The

Hermitage, St Petersburg, is a good example.[21] The smile was well used by Leonardo's pupils of the Milanese school, and is unmistakable in Leonardo's pre-Lisa Burlington House cartoon of St Ann.

One of the great attributes of the *Mona Lisa* portrait is Leonardo's exceptional treatment of Lisa's skin. Recognizing that skin consists of semi-transparent layers, he built up her face accordingly, with a series of translucent colour glazes. In this way, he achieved his *sfumato* blurring of contours into soft transitions between light and shade. There is good evidence of this around the lateral canthus (outer edges) of Lisa's eyes, which gives rise to a semblance of animation – but it plays only a part in the ambiguous *Mona Lisa* smile. Those things already mentioned set the framework for the intriguing countenance, and it is the shaping of the mouth which does the rest. Used originally for the playful look of youthful Greek gods, the principle is to elongate and slightly turn up just one side of the mouth extremity, whilst leaving the other side shorter and comparatively straight. The application of more under-shadow to the upturned side of the top lip exaggerates the illusion, and the result is an expression that is both quizzical and knowing at the same time.

A while after Leonardo's death, King François I of France (1515–47) purchased *Mona Lisa* for 4,000 gold crowns for the palace at Fontainebleau. In the later times of Louis XIII (1610–43), England's Duke of Buckingham tried to buy the portrait, but the King would not part with it. The painting is catalogued as having been at the palaces of Fontainebleau, Versailles and Paris. It was lodged at The Louvre after the

French Revolution, but Napoleon Bonaparte subsequently claimed it to hang over his bed.[22] When he was exiled in 1815, Lisa went back to the Louvre. She has remained there for most of the time since, but has undergone some appalling ordeals.

At some early stage, about 7 cm were cut from each side of the panel, thereby ruining Leonardo's overall proportions for the image. There used to be side columns which made it apparent that Lisa was sitting on a terrace. On 21 August 1911, an eccentric Italian painter, Vincenzo Peruggia, stole the portrait to return Lisa to her native country. After a two-year police enquiry, during which any number of people were suspected, including the poet Guillaume Apollinaire (who had one day shouted that 'the Louvre should be burnt'), the painting was discovered in Italy.

Returned eventually to The Louvre, Lisa was vandalized and damaged with acid in 1956. Then, in the 1960s, she was slashed with a knife. At the better end of things, however, in 1963 she went to the United States, and in 1974 to Japan. The receptions were extraordinary and, in both places, Lisa was greeted and treated like a Hollywood movie star.

In the course of all this, a number of poor repairs were made; there are some badly discoloured retouchings, and an unsatisfactory varnish that quickly bloomed was applied without removing the previous darkened glaze. Leonardo would not be at all happy to see *La Joconde* as she exists so grubbily today. Desperately in need of cleaning and proper repair, suggestions to nurse her back to health and vitality have been rejected even though her poplar wood panel is now becoming very fragile. Instead, the *Mona Lisa* is now kept behind thick bulletproof glass – a fate that no such masterwork should endure. For all that, however, she remains the mistress of the most famous countenance in the world.

Virgin of the Rocks

Another Leonardo image discussed in *The Da Vinci Code* is his *Virgin of the Rocks* – specifically the version that hangs in The Louvre. Professor Langdon and the book's heroine, Sophie Neveu, encounter this painting soon after studying the *Madonna Lisa*. It is described as a representation of the 'Virgin Mary sitting with baby Jesus, John the Baptist, and the Angel Uriel on a perilous outcropping of rocks'.[23] This is followed with an explanation by Langdon that Leonardo had painted it for the nuns of the church of San Francesco in Milan, who gave the precise instructions for their requirement as being: 'The Virgin Mary, baby John the Baptist, Uriel and baby Jesus sheltering in a cave'.

Before progressing further, it has to be said that actually there were no nuns involved in this commission. Leonardo received his brief on 25 April 1483 from the Confraternity of the Immaculate Conception.[24] This was a small brotherhood of Franciscan monks, elected by canonical authority to promote the newly proclaimed Vatican doctrine of Mother Mary's Immaculate Conception.[25] They were based in the Milanese diocese of San Francesco, where they established a small chapel. Leonardo's *Madonna of the Rocks* painting for the 'church' of San Francesco was a different and subsequent work, to which we shall return.

Leonardo da Vinci

Leonardo (specified as Il Fiorentino, Leonardo di Ser Piero) was one of three artists commissioned by the Confraternity to paint a triptych altarpiece for their chapel. He was to paint the centre panel, while Ambrogio and Evangelista de Predis would paint the side panels – one 'an angel in green with a viola', and the other 'an angel in red with a lute'. In terms of the commission itself, the instructions were indeed very specific, but they were nothing whatever to do with a holy threesome and an angel in a cave. The frames had already been made by the brethren, and so even the shapes and sizes of the paintings were inherent in the contract and instruction, which runs to several pages of both Latin and Italian. It reads, in part:

318

Our Lady, flanked by two prophets, will occupy the centre of the painting portrayed to perfection. The cloak of Our Lady in the middle be of gold brocade and ultramarine blue. Also that the gown be of gold brocade and crimson lake, in oil … Also the seraphim done in *sgrafitto* work.[26] Also God the Father to have a cloak of gold brocade and ultramarine blue … the angels above them to be decorated and with their garments fashioned after the Greek style … Our Lady shall be decorated like the one in the middle, and the other figures are to be in the Greek style, decorated with various colours … all of which shall be done to perfection … in garments differentiated from each other … Our Lady with her son and the four angels shall be done in oil to perfection with the two prophets painted on flat surfaces in colours of fine quality … Also in the place where the infant is, let there be put gold worked to look like *spinnchristi*.[27]

So, that was the required line-up: Mary, God, four angels, and Jesus, with their individual clothing and decorations explicitly defined. What the priors got, however, was Mary, the naked boys Jesus and John, and one angel – all sat within a rocky grotto, and not a halo in sight (*see* plate 44). The backdrop was an inspired combination of features from the works of Botticelli's master, the Florentine artist Fra Filippo Lippi (1406–69) who, like Leonardo, received the patronage of the Medicis. The dark surrealism of Leonardo's uncanny grotto comes from Lippi's *Madonna in the Forest*,[28] while the rock formation itself was inspired by the rocks in Lippi's *Madonna and Child with Two Angels*.[29]

The problem faced by Leonardo was that he was given less than eight months to design and complete the work, which was to be unveiled on the Feast of the Immaculate Conception on 8 December 1483. With an arched top, the painting was to be 199 x 122 cms. (That is a little over 6½ ft tall, as against the 5ft height as given in *The Da Vinci Code*.) Within the same time frame, the Predis brothers were expected to paint the side-panels and to gild and paint the *ancona* (a carved wooden altar table). They must all have known from the outset that the project was an impossibility with such a deadline, and it is a wonder they agreed to it. By virtue of these things, however, certain short cuts were contrived. Leonardo decided to ignore completely the commission as received, and to make use of a composition he had already prepared for another purpose. (In *The Da Vinci Code*, this painting is described as being on canvas with a stretcher, behind which a key is hidden. This is a fictional departure, however. *The Virgin of the Rocks* is actually painted on a solid wooden panel.)

It has been suggested that perhaps Leonardo's *Virgin of the Rocks* image is a representation of a popular 14th-century tale about Mary in the desert, but Leonardo never said so, and the portrayal is significantly different to the tale in question. The story related Joseph and Mary's flight into Egypt with baby Jesus to avoid King Herod's slaying of the infants. It told of how they had met in the desert with Mary's cousin Elisabeth, her infant John, and the angel Uriel. In Leonardo's picture, however, there is no desert – just a rocky hollow with mountains beyond. Elisabeth is nowhere to be seen, and neither is Joseph. Moreover, Uriel (always depicted as man) is not present. Instead, there is a girl whose wings are barely discernible against the rocks. Leonardo's original study of the angel, entitled *Head of a girl*, can be seen in plate 23. This is catalogued by the College Léonard de Vinci of St Michel sur Orge for the Académie Versailles as *'Etude de la tête de l'ange pour La vierge aux rochers'* (Study of the head of the angel for the virgin with the rocks).

The finished portrayal was, therefore, a complete mystery to the Confraternity. Leonardo had agreed a price of 100 ducats,[30] but was given only 25 ducats.[31] Brother Agostino refused to pay an agreed 800 lire for general expenses incurred in decorating the altar, and further declined to acknowledge a sum of 300 ducats for the overall commission. (For the purposes of the conspiratorial plot of *The Da Vinci Code*, it is suggested that the painting was rejected because it contained 'explosive and disturbing details',[32] but nothing of the kind is mentioned by any of the parties concerned in the documents pertaining to this affair.)[33]

The painting, which eventually became known as *Vierge aux Rochers* (Virgin with the Rocks – not Madonna of the Rocks), was recorded at that time with the title *La Nostra Signora* (Our Lady). It remained with Leonardo for a while, but subsequently became the subject of a court case about the unpaid fees, and was held in legal custody. By 1490 (seven years after the commission), the Predis bothers were still working on their side panels, but during that year Evangelista de Predis died. Then, in 1506, the court case against the Confraternity was settled in Leonardo's favour, and the *Nostra Signora* painting was forfeited to him. Intent that the work should have historical prestige, even if produced for no payment, he liaised with Ludo-vicio Sforza for it to be lodged with King Louis XII of France for the royal collection at Fontainebleau.[34]

Meanwhile, in 1503, at the height of the court case, the officials of the Church of San Francesco il Grand (quite separate to the Confraternity) came onto the scene. The fate of *La Nostra Signora* was at that time uncertain, but Ambrogio de Predis still had the angelic wing pieces. The San Francesco church authorities agreed to make use of these if Leonardo would paint another centre-piece. This led to the second *Vierge aux Rochers* painting – the one which (to distinguish it from the first) is better known today as *Madonna of the Rocks*. It appears that Leonardo still had his original outline cartoon of the subject, but once again it was not suitable because of its incorrect size. The second painting still had to fit between the Predis brothers' two side-panels.

Madonna of the Rocks

It is with this second painting (completed in 1508) that my own close quarters introduction to Leonardo da Vinci occurred in 1961. Then at the National Gallery in London (where it remains today with the side-wings), *Madonna of the Rocks* (189.5 x 120 cm) had first come to England in 1785. After the church of San Francesco il Grand was closed in 1781, it went to the hospital archivists of Santa Caterina in Milan, who later sold it to the English painter Gavin Hamilton. Subsequently it went to the Marquess of Lansdowne Collection; then to Henry Howard, Earl of Suffolk, and entered the National Gallery in 1880 (*see* plate 45). The side-wings to complete the triptych were acquired in 1898.

In 1934, Sir Kenneth Clarke, director of the National Gallery invited the noted German picture restorer, Helmut Ruhemann of the Berlin State Galleries, to head up a new Scientific Department following his conservation course lectures at the Courtauld Institute. By 1947, a number of prized masterpieces had been cleaned and an exhibition was held which stunned museum curators from around the world. A year after that, in 1948, Leonardo's *Madonna of the Rocks* was restored, and it was one of the first paintings that I was obliged to study when I began my conservation of paintings training in the early 1960s. I, therefore, came to know the painting especially well.

The National Gallery's dossier of this restoration amounts to seven volumes of description, with 144 12 x 10 inch photographs. It was first examined and tested from February to March 1948, and then cleaned and consolidated from May 1948 to January 1949. There are still a couple of small half-inch squares left uncleaned by the frame edge to record the pre-restoration surface. Previously, said Ruhemann, 'it was impossible to know that the flowers were white, or that they had yellow centres'.[35] This is still very much the situation with the *Vierge aux Rochers* at The Louvre which was very timidly undercleaned, and remains cloudy and dull by comparison.[36]

Before restoration, the *Madonna of the Rocks* was discovered to have significant elements of overpainting by other artists. This had been a common practice in the days before cleaning techniques were perfected. When paintings became dull and their varnish darkened, artists would simply overpaint certain areas to brighten them up before applying another layer of varnish. The *Mona Lisa* still suffers from this, and Leonardo's *The Last Supper* was mostly overpainted before being brought back to base in a recent restoration. Even now, in the National Gallery's *Madonna of the Rocks*, Mary's right hand (with the exception of her thumb) is an overpainting, which was intentionally left for the sake of instructional interest.[37] A very narrow cleaned band can be seen at the tip of her third and fourth fingers to reveal Leonardo's much lighter original.[38]

Another overpainted item that was left in situ is the reed cross held by St John. Unlike The Louvre version, which was entirely by Leonardo, the second was a collaborative work by Leonardo and Ambrogio de Predis. The reed cross, however, was by neither of them. It was added in later times because viewers were not sure which of the boys was which. In both paintings, John is seemingly with Mary, and Jesus is with the angel – but this is not what people expected to see and they could not understand why the boy with Mary looked to be the elder of the two.

The reed cross was inserted, along with a small scroll relating to the other child, which states in Latin, 'Behold the Lamb of God'. But how did that artist know that the boy with Mary was supposed to be John? And why did he presume that the other was Jesus? Leonardo had never said so. These were presumptions based on the premise that Leonardo had depicted the meeting of Mary and Elisabeth in the desert. But there was no Elisabeth; there was no Joseph; there was no Uriel, and Leonardo had certainly not depicted the desert tale. His scene was entirely different, and the difference is enhanced in the second painting, which revealed after cleaning that the rocks sit at the edge of a blue glacial lake. Some have suggested that the larger boy must be John because John was a popular saint in Florence, but the paintings were not for Florence, they were for Milan.

In both paintings, the pyramidal grouping is the same, with the smaller child seemingly blessing the larger. In the second painting, halos that were omitted from the first work now appear – but again these are the work of a later hand, so they should be discounted along with the reed cross and the scroll. In each painting, Mary or (to refer back to Leonardo's description) *La Nostra Signora* is wearing blue and gold, although a lighter blue in the second work. In both paintings, her left hand is poised protectively above the smaller child. The girl, who points at the larger boy in the first painting, is not pointing in the second – and a major change has been made in her clothing. Originally, when painted by Leonardo, she wore the green and red colours of the Magdalene, but in the second painting (which has been thoroughly cleaned) the dress colours, painted by Ambrogio, are surprisingly fudged and indistinct.

Back now to *The Da Vinci Code*. Referring to the Paris painting, Professor Langdon explains that the smaller child is not Jesus, but John the Baptist, and that Mary is threatening him with a hand 'like an eagle's talons gripping an invisible head', which the angel is severing 'with a cutting gesture'. He then states that Leonardo had to produce a second painting (the London *Madonna*) – a 'watered-down version' for the Confraternity – because the original was too hostile towards Jesus.[39] The records confirm none of this, and these things are certainly not conveyed by the painting. Apart from that, the commissions were from two different organizations. So again, it has to be remembered that *The Da Vinci Code* is a fictional novel, not an art historian's text book.

Notre Dame

We have seen that Leonardo appears to have had the composition for his Lippi-inspired *La Nostra Signora* painting in place before receiving the Confraternity commission in 1483. At any time he might have decided to complete this work, whether alone or with another artist. If not, it is plausible that the School of Leonardo might have completed it after his death. Indeed, Leonardo's biographers have mentioned a third *Virgin of the Rocks* painting,[40] but they say it is difficult to know where it might exist because there are some very good copies. The common feature of copies however is that, by their very nature, they replicate originals. In this case, the known copies replicate either the Louvre painting or the

National Gallery painting. But the latter is not itself a copy of the former because they are markedly different in certain respects. A third legitimate *Virgin of the Rocks* would, therefore, be different in some ways from the other two – and there is indeed such a painting at the Musée des Beaux Arts de Caen (*see* plate 46).

In this version there is a very obvious difference although it depicts the same scene. In basic construction, it resembles Leonardo's original, the Louvre painting. The larger boy is without the reed cross; the halos are again non-existent, and the angelic girl has returned to her pointing pose. She is also, very apparently, back in her green and red Magdalene colours. But, most surprisingly, Mary is now wearing green and red too, along with gold, and her hair is much more red. In fact, she is now a perfect representation of the traditional Magdalene figure.

In the previous National Gallery version, a distinctive flower was added at the base of Mary's dress – a single Arum Lily (sometimes called the Calla Lily). This is the flower with a pure white spathe and a long, cone-shaped yellow spadix. These days it is correctly named *Zantedeschia* after the Italian botanist Giovanni Zantedeschi (1773–1846). Much is made in the painting of the exaggerated *Spadix*, which stems from the Greek for 'Palm Tree',[41] the Semitic equivalent of which was Tamar[42] (the name of Mary Magdalene's daughter). In parts of Australia, the Arum Lily is a 'declared plant' (a weed), and in America it appears in part to have a funerary connotation. In Mediterranean Europe, South Africa and Britain, however, it has long been a traditional flower of the bridal bouquet.

It is also perhaps relevant to note that Leonardo was influenced in his rocky setting by the Old Testament Song of Solomon 2:13–14 which (translated from the Greek text of his time), reads: 'The vines put forth the tender grape … Arise, come my consort, my fair one … Thou art my dove in the shelter of the rocks'.[43]

In these respects, the Arum Lily is pure Magdalene iconography. Leonardo never claimed that his central figure was Mother Mary; she was simply assumed to be. He called her *La Nostra Signora* – Our Lady (*Notre Dame*), which is precisely what Mary Magdalene had been called by the Templars and the Troubadours. Neither did Leonardo ever personally state that the boys were Jesus and John. This was presumed to be the case by others. Moreover, the angelic figure had been portrayed as a girl in each of the paintings from the outset.

Accepting that the girl's wings, which were no more than a gesture in the Louvre painting because the Confraternity wanted 'angels', we are left with an intriguing scenario that is significantly heightened in the second and third paintings. We have a maternal figure, who is rather more like Mary Magdalene than she is like her namesake. We have a girl, clearly older than the boys. We have two boys, one larger and older than the other, with the girl pointedly directing our attention towards the elder boy in two of the depictions. And we have a landscape which, although bordering on the unreal, looks far more European than any Holy Land or Egyptian setting.

In consideration of all this, a possibility emerges. Mary Magdalene had three children – a daughter and two sons, each some years apart. Given that, as we shall see later, Leonardo da Vinci was involved with an esoteric Rosicrucian fraternity of Magdalene adherents, it is just possible that this rocky scene was always a romanticized portrayal of the Magdalene family.

16

The Last Supper

A Tragic History

We should now look at *The Last Supper* – the Leonardo painting that sits at the very heart of *The Da Vinci Code*. Despite being created by one of the great masters of the Renaissance, this extensive wall-painting has suffered like no other at the hands of its owners. The *Mona Lisa* was attacked with a knife and with acid, as others have been, but *The Last Supper* had a doorway cut right through it! This is generally not shown in reproductions, which are much shallower than the original, but the door extends up into the bottom quarter of the painting, with its curved top frame well into the tablecloth just below Jesus' plate.

Ludovico Sforza (1452–1508), Duke of Milan, used to worship at the church nearest to the Castello Sforzeco – the church of Santa Maria delle Grazie. Disliking the austere old building, he had the main chapel and choir demolished, and proclaimed that the new chapel would have wonderful frescoes to brighten its walls. Plans were also made for the attached Dominican monastery, and in 1495 Leonardo da Vinci was commissioned to paint a mural of the *Last Supper* on an end wall of the new refectory. There was good daylight from the left-side windows, which lit up the right side of the picture area, and Leonardo customized his composition accordingly, so that the light and shadings in his work took account of this natural feature. Judas, for example, was customarily painted so that his full face was never presented 'lest the viewer gaze into the eyes of evil'. But, since Leonardo's painting was to remain in a fixed position, he contrived to have Judas in a strategic spot that was always in shadow, with just one eye showing.[1]

The plan was for the Prior's table to be set up at the other end of this dining-room (where there were other wall paintings) in such a way that it faced Jesus and the apostles, below whom was a doorway through which the monks would enter. Their long tables were established lengthwise on either side of the room, and it was to be as if it were a communal meal, with Jesus presiding at one end and the Prior at the other.

Unfortunately, however, Leonardo used this work to experiment with some risky techniques instead of going for a straightforward fresco and applying tempera colours into a wet plaster surface. In his enthusiasm, he used pigments mixed with egg, oil or varnish on a dry mortar wall – an unconventional media combination that was not absorbed. Hence the bonding of his mural was only superficial, and the work soon began to flake off as dampness from upwelling groundwater caused salts to leech out behind the paint layer. Pictorially, it might have been a great work, but in terms of engineered method it was (unusually for Leonardo) a disaster. As recently stated by art historian Leo

Steinberg, 'Leonardo da Vinci's *The Last Supper* is the greatest work of art there never really was'.[2]

As early as 1540, the painting was described as being 'half obliterated', and by 1560 it was recorded that the majority of colour had disappeared, leaving intermittent patches of paintwork and the under-drawing clearly visible. In 1568, the historian Paolo Lomazzo wrote, 'Today the painting is in a state of total ruin'. A decade later, after visiting the monastery, Giorgio Vasari lamented, 'It is nothing but a blurred stain'. During the following centuries, things got progressively worse: nineteen successive painters put their brushes to Leonardo's mural, obscuring it totally behind a thick mess of paint and adhesives.

By 1624, the painting was regarded pretty much as a non-event, and the friars had no qualms in cutting a much bigger door for better access. Not only did this chop off the feet of Jesus and the apostles to his either side, but the pounding of hammers loosened even more paint, which was just swept away with the workmen's debris.[3]

These days, a superficial wall-painting in the early stages of such decay could easily be saved. But in those times, if a painting was on a leeching wall, that is where it had to stay, even if the salts were killing it by breaking down the adhesion. In 1726, it was decided that some action should be taken and, unbeknown to the monks, a further death knell was sounded with that decision. They brought in a second-rate artist called Michelangelo Bellotti, who said he had a great secret that could bring the painting back to life. They allowed him to screen off his working area with sheets of canvas, subsequent to which he disappeared behind the cloth to work his magic. Meanwhile, as the weeks went by, no one dared to look at what was happening because they had been warned against it.

Eventually, the day came when Bellotti removed the screening to reveal a complete and brilliantly coloured image such as the monks would never have imagined. They were delighted, and Bellotti left with a very handsome fee. In fact, all he had done was to paint his own completely new picture over the top of Leonardo's work.

Before long, Bellotti's crude colours were fading from the bright window light, and the flaking was rampant again. Different hands made various attempts to stick the work together with distemper but, in 1770, another major repair was commissioned. In came Guiseppe Mazza with a poker! His technique was to scratch the whole surface with this to get rid of any loose paint or mortar. He then filled the resultant holes and scumbled in random colour tones so that it looked roughly altogether from a distance.

Then 1796 arrived, and with it the army of Napoleon Bonaparte. They figured that the large refectory would make a wonderful stable and a good place to store fodder. The French biographer and travel writer, Henri Stendhal, recorded that the dragoons amused themselves with a competitive game of throwing bricks at the apostles' heads.[4] As if all that were not enough, there was more to come!

In 1800, the big door under Leonardo's mural was walled up, as it remains today. But soon afterwards the room was flooded, leaving the refectory sodden from top to ground, and the painting loosened even more. A few years later, in 1807, the monastery of Santa Maria delle Grazie was converted into a military barracks, at which time the refectory was dried, aired, cleaned, and renovated. *The Last Supper* was not improved, but at least it was finally being treated with some care. Then, in 1821, along came Stefano Berazzi with a plan to remove the painting in its entirety from the wall. But he soon gave up after losing a chunk of the tablecloth in the early stages.

Extensive renovation work was undertaken by the fresco craftsman Luigi Cavenaghi in 1906–08 but, since it was a mural not a fresco, he repaired only the most unsightly areas, leaving the previous inpainting and overpainting in place. He was followed by the restorer Oreste Silvestri in 1924, who sealed the edges most at risk with black-tinged stucco. Then on, 15 August 1943, the refectory was hit by a wartime bomb and largely demolished. Fortunately a steel framework filled with sandbags had been erected before-hand to protect the painting, and the northern wall of *The Last Supper* remained intact. But left to contend with the el-ements, the sand became wet and for over a year the paint-ing suffered more harsh conditions.

When the refectory was eventually rebuilt, Mauro Pelliccioli gave the painting a clean, and treated it for severe mildew damage, anchoring it wherever he could with a shellac fixative. Working until 1954, he consolidated the sur-face and revived the colours, but he did not remove any of the old repainted layers. Reasonably presentable from that time, photographs were taken and *The Last Supper* joined the *Mona Lisa* as one of the most popular classical prints of the latter 20th century. What few people realized, however, was that scarcely anywhere in the picture were they looking at anything painted by Leonardo da Vinci. From the 'blurred stain' that Vasari had recorded in 1560, a good deal more of Leonardo's original had since been lost, and what remained beneath all the adhesives and overpainting was about one-fifth of the original work, which was still deteriorating.

No other major painting has undergone such mistreatment – from the artist's own unfortunate choice of method, to the ravages of the Second World War. But the time had come to spare no effort or expense in an endeavour to reclaim what little there was left. In 1978, the renowned restorer of masterworks, Dr Pinin Brambilla Barcilon, was commissioned to undertake the most daunting of projects. Her task was to permanently stabilize the painting, and to reverse the damage caused by centuries of dirt, pollution, water, vibration, and all the misguided renovation attempts of the past. In short, she was to get rid of every scrap of material that was not put on the wall by Leonardo. If this left just one-fifth of the painting, then so be it. At least it would be Leonardo's painting.

The Adoration Dispute

Another Leonardo work notorious for its spurious over-painting is the *Adoration of the Magi*. Once the pride of the Uffuzi, this panel is now confined to a storeroom awaiting remedial treatment. It was originally a commission from the monks of San Donato a Scopeto, and was begun by Leonardo in 1481. He took it with him, from Florence to Milan, in the following year, but never progressed it beyond

the drawing stage. Quite unlike the usual Nativity renditions, this one is a large, open-air crowd scene incorporating
various individual activities. Apart from the main preparatory work, there is a perspective study at the Uffizi in
Florence, along with figure studies at The Louvre, at the
Kunsthalle in Hamburg, and at the Metropolitan Museum
of Art in New York. Additionally, there is a composite
design for the painting at The Louvre, and related sketches
at the Musée des Beaux-Arts in Paris, and the Fitzwilliam
Museum in Cambridge.

An enormous amount of work went into planning this
painting, but contractual disputes and Leonardo's eventual
loss of interest caused him to abandon the project. Just
recently, however, a significant discovery was made when
the unfinished work was taken to the Uffizi's restoration
studio for conservation procedures. To everyone's horror, it
was revealed that Leonardo's original drawing had been
overpainted, possibly a century after his death, by an artist
of comparatively modest talent.[5]

It is suggested in *The Da Vinci Code*, with the usual literary licence, that the painting 'was hiding a dark secret
beneath its layers of paint'. The novel states that 'Italian art
diagnostician Maurizio Seracini had unveiled the unsettling
truth, which the *New York Times Magazine* carried prominently in a story titled "The Leonardo Cover-Up".' Embarrassed
officials at Florence's Uffizi Gallery immediately banished
the painting to a warehouse across the street.[6]

True, there was indeed such an article; it was published
on 21 April 2001, but the banishment had nothing whatever
to do with any 'dark secret' or 'unsettling truth'. It occurred

because of a major division of opinion in the art world. In practice, the offending item does not consist of 'layers of paint'. It is little more than a transparent layer of orange-brown laid over Leonardo's drawing, which is in no way obliterated and is entirely visible throughout. The secondary artist might have intended to finish the picture after laying this ground, but in the event he went no further.

There was, therefore, no new discovery of any kind in terms of what Leonardo had drawn. The unsettling discovery was simply that his work was embedded behind another artist's transparent overlay, which had previously been thought done by Leonardo. What happened was that the organization ArtWatch International, with wide support, suggested that since the panel was so fragile there should be no rush to clean off the spurious layer regardless. After more than half a millennium in that state, the work surely justified further analysis to determine the viability of such an exercise. The *New York Times* was advised by ArtWatch in January 2002 that its article was misleading, and documentary evidence was provided to show that certain pictorial aspects which the magazine had sensationally announced as being 'newly discovered' were known about and recorded as far back as 1951.[7]

The Da Vinci Code

At Santa Maria delle Grazie, restoration of *The Last Supper* began in 1979, and in 1982 the office equipment company Olivetti agreed to fund the whole cost of the project, which finally amounted to 7 billion lire. The work was completed after twenty years and, protected now by a sophisticated air filtration system, the mural went back on display on 28 May 1999. What remains is about twenty per cent of the original, but Dr Barcilon has used soft blended watercolours, based on Leonardo's preparatory drawings, to fill the missing areas. These do not attempt in any way to look like standard retouchings that are indistinguishable from the original. They have been laid in as simple, removable colour-washes so as to make Leonardo's personal work apparent, while at the same time giving the general impression of a complete image.[8]

In 1994, five years before Leonardo's restored painting of *The Last Supper* was unveiled, attention was drawn to the apostle on Jesus' right (on his left to the viewer). Traditionally accepted as being John Boanerges, the character looked somewhat female, and the possibility was suggested that it might not be John, but Mary Magdalene.[9] At the time this was an intriguing concept and, although unlikely for a number of reasons, the figure did indeed look a little feminine. The character was of slighter build than the other apostles, with longer hair than most, and there appeared to be a necklace of some sort, along with the semblance of a light bosom.

In opposition to this speculation, a valid scenario posed from the outset was that if it is possible in a substantially deteriorated, 500 year-old painting to discover that one of the characters is not a man, but a woman, then this would clearly have been most apparent when the painting was in its prime, and would have become part of the painting's history.

Since 1999, however, with the painting brought back to Leonardo's base, it can be seen that these things are not as they appeared inprerestoration prints. For detailed inspection, we now have the advantage of Dr Barcilon's superb high-resolution close-up photographs, from which we can see there is no necklace, and the bosom effect was caused by a crack in the wall. Today, we also know that the 1994 hypothesis was based on a character substantially over-painted by other artists, whereas we can now view the figure as originally painted by Leonardo.

The unfortunate aspect of this is not that an ostensibly intriguing concept has now been invalidated, it is that of all the important novelistic revelations in *The Da Vinci Code* the notion of Mary Magdalene's presence in Leonardo's *The Last Supper* is the foremost. In fact, it could be said that it constitutes the very essence of 'the Code'. Since the idea is based on a superseded, pre-restoration theory, however, it has to be said yet again that, although *The Da Vinci Code* has a factual base in *Desposynic* terms, its comments and conjectures relating to Leonardo's artwork are largely inaccurate.

When planning his lay-up for *The Last Supper*, Leonardo made numerous notes and some preparatory drawings. He split his apostles into four groups of three at the table, with Jesus central and the apostles six to his either side. Describing the individual activities when preparing for the work, he wrote notes pertaining to each, such as:

> One who was drinking has left his glass in
> its place and turned his head towards the
> speaker. Another wrings the fingers of his

> hands and turns with a frown to his
> companion … Another speaks into his
> neighbour's ear, and the listener turns his
> body round to him, and lends an ear
> while holding a knife in one hand.

The individual apostles are thus described and, in determining how to portray the younger characters (such as the brothers James and John) as distinct from the older, more swarthy men with beards, Leonardo wrote:

> Therefore make the hair on the head play
> in the wind around youthful faces, and
> gracefully adorn them with many
> cascades of curls.[10]

Although not described as being especially young in the New Testament, it became an artistic tradition to portray James, John and Philip as younger men than the others. John in particular is a mere youth in a good many Last Supper portrayals, and is even a young boy in a number of them. Leonardo's depiction is no different. His John is youthful and corresponds to his notebook description. Good examples of Leonardo's young men are his drawing of Philip (*see* plate 22) and his colour-wash portrayal of Jesus (plate 26). Another study for James is much the same. A close-up of the restored John, as in *The Last Supper*, is shown in plate 27.

Returning to *The Da Vinci Code*, we meet another of the book's characters, Grail enthusiast Sir Leigh Teabing,[11] who explains to Sophie Neveu that the figure of John is really

Mary Magdalene.[12] He draws her attention to the fact that Peter (sitting adjacent) is slicing his blade-like hand across Mary's neck.

In the world of fine art, there are various scenes associated with the Last Supper as detailed in the Gospels.[13] Leonardo elected to portray the moment in John 13:21, when Jesus announced that one of the apostles would betray him. The text follows: 'Then the disciples looked one on another, doubting of whom he spake', and it is explained that Peter consulted another (generally reckoned to be John), and 'beckoned to him, that he should ask who it should be of whom he spake' (John 13:24).

Leonardo's portrayal shows Peter asking this question. There is no sign of any menace between him and his neighbour, and the apostle concerned leans towards him, listening. There is no blade-like cutting by Peter's hand as it might have seemed in the 1994 pre-restoration prints; it is simply resting gently on the apostle's shoulder (*see* plate 24). This same scene was painted by various other artists – Hans Holbein for example (plate 25) where, once again, John is younger, more attractive, and longer-haired than the ageing Peter.

In the same sequence of *The Da Vinci Code*, a 'disembodied' hand 'wielding a dagger' is mentioned.[14] It appears in the painting between Andrew and Judas, and before the 1979–99 restoration it was indeed difficult to determine to whom it belonged. Its owner, Peter, is now rather more apparent, however, although it is not a dagger; it is a knife. Fortunately, there were a number of individual copies of the painting made by students of Leonardo within the first

Detail of *The Last Supper* (1495), copied in 1524 from Leonardo da Vinci by Marco d'Oggiono, showing Peter's left hand on John's shoulder and his right hand concealing a knife

30 years of its life, before the decay set in. They each make it plain that Peter has his right arm twisted awkwardly as he leans behind Judas to speak to John. It was Peter who subsequently drew his sword and cut off Malchus' ear when Jesus was arrested at Gethsemane (John 18:10), and Leonardo's painting paves the way for this event. The scenario is that Peter conceals the knife behind him whilst asking John the name of Jesus' betrayer, with the irony being that Judas is the very man who sits between them and turns to listen to their conversation.

These same early copies (made around 1520) also serve to identify Peter's left hand resting gently on John's shoulder, and they also depict Jesus' drinking vessel. *The Da Vinci Code* makes the point that Jesus should have had a Grail chalice for his wine, as suggested in the Bible.[15] But the fact is the Bible makes no such claim. The three Gospel entries concerning the communion at the table refer only to 'a cup',[16] and the Gospel of John (whose account Leonardo portrayed) does not mention the wine and blood communion in any event.

The unfortunate aspect of *The Da Vinci Code* premise in all respects, when related to this painting, is that it is an out-of-date premise. The text relates specifically to *The Last Supper* painting as it appeared after the 1954 cleaning by Mauro Pelliccioli, and states, in the words of Teabing: '… many of the pictures in art books were taken before 1954, when the details were still hidden beneath layers of grime and several restorative repaintings done by clumsy hands … Now at last the fresco has been cleaned down to Da Vinci's original layer of paint'.[17] The truth is, however, that Pelliccioli did not remove any of the previous overpaintings and, following his superficial cleaning, there was still none of Leonardo's original work to be seen. This has only become the case since the 1979–99 restoration, and *The Da Vinci Code* takes no account of this, while perpetuating an old Magdalene theory that has now been overturned by the revelatory results of the Barcilon project.

On a strictly historical note, it is worth stressing that the Last Supper of Jesus and the apostles was not actually a Passover meal as is customarily supposed. Neither did Jesus introduce the communion wine ritual. As evidenced by the *Community Rule* of the Dead Sea Scrolls, the Last Supper corresponds, in fact, to the Messianic Banquet (the Lord's Supper). That it occurred at the same time as the Passover celebration in Jerusalem was entirely coincidental for the Messianic Banquet had a quite different significance. The primary hosts of the banquet were the High Priest and the Messiah of Israel.[18] The people of the community were represented by twelve delegate apostles who were called the Council of the Community. The *Community Rule* (one of the oldest documents of Essene record, sometimes called the *Manual of Discipline*) lays down the correct order of precedence for the seating, and details the ritual to be observed at the meal. It concludes:

> And when they gather for the community
> table … and mix the wine for drinking, let
> no man stretch forth his hand on the first
> of the bread or the wine before the Priest,
> for it is he who will bless the first fruits of
> the bread and wine … And afterwards,
> the Messiah of Israel shall stretch out his
> hands upon the bread, and afterwards all
> the congregation of the community will
> give blessings, each according to his
> rank.[19]

From picture to picture, most artists stay fairly close to a character ideal once established in their minds – and there is no reason to suppose that Leonardo was any different. He is reckoned to have painted Mary Magdalene while in France, and tradition relates that the painting went to Burgos in Spain, but I have never managed to trace it. There are, however, two extant Magdalene drawings by Leonardo, and they share no similarity with the suggested Magdalene in *The Last Supper*. One of these is at the Galleria degli Uffizi in Florence, and the other – a sketch of Mary with her alabaster jar – is at the Courtauld Institute in London (plates 19 and 20).

Another suggestion in *The Da Vinci Code* is that a clue to the apostle's true Magdalene identity is found in an M-shape formed by the bodies of Jesus and the apostle in question (*see* plate 28). Again, this is not unique in Last Supper paintings. It is even more pronounced in *The Last Supper* by Philippe de Champaigne (1602–74), where the arm positions give rise to another smaller M within the larger – a double-M (MM). But this does not constitute a code for Mary Magdalene (plate 29). Again, in the Philippe de Champaigne painting, John looks fresh and youthful compared to the others. Indeed, this particular countenance (just as in Leonardo's work) exemplifies John Boanerges as he is customarily shown in Apostolic groupings (*see* examples in plates 30, 31, 32, 33). The so-called feminine aspect is integral to his popular image. It is not feminine; it is simply a Renaissance interpretation of youth. John is often seen leaning on Jesus or even, in some cases (where he is shown as a boy), sitting on Jesus' lap.

The main question that has always arisen in connection with the Magdalene theory from the time it was first put forward over ten years ago is that if she is at Leonardo's table, then who is missing? There are only twelve apostles in all. In 1810, the notes for Leonardo's line-up were discovered by the Milanese artist Guiseppe Bossi (Secretary of Brera Academy) at the church of Ponte Capriasca near Lake

The Last Supper from *The Grand Passion* by Albrecht Dürer
(1471–1528) – Jesus with young John on his lap and thirteen
apostles in all

Lugano. Reading from left to right (not all the apostles are shown in our plate 28 detail), the seating arrangement is: Bartholomew, James of Alphaeus, Andrew, Peter, Judas, John, Jesus, James Boanerges, Thomas, Philip, Matthew, Thaddaeus, and Simon Zelotes.[20] In two instances – Peter and Judas, and James and Thomas – one of each pair leans across the other so that their heads reverse the order of their seats. On that basis, the apostle whom Mary Magdalene supposedly replaces is indeed John. But Leonardo would certainly not have missed out anyone, especially not John; the Gospels are explicit in stating that Jesus and 'the twelve' were at the supper.[21]

If Leonardo had wanted to have thirteen apostles in his scene instead of twelve, he could easily have done so, even if it was not canonically correct. Albrecht Dürer put thirteen apostles in the *Last Supper* woodcut for his *Grand Passion* series. Moreover, if Leonardo had desired to introduce Mary Magdalene, he could have done this also, and it would not have been unique.[22] After all, Santa Maria delle Grazie was a Dominican monastery and, as we have seen, Mary Magdalene was the Mother Protectress and patron saint of the Order.[23] The choice was Leonardo's. He would certainly not have had to include her surreptitiously as *The Da Vinci Code* suggests. Dressing Mary in a suitably conventual style (as in the red egg portrayal that we looked at earlier),[24] the Dominican friar, Fra Angelico, had no qualms about including her in his *Last Supper* fresco at the Muséo di San Marco in Florence (*see* plate 50).

Sacred Allegory

A Mysterious Panel

In the world of pictorial fine art, some of the best known and most popular paintings are often those about which very little is known. The *Virgin of the Rocks* comes under this heading since, although its provenance is recorded, the subject matter remains mysterious and is constantly being debated.

One of the world's most recognizable paintings, and artistically one of the finest, is a work familiar even to those who have never studied art for its own sake. From the hand of the Flemish artist Jan van Eyck, and painted in 1434, it is a 32.5 x 23.5 inches (82 x 60 cm) oil painting on an oak panel, which resides at the National Gallery in London. Classified as a 'double portrait', it is set in a strangely adorned bedroom, and is known as *The Arnolfini Marriage* (*see* plate 47).

The main subjects of depiction are a slightly-built man in a fur-trimmed claret cape and a large black hat – along with a young woman dressed in a long green gown, trimmed with white, and a white headdress. The woman is pregnant, and the man supports the woman's open hand, creating a cup-shaped frame for a convex mirror beyond. But,

The 'double portrait' signature of Jan van Eyck, 1434 –
'Johannes de eyck fuit hic'

although these things are superficially obvious, the work is
full of questionable ambiguities.

The painting was acquired by the gallery in 1842 from
a Colonel Hay, who had bought it in Brussels, and it was
originally catalogued as *A Gentleman and his Lady*. But in a
subsequent National Gallery catalogue of 1862 it was stated
that the research of WH James Weale (a consultant on
Netherlandish art) had proved that 'the personages represented in this picture are Giovanni Arnolfini and Jeanne de
Chenamy, his wife'.[1] Henceforth, the painting was called
The Arnolfini Marriage – as it still is today. The fact is, however, that no one really has the slightest clue as to what this
uniquely esoteric picture is about.

The attributed 'Arnolfini' title has nothing to do with
anything that Jan van Eyck ever said or wrote about the
painting. He is not on record as having commented on the
work, and he certainly did not use the title by which it
has become known. So, who was Giovanni Arnolfini? It

transpires that he was an Italian banker and merchant who moved to Bruges in 1420. But why were he and his lady painted in such an unusual fashion?

Historically, this is the first ever painting of a contemporary couple in a contemporary interior. Nothing like it exists from before, and it represents a landmark in Renaissance artwork. When painted in 1434, Leonardo da Vinci had not yet been born, and pictorial art was, in the main, religiously based or concerned with royalty and high nobility. But here, in a work which remains in superb condition and technically far in advance of its time, is a domestic scene with two wealthy-looking but seemingly everyday people.

The trend set by this painting was remarkable and, alongside the Italian-led, religio-aristocratic art movement, Dutch and Flemish artists were soon claiming their own niche with homespun interiors, rural landscapes, village scenes and still-life representations. Along with some artists from Germany, they constituted the movement known as the Northern Renaissance which, although less fiery and alive than the Italian movement, produced work with the finest of intricate and exquisite detail.

Jan van Eyck was the appointed court painter to John, Duke of Bavaria, Prince of Liège, and was also retained by the Duke of Burgundy. His greatest work, the Ghent Altarpiece, appeared in 1432. This magnificent and highly esoteric two-tiered polyptych, incorporating biblical characters from Adam and Eve to Jesus, was painted by Jan for the Cathedral of St Bavo. He was aided in this by his artist wife Margaretta, especially with the large panel entitled *Adoration of the Lamb* – a mystical outdoor portrayal from

The Revelation. In fact, the whole of the altarpiece, with its twenty-four individual panels, is imbued with intellectual significance, and represents 'the new heaven and the new earth' from the book of The Revelation 21:1.

Art books relate that Jan had an older brother called Hubert, who assisted with some of the painting – but Hubert is a myth. His name appeared nowhere in 1432, and not for more than a century after installation of the altarpiece. But as Hubert's contrived legend became established, Margaretta was sidelined in his favour.

The switch of personalities began when the *Adoration of the Lamb* was commended in the Cathedral at a Chapter meeting of the Order of the Golden Fleece on 23 July 1559. This prestigious award led to a greater public awareness of the altarpiece but, for some reason, the Cathedral authorities had a problem in admitting that a woman might have been involved. By 1568, a brother had been invented for the artist and, since the originators were all long deceased, Hubert (actually a brother of Margaretta, and thought to have been a sculptor) was spuriously introduced as the brother of Jan. The final nail was driven home in 1616 when Hubert's name was mentioned in respect of a recently written stanza that was painted onto a shutter of the famous Ghent Altarpiece.[2] At much the same time, a bogus tomb was also ascribed to him in the Cathedral, although the tomb's inscription plate had apparently been lost!

A painting signed by Margaretta van Eyck, entitled *Madonna and Mary Magdalene with a Donor* was catalogued at the Bruges Exhibition in 1867, and another *Madonna* by her was catalogued in London's National Gallery subsequent to its opening in 1824. In later times, however, her name was removed from the catalogue and, without justification or explanation, the *Madonna* was reassigned to an unknown artist. These days, the fictitious Hubert lives on as Jan's supposed collaborator, and Margaretta has successfully been expunged from artistic record.

As WH James Weale had said, Giovanni Arnolfini did indeed marry Jeanne Cenami in Bruges but, in recent times, Weale's information has been proved erroneous as far as this particular painting is concerned. In fact, a good deal of debate has ensued, to the extent that, in 1997, an investigation was made as a part of Britain's Open University art course. Televised on BBC2, the conclusion of the panel was: 'Everything this painting seems to be, it isn't'.

The 15th-century Burgundian State archive dates the marriage of the Arnolfinis as being in 1447 – thirteen years after the picture was dated – by which time Jan van Eyck had been dead for six years. And yet Jan's signature on the panel is not only beyond question, it is unique since it forms an integral part of the painting itself. Written in Latin on the back wall above the convex mirror (with the added date of 1434), is: *Johannes de eyck fuit hic* – 'Jan van Eyck was here'.

The Open University investigators were Craig Harbison, professor of art history at the University of Massachusetts, Evelyn Welch of the School of European Studies at the University of Sussex, Martin Kemp, professor of art history at Oxford University, and Jacques Piviot, professor of history at the Sorbonne in Paris. They discussed the fact that, although there is not an error to be seen in this near-photographic masterpiece, there are numerous anomalies and it is loaded with esoteric symbolism. In wrapping-up the investigation, which came to no real conclusion, the point was made that 'This painting holds a secret'.

One thing which has become apparent since the Arnolfini marriage entry was found is that, despite the National Gallery decision to change the painting's title in 1862, this is definitely not a picture of Giovanni and Jeanne Arnolfini. Indeed, it is now known that Weale made this assumption from an archival note dated 1516 when the panel was owned by Margaret of Austria, Regent of the Netherlands. Written in her inventory in relation to the painting were the words *'Hernoul le fin'* (seemingly, '[?] the end'). Various unsuccessful attempts have been made to ascertain the meaning of *Hernoul*, but what Weale decided for his 'proof' in 1862 was that *Hernoul le fin* was phonetically similar to Arnolfini![3]

So, if they are not the Arnolfinis, who then are these people? It has been suggested that maybe it is actually a picture of Jan and Margaretta van Eyck, but the woman looks nothing like the portrait that Jan painted of his wife shortly after the bedroom scene. The only similarity is the headdress, which was a common type of the period. Also, if the double portrait is indeed a betrothal portrayal as supposed, then it is unlikely to be Jan and Margaretta. They were married nine years earlier in 1425.

Alongside this work, and acquired by the Berlin Museum in 1886, was an unsigned, half-length portrait of a similar-looking man. Originally, it had been at Alton Towers in England, but was sold abroad for the Earl of Shrewsbury by Christies auctioneers. The man, wearing a loose turban-like red headwrap, was not named before arriving in Berlin. But once there (in view of the new title given to the National Gallery couple), the portrait has since been catalogued as *Giovanni Arnolfini* and credited to Jan van Eyck.

It is generally accepted, by virtue of the *Ghent Altarpiece*, that Jan van Eyck was a master (if not the originator) of sophisticated pictorial allegory. The bedroom painting represents an artistic turning-point of the Renaissance when the first complete oil paintings were introduced, as against egg tempera or oil and tempera methods. For his pioneering role in this, Jan emerges as one of the most significant artists of the era.

As in the Ghent panels, symbolism and iconography abound in the double portrait and, as Professor Harbison states in the Open University film, 'There are so many things that seem to be woven into this painting that it seems almost like the challenge of a lifetime to really come to terms with it'.

Both the man and the woman are formally dressed, and the man is plainly wearing outdoor clothes – yet they are in a bedroom environment. Two pairs of patten-style house shoes lie separately at the back and front of the room, presumably to denote their double occupancy. Although it is broad daylight, there is a single candle burning in the chandelier. There are three oranges on the table and one on the window sill. Oranges are generally emblematic of innocence, although the woman is pregnant. In the foreground is a small Bolognese dog and, in the background, a string of amber beads with green tassels hung from a nail in the wall. Within a generally quiet room, the bed's coverlet and hanging drapes are bright crimson – as are the cover and cushion of a nearby bench. Through the open window is a tree bearing ripe red fruit. The uprights of the shining brass chandelier are designed as *fleur-de-lis*, crosses and crowns, and there is a high-backed chair by the bed, with a carved top depicting a woman triumphing over a dragon. From this hangs a utility dusting brush. To complete the scene, the man's hand is raised in a deictic gesture as a mark of his principal status.[4]

Throughout the 20th century, various researches have admitted that, for all they can see in the picture, there is something they are missing – an underlying message or meaning of some sort: 'Although there has been written more about this painting than about most famous masterpieces, we are left with a feeling that there is still something hidden'. There is, however, a possibility in this regard.

As Dutch and Flemish religious art grew to prominence in the Renaissance era, it took on a distinctive look of its own, quite different to the Italian lead which it followed. Whether through artistic design or simple ignorance of the past, there was a tendency to set biblical scenes in a contemporary environment. A few examples include *The Numbering at Bethlehem* by Pieter Bruegel the Elder – a scene of Joseph, Mary and the pre-Nativity census set amid red brick houses and churches with distinctive Dutch roofing. Then there is *St Luke Drawing the Madonna* by Rogier van der Weiden – a Flemish interior with 15th-century costumes. *The Marriage of Mary* by the Master of Flémalle (again with 15th-century costumes) is set within ornate Gothic architecture. *The Holy Family* Nativity by Joos van Cleve has a Joseph in a Dutch farmer's hat and a pair of spectacles, while other Gospel scenes include such subjects as windmills and knights in shining Middle Ages helms and plate armour.

Netherlandish artists of the period often depicted biblical scenes in their own familiar surroundings – but most of them are recognizable because of the subject matter. A man on a cross with three women beneath is understandably Jesus, even if there is an armoured knight and a windmill there too. But what about unfamiliar scenes such as Rogier van der Weiden's *Mary Magdalene Reading* (plate 38)? The furniture, the book, and the costume are all of the era when painted. Without the inclusion of the ointment jar, there would be absolutely no way of telling who was portrayed here. Another clue, of course, might be the woman's green dress and white headdress – which is precisely what the woman in Jan van Eyck's double portrait is wearing in a similarly unfamiliar scene. Perhaps we should look again to see what we might have been missing.

The Bedroom Heresy

The bedroom couple are surrounded by symbols of fertility and royalty, especially French royalty with the *fleur-de-lis* in the chandelier. But the chandelier's crowns are turned upside-down to denote a termination of reign. The red fruit is ripe on the tree and the woman is pregnant. With a candle burning, even though daytime, it is clearly a sacred occasion and, in pictorial symbolism, dogs are a sign of fidelity. In contrast to the apparent solemnity of the scene, there is the great heresy of the red bed, while the woman carved on the chair is seen as triumphant against a dragon – reminiscent of The Revelation scene concerning the *Desposynic* persecution.

Let us now delve into the backdrop, since the central focus of this work is not so much the couple, but the mirror on the wall behind them, framed within the V of their arms. (Unfortunately, our small reproduction does not help with a close inspection, but large prints of this work are easy to obtain.)

The paintwork on this mirror is extraordinarily detailed. Being convex, it shows the whole scene of the picture in reverse, including a doorway in front of the couple where two other people are entering the room. More intriguing, however, is the mirror's frame, for it is here that we find an incongruous Gospel connection. Within what appears to be a single scene of an interior, we now discover there are ten more complete miniature paintings set in medallions around the mirror. They depict the story of Christ's Passion and, travelling clockwise from the bottom left they are: 1) The Gethsemane betrayal, 2) Jesus before Caiaphas, 3) His scourging by the Roman soldiers, 4) Carrying the cross to Calvary, 5) The Crucifixion, 6) The Deposition, 7) The Entombment and Lamentation, 8) Descent into limbo, 9) The Resurrection, and 10) The sepulchre garden. The latter, sitting squarely at bottom centre, is the scene outside the tomb, in readiness for the *Noli me tangere* encounter between Jesus and Mary Magdalene.

This Jesus and Magdalene encounter is a customary Passion image that is not shown in these medallions. In the Baroque tradition, it was commonplace for Jesus to be depicted with a wide-brimmed hat for this scene – as in the Renaissance paintings of Lavinia Fontana, Giovanni Caracciolo, Rembrandt van Rijn, Bartholomeus Spranger, and the woodcut of Albrecht Dürer, among others. Many art books describe the double-portrait couple as holding hands, but in fact they are not. The woman's hand is seen in full, palm uppermost and empty. The man is simply supporting her hand and presenting it to the onlooker. Open hands depicted in this manner are the sign of openness – no threat; no secrets. The deictic gesture of the man's other hand is an artistic standard denoting a 'staying' influence on the situation – a control without words.

At this stage, it is worth looking at some other paintings by Jan van Eyck – the master of pictorial allegory and iconography, as demonstrated by the *Ghent Altarpiece*. There are only two images to consider here: *The Crucifixion* (at the Metropolitan Museum of Art, New York) and *The Three Marys at the Tomb of Jesus* (at the Museum Boijmans van Beuningen, Rotterdam). Mary Magdalene features prominently in each of these, and in both portrayals she is again wearing the green gown with the same white trim. All things considered, there is reason enough to postulate that Jan van Eyck's double portrait which 'holds a secret' that has never been discovered, might well be a cleverly conceived Magdalene allegory.

The *fleur-de-lis* and upturned crowns of the overthrown dynasty (as featured in the chandelier with its single candle of remembrance) both relate to the Merovingian Kings of the Franks. In this respect, *Hernoul* becomes identifiable as Hernoul of the Franks (580–640). He is featured in a medieval French manuscript in the Queen's College library at Oxford University.[5]

Variations of Hernoul's name are Hernault, Arnault, Arnaud, Arnou, Arnould, Arnoud, Arnaux, Arnold and

Arnulf. He was a senior court officer of the kings Theodebert II of Austrasia and Clotaire II of Neustria (*see* Map of Medieval France, page 112), and became Bishop of Metz in 626. Prior to that, he was tutor to Clotaire's son Prince Dagobert, but was not a supporter of his eventual kingship. In fact, Hernoul led what was to become the ultimate downfall (*le fin*) of the Merovingians, establishing a conspiratorial chain of events which led to the *Donation of Constantine* and the papal appointment of his descendant, King Pepin, the father of Charlemagne.[6] (Details of the Merovingian deposition are given in Appendix VI, page 462.)

Margaret of Austria's inventory entry, '*Hernoul le fin*', was not therefore a title for the painting, nor anything to do with the characters portrayed. It was her note of recognition of the painting's allegorical meaning. It marked the end of the Fisher Kings' reign in Gaul, and the termination of the Magdalene legacy of the *Desposynic* kingdoms.

In strictly pictorial terms, there is a remarkable similarity between the bedroom painting and a stained-glass window at Kilmore Church, Dervaig, on the Scottish Isle of Mull. The window portrays Jesus and Mary Magdalene holding hands

The Magdalene window legend at Kilmore church

in an intimate pose (*see* plate 48). The pregnant woman in the painting wears her belt above her waist, whereas the window's Mary Magdalene allows her sash to fall well below her abdomen, indicative of the same condition. The legend beneath this window is taken directly from Luke 10:42, when Jesus speaks to Martha about Mary when visiting Martha's house: 'Mary hath chosen that good part, which shall not be taken away from her'.

At this stage, the question remains: Did Jan van Eyck have a personal link with the Magdalene legacy? Was he perhaps associated with a Magdalene movement of some kind? The answer, as we shall see in the next chapter, is 'yes, he certainly did'.

Rod of Jesse

Some paintings are allegorical in a very obvious way since they have titles which convey the fact. *The Sacred Allegory* by the Flemish Northern Renaissance painter Jan Provost (sometimes called the *Christian Allegoria*) is a good example in a Magdalene context.[7] This 15th-century esoteric painting shows Jesus with a sword, together with Mary Magdalene, who wears a golden crown, while holding an open casket of black grapes on which is perched the dove of the Holy Spirit. Central to the portrayal is the blue Universal Globe, with the earth, sun and moon in separated positions on the surface. The Italian artist Ventura Salimbeni used a similar globe in his *Exaltation of the Eucharist* at the church of San Pietro at Montalcino, as did Johann Heinrich Schonfeld in his

L'Adoration de la Sainte Trinité (1640) and the Spanish painter, Juan Carreño de Miranda, in *La Messe de fondation de l'ordre des Trinitaires* (1666), both now at The Louvre. Symbolism of this sort is an example of how the enlightened artists of the Renaissance (Rebirth) actually worked in practice because, although many such images were for the adornment of churches, they were contrary to the orthodox dogma that the earth was at the centre of the universe.

The small casket that Provost introduced for Mary Magdalene was a true break from convention. Although the Grail significance of its grapes is readily apparent, her alabaster box (as mentioned in the Gospels) was generally substituted by a jar. Either way, as we have seen, the correct rendition in translation should have been an *alabastron*, but, in any event, the Church was adamant in its dislike of saintly women with boxes. The connotation was too close to the legend of Pandora.

In the ancient Greek tradition (or at least the tradition as it was told), Pandora had been the first woman on earth, and she had come with a box containing all the evils of the world. But when she opened the lid to look inside, the evils all escaped to beset mankind – all except Hope which remained trapped in the box. Actually, this Christianized version of the story is quite illogical because Hope is hardly an evil, and would therefore not have been in the box. The original story was different: Sent into the world by Jupiter, Pandora arrived not with a box of evils, but with a jar that was filled with all the great blessings, which she released into the world.

The problem with this was that it cut right across the clerical story of Eve who, as a woman, was said to have introduced sin in the Garden of Eden. Not only did Pandora take Eve's place as the first woman (which was heresy enough) but, contrary to ecclesiastical requirement, she was a bringer of good things, which was impossible for a woman! And so her story was corrupted and her jar of blessings became a box of evils, with religious artists obliged not to portray saintly women with boxes.

The French artist Jean Cousin broke with tradition to some degree in 1550 by painting the Greek *Eva Prima Pandora* (now in The Louvre), but even then she did not have a box. Reverting to the original story, Cousin gave her a jar – in fact two jars – along with a skull. Even though he painted her name into the picture, this Pandora escaped any direct criticism because she looked for all the world like another Magdalene in her grotto, and became reputed as the first great French reclining nude. It was not really until the 1800s that Pandora came to any artistic prominence. This evolved from an English-led movement in the romantic Victorian age, with some contributions from France and America.

There is another painting with the title *Sacred Allegory*, which ranks along with the *Arnolfini Marriage* as one of the great puzzles of the art world. Unlike Jan van Eyck's double portrait, however, this one is blatantly obvious in its portrayal. The reason why it continues to baffle some is that to understand it one has to acknowledge Mary Magdalene's position in the scheme of things. It was painted on a panel in about 1500 by the Venetian artist Giovanni Bellini, a contemporary of Leonardo.

In the world of Christian art, there is really only one true allegory. As with Jan Provost's interpretation, it is the relationship between Jesus and Mary Magdalene. Other Christian representations can be allegorically portrayed, and the pictures filled with symbolic iconography, but the base subject matter is always recognizable. Magdalene-related allegory, however, appears always like a parable: it is immediately apparent for those with eyes to see, but if one is not familiar with the subject, then the portrayals will remain forever baffling.

The story of the Vine of the royal bloodline, which became a part of Grail tradition, begins in the Old Testament book of Isaiah 11:1 – 'And there shall come forth a rod out of the stem of Jesse, and a branch shall grow out of his roots'. Jesse, the father of King David of Israel, was the grandson of Boaz and his wife, Ruth the Moabite. From this branch of the root of Jesse, the Royal House of Judah emerged, descending like a vine through the generations and progressing, in biblical terms, to Jesus' statement: 'I am the true vine' (John 15:1).

Bellini's *Sacred Allegory* (*see* plate 49) conveys this descendant theme within a single painting, while also expressing its continuation via Mary Magdalene. Jesse is seen wearing red with a sword (symbolic of royalty, as in the Provost painting), and the root of the line is shown, as described in Isaiah, by a new branch growing from his arm ('out of the stem of Jesse'). To the left of the picture, Ruth (the widow lady of tradition) looks on, while Jesus' mother Mary sits, raised upon a stone-carved throne. Our plate reproduction is just a detail of the whole painting in which, to the left behind Mary, Jesus stands gazing out across a lake, while to the right, beyond Jesse, Mary's husband Joseph leans on the balustrade, watching some young children at play. Central to the action however – being honoured by Mary and Jesse – sits a modest and contemplative Mary Magdalene wearing her crown of Messianic bridal office.

The Repentant Courtesan

Galleries and art museums are rich these days with portrayals of Mary Magdalene. She is one of the most painted of popular classical figures, but the artists concerned did not paint their pictures for galleries and museums. Clearly, there were some speculative projects, but a majority of the works were specifically commissioned. The key patrons and sponsors of the Renaissance era were the wealthy nobility and the royal houses, along with the Church from which most of the Italian commissions emanated. But there is something of a paradox here. Why would the Church authorities request and pay for paintings and sculptures of a woman whose legacy they sought to undermine at every turn? The bishops said that Mary was a sinner and a prostitute, so why would they want her adorning their sanctified walls?

In recent times, Professor Christopher Witcombe of the Department of Art History at Sweet Briar College, Virginia, followed the course of a particular 16th-century commission, and subsequently published a fascinating report on how the Church and Mary Magdalene were connected in the world of art. His article, 'The Chapel of the Courtesan', appeared in *The Art Bulletin* in June 2002,[8] and concerned the studio of the High Renaissance artist Raphael.

A student of Leonardo and Michelangelo, Raphael produced an extraordinary volume of work in his short lifetime – mainly during his last ten years from 1510. He had been called to Rome late in 1508 by Pope Julius II at the suggestion of the architect Donato Bramante, and became revered there as 'the prince of painters'. Raphael died, however, on his 37th birthday in 1520, at which time his studio was jointly inherited by his two best pupils, Giulio Romano and Gianfrancesco Penni. Soon afterwards, they received a commission to decorate a chapel dedicated to Mary Magdalene in the Church of Trinita dei Monti in Rome. Their brief was to paint an oil altarpiece of the *Noli me tangere* scene, and four Magdalene-related wall frescoes. Writing about this project in 1568, Giorgio Vasari confirmed that the artists were commissioned in this regard by 'a prostitute' (*una meretrice*) and that, at his time of writing, the chapel contained the carved marble likeness of 'a very famous courtesan of Rome' (*una famosissima cortigiana di Roma*).

In 1537, the artist Perino del Vaga was called in to paint more Magdalene images at the chapel, and the whole collection survived until the 19th century, when the chapel was redecorated. It seems inconceivable today that not so long ago artworks from the studio of Raphael would have been treated simply as decoration – discarded as one might change the furnishings of a living room. Fortunately, though, a couple of the works have survived. The *Noli me tangere* altarpiece is now in the Museo del Prado, Madrid, and one of the frescoes depicting Mary borne up by angels, is at the National Gallery in London. Before the chapel was redecorated, Pierre-Jean Mariette (1694–1774), publisher of the encyclopaedia *L'architecture a la mode*, wrote that the other frescoes in the chapel were of Mary anointing Jesus' feet in the house of Simon, along with Martha, Mary and Jesus, and a scene of Mary in the wilderness.

It seems that, during that period, professional courtesans were very much part of Roman high society, and were actively encouraged by the Church so long as they were repentant at the same time! On that basis, if a rich prostitute was paying the bill at Trinita dei Monti, the bishops were content to accept that scenes from the life of Mary Magdalene were suitable decorations for the chapel.

The word *cortigiana* (courtesan) evolved within 15th-century court society and, although defining a high-priced prostitute, was the female equivalent of *cortigiano* – a male courtier. Such women, it seems, could become extremely wealthy and, by virtue of this, were enabled to sponsor a good deal of Magdalene artwork in the churches. The reason for the great volume of non-biblical *Penitent Magdalene* depictions now becomes apparent. They provided the Church and the *cortigiana* women with a formal absolution. Popes, bishops or whoever, were automatically forgiven for retaining their mistresses so long as they repented.

In that era, the Popes were rather more vigorous men than the aged characters of latter years. Despite all the celibacy regulations, there were even advantages for priests with children because they had an apparent reason to display an open penance. It was even recorded as far back as the 11th century that, under such circumstances, the Papal Court would grant hereditary priesthood to their offspring.[9]

And the proof of repentance was yet another painting of the penitent Mary Magdalene!

The mistresses of Pope Alexander VI (Rodrigo Borgia) were openly acknowledged, especially the renowned Vannozza dei Cattanei, who gave him four children including the notorious Lucrezia Borgia.[10] Vannozza was followed as the Pope's concubine by Giulia Farnese.

Subsequently, Pope Julius II (Giuliano della Rovere) maintained a mistress also named Lucrezia, who bore him three daughters, along with another professional courtesan named Masina. These women lived in the greatest of papal luxury, with houses, vineyards and all manner of wealth lavished on them. Notwithstanding the celibacy rule that applied within the Church, a sexually extravagant lifestyle prevailed, and this was fully absolved by commissioning paintings of the penitent Magdalene.

The papal courtesans of Rome enjoyed an extraordinary social position, and it is clear that many of them used their positions to exercise their own intellectual abilities and display attributes that would otherwise be denied because of their status as women. Gaspara Stampa (1523–54), Veronica Franco (1546–91) and Tullia d'Aragona (1510–56), for example, each made significant contributions to the poetry of the period.

To be such a protagonist in an elite environment, the courtesan had to emulate the aristocratic society that supported her. She rendered herself desirable by replicating courtly behaviour, publicly acting the lady and transforming her home into a miniature Urbino where she discussed art, philosophy and music. She was established within the women of noble society, but was still a whore as far as those women were concerned. A door that was open to her, however – but unavailable to those women whose activities were constrained – was that she could become a goddess for posterity by having her face and body preserved on canvas. Identification with nymphs and divinities polished the courtesan's veneer of socioeconomic success, and society artists such as Raphael thereby acquired the very best of models for their religious and mythological paintings. A large number of Mary Magdalene portraits from the Italian Renaissance are actually studio representations of the beautiful pseudo-aristocratic courtesans of the papal palace.

Vasari did not name the particular courtesan who commissioned the Magdalene chapel paintings in the Church of Trinita dei Monti. It is likely, however, that she was Lucrezia Scanatoria, whose name appears in the surviving records of the convent and church. She died sometime before 14 February 1522, at which time her executors purchased a house in the Ponte district of Rome that subsequently became known as *La Maddalena*. Another *cortigiana* named Fiammetta – the courtesan of Cesare Borgia – had previously endowed a chapel dedicated to Mary Magdalene in the Church of St Agostino, and gave instructions that she be buried there.

Prostitution within the papal court was not a Renaissance novelty. It was a legacy of the Imperial Roman culture, and the early Church Fathers were necessarily ambivalent over the legal status of courtesans in the Roman civil laws of Emperor Theodosius in the 5th century and Justinian in the 6th, as codified in the *Corpus Juris Civilis*. It was during this era that Mary Magdalene was first defined in her non-biblical role as a prostitute, and it can now be seen that this was a strategic manoeuvre by the clergy to justify their own activities. Mary was a scapegoat and the anomaly of her ambiguous legacy is revealed. She was vilified by the Church on the one hand but, in inventing her repentance for sins she did not even commit, the bishops contrived their own perpetual source of vindication.

A Secret Priory

Conspiracy of Sion

There are references in *The Da Vinci Code* to a secret society of Magdalene adherents called the Priory of Sion. It is said in the novel to be in existence today, and to have been operative from the time of the Crusades. Again, it has to be remembered that *The Da Vinci Code* is a fictional story which happens to embody some elements of fact. But this is not one of them – at least not in the way it is presented.

There has only ever been one organization called the Priory of Sion (*Prieuré de Sion*). It was founded and registered as a society in France on 7 May 1956, and it folded in 1984 when its co-founder and secretary, Pierre Plantard, resigned. The society's president, André Bonhomme, had already confirmed his departure in writing eleven years earlier.[1]

Apart from Plantard, Bonhomme and a handful of colleagues, there were no outside members, and the Prieuré's purpose had nothing whatever to do with Mary Magdalene. It was nominally conceived as a Catholic pseudo-Order but, as detailed in the registration statutes, and confirmed in the society's news bulletin *Circuit*, it was no more than a club

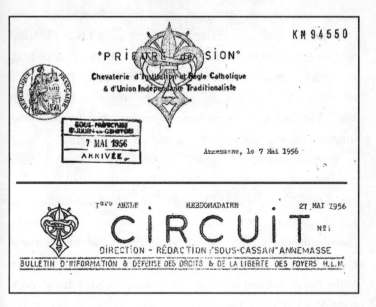

Priory of Sion headers from May 1956 – registration document
and the first issue of *Circuit*

established to discuss such matters as poor rental accommo-
dation and low-cost housing.[2] According to Bonhomme, it
was named after the hill of Mont Sion outside the town of St-
Julien-en-Genevoise, where the Prieuré was registered.[3]

It is apparent, however, that the *modus operandi* soon
changed, and Bonhomme's formal resignation on 7 August
1973 made it clear that he and two other co-founders (Jean
Deleaval and Armand Defago) had actually parted company with Plantard back in 1957. Bonhomme's letter,
addressed to the Sub-Prefecture of St-Julien-en-Genevoise,
had been prompted by an article in *Le Charivari*, which
brought to light dubious past activities of Pierre Plantard.[4]

These were subsequently reported in a Montpellier press issue of the *Midi Libre*.[5] The articles explained that Plantard was an adherent of the Vichy regime in wartime France and, in furtherance of anti-Semitic activities, had established a spurious Order of knighthood called the *Alpha Galates* in 1942. He had been imprisoned for this, and in 1953 was imprisoned yet again for fraud and embezzlement.[6]

It transpired that Plantard had used the Prieuré de Sion as a vehicle to publish a fabricated genealogy of his family, wrongfully attaching it to the House of St Clair and claiming a descent from the Merovingian royalty of early medieval times. This, along with details of his extreme right-wing pursuits was made known by the researcher Jean-Luc Chaumeil in 1984,[7] as a result of which the remnant of the Prieuré fell apart.

In the meantime, certain supposed historical parchments held by the Prieuré were announced as being forgeries by Plantard's associate Philippe de Chérisey. Not only that, but Chérisey actually admitted to having forged the parchments himself. This announcement was, in essence, an act of retribution because Chérisey had not been receiving his cut of the royalties due from a book which had published details of these ostensibly coded documents. In the light of this, no one was wholly sure of the truth: Had Chérisey fabricated the parchments, or was he just claiming this to spite the author?

The book in question was entitled *L'Or de Rennes*, produced in 1967 by Gérard de Sède. It concerned a mysterious discovery in the 1890s by Bérenger Saunière, a priest in the little village of Rennes-le-Château in Languedoc. As a result of his discovery, Saunière became extremely wealthy, although no one seemed to understand why or how. From 1896, he used the equivalent of millions of pounds to restore his church, as well as funding extensive public works projects to improve his parish for the community.

This local mystery was good ammunition for Pierre Plantard, who claimed to be in possession of Saunière's secret and, in 1989, he endeavoured to revive the Prieuré de Sion with yet another set of concocted documents. At that stage, he also confirmed that the originally produced Rennes-le-Château parchments were indeed forgeries. Real ones did exist, he added, although they were inaccessible. Once again, no one knew whether to believe him or not because, by that time, he was announcing publicly that he was the King of France!

In the course of investigating an associated financial scandal, Judge Thierry Jean-Pierre had Plantard's house searched, confiscating papers and subsequently issuing an official instruction that Prieuré-related activities must be terminated immediately. From that day, in 1993, the society moved into total obscurity, but the mystery of Bérenger Saunière remains. It was from this that the presumed Magdalene link of the Prieuré came to the fore because Saunière had been the priest at the Rennes-le-Château church of St Mary Magdalene, which was originally dedicated in 1059.

In 1996, a BBC2 Timewatch television documentary, *The History of a Mystery*, used film footage of Philippe de Chérisey, along with material evidence from Jean-Luc Chaumeil and various other sources, to discredit Pierre

Plantard and expose the whole Prieuré de Sion charade. Plantard kept a very low profile after that, moving in and out of hiding, and ultimately died on 3 February 2000 in Paris.

The Saunière Mystery

In recent times, there has been a plethora of books concerning the mystery of Saunière's unearthings, and any number of possibilities have been put forward. Some suggest that whatever Saunière discovered still lies buried within the church confines, as a result of which a competitive treasure-hunt prevails.[8] As might be expected, however, there are those who pose a counter-case, insisting that Saunière made no discovery, and became wealthy simply by wholesale trafficking in Masses.

Saunière began his Rennes-le-Château ministry in 1885 with a hamlet population of around only 200 people. Initially, he was a meticulous record keeper, noting down the smallest items of personal income and expenditure. But, from 1894, his accounts were nowhere near so concise through a period when he somehow amassed a great deal of money.

The parish notebooks that are readily accessible prove that he did indeed take contributions for Masses. This was a normal practice for which curés would receive about 50 centimes per Mass. Saunière seems to have done rather better than this at an average of three times that amount. It took about 2.5 hours to celebrate a Mass, and the allowable maximum was three per day, although generally fewer in practice. As a rule, therefore, it was not possible to become rich by this means. The only way to accrue wealth in this manner would be to take far more money per day than it was possible to say Masses for – and to do this over a very long period.

There seems to be little doubt that Saunière did indeed fall into this lucrative practice, and there are records of many more requests and postal orders being received each day than it was possible to accommodate. It is also a fact that, being unhappy with the financial management of the Diocese of Carcassonne, Saunière advertised Masses in various journals. And, of course, there were the usual benevolent donations for church repairs and the like.

At Saunière's related 1911 hearing in the Bishop's Court of Carcassonne,[9] it emerged that, rather than curtail his Mass requests, he would pass them and the money on to colleagues at other churches who were not so fortunate in their receipts. To what extent this is true cannot now be proven or disproven, but it is apparent that, to have acquired sufficient funds from Mass trafficking to account for his restoration and building expenditure at Rennes-le-Château, Saunière would need to have received money for about 1.4 million Masses in ten years.

The debate into this began at the 1911 hearing, and continues today, nearly a century later. Fuelling the debate, however, there appears to have been an underlying intrigue of some sort. Having charged Saunière with trafficking in Masses, the Bishop of Carcassonne had him suspended from duty, but it took very little effort for the priest to get the Vatican to overrule the decision and reinstate him. On the face of it, Saunière was by no means influential, but somehow he had enough sway at the highest level to overturn a decision of the Bishop's Court.

In chapter 6, we saw how the Templar commandery and alchemical workshops at Bézu had been hurriedly vacated as a result of the Order's persecution by Philippe IV of

TABLEAU

DES OFFICIERS ÉLUS PAR LA R.·. L.·.

DES COMMANDEURS DU TEMPLE,

A L'O.·. DE CARCASSONNE,

Pour diriger fes Travaux depuis le 24ᵉ jour du 4ᵉ mois de l'an de G.·. L.·. 5785, jufqu'à pareil jour de l'an 5786.

N.·. DE FAMILLE.	QUAL.·. CIVILES.	QUAL.·. MAÇONIQUES.
F.·. LE DOCTEUR FRANKLIN,	Ambaffadeur des Etats-Unis de l'Amérique,	*Vénérable d'honneur.*
F.·. DE VALETTE,	Confeiller du Roi, Magiftrat en la Sénéchauffée & Siége Préfidial de Carcaffonne,	*Vénérable.*
F.·. ASTOIN,	Avocat au Parlement,	*Premier Surveillant.*
F.·. L'ABBÉ MERIC DE RIEUX,	Prieur de Notre-Dame de Roumanou, Avocat au Parlement,	*Second Surveillant.*
F.·. NICOLAS-ALEXIS PRINCE DE GALLITZIN,	. . . .	*Ex-Vénérable d'honneur.*
F.·. SARRAN,	Receveur du Canal de Languedoc, au Port de Foucaud,	*Ex-Maître.*
F.·. CAZES,	Avocat au Parlement,	*Orateur.*
F.·. VIDAL DE Sᵀ-MARTIAL,	Avocat au Parlement,	*Secrétaire.*
F.·. GOURG,	Procureur au Sénéchal & Siége Préfidial de Carcaffonne,	*Tréforier.*
F.·. DAVID DE LAFAJEOLE,	Confeiller du Roi, fon Lieutenant-Particulier au Sénéchal & Siége Préfidial de Carcaffonne,	*Premier Expert.*
F.·. REBOUILH,	Docteur de la Fa....	
F.·. DAVID DE LAFAJEOLE		

Commanders of the Temple of Carcassonne, 1786, showing Benjamin Franklin's name at the top of the list

France in 1307. Since the anticipated Templar treasure had never been found at Bézu, it had long been suspected by Vatican officials that the Knights might have made a burial at nearby Rennes-le-Château. This theory had been heightened since June 1786, when archival documents from Bézu, Rousillon and other Templar preceptories were collated by the newly instituted Commandery of the Temple of Carcassonne. This Order had been formally constituted by Dr Benjamin Franklin, who was then United States Ambassador to France. He achieved that office following his appointment as a secret agent ten years earlier by Thomas Jefferson's Committee of Secret Correspondence. It was during the period from 1776 that Franklin put together the group which eventually became formalized as the Commandery of Carcassonne.[10]

From that time, the Vatican hierarchy had been watching events in Languedoc carefully, and when word reached Rome that Saunière had made an interesting discovery while undertaking repairs, the Cardinals became especially interested. Saunière's initial findings at the church were two documents of genealogical record dating from 1244 and 1644 respectively,[11] but it is not certain if he ever found anything else. The Cardinalate duly acquired these documents, and then applied substantial sums of money in Saunière's direction to encourage his continued work. They had their local emissary, Abbé Henri Boudet of nearby Rennes-le-Bains, keep a close eye on the proceedings. He was responsible for passing Vatican funds to Saunière in large, regular amounts over a long period of time. Maybe the Cardinals even thought there was a possibility of finding the Ark of the

Covenant. Certainly, it had not been heard of in France for nearly 600 years.

Commandery of the Revolution

In practical terms, the Vatican officials need never have been concerned about the reinstated Templar Commandery at Carcassonne. It had nothing to do with any physical treasure, and was essentially a political unit which, prior to its formalization, was linked to the War of Independence in America.

Before his visits to France, Benjamin Franklin had become a Fellow of the scientific and philosophical Royal Society in London. Although then under Hanoverian control, an element within the Society (originally chartered by King Charles II in 1662) was still operating as a Rosicrucian college with a strong affiliation to the Royal House of Stuart. When Franklin reached France in 1776, the Head of the Royal House was Charles Edward Stuart (*Bonnie Prince Charlie*), whose grandfather, James VII of Scots (James II of England) had been deposed in 1688 and exiled to the palace of St Germain-en-Laye in Paris. Charles Edward's Rosicrucian chancellor was the Marquis de Montferrat, the prevailing Count of St Germain. In September 1745, Charles had been installed at Hollyrood Abbey as Grand Master of the Jacobite Templars and, along with the Count, had founded the Rose-Croix Chapter in France soon afterwards. In this, they had used Robert the Bruce's 1317 model of the Elder Brethren of the Rosy Cross, which had itself evolved into the latter-day Royal Society.

Franklin's interest in these men was that the Jacobite attempt against King George II had failed at the Battle of Culloden in 1746, subsequent to which tens of thousands of Scots had fled to America to escape the brutal Highland Clearances in Scotland. Franklin offered Charles Edward another chance against the Georgian House of Hanover if he could get the French and Scottish Templars to assist with the American Revolution against that same royal house.

Plans were laid, bringing in such notable French Templars as the Marquis de Lafayette, and they set up conspiratorial headquarters at one of Count St Germain's workshops – the old Templar preceptory at Bézu in Languedoc. The records detail the Count as being President of the Parliament of the Temple. The net result of the establishment was that, in conjunction with Jacobite Royal Society members in London and adherents at the Académie Française, the American War of Independence was largely strategized at Bézu, and the French joined the Revolution in 1778.

Suspect Dossiers

Returning to the Prieuré documents as put forward by Pierre Plantard, Philippe de Chérisey and friends, there are two items in particular, apart from the coded parchments that have caused significant interest and investigation in recent years. The first, known as *Les Dossiers Secrets* (The Secret Dossiers), lists a series of Prieuré Grand Masters from 1188 to 1918. Although fabricated in its manner of portrayal, it does have some basis in fact, but not in the way it has been so conveniently strung together as a running sequence for a single organization. Various different historical groups and their branches are actually represented here.

The second document is entitled *Le Serpent Rouge* (The Red Serpent). A compilation work, allegedly by three authors,[12] it includes a couple of medieval French maps, a Merovingian genealogy, a ground-plan of the Paris seminary of Saint Sulpice, and thirteen Zodiac-related prose poems. Overtly cryptic in style, the verses incorporate references to numerous aspects of the Saunière mystery and the Magdalene church at Rennes-le-Château.[13]

There are distinct nominal references in this work to Mary Magdalene, likening her to Queen Isis and defining her as *Notre Dame des Cross*. The spelling of 'cross' is unusual, and one would expect the French to be *croix* in a cruciform sense. But the real enigma of *Le Serpent Rouge* lies in the fact that its three alleged authors were found individually hanged early in March 1967 – the same month that *Le Serpent Rouge* was lodged at the Bibliothèque Nationale in Paris with a front-page date of 17 January.

Of all the Prieuré documents, *Le Serpent Rouge* emerged as the most fascinating. The trouble was that the Prieuré de Sion (wholly under Plantard's control in 1967) was not to be trusted. It would have been easy enough to find three mysteriously similar, but unconnected, suicides in the obituary columns and to ascribe the names of the deceased parties to the document before lodging it in the national archive. But in fact, suspicion is certainly warranted since the archival deposit was actually made on 20 March, two weeks after the said authors' deaths.

Whatever the truth of its authorship, *Le Serpent Rouge* succeeded in postulating a link between Mary Magdalene and the Prieuré de Sion, while at the same time associating the enigmatic document with sinister deaths. It was a very powerful and compelling scenario, which has been reflected in *The Da Vinci Code*, whose strategically named museum curator and guardian of Prieuré secrets, Jacques Saunière, is murdered in The Louvre.

The heritage of Saint Sulpice dates back to Merovingian times when Sulpice was Bishop of Bourges 624–47. Commenced in 1646, the church's ground-plan and size are much the same as the Cathedral of Notre Dame de Paris. Interesting internal features include Old Testament wall frescoes (painted under the supervision of Eugene Delacroix) in the Chapel of the Holy Angels. There is a wonderful organ dating from 1781, and a 4.5 mm inlaid copper line through marble bands in the choir floor marks the zero meridian Rose Line of Paris. It has been suggested that maybe a 17th-century political movement, the *Compagnie du Saint-Sacrement* (of which the Saint Sulpice builder, Jean-Jacques Olier, was a member), was perhaps an early front for the Prieuré de Sion, but there is no evidence to support even the slightest connection. On being denounced by Louis XIV, the *Compagnie's* records were hidden, supposedly at Saint Sulpice, and this created an air of 'secret society' mystery that clearly appealed to Plantard.

The Original Prieuré

Leaving aside the erroneous concept of a modern Priory of Sion, the chivalric fraternity to which Dan Brown seemingly refers in *The Da Vinci Code* was founded in 1099 by Godefroi de Bouillon. He was installed as King of Jerusalem and Defender of the Sacred Sepulchre after the First Crusade. It was called the *Ordré de Notre Dame de Sion* (Order of Our Lady of Sion) and although it had no initial connection with Mary Magdalene, it did achieve a Magdalene association in later times.

The Order was initially headquartered at Godefroi's new Abbey of Mount Sion near Jerusalem. From around 1118, it was affiliated to the Order of the Knights of the Temple of Solomon and, by 1152, was operative in France under charter from King Louis VII at Orleans. Meanwhile, back in Jerusalem, the original *Ordré de Notre Dame* was used as a branch facility to accommodate Muslim and Jewish attachment to the Christian parent Order of the Temple.

Later that century, in 1188, a schism occurred following an internal dispute, and the French *Ordré de Notre Dame* sought independence from the Templars. But in forcing this issue, it ceased to be a recognized Order under royal charter. Instead, it became simply a Priory (an off-shoot branch), and was no longer afforded the privilege of a sovereign Grand Master. It became known as the *Prieuré Notre Dame de Sion*, and its principal figureheads were dubbed *Nautonniers* (Helmsmen).

In operative terms, the Prieuré maintained its links with the Templars in France, and it became a type of academy. Its members were particularly interested in matters of natural philosophy and alchemy. They became especially concerned with monatomic gold and the chemistry of *Ormus* (*see* chapter 6, page 119).[14] This related to documents which the Templars had brought back from Jerusalem, and was the reason for their original establishment of the Bézu foundation.

It is not surprising, therefore, that characters such as Nicolas Flamel, Leonardo da Vinci, Robert Boyle and Isaac Newton were involved with this esoteric fraternity, along with the 17th-century alchemical mentor of the Royal Society, Erenaeus Philalethes.[15] It was he who wrote the treatise, *Secrets Revealed*, concerning the nature of the Philosophers' Stone and the magical white powder of gold.

What is clear is that during that early Royal Society era, there was another change of direction within the Prieuré Notre Dame, leading to yet another schism. This seems to have occurred because the original fraternity were politically involved with affairs in France and worked in league with the Académie Française, which was in scientific competition with Boyle and Newton's Royal Society in England. It took Charles Radclyffe of Derwentwater, a Stuart nobleman in France, to hold things together within the Prieuré. Then came the American Revolution and Benjamin Franklin's involvement at Carcassonne at a time when the *Nautonnier* of the Prieuré was the Jacobite protagonist Charles, Duc de Lorraine.

The Prieuré's Stuart link and the affairs in America became paramount at this stage, but the succeeding *Nautonnier*, Maximillien de Lorraine, had no interest in politics or science – he was a patron of the arts, especially music and literature. And so, from that time, men such as Charles Nodier, Victor Hugo, Claude Debussy and Jèan Cocteau took the Prieuré helm, leading it into total obscurity after the First World War.

Meanwhile, during the early course of the schism, with the Prieuré under Robert Boyle, the scientific arm of the institution had passed to the Stuart Grand Mastership of the exiled King James VII of Scots at the Palace of St Germain. By virtue of having a sovereign head once again, this branch was inaugurated as a Royal Order (instead of just being a Priory), and it became reconstituted as the *Order of the Realm of Sion*. Day-to-day affairs were then managed not by Helmsmen, but by royally appointed Regents.

George Keith, Earl Marischal of Scotland (1692–1778) was Regent until he transferred the office to Seignelay de Colbert Traill, Bishop of Rodez (the younger son of Lord Castlehill). Later, Sir Robert Strange was Regent, and in 1848 Lord Elphinstone. At some later point, Bertram, 5th Earl of Ashburnham (1840–1913) became the Grand Master's Regent, and was succeeded in 1908 by Melville Henri Massue, the Marquis de Ruvigny et Raineval, who produced *The Jacobite Peerage* and the *Register of The Blood Royal of Britain*. After that, and subject to conditions of the British Mandate on behalf of the League of Nations in 1919, the foundation merged with the *Order of the Sangréal* in Europe.[16]

As given in the 1921 Register of *The Jacobite Peerage*, the *Order of the Sangréal* (The Sovereign Order of the Holy Grail) was an exclusive Household Order of the Royal House of Stuart. Today, these combined Orders reside within the protectorate of The Noble Order of the Guard of St Germain, constituted by King James VII (II) Stuart in 1692.

What has all this history from 1099 to do with a private society called the *Prieuré de Sion*, registered in France in 1956? Absolutely nothing. What has it to do with a secret plot to re-establish the Merovingian monarchy in France, as is often surmised? Again, nothing. What has any of this to do with goddess worship, as suggested in *The Da Vinci Code*? Nothing whatever. And what has it to do with Mary Magdalene? Also nothing – on the face of it. But, by default of the 1307 Templar Inquisition, the Magdalene legacy was brought firmly into the embrace of the *Prieuré Notre Dame de Sion* in France, and so the information in *The Da Vinci Code* is partially correct. But it is not a connection which lives on today because that particular organization ceased to exist when Maximillien de Lorraine took it in a very different, dead-end direction from 1780.

God and the Magdalene

In comparatively recent times, there have been two major art exhibitions dedicated to Mary Magdalene. The first, held at the Florence Exhibition Centre in 1986, was entitled, *The Magdalene between Sacred and Profane – An identity veiled and violated*. Shortly afterwards, in 1988, came *Marie Madeleine – A temptress of desire* at the Petrarch Museum, Fontaine-de-Vaucluse. The latter caused Mary's link with the royalty of France to be brought to the fore, especially in connection with Joan of Arc's extraordinary military campaign in the 15th century.

The man behind this campaign was one of the most amazing characters on historical record – a king whose own story was a match for any Grail adventurer. He was the Count of Provence, Duke of Anjou and King of Naples; also, Duke of Calabria and Lorraine, Count of Bar and Guise, and titular King of Hungary, Sicily, Aragon, Valencia, Majorca, Sardinia and Jerusalem. He was a renowned artist, writer, legislator, musician, architect, linguist, agriculturalist and knightly champion of the Lists. And he gave Christopher Columbus his first ship's commission.

Such impressive credentials would be a fine introduction to any romantic hero, but this was no character from the pages of mythic romance. He was King René d'Anjou (born in 1408), Grand Master of the navigational Order of the Crescent, whose sister Maria was married to King Charles VII of France, and whose daughter Margaret was the wife of King Henry VI of England.

René d'Anjou introduced the famous double-barred Cross of Lorraine, which became the lasting symbol of Free France and was the emblem of the French Resistance during the Second World War. He was the author and illustrator of *The Manual for the Perfect Organization of Tournaments*, along with *Battles and the Order of Knighthood and the Government of Princes*. A translation of the latter, known as the *Rosslyn-Hay Manuscript*, is held in the library of Lord William Sinclair at the 15th-century Rosslyn Chapel, near Edinburgh in Scotland, and it is the oldest work of Scottish prose in existence. The book's leather-bound oak cover bears the names *Jhesus–Maria–Johannes* (Jesus–Mary–John), as does a mason's inscription at Melrose Abbey in Scotland.[17]

Along with Mary Magdalene, St John the Divine (author of The Revelation) was greatly revered by René and the Grail adherents of the *Albi-gens*. John was said to be the guardian of 'the wine of the wrath of God', and is often depicted in artwork with a chalice containing a serpent. This alludes to Revelation 14:10 and to the cup of God's indignation. It was said that John had drunk from this very cup, but was not overcome because of his own divinity. In respect of this, the Rosslyn manuscript symbolizes St John by way of a Gnostic serpent of wisdom and a scalloped Grail emblem.

René d'Anjou's artistic career involved him with notables of the early Renaissance such as Jan van Eyck, Fra Angelico, Filippo Lippi and Paolo Uccello. He worked on a number of altarpieces, including the celebrated triptych at the Cathedral of Aix, which also includes work by Nicolas Froment.[18] Among René's colleagues were the great ruling houses of Italy – the families of Sforza and Medici – and his colourful painting of *Marie Madeleine Preaching to the King and Queen of Marseilles* is at the Cluny Museum in Paris.

King René therefore provides the missing link to the Jan van Eyck mystery of the National Gallery bedroom portrait with its distinctive Magdalene undertones. Jan and René were more than just associates, they were friends with mutual interests and acquaintances, and it was Jan van Eyck who taught René d'Anjou to paint.[19] The Dominican artist, Fra Angelico, was another in their circle, and it was he who placed the three red crosses in his *Noli me tangere* fresco (plate 5), while also introducing Mary Magdalene into his painting of *The Last Supper* (plate 50).

Along with his queen-consort, Jehanne de Laval, René

Marie Madeleine Preaching to the King and Queen of Marseilles
from a painting by René d'Anjou (1408–80)

arranged Magdalene pilgrimages, and had Mary
Magdalene's right arm-bone set into the silver-gilt casing in
which it is still displayed.[20] René designed and made this
casing in 1473 before the new basilica of St Maximus la
Sainte-Baume was opened, and in the light of this information we can now answer the question (posed at the end of
chapter 6) as to who held the Magdalene relics after the fall
of the French Templars in 1307 until the new basilica of St
Maximus la Sainte-Baume was consecrated and opened in
the late 1400s.

In 1307, the Helmsman of the Prieuré Notre Dame de
Sion is listed as having been Edouard de Bar, with his uncle

Jean, Comte de Bar, as his deputy. Edouard's sister, Jeanne de Bar, subsequently held the office until 1351.[21] A couple of generations later (after a period of Sinclair involvement by way of marriage) the helmsmanship fell to Cardinal Louis de Bar, whose deputy appears to have been the French chemist Nicolas Flamel. Then, from 1428, René of Anjou and Bar took the *Nautonnier's* helm. In this capacity he was succeeded, in 1480, by his daughter Yolande, whose own successors are given as Sandro Filipepi (Botticelli) and Leonardo da Vinci. Botticelli had been a student of René's artist friend, Filippo Lippi, and had also worked with the goldsmith/artist Andrea del Verrocchio, who was the tutor of Leonardo. The common patronage in all this was the Florentine House of Medici.

Throughout this period, King René's house of Anjou and Bar was paramount in the activities of the Prieuré, and since he had access to the Magdalene relics in 1473, it would appear that their safe-keeping from 1307 until the opening of the St Maximus basilica had been entrusted by the Templars to the Prieuré Notre Dame de Sion. Indeed, *Notre Dame de Sion* (Our Lady of Sion) emerges as being Mary Magdalene herself – the same *La Nostra Signora* painted by Leonardo in his *Madonna of the Rocks* while his friend Botticelli was *Nautonnier* of the Prieuré. It was Botticelli who placed ripe, open pomegranates in Jesus' hand to denote the fertility of his line, and who painted the scallop-shell masterwork, an allegory of Mary Jacob, which subsequently became known as *The Birth of Venus*.

During his Prieuré era, René d'Anjou became thoroughly immersed in the heritage of Mary Magdalene and *Les*

Saintes Maries de la Mer. He designed and built the ship-like collegiate church for St Martha's remains at Tarascon,[22] while at Reculée, near Angers, he founded the hermitage-shrine of *La Madeleine de St Baumette*.[23] Not only did King René revere and paint Mary Magdalene, he also became the principal benefactor of her tradition in Provence, and gave her name to one of his daughters. He arranged popular Bethany festivals at Marseilles, Tarascon and Aix, and was president of the Feast celebrations of *Les Saintes Maries*.

Among René's closest colleagues was the intrepid Maid of Orléans, Jehanne d'Arc (Joan of Arc). Born in 1412, she was the daughter of a Domrémy farmer in the Duchy of Bar. In the following year, Henry V became King of England – described by his own nobles as a cold, heartless warmonger, even though historical propaganda has since conferred on him the mantle of a patriotic hero. At the time of his accession, the Plantagenet war against France had subsided, but Henry decided to revive his ancestor Edward III's claim to the kingdom of France. This he did on the basis that Edward's mother of a whole century before was the daughter of King Philippe IV, the man who had persecuted the Knights Templars in 1307.

Henry V, with 2,000 men-at-arms and 6,000 archers, swept through Normandy and Rouen, defeating the French at Agincourt in 1415. He was subsequently proclaimed Regent of France at the Treaty of Troyes. With the aid of the faithless French Queen Isabau, Henry married the French King's daughter, Katherine de Valois. He then set a course towards overthrowing her brother, the

Dauphin, who was married to René d'Anjou's sister Mary. But Henry V died two years later, as did King Charles VI of France.

In England, the heir to the throne was Henry's infant son, whose uncles – the Dukes of Bedford and Gloucester – became Overlords of France. The French people were concerned about their future prospects, but, in 1429, Joan of Arc appeared at the fortress of Vaucouleurs, near Domrémy, announcing that she had been commanded by the saints to besiege the English at Orléans.

At the age of seventeen, Joan departed for the Royal Court of the Château du Milieu at Chinon, along with the Dauphin's brother-in-law, René d'Anjou. Once at Chinon on the Loire, she proclaimed her divine mission to save France from the invaders. At first, the Court resisted Joan's military ambitions, but she gained the support of Yolande d'Aragon, who was the Dauphin's mother-in-law and the mother of René d'Anjou. Joan was then entrusted with the command of more than 7,000 men, including the prestigious Scots Royal Guard of the *Gendarmes Ecossais* and the most prominent captains of the day. With René d'Anjou at her side, Joan's troops destroyed the blockade at Orléans and overthrew the English garrison. Within a few weeks, the Loire Valley was again in French hands.

On 17 July 1429, Charles the Dauphin was crowned at Reims Cathedral by Archbishop Regnault of Chartres. Alongside him, on that auspicious occasion, stood the brave shepherdess of Lorraine with her famous banner. Described in detail at her subsequent trial and painted by the Scotsman Hamish Power, it bore the names *'Jhesus Maria'*, the very same as on the sacred *Jesus Maria* stone at the Glastonbury chapel.

Less than a year after her success, the Maid of Orléans was captured while besieging Paris, and the Duke of Bedford arranged for her trial by Pierre Cauchon, Bishop of Beauvais, who condemned her to life imprisonment on bread and water. When Joan refused to submit to rape by her captors, the Bishop pronounced her an ungrateful sorceress and, without further trial, she was burned alive in the Old Market Square at Rouen on 30 May 1431.

When embarking on her Orléans campaign, Joan had selected her commander-in-chief with the request, 'Give me Duke René de Bar'.[24] To him she had said, 'There is none other here in whom I know I can put my whole trust … We will traverse France together', and for the ensuing months the pair were virtually inseparable.

Although remembered today for his wonderfully illuminated manuscript of the Knight of Love, *le Livre du Cueur d'Amours Espris*,[25] René d'Anjou's reputation suffered at the same stake that saw the end of his beloved Joan. She had been discredited by the powerful clergy of France and, in consequence of this, René became the victim of a purposeful literary Inquisition. The Church perceived him as the epitome of everything it detested in terms of the Grail tradition. Despite all the fame and importance of his lifetime, René was more or less expunged from academic records, and he is rarely mentioned in the schoolrooms of today. The great irony of this is that, as recently as 1920, the Church reconsidered Joan of Arc's case and, in the light of hypocritical hindsight, she was not only pardoned, but canonized!

Like Mary Magdalene before him, King René d'Anjou died at Aix en Provence on 10 July 1480. Queen Jehanne placed the sovereign jewel around her husband's neck in his casket – for although he had daughters, there was no legitimate male heir to the line of Anjou de Bar. His eldest daughter, Yolande, assumed his titles for a while, but conceded when they were claimed by Louis XI of France.

René's personal bequests to his wife, Jehanne, included collars of diamonds and rubies, caskets of silver and great bowls of gold encrusted with precious gems. But above all was valued a simple goblet – a rock-crystal wine cup, which René had engraved:

> Who drinks well,
> God shall see.
> Who drains at a single draught,
> Shall see God and the Magdalene.[26]

The inference of René's inscription is that disconnected aspects of learning are sufficient to present an image of Jesus as determined by conventional doctrine. But when the scriptural records are embraced as a whole, Mary Magdalene moves equally into the picture.

It was René's contention that, irrespective of alabastrons and spikenard, Mary Magdalene, the Patroness of Provence, was herself the Holy Balm of which *La Sainte-Baume* had been named. Her physical balm was manifest in the dynastic heritage of the *Desposyni*, but her spiritual balm was the true nature of the *Sangréal* – the abiding Light of the holy vessel. René maintained that the route to that enlightenment was indeed the Quest of the Holy Grail, and that the secret of its achievement constitutes the eternal legacy of Mary Magdalene.

NOTES AND REFERENCES

CHAPTER 1: SAINT OR SINNER?

1 Matthew 27:55–56, Matthew 28:1, Mark 15:40–41, Mark 16:1, Luke 8:2–3, Luke 24:10, John 19:25.
2 John 19:25.
3 John 20:1.
4 Mark 15:41, Luke 8:3.
5 Mark 16:9, John 20:16.
6 Luke 8:2.
7 John 11:1–5.
8 In standard Bible editions, *Noli me tangere*, is generally translated as 'Touch me not' or 'Do not touch me'. A translation from the original Greek text of John reveals, however, that the correct translation is 'Do not cling to me' or 'Do not embrace me'. The word *touch* is not applicable. *See* Professor Hugh J Schonfield, *The Original New Testament*, Waterstone, London, 1985, p 529 – John 20:17 and page note 7.
9 *The Catholic Encyclopedia*, Robert Appleton, New York, NY, 1910, vol IX – Mary Magdalene.
10 *Oxford Dictionary of Saints* (ed, David Farmer), Oxford University Press, Oxford, 1997.
11 R McL Wilson, *The Gospel of Philip: Translated from the Coptic Text*, AR Mowbray, London, 1962, pp 35, 97. *See* also, Chapter 8 – Consort of the Saviour, and related note references.
12 Barbara Thiering, *Jesus the Man*, Transworld, London, 1992, ch 17, pp 88–9; appendix III, p 355.
13 James Hastings, *Dictionary of the Bible*, T & T Clark, Edinburgh, 1909.
14 Flavius Josephus, *The Wars of the Jews* in *The Works of Flavius Josephus*, (trans, William Whiston), Milner & Sowerby, London, 1870, bk II, ch XXI:4.
15 *Ibid*, bk III, ch X:1–10.
16 J Hastings, *Dictionary of the Bible* – Galilee.
17 Voragine is now Varazze, near Genoa, Italy.
18 Jacapo di Voragine, *Legenda Aurea (Golden Legend)*, (trans, William Caxton, 1483; ed, George V O'Neill), Cambridge University Press, Cambridge, 1972.
19 B Thiering, *Jesus the Man*; appendix III, p 369.
20 Margaret Starbird, *The Woman with the Alabaster Jar*, Bear, Santa Fe, 1993, ch 3, pp 50–1.
21 Mark 1:21–28.
22 2 Samuel 20:25–26.
23 Numbers 32:41.
24 Also in Mark 5:22–43 and Luke 8:41–56. *See* further information in this regard, from interpretations of the Dead Sea Scrolls, in B Thiering, *Jesus the Man*, ch 17, p 89; appendix I, p 215, and appendix III, pp 338–9.

or, *The Coming of the Saints*, Covenant Books, London, 1969,

ources for the Hasmonaeans are the apocryphal books of
s, for instance in *The Septuagint with Apocrypha* (trans, Sir
CL Brenton), Samuel Bagster, London, 1851. They also feature
in ry. phus, *The Antiquities of the Jews* in *The Works of Flavius Josephus*.

27 *The Catholic Encyclopedia*, vol XII – Rabanus Maurus.

28 Matthaei Parisiensis, *Chronica Majora*, Longman, London, 1874.

29 *Scriptorum Ecclesiasticorum Historia literaria Basilae*, vol II, p 38 (folio),
Oxford, 1740–43.

30 A good source for the history of Magdalene College is Peter Cunich,
David Hoyle, Eamon Duffy and Ronald Hyam, *A History of Magdalene
College Cambridge 1428–1988*, Magdalene College Publications,
Cambridge, 1994. Soon after the Cambridge foundation, and as a direct
result of it, a new word entered the English language. The word, which
related to a tearful or sentimental aspect and derived from the image of
Mary Magdalene weeping, was 'maudlin' ('And they say unto her,
Woman, why weepest thou? She saith unto them, Because they have
taken away my Lord, and I know not where they have laid him' – John
20:13.) The famous *Nathan Bailey's Universal Etymological Dictionary*, T
Cox at The Lamb, Royal Exchange, London, 1721 (as used by Samuel
Johnson), explains the word as: 'Half drunk, tipsy; contracted of
Magdalene'.

31 This book has recently been republished in conjunction with Emmanuel
College, Cambridge – Barry Windeatt (ed), *The Book of Margery Kempe*,
Longman, London, 1999.

32 Père Lacordaire, St *Mary Magdalene*, Thomas Richardson, Derby, 1880.

33 Laurence Gardner, *Bloodline of the Holy Grail* (Element Books, 1996).
Revised edition, Thorsons–Element/HarperCollins, London, 2002.
http://www.Graal.co.uk/bloodline.html.

CHAPTER 2: PERSECUTION

1 Malachi Martin, *The Decline and Fall of the Roman Church*, Secker &
Warburg, London, 1982, pp 42–3.

2 Matthew 1:17, Luke 3:23–38.

3 In the public domain, *see* Eusebius of Caesarea, *An Ecclesiastical History*
(trans, Rev CF Crusè), Samuel Bagster, London, 1838, bk 3, p 84.

4 *The Catholic Encyclopedia*, vol I – Abdias.

5 Eusebius of Caesarea, *The History of the Church from Christ to Constantine*,
Penguin, London, 1989, bk 1, p 22.

6 Tacitus, *The Annals of Imperial Rome* (trans, Michael Grant), Penguin,
London, 1996, ch 14, p 365.

7 Irenaeus of Lyon, *Adversus Haereses*, V, 30, 3 – as in Eusebius, *The History
of the Church from Christ to Constantine*, bk 3, p 81.

8 *Ibid*, bk 3, p 82.

NOTES AND REFERENCES

9 Revelation 12:17.

10 Acts 12:23 states that Herod-Agrippa was smote by an angel and 'eaten of worms'. *See* also, Stewart Perowne, *The Later Herods*, Hodder & Stoughton, London, 1958, ch 10, p 83.

11 F Josephus, *The Wars of the Jews*, bk II, ch VII:3. There is a genealogical chart showing the family descent of the 'House of Herod' in Laurence Gardner, *Lost Secrets of the Sacred Ark*, Thorsons–Element/HarperCollins, London, 2004, pp 344–5.

12 Revelation 12:2.

13 *The Nag Hammadi Library – On the Origin of the World* (trans, James M Robinson and the Coptic Gnostic Project), Institute for Antiquity and Christianity, EJ Brill, Leiden, 1977, Codex II, 5 & XIII, 2, p 161.

14 Margaret Starbird, *The Woman with the Alabaster Jar*, ch 1, p 28.

15 Bernard de Clairvaux, *Patriologia Latina* (ed, JP Minge), Paris, 1854, vol 183, cols, 1050–55.

16 J Hastings, *Dictionary of the Bible – Shulamite*.

17 Ean CM Begg, *The Cult of the Black Virgin*, Arkana, London, 1985, ch 4, provides good reference for 'The whore wisdom in the Christian era'.

18 Revelation 12:3.

19 The stories of these kings are in Titus Livius ('Livy' c59 BC–AD 17), *Ab Urbe Condita* (From the Founding of the City) – vol I, Loeb Classical Library, Harvard University Press, Cambridge, MA, 1919; vol II, Bristol Classical Press, Bristol, 1998; vols III, IV, Loeb Classical Library, 1989.

20 M Martin, *The Decline and Fall of the Roman Church*, pp 42–4.

21 F Josephus, *The Antiquities of the Jews* in *The Works of Flavius Josephus*, bk XX, ch IX:1.

22 *Ibid*, bk XVIII, ch III/3. This particular entry has been claimed by some commentators as a later interpolation – an assumption based on the fact that the entry expresses a Christian sympathy, whereas Josephus was a Hebrew. Origen (writing before AD c245) does not mention this entry, although Eusebius, in his *Demonstration of the Gospel* (written AD c320) does mention it. Any interpolation, therefore, would have to have been made between the times of Origen and Eusebius. In real terms, however, the entry is not at all Christian in sentiment. It does not refer to Jesus in any divine context – simply that he was a wise man, a worker of marvels and a teacher, in much the way that anyone of the era would have perceived him. *See* also AN Wilson, *Jesus*, Sinclair Stevenson, London, 1992, ch 4, p 89.

23 Tacitus, *The Annals of Imperial Rome*, ch 14, p 365.

24 Epiphanius, *Panarion* (trans, F Wilkins), EJ Brill, Leiden, 1989–93, 78:8:1 & 78:9:6; *Ancoratus* (trans, Karl Hol), Walter de Gruyter, Berlin, 2002–4, 60:1.

25 *Protevangelion of James* 19:3–20; 4; *See* also in Richard Bauckham, *Jude and the Relatives of Jesus in the Early Church*, T & T Clark, Edinburgh, 1988, ch 1, p 37.

26 Philip 59:6–11 in *The Nag Hammadi Library*.

27 AN Wilson, *Jesus*, ch 4, p 79.
28 Nancy Qualls-Corbett, *The Sacred Prostitute*, Inner City Books, Toronto, 1988, ch 2, p 58.

CHAPTER 3: APOCALYPSE

1 A good example is *The Wine Press* by John Spencer Stanhope, 1864. A colour reproduction of this image is in the plate section of the 2002 HarperCollins edition of Laurence Gardner, *Bloodline of the Holy Grail*.

2 Harold Bayley, *The Lost Language of Symbolism*, Williams & Norgate, London, 1912, contains comprehensive details of medieval watermarks in Provence.

3 Marjorie Malvern, *Venus in Sackcloth*, Southern Illinois University Press, Carbondale, IL, 1975, ch 1, p 3.

4 The story of the Provençal paper trade is told in Harold Bayley, *A New Light on the Renaissance*, John Dent, London, 1909.

5 H Bayley, *The Lost Language of Symbolism*, ch 1, p 2.

6 Elaine Pagels, *The Gnostic Gospels*, Weidenfeld and Nicolson, London, 1980, ch 3, pp 50–1.

7 The earliest genuine text of a Marian litany is in a 12th-century codex in the Mainz Library, entitled, *Letania de domina nostra Dei genitrice virgine Maria: oratio valde bona: cottidie pro quacumque tribulatione recitanda est.*

8 Riane Eisler, *The Chalice and the Blade*, Harper & Row, New York, 1987, p 72.

9 Recommended reading in respect of the Troubadours and the Grail, and for further study with regard to early watermarks and X-marks, is Margaret Starbird, *The Woman with the Alabaster Jar*.

10 For more on this subject, *see* Robert Graves, *The White Goddess*, Faber & Faber, London, 1961, ch 22, pp 395–6.

11 Nisan is the first month of the Jewish calendar.

12 The constant symbol of Eostre, the spring goddess, was a rabbit. She was generally portrayed within an abundant array of spring flowers. On her feast day, spiced buns were baked, their tops decorated with solar crosses, and baskets were woven to represent birds' nests. All these old English customs were enveloped within Christianity – Easter eggs, Easter bunnies and hot cross buns – seemingly aligned with the Resurrection of Jesus, but actually having nothing whatever to do with him.

13 The history of the Royal Syths is recounted in Laurence Gardner, *Realm of the Ring Lords*, Thorsons–Element/HarperCollins, London, 2003. http://www.Graal.co.uk/ringlords.html.

14 Rosemary Radford Ruether (professor of theology, Garrett-Evangelical Theological Seminary), 'No Church conspiracy against Mary Magdalene' in *The National Catholic Reporter*, Kansas City, 9 Feb, 2001.

15 M Malvern, *Venus in Sackcloth*, ch 6, p 77.

16 A colour reproduction of this Sforza image is in the plate section of the 2002 HarperCollins edition of Laurence Gardner, *Bloodline of the Holy Grail*. The Sforzas were Dukes of Milan 1450–1535. Their richly illuminated *Book of Hours* was commissioned in 1490, and can be seen at the British Museum in London.

17 Udo Becker, *The Element Encyclopedia of Symbols*, Element Books, Shaftesbury, 1996 – Dove.

18 For a full explanation of the book of The Revelation, *see* Barbara Thiering, *Jesus of the Apocalypse*, Transworld/Doubleday, London, 1996.

CHAPTER 4: THE OTHER MARY

1 F Josephus, *The Wars of the Jews*, bk II, ch VIII:2.

2 *Ibid*, bk II, ch VIII:6.

3 F Josephus, *The Antiquities of the Jews*, bk XVIII, ch I:3.

4 *Ibid*.

5 JT Milik, *Ten Years of Discovery in the Wilderness of Judaea* (trans, J. Strugnell), SCM Press, London, 1959.

6 In the New Testament, 2 Corinthians 4:3–7 similarly states, 'If our Gospel be hid, it is hid to them that are lost … But we have this treasure in earthen vessels'.

7 Ahmed Osman, *The House of the Messiah*, HarperCollins, London, 1992, ch 5, p 31.

8 An Arabic alternative is *en Nusara* – *see* Rev John Fleetwood, *The Life of Our Lord and Saviour Jesus Christ*, William MacKenzie, Glasgow, 1900, ch 1, p 10.

9 This error is repeated in Luke 2:39.

10 *The Catholic Encyclopedia*, vol VI – Gabriel.

11 *The Book of Enoch*, (trans, RH Charles; revised from Dillmann's edition of the Ethiopic text, 1893), Oxford University Press, Oxford, 1906 and 1912, bk I, ch 10:9.

12 *The Catholic Encyclopedia*, vol I – Book of Enoch.

13 F Josephus, *Antiquities of the Jews*, bk XV, ch V:2.

14 JT Milik, *Ten Years of Discovery in the Wilderness of Judaea*, ch 3, pp 51–3.

15 John Allegro, *The Dead Sea Scrolls*, Penguin, London, 1964, ch 5, p 94.

16 F Josephus, *The Wars of the Jews*, bk II, ch VIII:7.

17 AN Wilson, *Jesus*, ch 4, p 83.

18 Genesis 32:28.

19 The further term, *Hebrew*, comes from *eber*, meaning 'other side'. It is referenced in Syrian texts as *Habirû*, and derived from *Eber han nahor* – from the 'Other side of the flood' (the River Euphrates), as explained in Joshua 24:3. That is to say that the original Hebrews (the family of Abraham) came into Canaan (Palestine) from across the Euphrates in Mesopotamia. Eber is given as the name of Abraham's 6th generational ancestor in Genesis 11:14–17, while Nahor was one of his brothers (Genesis 11:27).

20 Jan Provost's *The Sacred Allegory* is reproduced in colour in the HarperCollins 2002 edition of L Gardner, *Bloodline of the Holy Grail*.

21 An excellent appraisal of these dynastic structures, based on detailed information from the Dead Sea Scrolls, is given in B Thiering, *Jesus the Man*, appendix III, 'Hierarchy'.

22 Hebrews 7:14.

23 F Josephus, *The Wars of the Jews*, bk II, ch VIII:13.

24 *Ibid*, (same entry).

25 In the above mentioned appendix III, 'Hierarchy' of B Thiering, *Jesus the Man*, there are sections dealing specifically with Women in the Qumrân community structure as determined from the Dead Sea Scrolls.

26 The term *Catholic* means 'universal'.

27 Recommended reading in this regard is Norman J Bull, *The Rise of the Church*, Heinemann, London, 1967.

28 Notwithstanding the break between Rome and Constantinople, the independent status of the Western and Eastern Churches was not formalized until as late as 1945.

29 This Bellagambe painting of *The Immaculate Conception* is reproduced in Laurence Gardner, *The Illustrated Bloodline of the Holy Grail*, Barnes & Noble, New York, 2000, p 188.

CHAPTER 5: SEPULCHRE OF THE MAGDALENE

1 The Bishops of Rome were called *pontiffs* (bridge-builders – relating to a bridge between God and the people), but had long been referred to as Father (*Papa*). From 610 Boniface IV was the first to be styled Pope as a formality, although it is generally acceptable to apply the title to his predecessors.

2 George F Jowett, *The Drama of the Lost Disciples*, Covenant Books, London, 1961, ch 12, pp 125–6.

3 Relating to 'special insight' – from the Greek *gnosis*, meaning 'knowledge'.

4 *The Nag Hammadi Library*, Codex VII, 3.

5 Rev Lionel Smithett Lewis, *Joseph of Arimathea at Glastonbury*, AR Mobray, London, 1927, p 54.

6 Hugh Cressy's *The History of Brittany or England*, was published in Rouen in 1668.

7 Verulam or Verulamium was renamed St Albans after a 4th-century martyr. He was the Roman soldier Alban, who was beheaded by his military superiors in AD 303 for sheltering a Christian priest. Modern St Albans is a busy market city in Hertfordshire, with a spectacular abbey.

8 The exile of Herod the Great's son, Herod-Archaelus, to Vienne in France is recorded in F Josephus, *The Wars of the Jews*, bk II, ch VII:3. At much the same time (AD c39), his brother Herod-Antipas of Galilee was exiled to nearby Saint-Bertrand de Comminges in Aquitaine, near the Spanish frontier – *see* S Perowne, *The Later Herods*, ch 10, p 69. In F Josephus, *The Wars of the Jews*, bk II, ch IX:6, this is classified as being Spain.

9 Some commentators have suggested that the younger Aristobulus was Mary Magdalene's confederate, but he was acting as regent for the king in Lesser Armenia at the time.

10 The Abbey of St Maximus is around 30 miles (48 km) from Marseilles.

11 Malachi Martin, *The Decline and Fall of the Roman Church*, pp 63–5.

12 For further information about the Celtic Church, see Nora K Chadwick, *The Age of Saints in the Celtic Church*, Oxford University Press, 1961; Dom Louis Gougaud, *Christianity in Celtic Lands* (trans, Maud Joynt), Four Courts Press, Dublin, 1932, and EG Bowen, *The Settlements of the Celtic Saints in Wales*, University of Wales Press, Cardiff, 1956.

13 In Latin, it was the *Constitutum Constantini*.

14 The town of Ferrières was destroyed by Atilla the Hun in AD 461, but was substantially rebuilt by the Merovingians. *See* ECM Begg, *The Cult of the Black Virgin*, Introduction, pp 20–1.

15 They were so named after Meroveus (son of Clodion of Tournai), who died in AD 446 and was the founder of the Frankish dynasty. For a genealogical chart of the Merovingian Kings, *see* the revised 2002 HarperCollins edition of Laurence Gardner, *Bloodline of the Holy Grail*, pp 335–7.

16 Originally, the *fleur-de-lis* was emblematic of the Jewish covenant of circumcision.

17 Eusebius of Caesarea, *An Ecclesiastical History*, bk 3, p 84.

18 An English transcript of the *Donation of Constantine* is given in *Select Historical Documents of the Middle Ages* (trans, Ernest F Henderson), G Bell, London, 1925, pp 319–29.

19 In the 4th century (from AD 382), St Jerome made a Latin translation of the Bible from the earlier Hebrew and Greek texts for subsequent Christian usage. It was called the Vulgate because of its 'vulgar' (general) application – from *vulgata editio* (common edition). Emperor Constantine died before this in AD 337.

20 The earliest known manuscript of the Donation is in the *Codex Parisiensis Lat. 2778* in the *Collectio Sancti Dionysii*, found in the monastery of St Denis in France. *See* Christopher B Coleman, *The Treatise of Lorenzo Valla on the Donation of Constantine*, University of Toronto Press, Toronto, 1993, p 6.

21 *Ibid*, p 3. Nicholas of Cusa (Nicholas Cusanus) published his critical appraisal of the Donation in his *De Concordantia Catholica*.

22 *Ibid*, p 20ff, presents the *Treatise of Lorenzo Valla* (*Laurentii Vallensis*) as a translated discourse.

23 *Ibid*, p 25.

24 An account of Henry Edward Manning's life and Catholic conversion is given in David Newsome, *The Convert Cardinals*, John Murray, London, 1993, *passim*.

25 At the time of Christopher B Coleman's publication, he was professor of history at Allegheny College, Meadville, Pennsylvania, compiling his work with assistance from that College and from Columbia University, New York.

26 Père Lacordaire, *St Mary Magdalene*, ch VII, p 99.

27 *The Hutchinson Encyclopedia*, Hutchinson, London, 1997 – Saracens.

28 *The Macmillan Encyclopedia*, Macmillan, London, 1996 – Moors. The designation derived from 'Mauritania', the Roman name for NW Africa.

29 The most comprehensive account of the Septimanian kingdom is in Arthur J Zuckerman, *A Jewish Princedom in Feudal France*, Columbia University Press, New York, 1972.

30 The Jewish faith is represented here by the collective term *Torah*, being the first five scriptural books of the Hebrew Bible.

31 *Ibid*, ch VII, p 103. This account was prepared from Dominican records in the 19th century by Père Lacordaire, Dominican friar and member of the French Academy.

32 *Ibid*, ch VII, p 107.

33 Eudes, as mentioned in the inscription, was Eudes of Aquitaine, who had declared his independence from the attempt by the Carolingian, Pepin the Short (Charlemagne's father), to take control from the Merovingians in France. In this regard, Eudes was considered regionally to be King of France south of the Loire.

34 At that stage Charles's successor, Bene, was King of Naples and Provence.

CHAPTER 6: GUARDIANS OF THE RELIC

1 *The Catholic Encyclopedia*, vol XII – Friars Preachers.

2 *The Catholic Encyclopedia*, vol VIII – Lacordaire.

3 Père Lacordaire, *St Mary Magdalene*, ch VII, p 120.

4 Philippe VI of France, Alfonso IV of Aragon, Hugh IV of Cyprus, John of Bohemia, Robert of Sicily.

5 John XXII, Benedict XII, Clement VII, Urban V, Gregory XI, Urban VI, Boniface IX, Innocent VII.

6 Catalogued at the British Museum as *Piste Sophia Coptice*, MS Add. 5114.

7 Jean Doresse, *The Secret Books of the Egyptian Gnostics* (trans, Philip Mairet), Hollis & Carter, London, 1960, ch 2, p 64. It was not until the 10th century that Coptic gave way to the Arabic language, although it is still used by the Coptic branch of the Egyptian Church.

8 *Pistis Sophia: a Gnostic Miscellany* (trans, GRS Mead, 1921), reprinted Kessinger, Kila, MT, 1992, bk 1, ch 1, p 1.

9 *Ibid*, bk 1, ch 36, p 47.

10 *Ibid*, bk 2, ch 72, p 135. This is sometimes rendered as '… hateth our sex'.

11 *Ibid*, bk 1, ch 17, p 20.

12 For comprehensive information concerning the Knights of the Temple, *see* Desmond Seward, *The Monks of War*, Paladin/Granada, St Albans, 1974.

13 Louis Charpentier, *The Mysteries of Chartres Cathedral*, Research Into Lost Knowledge Organization and Thorsons, Wellingborough, 1992, ch 8, p 69.

NOTES AND REFERENCES

14 ECM Begg, *The Cult of the Black Virgin*, ch 4, p 103.

15 Palestine Exploration Fund, 2 Hinde Mews, Marylebone Lane, London, W1U 2AA.

16 Leen and Kathleen Ritmeyer, *Secrets of Jerusalem's Temple Mount*, Biblical Archaeological Society, Washington, DC, 1998, ch 5, pp 71–7.

17 These artefacts are now held by the Scottish Templar archivist, Robert Brydon. *See* Christopher Knight and Robert Lomas, *The Hiram Key*, Century, London, 1996, ch 13, p 267.

18 Even today there are a couple of ornamental caskets at the Basilica of Vézelay, which are spuriously purported to contain Mary Magdalene's relics.

19 L Gardner, *Lost Secrets of the Sacred Ark*, ch 15, pp 217–29.

20 Louis Charpentier, *The Mysteries of Chartres Cathedral*, ch 17, pp 137–43 gives a good overview of the properties of Gothic stained glass.

21 Michael Baigent, Richard Leigh and Henry Lincoln, *The Holy Blood and the Holy Grail*, Jonathan Cape, London, 1982, ch 5, p 92.

22 An alchemical process (discovered by modern scientists in the 1980s) which transposes Transition Group metals such as gold or platinum into a single atomic state. Rendered as a fine white powder and classified as 'exotic matter', the substance has unique anti-gravitational and superconductive attributes.

23 Subsequent to a modernization of his name in the 19th century, Vilars Dehoncort is now generally referred to as Villard de Honnecourt. There is good coverage of Villard de Honnecourt in French literature. In the English language, he may be found referenced in François Bucher, *Architector: The Lodge Books and Sketchbooks of Medieval Architects*, Abaris Books, New York, NY, 1979. And in Jean Gimpel, *The Medieval Machine: The Industrial Revolution of the Middle Ages*, Pimlico, London, 1976.

24 Catalogue shelf number: MS Lat. 1104. His accompanying manuscript notes are numbered MS. Fr. 19093.

25 There is a colour photo-print of this 13th-century sketchbook design for the Chartres labyrinth in the plate section of Laurence Gardner, *Lost Secrets of the Sacred Ark*.

26 Albertus was subsequently beatified as St Albertus by Pope Gregory XV in 1622.

27 *The Catholic Encyclopedia*, vol XIV – Albertus Magnus.

28 *The Catholic Encyclopedia*, vol II – Benedict XI, and vol XIV – Toulouse.

29 As a result of this, some people are still averse to the unlucky date of Friday 13th.

30 HRH Prince Michael of Albany, *The Forgotten Monarchy of Scotland*, Chrysalis/Vega, London, 2002, ch 5, p 62.

31 In the 19th century, the trainee Catholic priest Alphonse Louis Constant (1810–75) gave up his ecclesiastical schooling to become an occultist – adopting the Jewish pseudonym Eliphas Lévi. He wrote many books on ritual magic, in the course of which he reinvented Baphomet, based on the premise that it was a goat and terrible demon. His drawing of this is now

very well known, half male and half female, with the head of a goat and a pentagram on its forehead, it has become a universal symbol of black magic and evil. It has been used as a representation of the devil in Tarot decks. The device was so appealing to the 20th-century English occultist Aleister Crowley that he used Baphomet as his own magical name.

32 Twelve other works dating from the Scrolls period, and relating to the last part of the Old Testament era constitute the *Apocrypha* (Hidden things). Although included in the Greek *Septuagint*, they were not contained in the Hebrew canon. They originated in the Hellenist Judaism of Alexandria, but are not accepted by orthodox Jews. The books are, nevertheless, included in St Jerome's Latin Vulgate (AD c385) as an extension to the Old Testament, and are recognized by the Roman Catholic Church. They are omitted by almost all Protestant Bibles, having been sidelined by the prime reformer Martin Luther (1483–1546) and largely ignored by translators. The twelve books are: Esdras, Tobit, Judith, the Rest of Esther, the Wisdom of Solomon, Ecclesiasticus [of Jeremiah], Baruch with the Epistle of Jeremy, the Song of the Three Holy Children, the History of Susanna, Bel and the Dragon, the Prayer of Manasses, and Maccabees.

33 John Allegro, *The Dead Sea Scrolls*, Penguin, London, 1964, ch 5, p 93.

34 B Thiering, *Jesus the Man*, ch 4, pp 20–21. This is the finest work for describing precisely how the Essene scribal codes work in practice – written by Dr Thiering who discovered and perfected the process. There is also a simplified overview in the 2002 HarperCollins edition of Laurence Gardner, *Bloodline of the Holy Grail*, ch 2, pp 20–3.

35 *Eschatology* is the study (a branch of theology) that has to do with the end of the world – the Last Things (death and/or judgement).

36 Hugh J Schonfield, *The Essene Odyssey*, Element Books, Shaftesbury, 1984, introduction, pp 7–8, and ch 11, pp 66–68.

37 *Ibid*, appendix A, pp 162–165. Baphomet in Hebrew (right to left) is [*taf*] [*mem*] [*vav*] [*pe*] [*bet*]. Application of the Atbash cipher results (again right to left for Hebrew) in [*alef*] [*yud*] [*pe*] [*vav*] [*shin*] = Sofia.

CHAPTER 7: REMARKABLE TEXTS

1 John 11:1–53.

2 *The Catholic Encyclopedia*, vol IX – Mark.

3 B Thiering, *Jesus the Man*, ch 14, p 75.

4 For a fuller description of the Church of Saint Martha, *see* J W Taylor, *The Coming of the Saints*, ch 10, pp 195–7.

5 St Caesarius was abbot of a pre-Benedictine monastery at Arles in Southern France in Merovingian times. He also founded a convent at Arles, and became famous for his words, 'Match your behaviour to the words that you sing' – *Oxford Dictionary of Saints*.

6 *Sermo 26 de Verbis Domini*, from *Homilia sancti Augustini Episcopi* – A Homily by St Augustine the Bishop.

7 JR Porter, *Jesus Christ*, Duncan Baird, London, 1999, p 129.

8 M Baigent, R Leigh and H Lincoln, *The Holy Blood and the Holy Grail*, ch 12, pp 282–3, and note 12/5, p 432.

9 Nancy Qualls-Corbett, *The Sacred Prostitute*, p 56; Marjory Malvern, *Venus in Sackcloth*, ch 2, p 17 and note 2/10, p 186; *Oxford Annotated Bible* (eds, Herbert G May and Bruce M Metzger), Oxford University Press, Oxford, 1962, p 1238.

10 The definitive work on this subject is Morton Smith, *The Secret Gospel*, Victor Gollancz, London, 1974.

11 E Pagels, *The Gnostic Gospels*, ch 3, p 60.

12 There is a lengthy article featuring this discovery, entitled 'The Strange Case of the Secret Gospel According to Mark' (ed, David Fideler) in *Alexandria: The Journal for the Western Cosmological Traditions*, Phanes Press, 1995, vol 3, pp 103–29.

13 M Smith, *The Secret Gospel*, ch 7, p 51.

14 M Baigent, R Leigh and H Lincoln, *The Holy Blood and the Holy Grail*, ch 12, p 296.

15 Matthew 26:6, Mark 14:3, Luke 7:36 and 40, John 11:1 and 12:1.

16 F Josephus, *The Antiquities of the Jews*, bk XVIII, ch 3:2.

17 This is confirmed to have been the case in the Secret Gospel of Mark, where Lazarus is said to be 'wearing a linen cloth over his naked body'. He is also referred to as a 'young man'. There is a similar mention in connection with Jesus' Gethsemane arrest in Mark 14:51–52, which states: 'And there followed him a certain young man, having a linen cloth cast about his naked body'. In both cases this was symbolic of Simon having been unfrocked from his previous ecclesiastical rank, while for him to be described as a 'young man' relegates him to his newly demoted status as a Community novice following his excommunication.

18 Dondaine (1898–1987) was famed for his informative work *Les Heresies et L'Inquisition*.

19 Istituto Storico Domenicano http://www.op.org/curia/storico/ and http://www.op.org/curia/storico/afp/.

20 Yuri Stoyanov, *The Hidden Tradition in Europe*, Arkana/Penguin, London, 1994, ch 6, pp 222–3.

21 Robert Alter, *Genesis*, WW Norton, New York, NY, 1996, ch 36, p 204.

22 This subject is well covered in M Baigent, R Leigh and H Lincoln, *The Holy Blood and the Holy Grail*, ch 2, pp 19–34.

23 A good overview of Provence as a Cradle of Enlightenment is given in M Starbird, *The Woman with the Alabaster Jar*, ch 4, pp 67–78.

24 Eleanor of Aquitaine (1122–1204) is a good example of female equality in the region. Her importance and influence were a constant embarrassment to the Roman Church bishops.

25 Y Stoyanov, *The Hidden Tradition in Europe*, ch 4, p 159.

26 Selected works concerning the Albigensian Crusade are Jonathan Sumption, *The Albigensian Crusade*, Faber & Faber, London, 1978, and

Zoé Oldenbourg, *Massacre at Montségur* (trans, Peter Green), Pantheon, New York, 1961.

27 Jean Evenou, 'La messe de Sainte Marie Madeleine au Missel romain (1570–1970)' in Robert SJ Godding, *Grégoire le Grand et la Madeleine in Memoriam soctorum venerantes – Miscellanea in onore di Mgr. Victor Saxer*, The Vatican, Rome 1992, pp 353–65.

28 'De nativitate sancti Johannis Baptiste, et de beaetis apostolic Petro et Paulo, et de beata maria Magdalena fiat festum totum duplex; et magister ordinis cures de sequentiis providere' in *Acta capitulorum generalium ordinis praedicatorum* (ed, B Reichert), The Vatican, Rome, 1898, p 283.

29 Susan Haskins, *Mary Magdalene, Myth and Metaphor,* Harcourt Brace, New York, 1994, ch 5, p 147.

30 'In festo sanctae Mariae Magdalenae' in *Sermones festiui, Divi. Thomae Aquinatis opera LXXV,* Venice, 1787, p 113.

31 *The Dialogue of the Saviour* and the *Gospel of Mary* in this section are all to be found in English translation in *The Nag Hammadi Library.*

32 R McL Wilson, *The Gospel of Philip: Translated from the Coptic Text; See* also Chapter 8 – Consort of the Saviour, and related note references.

33 Published in 1892 under the care of M. Bouriant in vol IX, fac I, *Memoirs of the French Archaeological Mission at Cairo.*

CHAPTER 8: WOMEN AND THE CHURCH

1 F Josephus, *The Antiquities of the Jews*, bk XVII, ch 13:5, and bk XVIII, ch 1:1.

2 S Perowne, *The Later Herods*, ch 5, pp 26–9.

3 B Thiering, *Jesus the Man*, ch 8, p 48.

4 HJ Schonfield, *The Original New Testament*, p 136 – Luke 2:45–50. In the King James Bible, the word 'teachers' is translated as 'doctors', as would be those with academic doctorates.

5 These days, by virtue of cosmopolitan social structures, the BC and AD classifications are often replaced by BCE (Before the Common Era) and CE (Common Era).

6 B Thiering, *Jesus the Man*, appendix 1, p 178.

7 J Finigan, *Handbook of Biblical Chronology*, Princeton University Press, Princeton, NJ, 1964.

8 Similar traditions are still customary today. Queen Elizabeth II of Britain was born in April 1926, but her official birthday is celebrated in June, as were those of her predecessors since Edward VII's reign in 1748.

9 It is significant that in Acts 5:30, 10:39 and 13:29, the references to Jesus' torture all relate to his being 'hanged on a tree'.

10 As referenced in chapter 1, standard Bible editions generally translate *Noli me tangere* as 'Touch me not' or 'Do not touch me'. A translation from the original Greek text of John reveals, however, that this is incorrect. The correct translation is 'Do not cling to me' or 'Do not

embrace me'. The word *touch* is not applicable. *See* HJ Schonfield, *The Original New Testament*, p 529 – John 20:17 and Schonfield page note 7.

11 *The Oxford Compact English Dictionary* (Oxford Word Library: OWL Micrographic), Oxford University Press, Oxford, 1971. Deriving from *con* (together) + *sortem* (lot), the noun 'consort' relates to 'holding title in common'. In the 1721 first edition of *Nathan Bailey's Universal Etymological Dictionary*, the term is given as 'The wife of a sovereign prince'.

12 In some *Gospel of Philip* translations, the Greek word *koinonôs* has been translated as 'companion'. Linguistic scholars have pointed out however that, although not wholly incorrect in the broader sense, *koinonôs* is a singular term with conjugal connotations that should more correctly be translated as 'consort'. *See* R McL Wilson, *The Gospel of Philip: Translated from the Coptic Text*, pp 35, 97.

13 *The Catholic Encyclopedia*, vol II – St Athanasius.

14 The Gospel of Thomas in *The Nag Hammadi Library*.

15 St Clement of Alexandria, *Clementine Homilies and Apostolical Constitutions* (trans, William Whiston), Ante-Nicene Library, T & T Clark, Edinburgh, 1870, introduction, p 3.

16 E Pagels, *The Gnostic Gospels*, ch 3, p 60.

17 Carla Ricci, *Mary Magdalene and Many Others*, Fortress Press, Minneapolis, MN, 1994, ch 1, p 23.

18 *Talmud*, sota 19a.

19 E Pagels, *The Gnostic Gospels*, ch 3, p 65.

CHAPTER 9: THE SACRED MARRIAGE

1 JR Porter, *The Illustrated Guide to the Bible*, Duncan Baird, London, 1995, p 12.

2 *Diatessaron*: Late Latin, from Greek – *dia tessaron khordon sumphonia* – 'concord through four notes', from *dia* (through) + *tessares* (four). For details, *see* WL Peterson 'Taitan's Diatessaron' in Helmut Koester, *Ancient Christian Gospels: Their History and Development*, SCM Press, London, 1990, pp 403–30.

3 Gospels were produced by the monks of Lindisfarne off the north-eastern coast of England in c950, while in Europe, elements were transcribed into Slavonic, the liturgical language of what is now called the Old Church.

4 In chapter 2 – 'Brothers and Sisters' and chapter 4 – 'Marriage Regulations'.

5 *Dr Smith's Bible Dictionary* – referenced in J Fleetwood, *The Life of Our Lord and Saviour Jesus Christ* – states that the original word signifies a 'lodging-place for the night'. Inns, in the Western sense, were unknown in the ancient Near East.

6 AN Wilson, *Jesus*, ch 4, p 80.

7 *The Oxford Concise English Dictionary* (ed, Della Thompson), Oxford University Press, Oxford, 1995 – Manger: 'A long open box or trough in a stable, etc., for horses or cattle to eat from'.

8 *The Oxford Compact English Dictionary* (Oxford Word Library: OWL Micrographic) – Harlot.

9 *Nathan Bailey's Universal Etymological Dictionary* – Harlot.

10 Samuel Noel Kramer, *The Sacred Marriage Rite*, Indiana University Press, Bloomington, AL, 1969, ch 4, p 84.

11 The city state of Ur of the Chaldees (or Ur of Chaldaea) was the site of the Inanna ziggurat tower in Sumer, north of the Persian Gulf (now southern Iraq).

12 Henri Frankfort, *Kingship and the Gods*, University of Chicago Press, Chicago, IL, 1948, p 246. The term *lugal* stems from From *lu* (man) and *gal* (great) – so, 'great man'.

13 Colin Wilson and John Grant, *The Directory of Possibilities*, Webb & Bower, Exeter, 1981, p 37.

14 A Phoenician coin bearing this emblem is illustrated in the HarperCollins 2003 edition of Laurence Gardner, *Realm of the Ring Lords*, ch 5, p 54.

15 AN Wilson, *Jesus*, ch 2, p 26.

16 Michael Baigent, Richard Leigh and Henry Lincoln, *The Messianic Legacy*, Jonathan Cape, London, 1986, ch 6, p 67.

17 This has been made apparent in recent times by the Campaign for the Ordination of Women in the Roman Catholic Church http://www.womenpriests.org.

18 John Wijngaards, *No Women in Holy Orders?* Canterbury Press, Norwich, 2002, p 158.

19 2 Thessalonians 2:2.

20 JR Porter, *The Illustrated Guide to the Bible*, p 239.

21 *Ibid*, p 241.

22 1 Timothy 2:11–12 – 'Let the woman learn in silence with all subjection. But I suffer not a woman to teach, nor to usurp authority over the man, but to be in silence'.

23 J Wijngaards, *No Women in Holy Orders?* appendix 'The Texts', pp 156–205.

24 *The Catholic Encyclopedia*, vol XI – St Olympias.

25 'Women in the Christian Revision' in B Thiering, *Jesus the Man*, appendix III, pp 366–71.

26 In relating Jesus' lineage, Matthew and Luke do not agree on the genealogy from King David. Matthew gives the kingly line from Solomon, whereas Luke details a descent from Nathan, another of David's sons. This segment of the list in Matthew contains twenty two ancestors, against twenty in Luke. However, both lists eventually coincide at Zerubbabel, whom they agree was the direct and immediate heir of Shealtiel. But even this is subject to debate for, whereas the Old Testament books of Ezra 3:2 and Haggai 1:1 confirm that Zerubbabel was

born into Shealtiel's family, there could have been a generation between the two – a possible son of Shealtiel named Pedaiah, who would then have been Zerubbabel's father. The account in 1 Chronicles 3:19 is confusing in this regard.

The main difference between Matthew and Luke concerns the ancestors from the time of David to the era of the Israelites's return from Babylonian captivity. For this term, the equivalent list in 1 Chronicles is in general accord with Matthew's genealogy. Then, having converged on Zerubbabel, the lists in Matthew and Luke diverge again. Matthew traces Jesus' descent through a son named Abiud, while Luke takes a course via a son called Rhesa.

Jesus' paternal grandfather is called Jacob according to Matthew 1:16 but, in Luke 3:23, he is said to be Heli. Both versions are correct, however, for Joseph's father, Heli, held the distinction of 'Jacob' in his patriarchal capacity (*see* B Thiering, *Jesus the Man*, ch 5, p 29.)

The genealogical list in Matthew, from David to Jacob-Heli (spanning about 1,000 years) contains 25 generations at 40 years each. Luke, on the other hand, gives 40 generations at 25 years each. Hence, Luke places Jesus in the 20th generation from Zerubbabel, whereas Matthew places him in the 11th. Through this latter period of around 530 years, the Matthew list supports a 53-year generation standard, while Luke is more comprehensible with its 28-year standard.

27 J Fleetwood, *The Life of Our Lord and Saviour Jesus Christ*, ch 1, pp 10–11. An extract by Dr Paxton outlines the customary rules of Jewish matrimony as distinct from the more restrictive dynastic regulations.
28 B Thiering, *Jesus the Man*, ch 8, pp 43–49, and appendix I, p 177.
29 F Josephus, *The Wars of the Jews*, bk II, ch 8:13.
30 B Thiering, *Jesus the Man*, ch 7, p 42, and appendix I, p 209.
31 William Barclay, *The Mind of Jesus*, SCM Press, London, 1971, ch 9, pp 87–8.
32 'The Community Rule' in Geza Vermes, *The Complete Dead Sea Scrolls in English*, Penguin, London, 1998, pp 105, 120.
33 B Thiering, *Jesus the Man*, ch 4, p 24.
34 John Shelby Spong, *Born of a Woman*, HarperSanFrancisco, San Francisco, CA, 1992, ch 13, pp 187–99.
35 The complete time-frame and dates for these events is given in appendix I, 'Chronology' in B Thiering, *Jesus the Man,*, pp 221–2.
36 *Ibid*, appendix III, p 367.

CHAPTER 10: THE INHERITORS

1 J Hastings (ed), *Dictionary of the Bible* – Messiah.

2 Michael Baigent and Richard Leigh, *The Dead Sea Scrolls Deception*, Jonathan Cape, London, 1991, ch 9, p 141. This 'Messiah' entry in *War Rule*, ch XI, is sometimes given as 'Thine Anointed' (for instance, in G Vermes, *The Complete Dead Sea Scrolls in English*, Penguin, London, 1998).

3 'The Messianic Rule' in Geza Vermes, *The Dead Sea Scrolls in English*, Penguin, London, 1995, pp 119–22.

4 *Lutterworth Dictionary of the Bible* (ed, Watson E Mills), Lutterworth Press, Cambridge, 1994 – Anointing.

5 Spikenard is a fragrant, sweet-smelling ointment compounded from the Himalayan nard plant. Growing only at heights of around 15,000 feet (about 4,570 metres), it was very expensive.

6 Anointing at Bethany – Matthew 26:6–13, Mark 14:3–9, John 12:1–7.

7 Previous anointing by Mary – Luke 7:36–50.

8 'Lexicon & Pesher' in B Thiering, *Jesus of the Apocalypse*, p 240.

9 Spikenard was also used as an unguent in funerary rites. It was customary for a grieving widow to place a broken vial of the ointment in her late husband's tomb. *See* M Starbird, *The Woman with the Alabaster Jar*, ch 2, pp 40–1. It was for this reason that Mary went to the tomb of Jesus (John 20:1).

10 Matthew 26:7, Mark 14:4, John 12:2–3.

11 The Psalm 23, verse 5.

12 M Starbird, *The Woman with the Alabaster Jar*, ch 11, pp 35–6.

13 Barbara G Walker, *The Woman's Encyclopedia of Myths and Secrets*, HarperSanFrancisco, San Francisco, CA, 1983, p 501 – Kingship.

14 AM Hocart, *Kingship*, Oxford University Press, Oxford, 1927, ch 8, p 103.

15 SN Kramer, *The Sacred Marriage Rite*, ch 5, pp 85–6.

16 Samuel Macauley Jackson (ed), *The Schaff-Herzog Encyclopedia of Religious Knowledge*, Baker Book House, Grand Rapids, MI, 1953 – Song of Solomon.

17 J Hastings (ed), *Dictionary of the Bible* – Song of Solomon.

18 Bernard de Clairvaux, *Patriologia Latina* (ed, JP Minge), Paris, 1854, vol 183, cols, 1050–5.

19 M Starbird, *The Goddess in the Gospels: Reclaiming the Sacred Feminine*, Bear & Co, Santa Fe, NM, 1998.

20 B Thiering, *Jesus the Man*, appendix I, 'Chronology', pp 177–8, 196.

21 Further prophecies also in Zachariah 12:10 and 13:6.

22 John Michell, *Dimensions of Paradise*, Thames and Hudson, London, 1988, ch 1, p 18.

23 John Michell, *The City of Revelation*, Garnstone, London 1971, p 91.

24 M Starbird, *Goddess in the Gospels*, appendix 2, pp 157–8.

25 *Ibid*, p 177.

26 B Thiering, *Jesus the Man*, appendix III, p 367.

27 Matthew 26:6–7, Mark 14:3, John 12:1–3.

28 The fact that Jesus is mentioned in connection with the 'times of restitution' (Acts 3:21) indicates that he had become a parent and was obliged to lead a celibate existence for a predetermined time. There is no suggestion that this child was a son, which means that the child was a daughter. Damaris is mentioned in Acts 17:34.

29 B Thiering, *Jesus the Man*, appendix I, p 297 and p 299; appendix III, pp 363–4.

30 Salem – *shalom*, as for Jerusalem (*Yerushalom*): City of Peace.

31 G Vermes, *The Complete Dead Sea Scrolls in English*, p 85.

32 Luke 1:34–36.

33 Matthew 3, Mark 1, Luke 3, John 1:32, 3:26.

34 For the Qumrân notion of the two Messiahs, *see* John Allegro, *The Dead Sea Scrolls*, Penguin, London, 1964, ch 13, pp 167–72.

35 Tetrarch: the ruler of a fourth part of a kingdom, as against Ethnarch: the ruler of a nation or tribe within a kingdom.

36 F Josephus, *The Antiquities of the Jews*, bk XVIII, ch 5:4.

37 B Thiering, *Jesus of the Apocalypse*, ch 6, pp 53–4.

38 The Gospel narrative was geared to comply with the prophecy of Micah 5:2, which dates from c710 BC: 'But thou, Bethlehem Ephratah [fruitful], though thou be little … yet out of thee shall he come forth unto me that is to be ruler in Israel'. *See* also B Thiering, *Jesus the Man*, ch 9, pp 50–2.

39 B Thiering, *Jesus the Man*, ch 29, p 133.

40 John 3:30.

CHAPTER 11: THE GRAIL CHILD

1 Simon is honoured as the first missionary priest in Cyprus. The main church in Larnaca is dedicated to him under his other New Testament name, Lazarus. He is said to have been the first Bishop of Larnaca.

2 Proselytes were Gentiles converted to Judaism.

3 B Thiering, *Jesus the Man*, ch 31, pp 143–4.

4 JW Taylor, *The Coming of the Saints*, ch 6, p 103.

5 Christopher Witcombe, 'The Chapel of the Courtesan and the Quarrel of the Magdalens' in *Art Bulletin*, New York, 1 July 2002, vol 84, no 2, pp 273–92.

6 *See* 'ancient texts' references in LS Lewis, *Joseph of Arimathea at Glastonbury*, pp 58–80.

7 Salome's baptismal name was Helena. As the spiritual adviser to Princess Salome, daughter of Herodias, she too was called Salome in accordance with custom. Helena-Salome was the mother of the apostles James and John Boanerges, the sons of Zebedee (by which name Simon was also known – *see* B Thiering, *Jesus the Man*, appendix III, p 333).

8 In medieval Britain, mermaids were called 'merrimaids', while in Ireland they were 'merrows'.

9 Originally *gypcian*, as per Egypcian – *Oxford Concise English Dictionary*.

10 R Graves, *The White Goddess*, ch 22, p 395.

11 *Ibid*, ch 22, p 395.

12 Gladys Taylor, *Our Neglected Heritage*, Covenant Books, London, 1974, vol 1, p 17.

13 B Thiering, *Jesus the Man*, ch 31, p 141.

14 Acts 18:7. *See* also B Thiering, *Jesus the Man* appendix I, p 268.

15 The colour black, as used for ecclesiastical garb, has associations far older than Christianity. The tall black statue of Isis at the Church of St Germain, Paris, was identified as the Virgin of Paris until the 16th century. The original abbey on the site was built for the Merovingian King Childebert I above a Temple of Isis. It housed Childebert's relics from the treasures of Solomon and was a burial-place for the Merovingian Kings of the Franks. *See* ECM Begg, *The Cult of the Black Virgin*, ch 2, p 66. The Benedictine monks of St Germain-des-Prés wore black cassocks in the Nazarite tradition. A statue of St Genevieve was erected in the Benedictine chapel. She was perceived as a successor to Isis in France, and was a close friend of King Clovis.

16 It was in AD 62 that Ananus the younger, a Sadducee brother of Jonathan Annas, became High Priest. As such, he was predisposed towards furthering the Sanhedrin's opposition to James and his Nazarene ideals.

17 The stoning took place in AD 62 according to F Josephus, *The Antiquities of the Jews*, bk XX, ch 9:1.

18 The only time that Jewish forces ever dented Roman military pride again was in AD 132, when they revolted once more under the leadership of Simon Ben Kochba, Prince of Israel. Simon assembled a large army of native volunteers, together with professional mercenary soldiers from abroad. His battle plan included many strategic operations, some of which made use of tunnels and underground chambers beneath Jerusalem. Within one year, Jerusalem was recaptured from the Romans. Jewish administration was established and maintained for two years. But outside the city the struggle continued and the final strategy depended on military assistance from Persia. However, when the Persian forces were ready to set out for the Holy Land, Persia was invaded. Its troops had to stay and defend their own territory, with the result that Simon and his gallant band were not able to counter the advance of the twelve Roman legions, who had regrouped in Syria at the command of Emperor Hadrian. Simon's men were eventually overwhelmed at Battin, west of Jerusalem, in AD 135.

19 Edessa, now Urfa in Turkey, as opposed to Edessa in Greece.

20 Matthew 13:55, Mark 6:3.

21 Strictly speaking, a *paranymphos* was one who ceremonially conducted a bride to her bridegroom.

22 Professor Fida Hassnain, *A Search for the Historical Jesus – from Apocryphal, Buddhist, Islamic & Sanscrit Sources*, Gateway Books, Bath, 1994.

23 B Thiering, *Jesus the Man*, ch 33, p 151.

24 B Thiering, *Jesus of the Apocalypse*, ch 3, p 31. This work details the full sequence of events in respect of the Messianic family history as recounted in The Revelation.

25 John 21:7, 21:20.

26 *See* Chapter 7 – 'Martha'.

27 Revelation 1:4.

CHAPTER 12: REALM OF THE *DESPOSYNI*

1 *Dictionnaire étymologique des noms de lieux en France* – Aix.

2 G Vermes, *The Complete Dead Sea Scrolls in English*, Community Rule VII, pp 108–109. *See* also M Baigent and R Leigh, *The Dead Sea Scrolls Deception*, ch 9, pp 140–1, and Robert H Eisenman, *Maccabees, Zadokites, Christians and Qumrân*, EJ Brill, Leiden, 1983, p 42.

3 B Thiering, *Jesus the Man*, appendix II, 'Locations: The System for Boats', pp 325–31.

4 *Ibid*, ch 18, p 91.

5 There were not actually 5,000 people at this symbolic feeding. The 'Five Thousand' was the name applied to a body of non-Jews native to Palestine and who were described as the 'Sons of Ham' – regarded as the founder of the Hamitic tribes of the region. The Community's liaison officer with the Five Thousand was Jesus' apostle John Boanerges. *See* B Thiering, *Jesus the Man*, appendix III, p 357.

6 Again there were not 4,000 recipients involved. This 'Four Thousand' (the Men of Shem) was another particular group of Gentiles. Together with the Proselytes (converts to Judaism) called the 'Three Thousand', the Five Thousand and the Four Thousand were held to comprise part of the especially cosmopolitan tribe of Asher.

7 *The High History of the Holy Grail (Perlesvaus)*, (trans, Sebastian Evans), Everyman, London, 1912.

8 *Dictionnaire étymologique des noms de lieux en France* – Dax.

9 Watson E Mills (ed), *Lutterworth Dictionary of the Bible* – Bethlehem.

10 The Egyptian mountain-top temple of *Serâbît el Khâdim*, Sinai, discovered in 1904. *See* WM Flinders Petrie, *Researches in Sinai*, John Murray, London, 1906.

11 The treasure relief of Pharaoh Tuthmosis III, c1450 BC, at the Temple of Karnak.

12 1 Samuel 21:6.

13 Greek *Septuagint* Bible – Old Testament, 3 Kings 5:7.

14 *The Times Atlas of the Bible*, Times Books, London, 1994, p 147.

15 The route used by the Jewish metal traders was described by Diodorus Siculus in the days of Emperor Augustus (63 BC to AD 14): 'The tin ore is transported from Britain into Gaul, the merchants carrying it on horseback through the heart of Celtica to Marseilles and the city called Narbo[nne]'.It was then taken by ship across the Mediterranean Sea to any of several destinations. *See* JW Taylor, *The Coming of the Saints*, ch 8, p 143.

16 Matthew 27:57–60.

17 In modern terms of Western monarchical structure, this would be equivalent to the princely style, His Royal Highness.

18 B Thiering, *Jesus the Man*, appendix III, p 353.

19 LS Lewis, *Joseph of Arimathea at Glastonbury*, p 54.

20 A hide was an area of land reckoned agriculturally to support one family for one year with one plough – equal in Somerset (the Glastonbury shire) to 120 acres (about 48½ hectares).

21 The Tabernacle is described in Exodus 26 and 36.

22 LS Lewis, *Joseph of Arimathea at Glastonbury*, pp 15–16.

23 Writing in about AD 600, St Augustine described: 'There is on the western confines of Britain a certain royal island called in ancient speech Glastonia … In it, the earliest Angle neophytes of the Catholic doctrine – God guiding them – found a church not made by any man, they say, but prepared by God Himself for the salvation of mankind, which church the Heavenly Builder Himself declared (by many miracles and mysteries of healing) he had consecrated to Himself and to Holy Mary, Mother of God'. *See* William of Malmesbury, *The Antiquities of Glastonbury*, Talbot/JMF Books, Llanerch, 1980, p 1.

24 Willis Barnstone (ed), *The Other Bible*, HarperSanFrancisco, San Francisco, 1984, p 368.

25 Gregory of Tours, *A History of the Franks* (trans, Lewis Thorpe), Penguin, London, 1964, bk 1:21, p 82.

26 In the Howard collection at Naworth Castle in Cumbria.

27 Tin is essential to the production of bronze, and the most important tin mines were in south-west England – an area also rich in copper and lead, for which there was a great market in the expanding Roman Empire. The British Museum contains two splendid examples of lead from the Mendip mines near Glastonbury, dated AD 49 and AD 60 respectively. In Latin, one bears the name of 'Britannicus, son of the Emperor Claudius', and the other is inscribed, 'British lead: property of the Emperor Nero'.

28 Genesis 4:22 and Exodus 35:30–32, respectively.

29 Matthaei Parisiensis, *Chronica Majora* (rep, Matthew Paris, *The Chronicles of Matthew Paris*, Palgrave Macmillan, London, 1984).

30 Stoning was not generally a method of execution. It was more often a way of hounding a denounced victim out of an area of the city, or out of the city altogether.

31 LS Lewis, *Joseph of Arimathea at Glastonbury*, p 15. Following the union of Scotland with England and Wales, the king's title was adjusted to the less pious His Britannic Majesty.

32 The Cistercian *Vulgate Cycle* contains the *Estoire del Graal*, the *Queste del Saint Graal* and the *Livres de Lancelot*, as well as other tales of Arthur and Merlin.

33 In the 1st century, mainland Britain (England, Wales and Scotland) was generally known as Albion. The Irish called it Alba – a name which was later restricted to the Scottish North after the Irish Scots had settled in

the Western Highlands of Dalriada. By the 900s Alba had been adapted to Albany, and the alternative name, Scotland (or Scotia), emerged about a century later.

The Gaelic term *Scotia* (from which the names Scots and Scotland derive) was inherited from Princess Scota, daughter of Pharaoh Nechonibus (Nekau I) of Egypt (610–555 BC). She gained the name Scota (Scythian: *Sco-ta* = Ruler of people) when she married Galamh of Scythia (also known as Milidh). Thereafter, she moved to Ireland with her sons following Galamh's death in Spain. It was King Nial Noighiallach and the Dal Riàta who gave the name Scotia to Alba during the 4th century AD. *See* Geoffrey Keating, *The History of Ireland* (trans, David Comyn and Rev PS Dinneen), Irish Texts Society, London, 1904–14, vol I, p 102; vol II, pp 44, 46, 58, 78, 372, 374.

34 This has been mistakenly transcribed in some books as 'Isle of Glass'.
35 Roger Sherman Loomis, in *The Grail: From Celtic Myth to Christian Symbolism*, University of Wales Press, Cardiff, 1963, makes the point that proper names in manuscript transmission sometimes lose their initial letter – although mutation of the initial letters of names is a feature of the Celtic languages. By this process, Morgaine is sometimes found as Orguein and, with specific relevance to the present case, Galains (Galaain) becomes Alain (Alaain).
36 *The Grand Saint Grail* (*Estoire del Saint Graal*) confirms that, on the death of Alain, the Lordship of the Grail passed to Josue – although defining him as Alain's brother rather than his cousin.
37 The foremost chronicles of Glastonbury are: William of Malmesbury (1090–1143), *De Antiquitate Glastoniensis Ecclesiæ*, and John of Glastonbury, *Cronica sive Antiquitates Glastoniensis Ecclesie* (c1400), Boydell & Brewer, Woodbridge, 1985.

CHAPTER 13: THE HOLY BALM

1 Llanover MS B1, and Cardiff MS 16.
2 A selection of ancient Welsh manuscripts, in prose and verse, from a collection made by Edward Williams (known as Iolo Morganwg – Iolo of Glamorgan) 1747–1826, and proposed as materials for a new history of Wales. Published as: Taliesin Williams, Iolo Morganwg, Thomas Price, Owen Jones, and the Society for the Publication of Ancient Welsh Manuscripts. Abergavenny, *Iolo Manuscripts*, W. Rees, Llandovery and Longman & Co., London, 1848.
3 LS Lewis, *Joseph of Arimathea at Glastonbury*, pp 68–69, 78–79.
4 Chapter 5 – 'The Holy Balm'.
5 *Genealogies of the Welsh Princes* in Harleian MS 3859.
6 Siluria was part of the west of England and a part of South Wales.

7 G Taylor, *Our Neglected Heritage*, bk I, p 33.
8 Because of this, Alain is sometimes shown in family lists as the son of Brân the patriarch.
9 Saraz is now Gaza. *See* Professor S Hewins, *The Royal Saints of Britain*, Chiswick Press, London, 1929, p 18.
10 F Josephus, *The Antiquities of the Jews*, bk XX, ch 1:1.
11 RS Loomis, *The Grail: From Celtic Myth to Christian Symbolism*, ch 12, p 187.
12 *Ibid*, ch 12, p 179.
13 From *Corpus benedictum*.
14 For example – published in 1966: *The Good News Bible* and *The Jerusalem Bible* in English.
15 *Codex Vaticanus* MS 1209.
16 M Starbird, *The Woman with the Alabaster Jar*, ch 2, pp 40–41. (Mark 16:1 makes the point that anointing was the purpose of visiting the tomb.)
17 John 20:1.
18 James King Hewison, *The Isle of Bute in the Olden Time*, William Blackwood, Edinburgh, 1895, Chart XXIII.
19 *The Catholic Encyclopedia*, vol VI – Symbolism of the Fish.
20 J Allegro, *The Dead Sea Scrolls*, ch 7, p 110.
21 A transcript of Eleutherius' reply to King Lucius in AD 177 is given in JW Taylor, *The Coming of the Saints*, appendix K.
22 *The Anglo-Saxon Chronicle* (trans, Michael Swanton), JM Dent, London, 1997 – Winchester MS (A) & Peterborough MS (E), AD 167.
23 Lucius died on 3 December 201, and was buried at St Mary le Lode in Gloucester. His remains were later reinterred at St Peter's Church, Cornhill, in London. References in Roman martyrology to the burial of Lucius at Chur in Switzerland are inaccurate on two counts. They actually relate to King Lucius of Bavaria (not to Lucius the Luminary of Britain). Moreover, the Bavarian Lucius died at Curia in Germany, not at Chur in Switzerland.

CHAPTER 14: KINGDOMS AND COLOURS

1 For a full account of the history of this family and its various branches, *see* Laurence Gardner, *Bloodline of the Holy Grail* (HarperCollins, 2002 edition), ch 13, pp 150–9.
2 Brân the Blessed is often erroneously cited as being the father of Caractacus. They were indeed contemporaries in the 1st century AD, but Caractacus' father was Cymbeline of Camulod. As the Archdruid of Britain, Brân was the 'spiritual' father of the Pendragon, Caractacus.
3 Lucius was the grandson of Brân's daughter Penardun of Siluria. She is sometimes held to have been the daughter of Beli Mawr, or sometimes his sister. She was, however, the sister of the later Beli, son of Brân. Penardun was a protégée of Queen Boudicca.
4 Gabràn was a grandson of Fergus mac Erc, who was born of Gaelic Scots

royalty in descent from the High King Conaire Mór of Ireland. Fergus left Ireland in the latter 5th century in order to colonize the Western Highlands, taking with him his brothers Loarn and Angus. Loarn's family occupied the region of northern Argyll, thereafter known as Loarna (or Lorne), based at Dunollie, Oban.

5 Individual annals cite different names for this conflict and/or its location. Names for the location include Mount Badon, Mons Badonicus, Dun Baedàn and Cath Badwn (in which *mount* and *mons* imply a hill; *dun* implies either a hill or a hill-fort, and *cath* represents a stronghold). Names for the battle include *Bellum Badonis* and *Obsessio Badonica* (the first suggesting a war and the second a siege).

6 The battle is cited in the *Bodleian Manuscripts*, the *Book of Leinster*, the *Book of Ballymote* and the *Chronicles of the Scots*, and all give the date as 516. *See* William Forbes Skene, *Chronicles of the Picts and Scots*, HM General Register, Edinburgh, 1867.

The Scots commander is sometimes named as Aedàn mac Gabràn of Dalriada, but Aedàn had not yet been born. The leader was his father, Prince Gabràn, who became King of Dalriada in 537. Aedàn and his eldest son, Arthur, fought at the second battle of Dun Baedàn, which took place in 575.

Despite the definitive date of 516 cited in the chronicles, there has been a great deal of speculation about the first battle. This has arisen because researchers have been directed to Gildas I, who is mistakenly identified as the author of *De Excidio*. But he lived 425–512, and was thus already dead when Gildas II was born in 516 – the year of the battle, as he made a point of stating in his account.

Other selected works on the subject of Britain in the Dark Ages are Myles Dillon and Nora K Chadwick, *The Celtic Realms*, Weidenfeld & Nicolson, London, 1967; Nora K Chadwick and Hector Munro Chadwick, *Studies in Early British History*, Cambridge University Press, Cambridge, 1954; Hector Munro Chadwick, *Early Scotland: The Picts, Scots and Welsh of Southern Scotland*, Cambridge University Press, Cambridge, 1949; William Forbes Skene, *Celtic Scotland*, David Douglas, Edinburgh, 1886–1890; R Cunliffe Shaw, *Post-Roman Carlisle and the Kingdoms of the North-West*, Guardian Press, Preston, 1964; Eoin MacNeill, *Celtic Ireland*, (Martin Lester, Dublin, 1921), Academy Press, Dublin, 1981; Peter Hunter Blair, *The Origins of Northumbria*, Northumberland Press, Gateshead, 1948.

7 The title of Merlin ('Seer to the King') was long established in the Druid tradition. Prior to Emrys, the appointed Merlin was Taliesin the Bard, husband of Viviane I del Acqs. At his death in 540, the title passed to Emrys of Powys, who was the famous Merlin of Arthurian tradition.

Merlin Emrys was an elder cousin of King Aedàn and was, therefore, in a position to request that the new king take action against Gwenddolau's killer. Aedàn, therefore, complied and duly demolished Rhydderch's Court of Alcut at Dumbarton.

8 The name Arthur is sometimes reckoned to derive from the Latin *Artorius*, but this is quite incorrect. The Arthurian name was purely Celtic, emerging from the Irish *Artur*. The 3rd-century sons of King Art were Cormac and Artur. Irish names were not influenced by the Romans and the root of the name Arthur can be found as far back as the 5th century BC, when Artur mes Delmann was King of the Lagain.

9 The name Uther Pendragon was invented in the 12th century by the romancer Geoffrey of Monmouth (later Bishop of St Asaph), and the Gaelic word *uther* (or *uthir*) was simply an adjective meaning 'terrible'.

10 A more complete history of King Arthur can be found in Laurence Gardner, *Bloodline of the Holy Grail* (HarperCollins 2002 edition), ch 14, pp 160–73. From this, certain aspects concerning the Welsh tradition of King Arthur are expanded in Laurence Gardner, *Realm of the Ring Lords* (HarperCollins 2003 edition), ch 8, pp 91–102.

11 As note 6: WF Skene, *Chronicles of the Picts and Scots*.

12 Saint Adamnan, *A Life of Saint Columba* (trans, Wentworth Huyshe), George Routledge, London, 1908.

13 Tract on the 'Tributes Paid to Baedàn, King of Ulster' in WF Skene, the *Chronicles of the Picts and Scots*.

14 Tigernach hua Braein, *The Annals of Tigernach*, AD 595, Rawlinson 3rd fragment in *Revue Celtique 17* at Bodleian Library, Oxford.

15 The Celtic Church ecclesiastical seat of the Kings of Scots.

16 This was at a time before the unified nation of England. It was not until 927 that Alfred the Great's grandson, Aethelstan, was recognized as overall king by the majority of Anglo-Saxon territorial groupings.

17 HRH Prince Michael of Albany, *The Forgotten Monarchy of Scotland*, ch 2, p 18.

18 Whitley Stokes (ed), *Félire Óengusso Céli Dé (The Martyrology of Oengus the Culdee)*, Dublin Institute for Advanced Studies, Dublin, 1984, Item: January, note 27, p 53.

19 *The Catholic Encyclopedia*, vol V – Ecclesiastical Art.

20 S Haskins, *Mary Magdalen, Myth and Metaphor*, ch 3, pp 58–9.

21 An excellent book concerning the rules, regulations, fashions and traditions of Marian artwork is Anna Jameson, *Legends of the Madonna*, Houghton Mifflin, Boston, 1895.

22 *Ibid*, introduction, pp 40–1.

23 M Starbird, *The Woman With the Alabaster Jar*, ch 6, p 123.

24 A Jameson, *Legends of the Madonna*, introduction, p 21.

NOTES AND REFERENCES

CHAPTER 15: LEONARDO DA VINCI

1 Serge Bramly, *Leonardo the Artist and Man*, Penguin, London, 1994, p 362.
2 Dan Brown, *The Da Vinci Code*, Bantam Press, London, 2003, ch 26, pp 121–2.
3 Patrice Boussel, *Leonardo da Vinci*, Nouvelles Éditions Françaises, Paris, 1986, p 88.
4 Bülent Atalay, *Math and the Mona Lisa*, Smithsonian Books, Washington, DC, 2004, ch 9, p 177.
5 Housed at the National Gallery of Art, Washington, DC, this is the only Leonardo painting outside Europe. Ginevra was the daughter of Florentine banker Amerigo de' Benci.
6 Cecilia was the mistress of Duke Ludovicio Sforza of Milan.
7 Don Pierce, *How to Decorate Mats*, Cameron, San Raphael, CA, 1985, p 5.
8 For example, http://ccins.camosun.bc.ca/~jbritton/goldslide/jbgoldslide.htm.
9 Both of these paintings carry Leonardo's fingerprint, as does the *Madonna of the Rocks* at the National Gallery in London.
10 D Brown, *The Da Vinci Code*, ch 26, pp 118–21.
11 Vitruvius, *De Architecture*, Rome, bk III, ch 1.
12 P Boussel, *Leonardo da Vinci*, p 88.
13 B Atalay, *Math and the Mona Lisa*, ch 8, p 152.
14 Including Bernini, Artemisia Gentileschi, Nicolas Poussin, Simon Vouet, Pietro da Cortona, Anthony Van Dyck, and Alessandro Turchi.
15 S Bramly, *Leonardo the Artist and Man*, p 362.
16 Giuliano's tomb in the Medici chapel in the Church of San Lorenzo, is ornamented with the *Night and Day* of Michelangelo, along with a statue of Giuliano by Michelangelo. Due to the identical name he shares with his uncle (they are both Giuliano de Medici), whose tomb is also in the Medici chapel, this tomb is often mistaken for that of his uncle.
17 Giorgio Vasari, *Le Vite de' Piú Eccelenti Architetti, Pittori, et Scultori Italiani*, Firenza, 1550, part III – Leonardo.
18 B Atalay, *Math and the Mona Lisa*, ch 1, pp 1–2.
19 *Ibid*, ch 3, p 37.
20 Helmut Ruhemann, 'A refutation of Gombrich's contention that Leonardo deliberately cuts down on information by his sfumato, which G. conceives as an all-over blurring' in *The British Journal of Aesthetics*, I, 1961, pp 231–37.
21 Italian sculptor of the Florentine school (1427–79).
22 B Atalay, *Math and the Mona Lisa*, ch 9, p 176.
23 D Brown, *The Da Vinci Code*, ch 30, p 131.
24 Confraternità dell' Immaculata Concezione.
25 The Immaculate Conception became official dogma in 1584.
26 A form of decoration made by scratching through a surface layer to show a different coloured under-surface.

27 Martin Kemp, *Leonardo on Painting*, Yale University Press, New Haven, CT, 2001, pt VI, pp 268, 270. *See* also S Bramly, *Leonardo, the Artist and Man*, p 185, and A Bülent, *Math and the Mona Lisa*, ch 9, p 165. *Spinnchristi* is a flower representative of Christ's passion.

28 At the Staatliche Museen, Berlin.

29 At the Galleria degli Uffizi, Florence.

30 A valuable coin of either gold or silver minted in several European countries. Originally struck in the dominions of Dukes, they had a market value, but were not always legal tender.

31 M Kemp, *Leonardo on Painting*, pt VI, p 253.

32 D Brown, *The Da Vinci Code*, ch 32, p 138.

33 A folio list and concordance of all manuscript sources of the *Codex Urbinas* and 'Original Leonardo Manuscripts' is given in M Kemp, *Leonardo on Painting*, pp 297–310.

34 P Boussel, *Leonardo da Vinci*, p 27.

35 Helmut Ruhemann, *The Cleaning of Paintings*, Hacker Art Books, New York, NY, 1982, ch 7, p 230.

36 There is a write-up regarding the Louvre cleaning in Guy Iznard, *Les Pirates de la Peínture*, Flammarion, Paris, 1955, p 48.

37 H Ruhemann, *The Cleaning of Paintings*, ch 10, pp 231, 259.

38 National Gallery catalogue photograph no 1093 shows the enhanced detail of this.

39 D Brown, *The Da Vinci Code*, ch 32, p 139.

40 For example, S Bramly, *Leonardo, the Artist and Man*, p 189.

41 *The Oxford Concise English Dictionary* – Spadix.

42 *Oxford Concordance to the Bible* – Tamar.

43 *The Septuagint* (trans, LCL Brenton).

CHAPTER 16: THE LAST SUPPER

1 B Atalay, *Math and the Mona Lisa*, ch 9, p 167.

2 A comprehensive record of *The Last Supper* (its history and geometry, with details of copies) is given in Leo Steinberg, *Leonardo's Incessant Last Supper*, Zone Books, New York, NY, 2001.

3 P Boussel, *Leonardo da Vinci*, pp 70–1.

4 *Ibid*, p 71.

5 B Atalay, *Math and the Mona Lisa*, ch 9, p 182.

6 D Brown, *The Da Vinci Code*, ch 40, pp 169–70.

7 Information in this regard can be found at the ArtWatch International subscriber site http://www.artwatchinternational.org.

8 The complete story of this milestone restoration may be found in: Pinin Brambilla Barcilon, and Pietro C Marani, *Leonardo, The Last Supper* – English language edition (trans, Harlow Tighe), University of Chicago Press, Chicago, IL, 2001.

This book presents full-scale reproductions of details from the fresco that clearly display and distinguish Leonardo's hand from that of the restorer. With nearly 400 sumptuous colour reproductions, the most comprehensive technical documentation of the project by Barcilon, and an introductory essay by art historian and project co-director Pietro C Marani that focuses on the history of the mural, *Leonardo, The Last Supper* is an invaluable historic record, an extraordinarily handsome book, and an essential volume for anyone who appreciates the beauty, technical achievements and fate of Renaissance painting.

9 Lynn Picknett and Clive Prince, *Turin Shroud: In Whose Image?* Bloomsbury, London 1994, ch 5, p 105.

10 'The Invention and Composition of Narratives' in M Kemp, *Leonardo on Painting*, pt V, p 226.

11 An early book in the popular domain which discussed Mary Magdalene's intimate relationship with Jesus was the 1982 publication *The Holy Blood and the Holy Grail*. Two of its three authors were Richard Leigh and Michael Baigent. Sir Leigh Teabing's name comes from this source – *Leigh* from the surname Leigh, and *Teabing* an anagram of Baigent.

12 D Brown, *The Da Vinci Code*, ch 58, p 248.

13 Matthew 26:18–30, Mark 14:12–26, Luke 22:1–39, John 13:1–18:1.

14 D Brown, *The Da Vinci Code*, ch 58, p 248.

15 *Ibid*, ch 57, p 236.

16 Matthew 26:27, Mark 14:23–24, Luke 22:20.

17 D Brown, *The Da Vinci Code*, ch 58, p 243.

18 J Allegro, *The Dead Sea Scrolls*, ch 7, p 131; ch 12, p 164; ch 13, p 168.

19 *Scroll of The Rule*, Annex II, 17–22. For the citation as given, *see* the *Messianic Rule* within the *Community Rule*: G. Vermes, *The Complete Dead Sea Scrolls in English* ($_1$QSa=1Q$_2$8a), pp 159–60.

20 L Steinberg, *Leonardo's Incessant Last Supper*, appendix C, p 217.

21 Matthew 26:20, Mark 14:17, Luke 22:14.

22 On occasions, the Last Supper and Mary's anointing of Jesus have been brought together as a single compilation scene. *See* S Haskins, *Mary Magdalen*, ch 6, p 222.

23 Chapter 7 – The Magdalene Archive, and Chapter 6 – Daughter of France.

24 Plate 14.

CHAPTER 17: SACRED ALLEGORY

1 Maurice W Brockwell, *The Pseudo-Arnolfini Portrait*, Chatto & Windus, London 1952, p 10.

2 *Ibid*, ch 2, p 5. The inscription reads:

Pictor Hubertus e Eyck major quo nemo repertus
Incepit pondus: quod Johannes arte secundus
Suscepit letus, Judoci Vyd prece fretus Vers-V seXta Ma-I: Vos CoLLoCat
a Cta tVerI.

The faulty Latin of this cryptic inscription means: 'Hubert van Eyck, the greatest painter that ever lived, began this work [*pondus*], which John, his brother, second only to him in skill, had the happiness to continue at the request of Jodocus (Josse) Vydt. By this line, on the 6th of May, you learn when the work was completed, i.e., MCCCCXXXII'.

It was after 1559 that the quadruple was painted on the shutter, in which Hubert is commemorated as a more important master than Jan, and the last line is a chronogram, in which some of the letters give the year 1432 if read as Roman numerals. The lines are the earliest mentioned to have existed in a text by C van Huerne from about 1616, but were not mentioned by C van Mander in his *Het Schilder-boeck* (Haarlem 1604). When the frames of the altarpiece were restored in Berlin in 1823, some of the words were no longer legible.

3   *Ibid*, ch 6, p 64.
4   In primitive art, especially Italian religious art with multiple characters, the figure who is deemed to be directing the action often has a hand raised.
5   MS 305, France s xv 3/4, fols 106, 106r–108v.
6   RCH Davis, *A History of Medieval Europe*, Longmans, London, 1957, ch 6, pp 120–36.
7   Jan Provost's *The Sacred Allegory* is colour reproduced in the HarperCollins 2002 edition of Laurence Gardner, *Bloodline of the Holy Grail*.
8   C Witcombe, 'The Chapel of the Courtesan and the Quarrel of the Magdalens' in *The Art Bulletin*, vol 84, no 2, pp 273–92.
9   Henry Charles Lea, *History of Sacerdotal Celibacy in the Christian Church*, Watts & Co, London, 1867, pp 271–2.
10 Following Lucrezia, Pope Alexander's other children by Vannozza dei Cattanei were Giovanni, born in 1474, Cesare, born in 1476, and Goffredo, born in 1481.

CHAPTER 18: A SECRET PRIORY

1   This was done by way of a letter to the Sub-Prefecture of Saint-Julien-en-Genevoise.
2   Copies of *Circuit*, in original form, and as later restructured with new right-wing political emphases by Pierre Plantard, are held at the Bibliothèque Nationale de Paris.
3   The Statutes of the Prieuré de Sion were deposited at the Sub-Prefecture in Saint-Julien-en-Genevoise. The official announcement of formation on 25 June 1956 appeared in the *Journal Officiel de la Règublique Français* on 20 July 1956, p 6731.
4   'Les Archives du Prieuré de Sion', by Jean-Luc Chaumeil in *Le Charivari*, no 18, Oct–Dec 1973.
5   The largest circulation regional newspaper in south-west France.
6   Plantard was sentenced to six months' imprisonment on 17 December

1953 by the Court of St Julien-en-Genevoise for breaking the law of *Abus de Confiance*.

7 The Statutes of Alpha Galates were exposed and printed by Chaumeil in *Le Trésor des Templiers*, a reprint of his 1979 work *Le Trésor du Triangle d'Or*, with a new Appendix concerning Pierre Plantard.

8 The story of Saunière's unaccountable rise to wealthy status was brought to wide public attention in the book, *The Holy Blood and the Holy Grail*, by M Baigent, R Leigh and H Lincoln in 1982.

9 Details of the Bishop's hearing are held by la Semaine Religieuse de Carcassonne. On 3 February 1911, it was formally decreed that Saunière was no longer permitted to perform Masses.

10 Records of the Commandery of the Temple of Carcassonne are held in the bibliothèque collection of the Grand Orient de France, and Les archives secrètes des francs-maçons, in Paris.

11 *Ibid*, ch 1, p 5.

12 Pierre Fueugère, Louis Saint-Maxent and Gaston de Koker.

13 This connotation was first suggested in M Baigent, R Leigh and H Lincoln, *The Holy Blood and the Holy Grail*, ch 4, p 72.

14 Chapter 6 – Breath of the Universe.

15 For information concerning Isaac Newton and Royal Society interest in alchemy, *see* Michael White, *Isaac Newton, the Last Sorcerer*, Fourth Estate, London, 1998, chs 6 and 7, pp 104–62.

16 Some useful information concerning the Order of the Realm of Sion can be found in Melville Henry Massue, Marquis de Ruvigny & Raineval 1868–1921, *The Jacobite Peerage, Baronetage, Knightage & Grants of Honour* (1921), fac. reprint Charles Skilton, London, 1974.

17 Andrew Sinclair, *The Sword and the Grail*, Crown, New York, 1992, ch 7, pp 77–8.

18 Edgcumbe Staley, *King René d'Anjou and his Seven Queens*, John Long, London, 1912, ch 1, pp 20–1.

19 *Ibid*, introduction, pp 19–20.

20 *Ibid*, ch 9, p 334.

21 M Baigent, R Leigh and H Lincoln, *The Holy Blood and the Holy Grail*, ch 6, p 101, and appendix pp 375–6.

22 *See* Chapter 7 – Martha.

23 E Staley, *King René d'Anjou and his Seven Queens*, ch 9, p 334.

24 *Ibid*, ch 5, p 143.

25 Written in 1457, the story tells of the chivalric knight Cueur who, in the company of his page Desire, embarks on a perilous journey of courtship to liberate Sweet Grace (*la Dame Doulce-Mercy*) who is being held captive in the Fortress of Resistance by the three enemies of Love, namely Denial, Shame and Fear.

26 'Qui bien beurra, Dieu voira. Qui buerra tout d'une baleine, voira Dieu et la Madeleine'. *See* E Staley, *King René d'Anjou and his Seven Queens*, ch 1, p 29.

BLOODLINE OF THE HOLY GRAIL

Ancestors and Descendants of Jesus from King David to King Arthur

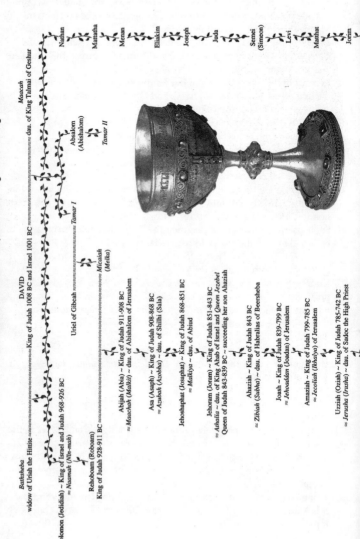

DAVID
~ King of Judah 1008 BC and Israel 1001 BC ~

Bathsheba
widow of Uriah the Hittite

Maacah
dau. of King Talmai of Geshur

Nathan

Mattatha

Menan

Eliakim

Joseph

Juda

Semei
(Simeon)

Levi

Matthat

Jorim

Absalom
(Abishalom)

Tamar II

Uriel of Gibeah

Tamar I

Miccaiah
(*Melka*)

olomon (Jedidiah) ~ King of Israel and Judah 968-926 BC
≈ *Naamah* (*Nin-mah*)

Rehoboam (Roboam)
King of Judah 928-911 BC

Abijah (Abia) ~ King of Judah 911-908 BC
≈ *Maachah* (*Malkit*) ~ dau. of Abishalom of Jerusalem

Asa (Asaph) ~ King of Judah 908-868 BC
≈ *Azubah* (*Azobha*) ~ dau. of Shilhi (Sala)

Jehoshaphat (Josaphat) ~ King of Judah 868-851 BC
≈ *Malkiya* ~ dau. of Abiud

Jehoram (Joram) ~ King of Judah 851-843 BC
≈ *Athalia* ~ dau. of King Ahab of Israel and *Queen Jezebel*
Queen of Judah 843-839 BC ~ succeeding her son Ahaziah

Ahaziah ~ King of Judah 843 BC
≈ *Zibiah* (*Subha*) ~ dau. of Habralias of Beersheba

Joash ~ King of Judah 839-799 BC
≈ *Jehoaddan* (*Joadan*) of Jerusalem

Amaziah ~ King of Judah 799-785 BC
≈ *Jecoliah* (*Ikhalya*) of Jerusalem

Uzziah (Oziah) ~ King of Judah 785-742 BC
≈ *Jerusha* (*Irusha*) ~ dau. of Sadoc the High Priest

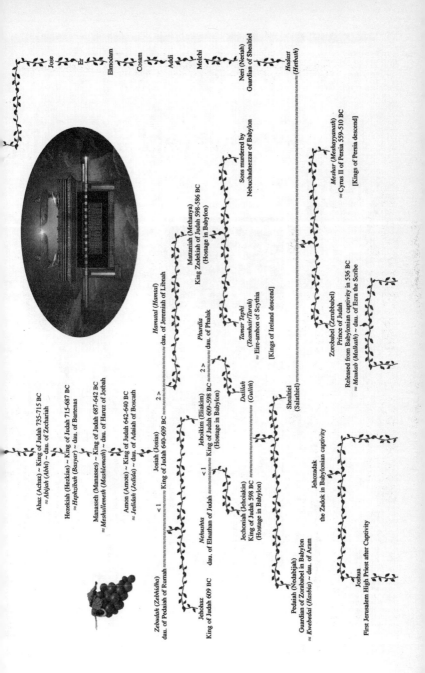

Jose

Er

Elmodam

Cosam

Addi

Melchi

Neri (Neriah)
Guardian of Shealtiel

Hadast (Hethath)

Ahaz (Achaz) ~ King of Judah 735-715 BC
≈ Abijah (Abhi) ~ dau. of Zechariah

Hezekiah (Hezekias) ~ King of Judah 715-687 BC
≈ Hephzibah (Bazyer) ~ dau. of Bartenas

Manasseh (Manasses) ~ King of Judah 687-642 BC
≈ Meshullemeth (Mashlemeth) ~ dau. of Haruz of Jotbah

Amon (Amos) ~ King of Judah 642-640 BC
≈ Jedidah (Jedida) ~ dau. of Adaiah of Boscath

Josiah (Josias) ~ King of Judah 640-609 BC

Zebudah (Zebhidha)
dau. of Pedaiah of Rumah

Hamutal (Hamtal)
dau. of Jeremiah of Libnah

< 1   2 >

Jehoahaz
King of Judah 609 BC

Jehoiakim (Eliakim)
King of Judah 609-598 BC
(Hostage in Babylon)

Mattaniah (Metharya)
King Zedekiah of Judah 598-586 BC
(Hostage in Babylon)

Nehushta
dau. of Elnathan of Judah

Phurdia
dau. of Phalak

Dalilah
(Galith)

Shealtiel
(Salathiel)

Tamar Tephi
(Teamhair/Tarah)
~ Eire-amhon of Scythia

[Kings of Ireland descend]

Sons murdered by
Nebuchadnezzar of Babylon

< 1   2 >

Jechoniah (Jehoiakin)
King of Judah 598 BC
(Hostage in Babylon)

Pedaiah (Nedabijah)
Guardian of Zorababel in Babylon
≈ Kwebedai (Hathia) ~ dau. of Aram

Jehozadak
the Zadok in Babylonian captivity

Zorobabel (Zerubbabel)
Prince of Judah
Released from Babylonian captivity in 536 BC
≈ Mankab (Malkath) ~ dau. of Ezra the Scribe

Meshar (Mesharyanah)
≈ Cyrus II of Persia 559-510 BC

[Kings of Persia descend]

Joshua
First Jerusalem High Priest after Captivity

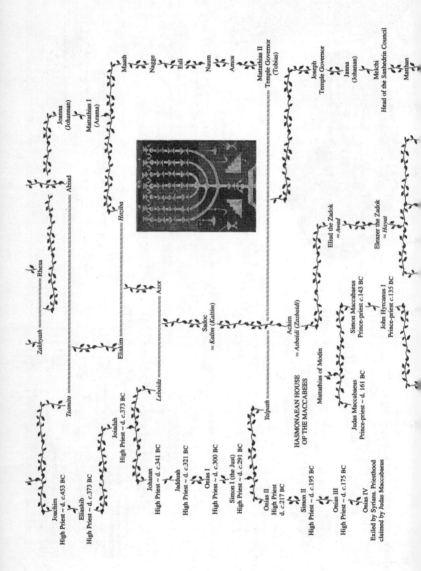

Joachim
High Priest ~ d. c.453 BC

Eliashib
High Priest ~ d. 373 BC

Joiadah
High Priest ~ d. c.373 BC

Johanan
High Priest ~ d. c.341 BC

Jaddnah
High Priest ~ d. c.321 BC

Onias I
High Priest ~ d. c.300 BC

Simon I (the Just)
High Priest ~ d. c.291 BC

Onias II
High Priest
d. c.217 BC

Simon II
High Priest ~ d. c.195 BC

Onias III
High Priest ~ d. c.175 BC

Onias IV
Exiled by Syrians Priesthood
claimed by Judas Maccabeus

Zabhyath ⚬ Rhessa ⚬ *Tsamita*

Abiud

Joanna
(Johannan)

Mattathias I
(Arama)

Maath

Nagge

Esli

Naum

Amos

Mattathias II
Temple Governor
(Tobias)

Joseph
Temple Governor

Janna
(Johanan)

Melchi
Head of the Sanhedrin Council

Matthan

Haziba

Eliakim

Azor

Lebaida

Sadoc
≈ *Kalim (Kalim)*

Achim
≈ *Asbaidi (Zazbaidi)*

Yalpath

HASMONAEAN HOUSE
OF THE MACCABEES

Mattathias of Modin

Judas Maccabeus
Prince-priest ~ d. 161 BC

Simon Maccabaeus
Prince-priest c.143 BC

John Hyrcanus I
Prince-priest c.135 BC

Eliud the Zadok
≈ *Awad*

Eleazer the Zadok
≈ *Hayat*

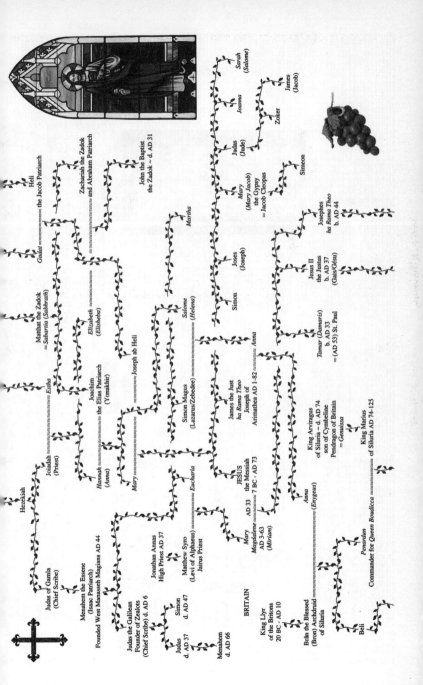

Hezekiah

Judas of Gamla
(Chief Scribe)

Menahem the Essene
(Isaac Patriarch)
Founded West Manasseh Magians AD 44

Judas the Galilean
Founder of Zealots
(Chief Scribe) d. AD 6

Simon
d. AD 47

Judas
d. AD 37

Menahem
d. AD 66

Joiadah
(Priest)

Hannah
(Anna)

Jonathan Annas
High Priest 37

Matthew Syro
(Levi of Alphaeus)
Jairus Priest

Heli
Gadal ══════════ the Jacob Patriarch

Matthat the Zadok
≈ Saburnia (Sobhrath)

Joachim
the Elias Patriarch
(Yonakhir)

Simon Magus
(Lazarus/Zebedee)

James the Just
ha Rama Theo
Joseph of
Arimathea AD 1-82 ══════

Esthe

Elizabeth
(Elisheba)

Mary

Salome
(Helena)

Martha

Anna

Zachariah the Zadok
and Abraham Patriarch

John the Baptist
the Zadok ~ d. AD 31

Joseph ab Heli

Mary
(Mary Jacob)
the Gypsy
≈ Jacob Cleopas

Simon

Joses
(Joseph)

Judas
(Jude)

Zoker

Joanna

Sarah
(Salome)

James
(Jacob)

Simeon

JESUS
the Messiah
7 BC - AD 73

Mary
Magdalene ══════
(Miriam)

AD 33

Tamar (Damaris)
b. AD 33
≈ (AD 53) St. Paul

Jesus II
the Nazara
b. AD 37
(Gais/Gesu)

Josephes
ha Rama Theo
b. AD 44

Eucharia

King Arviragus
of Siluria ~ d. AD 74
son of Cymbeline
Pendragon of Britain
≈ Genuissa

King Marius
of Siluria AD 74-125

BRITAIN

King Llyr
of the Briions
20 BC - AD 10

Brân the Blessed
(Bron) Archdruid
of Siluria

Beli

Anna
(Enygeus)

Penardun
Commander for Queen Boudicca ══════════

427

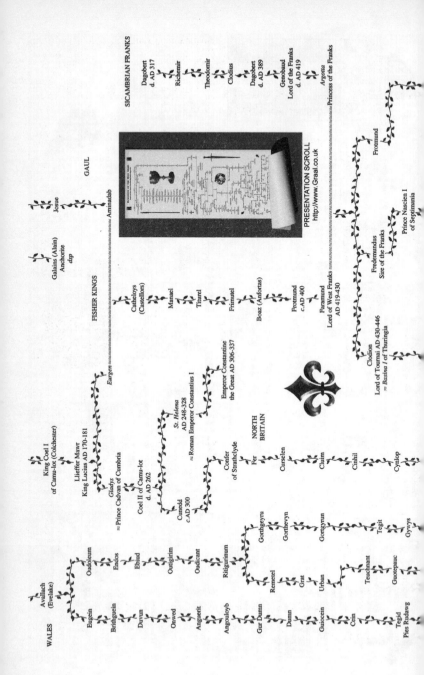

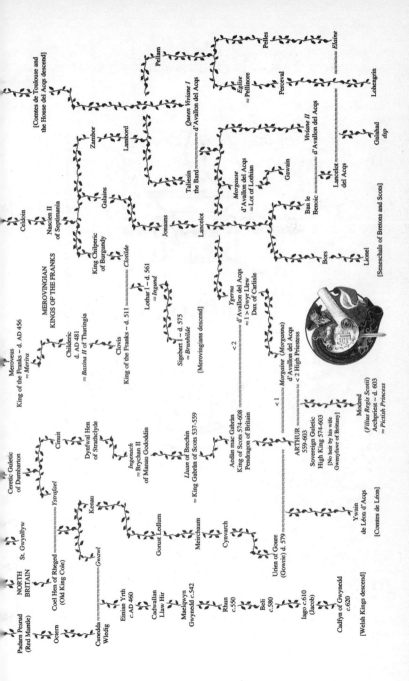

[Comtes de Toulouse and the House del Acqs descend]

Pellam
Eglise ≈ Pellinore
Peles
Elaine
Perceval
Lohengrin

Caldoin
Nascien II of Septimania
King Chilperic of Burgundy
Zambor
Lambord
Queen Viviane I d'Avallon del Acqs

MEROVINGIAN KINGS OF THE FRANKS

Galains
Taliesin the Bard
Jonaans
Lancelot
Morgause d'Avallon del Acqs = Lot of Lothian
Vivianne II d'Avallon del Acqs
Gawain
Ban le Benoic
Lancelot del Acqs
Galahad dap
Lionel
Bors

[Seneschals of Bretons and Scots]

Meroveus King of the Franks ~ d. AD 456 = Meriza
Childeric d. AD 481 = Basina II of Thuringia
Clovis King of the Franks ~ d. 511 = Clotilde
Lothar I ~ d. 561 = Ingund
Sigebert I ~ d. 575 = Brunhilde
[Merovingians descend]

Ygerna d'Avallon del Acqs =1> Gwyr Llew Dux of Carlisle
Morgaine (Morganna) d'Avallon del Acqs < 2   2 High Priestess
< 2
< 1
ARTHUR 559-603 Sovereign Guletic High King 574-603 [No heir by his wife Gwenyfawr of Brittany]
Modred (Filius Regis Scotti) Archpriest ~ d. 603 = Pictish Princess

NORTH BRITAIN

Paternus Pesrud (Red Mantle)
St. Gwynllyw
Ceretic Guletic of Dumbarton
Cinuit
Dynfwal Hen of Strathclyde
Ingenach = Brychan II of Manau Gododdin
Llvan of Brechin = King Gabrán of Scots 537-559
Aedàn mac Gabràn King of Scots 574-608 Pendragon of Britain

Coel Hen of Rheged (Old King Cole) = Gwawl
Octern
Kenau
Yzarfgael
Gorust Ledlum
Meirchaum
Cynvarch
Urien of Goure (Gowrie) d. 579
Yvain de Léon d'Acqs
[Comtes de Léon]

Cunedda Wledig
Einian Yrth c.AD 460
Cadwallan Llaw Hir
Maelgwyn Gwynedd c.542
Rhun c.550
Beli c.580
Iago c.610 (Jacob)
Cadfyn of Gwynedd c.620
[Welsh Kings descend]

429

APPENDICES

Son of God – Son of Man

How does the mortal figure of Jesus (the son of Mary and Joseph) reconcile with his Christian Church depiction as the divine son of God? Only the Gospels of Matthew and Luke discuss Mary's conception and the birth of Jesus. Mark and John ignore the events.

Although not discussing the Nativity as such, John 7:42 does comment regarding the ancestry of Jesus: 'Hath not the scripture said, that Christ cometh of the seed of David, and out of the town of Bethlehem, where David was.' In addition, St Paul's Epistle to the Romans 1:3–4 refers to 'Jesus Christ our Lord, which was made of the seed of David according to the flesh; and declared to be the Son of God'. Again, in Mark 10:47 and Matthew 22:42 Jesus is called the 'son of David'. In Acts 2:30, Peter (referring to King David) calls Jesus the 'fruit of his loins, according to the flesh'.

These entries, along with the male-line genealogical lists in Matthew and Luke, make it abundantly clear that Jesus was of straightforward human descent from King David. Over and above that, St Paul wrote that Jesus was 'declared' to be the son of God; while in the Annunciation sequence of

Luke 1:35, it is similarly stated that Jesus would be 'called' the son of God.

The fact of Jesus' Davidic paternal descent is made even more apparent in Hebrews 7:14, which relates to his appointment in the high priestly Order of Melchizedek. From the time of Moses and Aaron, only the tribe of Levi had any automatic right to Israelite priesthood. The tribe of Judah, which included David and his dynasty down to Joseph and Jesus, held the privilege of kingship, but not of priesthood.

In writing his epistle to the Hebrews, St Paul clarified the matter of Jesus' new priestly status with the following: 'It is evident that our Lord sprang out of Judah, of which tribe Moses spake nothing concerning priesthood' (Hebrews 7:14). Just before this, in Hebrews 7:12, the point is made that to accommodate this divergence from custom, there was 'made of necessity a change also of the law'. Nothing is mentioned here about Jesus being able to be whatever he wanted because he was the son of God – only that the law had to be amended because of his birth into the Davidic line of Judah.

Related to this is the *Coronation Psalm*, which concerns the Davidic throne – 'I will declare the decree: the Lord hath said unto me, Thou art my son; this day have I begotten thee' (Psalm 2:7). This Psalm is intimated when Jesus is baptized in the Jordan by John. Matthew 3:17, Mark 1:11 and Luke 3:22 all state that a voice from heaven said, 'This is [or Thou art] my beloved Son'.

When confronted by others as to whether he was the son of God, Jesus generally avoided the issue. In Matthew

26:63–64, when asked by the High Priest whether he was in truth the son of God, Jesus replied, 'Thou hast said' – implying that the priest had said it, not he. In Luke 22:70, Jesus answered in virtually identical terms: 'Then said they all, Art thou then the Son of God? And he said unto them, Ye say that I am'. On other occasions, Jesus responded to the effect that he was the 'son of man' (as in Matthew 26:63–64).

Apart from the Davidic Psalm reference, the perception of Jesus as the son of God emanates from things said about him by others in the text. For example, John 20:31 states, 'But these things are written, that ye might believe that Jesus is the Christ, the Son of God'. Similarly, in Acts 9:20 when Paul is said to have preached that Christ was the son of God. There are forty-five such entries in the New Testament, which state that Jesus was 'declared to be', 'preached as', 'believed to be', 'was called' the son of God. Alternatively, there are ninety mentions of his being the 'son of man', the majority of which references were made by Jesus himself.

The Greek biblical references to 'son of man' are: *huios ho anthropos*. The linguistic equivalents are: Aramaic, *bar nasha*, and Hebrew, *ben adam*. In each case the phrase means simply 'a man – a human being'.[1]

Luke 3:38 clarifies that Adam was the first of the line to be called the son of God. More important to the overall picture is that the Bible cites certain deserving people as being the 'children of God', commencing in the New Testament with Jesus' own words in Matthew 5:9: 'Blessed are the peacemakers, for they shall be called the children of God'. Once again, just as in the case of Jesus, the operative word is 'called'.

All things considered, the term 'son of God', as applicable to Jesus, was a figurative and symbolic description, whereas his physical lineage from King David is given on numerous occasions as being the human reality of his position. The most important thing here is that it was the kingly line of David which was especially considered to be God's offspring, not Jesus as a lone individual. This premise is laid down in 2 Samuel 7:13–14, where God is recorded as announcing in respect of King David: 'He shall build an house for my name, and I will stablish the throne of his kingdom for ever. I will be his father, and he shall be my son'.

1   William Barclay, *The Mind of Jesus*, SCM Press, London, 1971, ch 14, pp 148–9.

Trial and Crucifixion

The 1st-century *Annals of Imperial Rome*, compiled by Senator Cornelius Tacitus, state that the man called Christ, the originator of the 'notoriously depraved Christians', was crucified in the reign of Emperor Tiberius by the Governor of Judaea, Pontius Pilate.[1] The event is a matter of official record. No details of the trial are given, however; neither does Flavius Josephus detail the proceedings in his *Antiquities and Wars of the Jews*. The New Testament is the only known source of information in this regard.

As presented in the Gospels, Jesus' trial was hardly a trial at all, and the scenario is full of ambiguities. Matthew 26:57–59 states: 'They that had laid hold on Jesus led him away to Caiaphas the high priest, where the scribes and the elders were assembled … Now the chief priests, and elders, and all the council, sought false witness against Jesus.'

Even if all these priests, scribes and elders were somehow conveniently gathered together in the early hours at a moment's notice, the fact remains that it was against the law for the Jewish Council to sit at night. Luke 22:66 indicates that although Jesus was taken firstly to Caiaphas, the Sanhedrin did not meet until it was day. But the meeting would still have been illegal because the Sanhedrin Council was not allowed to sit during the Passover.[2]

The Gospels state that Peter followed Jesus to the house of high priest Joseph Caiaphas, where he denied his master three times as predicted. All accounts agree that Caiaphas then passed Jesus over to the Roman Governor, Pontius Pilate, whose presence facilitated an immediate interrogation. This is confirmed in John 18:28–31, only for a further anomaly to emerge:

> Then led they Jesus from Caiaphas unto
> the hall of judgement: and it was early;
> and they themselves went not into the
> judgement hall, lest they should be
> defiled; but that they might eat the
> Passover.
>
> Pilate then went out unto them, and said,
> What accusation bring ye against this
> man? They answered and said unto him,
> If he were not a malefactor, we would not
> have delivered him up unto thee. Then
> said Pilate unto them, Take ye him, and
> judge him according to your law. The
> Jews therefore said unto him, It is not
> lawful for us to put any man to death.

The truth is, however, that the Sanhedrin was fully empowered to condemn criminals and implement the death sentence if necessary. The Gospels also claim that Pilate offered to reprieve Jesus because 'it was customary for the Governor to release a prisoner at the feast of the Passover'. Again this is simply not true; there never was such a custom.

Although the Zealot apostles, Simon-Lazarus and Judas Sicariote (Iscariot), feature in the events leading to Jesus' arrest, it would appear that Thaddaeus (the third of the leaders in the revolt against Pilate)[3] is not mentioned after the Last Supper. But he does come into the story at the trial. Thaddaeus was a deputy of the Alphaeus succession and a devotional son of the Community Father. In Hebrew, the expression 'son of the father' would incorporate the elements *bar* (son) and *abba* (father) – so Thaddaeus might be described as *Bar-abba*, and a man called Barabbas is intimately concerned with the possibility of Jesus' reprieve by Pontius Pilate.

Barabbas is described in Matthew 27:16 as 'a notable prisoner'; in Mark 15:7 as one who had 'committed murder in the insurrection'; in Luke 23:19 as a man who 'for murder had been cast into prison', and in John 18:40 as 'a robber'. The John description is rather too vague, for everyday robbers were not customarily sentenced to crucifixion. However, the English translation does not truly reflect the original Greek implication, for *léstés* does not mean 'robber' so much as 'outlaw'. Mark's words point far more specifically to the insurgent role of Barabbas in the revolt.

What seems to have happened is that when the three prisoners Simon, Thaddaeus and Jesus were brought before Pilate, the cases against Simon and Thaddaeus were clear cut; they were known Zealot leaders and had been condemned men since the uprising. On the other hand, Pilate found it extremely difficult to prove a case against Jesus. Indeed, he was only in Pilate's custody because the Jewish contingent had passed him over for sentencing with the others. Pilate asked the Jewish hierarchy to provide him, at least, with a pretext: 'What accusation bring ye against this man?' But he received no satisfactory answer. Pilate then suggested that the elders should take him and 'judge him according to your law', at which the elders are said to have given the false excuse that 'It is not lawful for us to put any man to death'.

So Pilate then turned to Jesus himself. 'Art thou the King of the Jews?' he asked – to which Jesus replied, 'Sayest thou this thing of thyself, or did others tell it thee of me?' Confused by this, Pilate continued, 'Thine own nation and the chief priests have delivered thee unto me: what hast thou done?' The questioning progressed until, eventually, Pilate 'went out again unto the Jews, and saith unto them, I find in him no fault at all' (John 18:38).

At that point, Herod-Antipas of Galilee arrived on the scene (Luke 23:7–12). He was no friend of the priests and it suited his purpose for Jesus to be released in order to provoke his nephew, King Herod-Agrippa. Antipas therefore struck a deal with Pilate to secure the release of Jesus. The pact between Jesus' betrayer, Judas Sicariote, and the priests was thus superseded by a new agreement between the Herodian Tetrarch and the Roman Governor. From that moment, Judas lost any chance of a pardon for his Zealot activities and his days were numbered. In accordance with the new arrangement, Pilate said to the Jewish elders:

> Ye have brought this man unto me, as one
> that perverteth the people: and, behold, I,
> having examined him before you, have
> found no fault in this man touching those
> things whereof ye accuse him: No, nor yet
> Herod: for I sent you to him; and lo,
> nothing worthy of death is done unto
> him. I will therefore chastise him, and
> release him (Luke 23:14–16).

Had the members of the Sanhedrin waited until after the Passover, they could have conducted their own trial of Jesus in perfect legality. But they had strategically passed the responsibility over to Pilate because they knew there was no true charge to substantiate. They had certainly not bargained for Pilate's sense of justice, nor for the intervention of Herod-Antipas. But, in the course of this, Pilate managed to defeat his own objective. He tried to reconcile his decision to free Jesus with the notion that it might be regarded as a Passover dispensation and, in so doing, he opened the door to a Jewish choice: 'Jesus or Barabbas?' At this, 'they cried out all at once, saying, Away with this man, and release unto us Barabbas' (Luke 23:18).

Pilate pursued his course in favour of Jesus, but the Jews cried 'Crucify him!' Yet again Pilate asked, 'Why, what evil hath he done? I have found no cause of death in him'. But the odds were stacked against him and, giving way to his misguided commitment, Pilate released Barabbas (Thaddaeus). The Roman soldiers placed a crown of thorns on Jesus' head and wrapped a purple robe around him.

Pilate then handed him back to the priests, saying, 'Behold, I bring him forth to you, that ye may know that I find no fault in him' (John 19:4).

At that stage, things were going well for the Jerusalem elders, and their plan had all but succeeded. The ageing Thaddaeus may have been released, but both Simon Zelotes and Jesus were in custody along with Judas Sicariote.

* * *

The three crosses were duly erected in the Place of a Skull (Golgotha) and were set to bear Jesus and the two guerrilla leaders, Simon Zelotes and Judas Sicariote. But on the way to the Crucifixion site a significant event occurred when a mysterious character named Simon the Cyrene offered to carry Jesus' cross (Matthew 27:32). Many theories have been put forward about who the Cyrene might have been, but his real identity does not matter too much. What matters is that he was there at all. There is an interesting reference to him in an early Coptic tractate called *The Second Treatise of the Great Seth*, discovered among the books of Nag Hammadi. Explaining that there was a substitution made for one of the three victims, it mentions the Cyrene in this connection. The substitution apparently succeeded, for the tractate declares that Jesus did not die on the cross as presumed. Jesus is himself quoted as saying after the event, 'As for my death – which was real enough to them – it was real to them because of their own incomprehension and blindness'.[4]

The Islamic *Koran* (chapter 4, entitled 'Women') also specifies that Jesus did not die on the cross, stating: 'Yet they slew him not, neither crucified him, but he was represented by one in his likeness ... They did not really kill him'. Also, the 2nd-century historian, Basilides of Alexandria, wrote that the crucifixion was stage-managed with Simon the Cyrene used as a substitute.

In the event, however, it would seem that Simon the Cyrene was a substitute for Simon Zelotes, not for Jesus. The execution of two such prominent men as Jesus and Simon could not go unchallenged, and so a strategy appears to have been implemented to outwit the Jewish authorities. It is possible that Pilate's men might have been party to the subterfuge, which hinged on the use of a comatosing poison and the performance of a physical deception.

If any man could mastermind such an illusion, that man was Simon Zelotes, head of the Samaritan Magi and renowned as the greatest magician of his day. Both the *Acts of Peter* and the Church's *Apostolic Constitutions* recount the story of how, some years later, Simon levitated himself above the Roman Forum.[5] At Golgotha, however, things were very different – Simon was under guard and on his way to be crucified.

In the first instance, it would have been necessary to extricate Simon from his predicament – and so a substitution was organized in the person of the Cyrene, who would have been in league with the released Thaddaeus (Barabbas). The deception began on the way to Golgotha when, by accepting Jesus' burden, the Cyrene was able to incorporate himself in the midst of the assembly. The switch itself was probably made at the Crucifixion site, under cover of the general preparations. Amid the bustle of erecting the crosses, the Cyrene seemingly disappeared, but actually took Simon's place.[6] In the Gospels, the following sequence of events is carefully veiled by giving very few details about the men crucified alongside Jesus, other than describing them as 'thieves'. And so the scene was set: Simon Zelotes had achieved his freedom and could successfully handle the proceedings from then on.

* * *

Although the Crucifixion is generally portrayed as a relatively public affair, the Gospels affirm (for instance, Luke 23:49) that onlookers were obliged to watch the proceedings 'from afar off'. Western tradition has romanticized the place as 'a green hill far away' – a theme on which many artists have produced variations. Yet not one of the Gospels makes any mention of a hill. According to John 19:41, the location was a 'garden' in which there was a private sepulchre owned by Joseph of Arimathea (Matthew 27:59–60). Heeding the evidence of the Gospels instead of popular folklore, it is apparent that the Crucifixion was no hill-top spectacle with crosses against the skyline and an epic cast of spectators. On the contrary, it was a small-scale affair on controlled land – an exclusive garden that was, in one way or another, the 'place of a skull' (John 19:17). The Gospels have little more to say on the subject, but Hebrews 13:11–13 provides some very important clues to the location:

> For the bodies of those beasts, whose
> blood is brought into the sanctuary by the
> high priest for sin, are burned without the
> camp. Wherefore Jesus also, that he might

> sanctify the people with his own blood,
> suffered without the gate. Let us go forth
> therefore unto him without the camp,
> bearing his reproach.

From this we gather that Jesus suffered 'outside the gate' and 'outside the camp'. Also there is some association with a place where the bodies of sacrificed animals were burned. This reference is particularly important because the sites at which animal remains were burned were regarded as unclean. According to Deuteronomy 23:10–14, 'without the camp' described areas set aside as cesspits, middens and public latrines which were both physically and ritually unclean. By the same token, 'without the gate' defined other unclean places, including ordinary cemeteries.[7] Furthermore, the Dead Sea Scrolls make it clear that, because it constituted an act of defilement to walk over the dead, human graveyards were identified with the sign of a skull. It follows, quite naturally, that the 'place of a skull' (Golgotha/Calvary) was a restricted cemetery garden that contained an empty sepulchre in the charge of Joseph of Arimathea.

A further clue comes from Revelation 11:8, which states that Jesus was crucified in 'the great city which spiritually is called Sodom and Egypt'. This positively identifies the cemetery location as Qumrân, which was designated Egypt by the Therapeutate[8] and was geographically associated with the Old Testament centre of Sodom.

As detailed in the 'Divine Highness' section of chapter 11, Joseph of Arimathea (the patriarchal Joseph *ha Rama Theo*)

was Jesus' own brother James. It therefore comes as no surprise that Jesus was entombed in a sepulchre that belonged
to his own royal family.

From the time the Dead Sea Scrolls were first discovered at Qumrân in 1947, digs and excavations went on
well into the 1950s. During this period, important finds
were made in a number of caves. The archaeologists discovered that one cave in particular had two chambers and
two separate entrances quite a way apart. The access to the
main chamber was through a hole in the roof path, whereas the adjoining hollow was approached from the side.[9]
From the roof entrance, steps had been constructed down
into the chamber and, to seal the entrance against rainfall,
a large stone had to be rolled across the opening.
According to the *Copper Scroll*, this sepulchre was used as
a Treasury deposit, and as such it has been dubbed the
Rich Man's Cave. This was the sepulchre of the Davidic
crown prince, and it was sited directly opposite another
cave called the Bosom of Abraham.

* * *

The prophecy that the Saviour would ride into Jerusalem on
an ass was not the only prediction made concerning the
Messiah in the Old Testament book of Zechariah. Two other
prophecies (Zechariah 12:10 and 13:6) stated that he would
be pierced and mourned in death by all Jerusalem and that
he would be wounded in the hands as a result of his friends.
Jesus knew that by being crucified he would qualify in all of
these respects. As John 19:36 states, 'These things were done,
that the scripture should be fulfilled'.

Crucifixion was both punishment and execution: death by a torturous ordeal extended over a number of days. First the victim's outstretched arms were strapped by the wrists to a beam, which was hoisted into place horizontally across an upright post. Sometimes the hands were transfixed by nails as well, but nails alone would have been useless. Suspended with all his weight on his arms, a man's lungs would be compressed and he would die fairly quickly through suffocation. To prolong the agony, chest pressure was relieved by fixing the victim's feet to the upright post. Supported in this manner a man could live for many days, possibly even a week or more. After a while, in order to free up the crosses, the executioners would sometimes break the legs of the victims so as to increase the hanging weight and accelerate death.

On that Friday, the equivalent of 20 March AD 33, there was no reason for any of the three men crucified to have died within the day. Nevertheless, Jesus was given some vinegar and, having taken it, he 'gave up the ghost' (John 19:30). Soon afterwards, a centurion pierced Jesus' side with a spear and the fact that he bled (identified as blood and water) has been held to indicate that he was dead (John 19:34). In reality, vascular bleeding indicates that a body is alive, not dead; blood does not flow from a stab wound which is inflicted after death. At that stage, Judas and the Cyrene were still very much alive, so their legs were broken.

The Gospels do not say who gave the vinegar to Jesus on the cross, but John 19:29 specifies that the vessel was ready and waiting. A little earlier in the same sequence the potion was said to be 'vinegar mingled with gall' (Matthew 27:34) –

that is soured wine mixed with snake venom. Dependent on the proportions, such a mixture could induce unconsciousness or even cause death. In this case, the poison was fed to Jesus not from a cup, but from a sponge and by measured application from a reed. The person who administered it was undoubtedly Simon Zelotes, who was meant to be on one of the crosses himself.

Meanwhile, Joseph of Arimathea was negotiating with Pilate to remove Jesus' body before the Sabbath and place it in his sepulchre, in accordance with the rule of Deuteronomy 21:22–23 and confirmed in the Qumrân *Temple Scroll*: 'And if a man have committed a sin worthy of death, and he be put to death, and thou hang him on a tree: His body shall not remain all night upon the tree, but thou shalt in any wise bury him that day'.

Pilate therefore sanctioned the change of procedure from hanging (as manifest in Roman crucifixion) to the Jewish custom of burial alive. He then returned to Jerusalem leaving Joseph in control. (It is perhaps significant that in Acts 5:30, 10:39 and 13:29, the references to Jesus' torture all relate to his being 'hanged on a tree'.)

With Jesus in a seemingly lifeless coma and with the legs of Judas and the Cyrene newly broken, the three victims were brought down, having been on their respective crosses for less than half a day. The account does not state that the men were dead; it simply refers to the removal of their 'bodies' – that is live bodies as against corpses.

* * *

The next day was the Sabbath, about which the Gospels have little to tell. Only Matthew 27:62–66 makes any mention of that Saturday, but refers simply to a conversation between Pilate and the Jewish elders in Jerusalem, following which Pilate arranged for two guards to watch Jesus' tomb. Apart from that, all four Gospels continue their story from the Sunday morning thereafter. Yet, if any day was important to the ongoing course of events, that day was the Saturday: the Sabbath day we are told so little about. This respected day of rest and worship was the key to everything that happened – a sacred day on which it was utterly forbidden to work.

It appears that the Cyrene and Judas Sicariote had been placed in the second chamber of the tomb. Jesus' body occupied the main chamber. Within the confines of the double-hollow, Simon Zelotes had already taken up his station, along with lamps and everything else required for the operation. (Interestingly, a lamp was among the items found within this sepulchre during the 1950s.)

Then, according to John 19:39, Nicodemus arrived, bringing with him 'a mixture of myrrh and aloes, about an hundred pound weight'.[10] Extract of myrrh was a form of sedative commonly used in contemporary medical practice. The juice of aloes, as modern pharmacopoeias explain, is a strong and fast-acting purgative – precisely what would have been needed by Simon to expel the poisonous venom from Jesus' body.

It was of great significance that the day after the Crucifixion was the Sabbath day. Indeed, the timing of the whole operation to 'raise Jesus from the dead' (to release him from excommunication – 'death by decree') relied on the critical timing of the precise hour at which the Sabbath might be considered to begin.

In those days, there was no concept of any fixed duration for hours and minutes. The recording and measurement of time was one of the official functions of the Levites who programmed the course of hours by ground-shadows on measured areas. Also, since about 6 BC, they had made use of sundials. However, neither ground markings nor sundials were of any use when there were no shadows. Hence, there were twelve designated 'hours of day' (daylight) and, similarly, twelve 'hours of night' (darkness). The latter were measured by Levitical prayer sessions (like the canonical hours of the Catholic Church today. Indeed, the prevailing *Angelus* devotion – held at morning, noon and sunset – derives from the practice of the early Levite angels). The problem was however that, as the days and nights became longer or shorter, adjustments were necessary where hours overlapped.

On that particular Friday of the Crucifixion, a forward adjustment of a full three hours was required and, because of this, there is a noticeable discrepancy between the accounts of Mark and John over the timing of events on that day. Mark 15:24 states that Jesus was crucified at the third hour, whereas John 19:14–16 claims that Jesus was delivered for crucifixion at about the sixth hour. This anomaly occurs because Mark's Gospel relies on time as measured by Hellenist (solar) reckoning, whereas John's Gospel uses Hebrew (lunar) time. The result of the time-change was that (as Mark 15:33 describes) 'When the sixth hour was come, there was a darkness over the whole land until the ninth hour'. These three hours of darkness were symbolic only; they occurred within a split second (as do changes in time today when we cross between different time-zones, or when we put clocks forward or backward for daylight saving). So, on this occasion, the end of the fifth hour was followed immediately by the ninth hour.

The key to the Resurrection story lies in those three missing hours (the daytime hours that became night-time hours), for the newly defined start of the Sabbath began three hours before the old twelfth hour – that is at the old ninth hour, which was then renamed the twelfth hour.

In contrast, the Samaritan Magi of Simon Zelotes worked on an astronomical time-frame and did not formally implement the three-hour change until the original twelfth hour. This meant that, without breaking any of the rules against labouring on the Sabbath, Simon had a full three hours in which he could do what he had to do, even while others had begun their sacred period of rest. This was time enough to administer the medications to Jesus and to attend to the bone fractures of the Cyrene. Judas Sicariote was dealt with none too mercifully and was thrown over a cliff to his death (as obliquely related in Acts 1:16–18). The earlier reference in Matthew 27:5, which indicates that Judas 'hanged himself', refers more precisely to the fact that, at that stage, he set the scene for his own downfall.

1   Tacitus, *The Annals of Imperial Rome* (trans, Michael Grant), Penguin, London, 1996, ch 14, p 365.
2   Michael Baigent, Richard Leigh and Henry Lincoln, *The Holy Blood and the Holy Grail*, Jonathan Cape, London, 1982, ch 12, p 309.

3   *See* chapter 7 – Suppressing the Evidence.
4   JM Robinson and the Coptic Gnostic Project, *The Second Treatise of the Great Seth* in *The Nag Hammadi Library*, Institute for Antiquity and Christianity, EJ Brill, Leiden, 1977, Codex VII, 2, p 329.
5   St Clement of Alexandria, *Clementine Homilies and Apostolical Constitutions* (trans William Whiston), Ante-Nicene Library, T & T Clark, Edinburgh, 1870, bk VI:9.
6   Gnostic tradition maintains that Simon the Cyrene was crucified 'in the place of Jesus'. This does not mean instead of Jesus, but in what should have been Jesus' location. Understanding Jesus to represent the kingly Davidic heritage, with Simon to represent the priestly line, and therefore Judas to represent the line of the prophets, the positioning of the three crosses should have been made to observe the formal ranking. According to this scheme, the position of the King should have been to the west (on the left); the position of the Priest should have been in the centre; and the position of the Prophet should have been to the east (on the right). It would seem, therefore, that the Cyrene was placed in the west, 'in the place of Jesus' and, with Simon out of the picture, Jesus would have moved to the centre. This makes it ever more apparent that the Roman soldiers were also party to the subterfuge.
7   Barbara Thiering, *Jesus the Man*, Transworld, London, 1992, ch 24, p 113.
8   *Ibid,* appendix II, p 312.
9   *Ibid*, ch 26, p 122.
10 The translation to 'pound' in this case represents the Greek *litra* (a variant of the Roman *libra*), a measure of weight equal to one ninetieth of a *talantaios* (talent). In modern terms, this approximates to 330 grams or 12 ounces avoirdupois. 100 New Testament 'pounds' is thus roughly equal in modern terms to 33 kilograms or 75 pounds (more than 5 stones) avoirdupois – a considerable quantity for Nicodemus to manage alone.

Jesus and India

Published accounts concerning Jesus in India began with the 19th-century Russian scholar, Nicolai Notovich. It is said that he obtained information about this from a manuscript which he discovered at the Tibetan lamasery in Hemis. But Notovich did not actually read the manuscript, nor even handle it. The story was read to him by a lama in 1887, while an interpreter took notes in Russian. The lama explained to him that the Hemis biography of the prophet Isa (as likened to Jesus) had been translated from an original manuscript in the old Pali language, which was held in Lhasa.

Apparently, there were some 84,000 such biographical scrolls in Lhasa, which was a teaching lamasery, and one of its long-standing customs was that each student must copy one of the biographies to take back to his home monastery. That was how the copy of the Isa document came to Hemis. The problem was that many of the Lhasa scrolls were in old languages that the visiting pupils could not read, and it was well known that the majority of the writings they took home were not accurate translations of the originals. Since Notavich did not see the original Palian scroll at Lhasa, the Hemis translation was left without any provable provenance.

Thomas the apostle was known to have preached in Syria, Persia and India, and was eventually lanced to death at Mylapore, near Madras. So there was indeed an early Christian connection which added some weight to the possibility of Jesus following his footsteps.

The Notovich account came to light when a diary of the missionaries, Marx and Francke, was found by Professor Fida Hassnain (former Director of Archives, Archaeology, Research and Museums for Kashmir) at the nearby lamasery in Leh. This journal mentioned Hemis and recounted the story of Isa according to Notovich. Professor Hassnain's book on this subject is *A Search for the Historical Jesus – from Apocryphal, Buddhist, Islamic & Sanscrit Sources*, Gateway Books, Bath, 1994.

The story of Marx and Francke is interesting in itself. They were Christian missionaries who visited Kashmir in 1894 to study the lives of the nation's prophets. But their mission was at a time when much of India (outside the princely states) was controlled by Victorian Britain at the height of the Empire. Every effort was made to Christianize the native Hindus and Muslims, and Imperial policy attempted to undermine those religions by convincing the people that India had a past Christian history. Queen Victoria (of the German House of Hanover) masterminded this via her missionary colleagues in Germany.

Subsequently, Marx and Francke discovered the Notovich account of the prophet Isa – a Buddhist from Tibet who was in Kashmir around about Jesus' time. They related that Notovich had first been told about Isa by a lama in Moulbeck, and this had prompted his subsequent visit to the

Hemis monastery, where the lama read the story of Isa from the student's translated copy.

Marx and Francke figured that the names Isa and Jesus were similar enough and (since Notovich had associated them in accordance with the Hemis story) they sent word back to the West that Isa and Jesus were one and the same. But the Dalai Lama vehemently objected, and Queen Victoria did not want to upset him, so the Isa connection was dropped. In practical terms, a minor Buddhist prophet was of no use to the Imperial strategy anyway. What they really needed was a tomb (not just a name) on which to hang the Christian tag.

The odd thing about all this was that this strategy was quite out of keeping with the conventional Christian doctrine of the Crucifixion and Ascension. But, on a world scale, Queen Victoria was far more powerful than the Pope at that time, and no one argued.

In Srinagar, Marx and Francke then found an old tomb dedicated to a prophet called Yuza Asaf. This name was again considered close to that of Jesus, and since Yuza was a Muslim, not a Buddhist, the Dalai Lama had no say in the matter. In Turkey and Persia there are traditional stories of the holy man Yuza Asaf, whose miracles and teachings were not unlike those of Jesus, but what the missionaries failed to take into account was that there were no Muslims in the 1st century. Nevertheless, the local Kashmiris were not well versed in history, so it was announced that Jesus and Yuza Asaf were synonymous. Under the control of the British Imperial authorities, the Srinagar tomb was then publicized as being the tomb of Jesus, and pilgrims began to visit.

After that, another Victorian team found a mountain location in Kashmir called *Muqam-i-Musa*, and duly dubbed it the burial place of Moses. Then, in 1898, precisely the same was done at the town of Murree, on the Kashmir border, where another Muslim prophet was buried at Pindi Point. The town-name Muree was similar enough to Mary, so the British colonial Government sequestrated this site too, announcing that Jesus' mother was buried there.

Following the reinstatement of India's Hindu independence in 1947, and the establishment of a Muslim state in Pakistan, the border region of Kashmir has remained in a condition of Hindu–Muslim turmoil ever since.

It is now believed by some that the Muslim crypt of Yuza Asaf might contain another body, buried beneath that of the 6th-century Yuza in the Roza Bal building at Srinagar (*rauza bal* = tomb of a prophet). Since discovering the Marx and Francke diary, Professor Hassnain has continued his research and is currently writing an updated book on the subject.[1] In recent years, American researcher, Suzanne Olsson, has also been investigating sites in Northern India and Pakistan, and intends to publish her discoveries in the near future.

1   The presently available research is to be found in: Professor Fida Hassnain, *A Search for the Historical Jesus – from Apocryphal, Buddhist, Islamic & Sanscrit Sources*, Gateway Books, Bath, 1994.

IV

Saint Helena

In 1662, the *Congregatio Propaganda Fide* was instituted by Pope Gregory XV. This College of the Propaganda of Cardinals was established to enforce Church dogma, through its teachers and approved historians, where it disagreed with traditional or documented facts. Prior to that date, information concerning the birthright of Empress Helena was always obtained from British records.

As far as Britain was concerned, it was not until 1776 that the English historian, Edward Gibbon, promoted the 1662 Roman fiction of Helena's birth when issuing his *History of the Decline and Fall of the Roman Empire*. This was followed by a vindication in 1779, after his spurious accounts of early Christian development were criticised by academic scholars. But Gibbon had converted to Catholicism in 1753 and was bound to represent Helena in accordance with the official doctrine.

According to Gibbon, Helena was born into an innkeeping family from the small town of Naissus in the Balkans. Later, he was obliged to confess that this notion was a matter of conjecture but, notwithstanding this, his original claim has since been slavishly followed by subsequent writers of histories and encyclopedias.

All pre-Gibbon records in Britain relate that Princess Elaine (Greco-Roman: Helen; Roman: Helena) was born and raised at Colchester and she became renowned for her expertise at political administration. Her husband, Constantius, was proclaimed Emperor at York (Caer Evroc). In AD 290, he had enlarged the York archbishopric at Helena's request and was subsequently buried at York. In recognition of Helena's pilgrimage to the Holy Land in AD 326, the church of Helen of the Cross was built at Colchester, where the city's coat-of-arms was established as her cross, with three silver crowns for its arms.

From the time of the Reformation, and especially after the College of Propaganda was instituted, Rome undertook a structured programme of disinformation about many aspects of Church history, and this continued with increasing intensity. In practice, however, the revised Roman view of Helena is vague in the extreme, with various accounts contradicting one another. Many churchmen have put forward the Balkan theory, as repeated by Gibbon; some gave Helena's birthplace as Nicomedia, and others cited her as a Roman native.

Quite apart from the British records, the pre-1662 information from Rome also upheld Helena's British heritage, as did other writings in Europe. These included the 16th-century *Epistola* of the German writer, Melancthon, who wrote: 'Helen was undoubtedly a British Princess'. The Jesuit records (even the Jesuit book, *Pilgrim Walks in Rome*) state, when detailing Constantine's own birth in Britain: 'It is one of Catholic England's greatest glories to count St Helena and Constantine among its children – St Helena being the only daughter of King Coilus.'

The Roman document most commonly cited to uphold the anti-Britain message is a manuscript written in the late 4th century (after Helena's death) by Ammianus Marcellinus, from which the original information concerning Helena (AD c248–328) has gone missing. There is, nevertheless, a spuriously entered margin note from the 1600s, which gives the newly devised Church-approved details on which the Gibbonites and others based their subsequent opinions.

In all of this, the one person that the Church and its dutiful scholars have chosen to ignore is Rome's own Cardinal Baronius, the Vatican librarian who compiled the 1601 *Annales Ecclesiastici*. In this work, he explicitly stated: 'The man must be mad who, in the face of universal antiquity, refuses to believe that Constantine and his mother were Britons, born in Britain.'

Three Tables of the Grail

Tradition relates that 'Three Tables bore the Grail; they were round, square and rectangular. Each had the same perimeter, and the number of the Three was Two–One'.

The Three Tables have been likened to those of King Arthur, Grail Castle and the Last Supper. However, the 2–1 specification is an inherent tabular proportion of the *Golden Mean*, and has little to do with tables in the utility sense.

The *Golden Mean* is a geometric progression employed by the Greek mathematician Euclid in the 1st century BC. In practice, however, it dates back far beyond Euclid to the time of Plato. The *Golden Mean* has been used as an architectural standard for proportion, and is used today in sophisticated artwork, framing and design. Roughly speaking, it is a proportion of 5:8, but the precise mathematical ratio is 0.618:1.[1]

The *Golden Mean* is based on the division of space by root rectangle derivatives, and it needs no form of measurement. Root rectangles can be produced from a square with compasses only. A square is simply a $\sqrt{1}$ rectangle. A $\sqrt{2}$ rectangle is produced from a square by setting the compasses at the length of the diagonal, and extending the base line to meet the arc. A $\sqrt{3}$ rectangle is produced from the diagonal of the second, and so on. A √5 rectangle (double-square) has the Grail proportion of 2:1.

Although not measured with numbers, such rectangles are not irrational because they can be measured in terms of the squares produced from them. Calculation in terms of area instead of length was the basis of ancient geometry. The *Pythagoras Theorem* is understandable only in terms of square measure. For instance, the area of a √1 square is exactly one-fifth of the area of a square on the long side of its extended √5 rectangle. Hence, the relationship between the end and side of the √5 rectangle may be used as an expression of area.

Rectangles with strictly numerical ratios such as 3:2, 5:4, etc. can be defined as *Static*, but root rectangles are *Dynamic*. They establish a particular harmony by virtue of their related proportion. The *Static* and *Dynamic* attributes are both inherent in the square (1 = 1:1 = √1:1) and in the extended double-square (2 = 2:1 = √4:1).

The diagonal of the double-square (which is itself √5) has been widely used for constructing temples and sacred

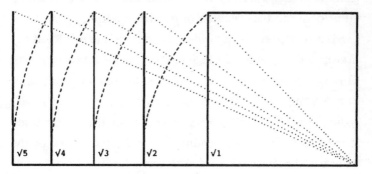

Rectangles of the Golden Mean

enclosures. It relates directly to the *Golden Mean* proportion of $(\sqrt{5} + 1) \div 2 = 1.618$.

The *Golden Mean* exists when the ratio between the larger and the smaller quantity is equal to the ratio between the sum of the two and the larger. The *Golden Number* 1.618 is mathematically symbolized by the Greek letter φ (*phi*). Numerically, it possesses exceptional mathematical properties: $1.618 \div 0.618 = (1 + 1.618) = (1 + 1.618) = (1.618 \times 1.618) = 2.618$. Thus $\varphi^2 = 2.618$.

In any increasing progression where φ is the ratio between the successive terms, each term is equal to the sum of the two preceding. This uniqueness affords the simple calculation of a series.

From any two successive terms, all others may be defined by the use of compasses. This additive sequence was first rationalized in arithmetical terms by the 12th-century Leonardo of Pisa (better known as Fibonacci, *see* page 314). It is generally known as the *Fibonacci Series,* with each successive figure being the sum of the previous two – i.e. 1, 1, 2, 3, 5, 8, 13, 21, 34, 55, 89, etc. This series is not only significant in practical terms, but has long been recognized as a fundamental principle in the structure of plant and animal organisms.

As a consequence of *Golden* calculation, the irrational figure of *pi* is achieved: $2.618 \: [\varphi^2] \times (12/10) = 3.1416 = pi \: [\pi]$. This is the constant factor which facilitates circumference calculation from a known diameter. Hence, the *Round Table of the Grail* can be calculated from its equally perimetered square and rectangular counterparts: Half the side of the square $\times \sqrt{1.618}$ = the radius. Therefore, (radius $\times$ 2) $\times \pi$ = the perimeter.[2]

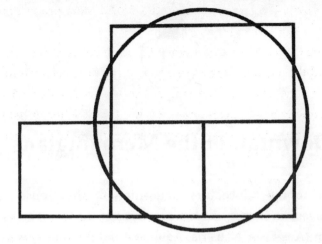

The Three Tables of the Grail

The symbolic *Round Table of the Grail* had its origin in the *Circle* – the ancient representation of wholeness. The famous figure of the *Vitruvian Man* is that of a circle encompassing man emblematic as a five-pointed star. From this, with a square and compasses, it is possible to derive all other geometrical figures, each in precise relation to the others. From the earliest times, hut-circles, fairy rings and megalithic temples were all *Round Tables* of cosmic unity.

Allegorically, the Round Table is the table of *Intuition;* the Square Table is that of *Intellect,* and the Rectangular Table is that of *Mysticism.*

1   The subject is fully covered in Nigel Pennick, *Sacred Geometry*, Turnstone, Wellingborough, 1980, ch 2, pp 25–8.
2   Various aspects of tabular calculation are in Louis Charpentier, *The Mysteries of Chartres Cathedral*, Research into Lost Knowledge Organization, and Thorsons, Wellingborough, 1972, ch 12, pp 83–90; ch 13, pp 91–111; and ch 15, pp 118–27.

Downfall of the Merovingians

Prior to the 8th-century deposition of the House of Meroveus in France, the key provinces of the Merovingian realm (Austrasia, Neustria, Aquitaine and Burgundy) were placed under the supervision of appointed mayors, who were themselves closely allied to the Catholic bishops. The Mayors of the Palace of Austrasia were the family of Hernoul (Arnulf) of Metz (*see* chapter 17), from whom the Carolingian dynasty of Charlemagne descended.

By 655, the Church of Rome was in a position to begin dismantling the Merovingian succession and, at that time, the mayors of the Austrasian Palace (akin to modern prime ministers) were firmly under papal control. The mayor at that time was Grimoald, the brother-in-law of Hernoul's son Ansegis, Lord of Brabant. The prevailing Merovingian King of Austrasia was Sigebert II, the son of Dagobert I.

When King Sigebert died, his son Dagobert was only five years old and Mayor Grimoald took the first step in the bishops' plan to usurp the reigning house. To begin, he kidnapped Dagobert and had him conveyed to Ireland, where he lived in exile among the Scots Gaels. Then, not expecting to see the young heir again, Grimoald told Queen Immachilde that her son had died.

Prince Dagobert was educated at Slane Monastery, near Dublin, and he married the Gaelic Princess Matilde when he was fifteen. Subsequently, he went to York under the patronage of St Wilfred, but then Matilde died and Dagobert returned to France, where he appeared much to the amazement of his mother. In the meantime, Grimoald had placed his own son on the Austrasian throne, but Wilfred of York and others spread word of the mayoral treachery and the House of Grimoald was duly discredited.

Having married his second wife, Gizelle de Razès (a niece of the Visigoth king), Dagobert was reinstated in 674, after an absence of nearly 20 years, and the Roman intrigue was thwarted – but not for long. Two days before Christmas 679, Dagobert was hunting near Stenay in the Ardennes when he was confronted in the forest and lanced to death: impaled to a tree by a henchman of his own powerful mayor, Pepin the Fat of Herstal (the grandson of Hernoul).

The Vatican was quick to approve the assassination and immediately passed the Merovingian administration in Austrasia to the ambitious Pepin. In due course, he was succeeded by his illegitimate son, Charles Martel, who sustained the Roman endeavour by gaining control of other Merovingian territories. When Martel died in 741, the only Merovingian of any notable authority was Dagobert's nephew Childeric III. Meanwhile, Martel's son, Pepin the Short, was the Mayor of Neustria.

Up to that point (except for the Grimoald affair), the Merovingian monarchy had been strictly dynastic, with its hereditary succession considered an automatic and sacred right – a matter in which the Church had no say whatsoever. But that tradition was destined to be overturned when Rome grasped the opportunity to 'create' kings by way of a spurious papal authority made possible by the *Donation of Constantine* (*see* chapter 5, page 95).

In 751, Mayor Pepin the Short, in league with Pope Zachary, secured Church approval for his own coronation as King of the Franks in place of Childeric. The Church's long-awaited ideal had come to fruition, and from that time onwards kings were endorsed and crowned only by self-styled Roman prerogative. And so it was that, with the full blessing of the Pope, Pepin became King of the Franks and Childeric was deposed. He was publicly humiliated by the bishops, and his hair (kept long in the Old Testament Nazarite tradition)[1] was cut brutally short. He was incarcerated in a monastery, where he died four years later, and thus began a new dynasty of French kings, the Carolingians – so named after Pepin's father, Charles (Carolus) Martel.

---

1 Nazarites were ascetic individuals (such as Samson) bound by strict vows through predetermined periods, as related in the law of the Nazarites, given in the book of Numbers 6:2–21.

THE LIBRARY
TOWER HAMLETS COLLEGE
POPLAR HIGH STREET
LONDON E14 0AF
Tel: 0207 510 7763

BIBLIOGRAPHY

Adamnan, St, *A Life of Saint Columba* (trans, Wentworth Huyshe), George Routledge, London, 1908

Addison, Charles G, *The History of the Knights Templars*, Adventures Unlimited, Kempton, IL, 1997

Albany, HRH Prince Michael of, *The Forgotten Monarchy of Scotland*, Chrysalis/Vega, London, 2002

Allegro, John, *The Dead Sea Scrolls*, Penguin, London, 1964

Alter, Robert, *Genesis*, WW Norton, New York, NY, 1996

Alviella, Count Goblet, *Migration of Symbols* (1892 facsimile), Aquarian Press, Wellingborough, 1979

Anderson, Alan Orr, *Early Sources of Scottish History*, (ed, Marjorie Anderson), Paul Watkins, London, 1990

Anderson, Flavia, *The Ancient Secret*, Research into Lost Knowledge Organization, and Thorsons, Wellingborough, 1953

Anderson, Joseph, *Scotland in Early Christian Times*, David Douglas, Edinburgh, 1881

Andressohn, John C, *The Ancestry and Life of Godfrey of Bouillon*, University of Indiana Press, Bloomington, IN, 1947

Anglo-Saxon Chronicle, The (trans, Michael Swanton), JM Dent, London, 1997

Aradi, Zsolt, *Shrines of Our Lady*, Farrar, Strauss & Young, New York, NY, 1954

Ashe, Geoffrey, *Avalonian Quest*, Methuen, London, 1982

Atalay, Bülent, *Math and the Mona Lisa*, Smithsonian Books, Washington, DC, 2004

Baigent, Michael, with Richard Leigh and Henry Lincoln, *The Holy Blood and the Holy Grail*, Jonathan Cape, London, 1982

— *The Messianic Legacy*, Jonathan Cape, London, 1986

Baigent, Michael, and Richard Leigh, *The Dead Sea Scrolls Deception*, Jonathan Cape, London, 1991

Barber, M, *The Trial of the Templars*, Cambridge University Press, Cambridge, 1978

Barber, Richard, *The Knight and Chivalry*, Longman, London, 1970

Barcilon, Pinin Brambilla, and Pietro C Marani, *Leonardo, The Last Supper* – English language edition (trans, Harlow Tighe), University of Chicago Press, Chicago, IL, 2001

Barclay, William, *The Mind of Jesus*, SCM Press, London, 1971

Baring-Gould, S and J Fisher, *The Lives of the British Saints*, Cymmrodorion Society, London, 1907–1913

Barnstone, Willis (ed), *The Other Bible*, HarperSanFrancisco, San Francisco, 1984

Bartrum, Peter C, *Early Welsh Genealogical Tracts*, University of Wales Press, Cardiff, 1966

Bauckham, Richard, *Jude and the Relatives of Jesus in the Early Church*, T & T Clark, Edinburgh, 1988

Bayley, Harold, *A New Light on the Renaissance*, John Dent, London, 1909

— *The Lost Language of Symbolism*, Williams & Norgate, London, 1912

Becker, Udo, *The Element Encyclopedia of Symbols*, Element Books, Shaftesbury, 1996

Bede of Jarrow, The Venerable, *The Ecclesiastical History of the English Nation* (trans, JA Giles), Dent/Everyman, London, 1970

Begg, Ean CM, *The Cult of the Black Virgin*, Arkana, London, 1985

Bernard de Clairvaux, *Patriologia Latina* (ed, JP Minge), Paris, 1854

— *On the Song of Songs* (trans, Kilian Walsh), Cistercian Publishers, Michigan, 1976

Bible, The Authorized King James Version with Apocrypha, Oxford University Press, Oxford, 1998

Blair, Peter Hunter, *The Origins of Northumbria*, Northumberland Press, Gateshead, 1948

Bogdanow, Fanni, *The Romance of the Grail*, Manchester University Press, Manchester, 1966

Bowen, EG, *The Settlements of the Celtic Saints in Wales*, University of Wales Press, Cardiff, 1956

Boussel, Patrice, *Leonardo da Vinci*, Nouvelles Éditions Françaises, Paris, 1986

Bowen, EG, *The Settlements of the Celtic Saints in Wales*, University of Wales Press, Cardiff, 1956

Bramly, Serge, *Leonardo the Artist and Man*, Penguin, London, 1994

Brandon, SGF, *The Fall of Jerusalem and the Christian Church*, SPCK, London, 1951

— *Jesus and the Zealots*, Charles Scribner's Sons, New York, NY, 1967

Branner, Robert, *Chartres Cathedral*, WW Norton, London, 1996

Brockwell, Maurice W, *The Pseudo-Arnolfini Portrait*, Chatto & Windus, London 1952

Brooke, G, *Temple Scroll Studies*, Sheffield Academic Press, Sheffield, 1989

BIBLIOGRAPHY

Brown, Dan, *The Da Vinci Code*, Bantam Press, London, 2003

Bryant, Nigel (trans,), *Perlesvaus*, DS Brewer, Cambridge, 1978

Bucher, François, *Architector: The Lodge Books and Sketchbooks of Medieval Architects*, Abaris Books, New York, NY, 1979

Bull, Norman J, *The Rise of the Church*, Heinemann, London, 1967

Bultmann, Rudolf, *Primitive Christianity in its Contemporary Setting* (trans, RH Fuller), Fontana/Collins, Glasgow, 1960

Burchardt, Titus, *Chartres and the Birth of a Cathedral*, Golgonooza Press, Ipswich, 1995

Burns, Jane E (ed), *The Vulgate Cycle*, Ohio State University Press, 1985

Butterworth, GW (trans,), *Clement of Alexandria*, Heinemann, London, 1968

Capellanus, Andreas, *The Art of Courtly Love* (trans, JJ Parry), Columbia University Press, New York, NY, 1941

Carpenter, Clive, *The Guinness Book of Kings, Rulers and Statesmen*, Guinness Superlatives, Enfield, 1978

Castries, Duc de, *The Lives of the Kings and Queens of France*, (trans, Anne Dobell for Académie Francaise), Weidenfeld & Nicolson, London, 1979

Catholic Encyclopedia, Robert Appleton, New York, NY, 1910

Chadwick, Hector Munro, *Early Scotland: The Picts, Scots and Welsh of Southern Scotland*, Cambridge University Press, Cambridge, 1949

— *Studies in Early British History*, Cambridge University Press, Cambridge, 1954

Chadwick, Nora K, *The Age of Saints in the Celtic Church*, Oxford University Press, 1961

— *Early Brittany*, University of Wales Press, Cardiff, 1969

Challine, Charles, *Recherches sur Chartres*, Société Archéologique d'Eure & Loir, Chartres, reprinted 1994

Charles, RH (trans,), *The Book of Enoch*, (revised from Dillmann's edition of the Ethiopic text, 1893), Oxford University Press, Oxford, 1906 and 1912

Charlsworth, MP, *The Lost Province*, University of Wales Press, Cardiff, 1949

Charpentier, Louis, *The Mysteries of Chartres Cathedral*, Research Into Lost Knowledge Organization and Thorsons, Wellingborough, 1992

Chevalier, Jean, and Gheerbrant, *Dictionnaire des Symboles*, Robert Laffont, Paris 1997

Chrétien de Troyes, *Le Conte del Graal*, (trans, Ruth Harwood Cline), University of Georgia Press, Athens, GA, 1985

Church, Rev Leslie F (ed), *Matthew Henry's Commentary on the Whole Bible*, Marshall Pickering, London, 1960

Clébert, Jean-Paul, *The Gypsies*, Vista Books, London, 1963

Clement of Alexandria, St, *Clementine Homilies and Apostolical Constitutions* (trans, William Whiston), Ante-Nicene Library, T & T Clark, Edinburgh, 1870

Coghlan, Ronan, *The Illustrated Encyclopaedia of Arthurian Legends*, Element Books, Shaftesbury, 1993

Cohn-Sherbok, Lavinia and Dan, *A Short Reader in Judaism*, Oneworld, Oxford, 1997

Coleman, Christopher B, *The Treatise of Lorenzo Valla on the Donation of Constantine*, University of Toronto Press, Toronto, 1993

Cruden, Alexander, *Complete Concordance to the Old and New Testament and the Apocrypha*, Frederick Warne, London, 1891

Cunich, Peter, with David Hoyle, Eamon Duffy and Ronald Hyam, *A History of Magdalene College Cambridge 1428–1988*, Magdalene College Publications, Cambridge, 1994

Danielou, Jean, *The Dead Sea Scrolls and Primitive Christianity* (trans, Salvator Attansio), New American Library, New York, NY, 1962

Davidson, Marshall B, *The Concise History of France*, American Heritage, New York, NY, 1971

Davis, RCH, *A History of Medieval Europe*, Longmans, London, 1957

Deanesly, Margaret, *A History of Early Medieval Europe 476–911*, Methuen, London, 1956

Dill, Sir Samuel, *Roman Society in Gaul in the Merovingian Age*, Macmillan, London, 1926

Dillon, Myles, and Nora K Chadwick, *The Celtic Realms*, Weidenfeld & Nicolson, London, 1967

Dobbs, Betty JT, *The Foundations of Newton's Alchemy*, Cambridge University Press, Cambridge, 1975

Doresse, Jean, *The Secret Books of the Egyptian Gnostics* (trans, Philip Mairet), Hollis & Carter, London, 1960

Dupont-Sommer, André, *The Jewish Sect of Qumrân and the Essenes*, Vallentine Mitchell, London, 1954

– *The Essene Writings from Qumrân* (trans, Geza Vermes), Basil Blackwell, Oxford, 1961

BIBLIOGRAPHY

Ehler, Sidney Z, and John B Morral (eds), *Church and State through the Centuries*, Burns & Oates, London, 1954

Eisenman, Robert H, *Maccabees, Zadokites, Christians and Qumrân*, EJ Brill, Leiden, 1983

— *The Dead Sea Scrolls and the First Christians*, Element Books, Shaftesbury, 1996

Eisler, Riane, *The Chalice and the Blade*, Harper & Row, New York, NY, 1987

Engnell, Ivan, *Studies in Divine Kingship in the Ancient Near East*, Basil Blackwell, Oxford, 1967

Epiphanius, *Panarion* (trans, F Wilkins), EJ Brill, Leiden, 1989–93

— *Ancoratus* (trans, Karl Hol), Walter de Gruyter, Berlin, 2002–4

Eusebius of Caesarea, *An Ecclesiastical History* (trans, Rev. CF Crusè), Samuel Bagster, London, 1838

— *The History of the Church from Christ to Constantine*, Penguin, London, 1989

Evans, Sebastian (trans), *The High History of the Holy Grail*, Everyman, London, 1912

Farmer, David (ed), *Oxford Dictionary of Saints*, Oxford University Press, Oxford, 1997

Fideler, David (ed), *Alexandria: The Journal for the Western Cosmological Traditions*, Phanes Press, 1995

Filliette, Edith, *Saint Mary Magdalene, Her Life and Times*, Society of St Mary Magdalene, Newton Lower Falls, MA, 1983

Finigan, J, *Handbook of Biblical Chronology*, Princeton University Press, Princeton, NJ, 1964

Fleetwood, Rev John, *The Life of Our Lord and Saviour Jesus Christ*, William MacKenzie, Glasgow, 1900

Frankfort, Henri, *Kingship and the Gods*, University of Chicago Press, Chicago, IL, 1948

Frappier, Jean, *Chrétien de Troyes and his Work* (trans, Raymond Cormier), Ohio State University Press, 1982

Freese, JH (trans), *The Octavius of Marcus Minucius Felix*, Macmillan, New York, NY, 1919

Furnival, Frederick J (ed), *The History of the Holy Grail – from Roman l'Estoire dou Saint Graal* by Sires Robert de Boron (trans, Henry Lonelich Skynner), Early English Text Society/N. Turner, London, 1861

Gardner, Laurence, *Bloodline of the Holy Grail*, Thorsons–Element/HarperCollins, London, 2002

— *Realm of the Ring Lords*, Thorsons–Element/HarperCollins, London, 2003

— *Lost Secrets of the Sacred Ark*, Thorsons–Element/HarperCollins, London, 2004

Gibson, Michael, *The Symbolists*, Harry N Abrams, New York, NY, 1988

Gibson, Shimon, and Jacobsen, David M, *Below the Temple Mount in Jerusalem*, Tempus Reparatum, Oxford, 1996

Gildas, *De Excidio et Conquestu Britanniae* (trans, Michael Winterbottom), Phillimore, Chichester, 1978

Gilson, Etienne, *The Mystical Theology of Saint Bernard* (trans, AHC Downes), Sheed & Ward, London, 1940

Gimpel, Jean, *The Medieval Machine: The Industrial Revolution of the Middle Ages*, Pimlico, London, 1976

Godding, Robert SJ, *Grégoire le Grand et la Madeleine in Memoriam soctorum venerantes – Miscellanea in onore di Mgr. Victor Saxer*, The Vatican, Rome 1992

Gougaud, Dom Louis, *Christianity in Celtic Lands* (trans, Maud Joynt), Four Courts Press, Dublin, 1932

Grant, M, *Herod The Great*, Weidenfeld & Nicolson, London, 1971

— *The Jews in the Roman World*, Weidenfeld & Nicolson, London, 1973

Graves, Robert, *The White Goddess*, Faber & Faber, London, 1961

Gregory of Tours, *A History of the Franks* (trans, Lewis Thorpe), Penguin, London, 1964

Gustafson, Fred, *The Black Madonna*, Sigo Press, Boston, MA, 1991

Halsberghe, GS, *The Cult of Sol Invictus*, EJ Brill, Leiden, 1972

Haskins, Susan, *Mary Magdalene, Myth and Metaphor,* Harcourt Brace, New York, NY, 1994

Hassnain, Professor Fida, *A Search for the Historical Jesus – from Apocryphal, Buddhist, Islamic & Sanscrit Sources*, Gateway Books, Bath, 1994

Hastings, James (ed), *Dictionary of the Bible*, T & T Clark, Edinburgh, 1909

Henderson, Ernest F (trans), *Select Historical Documents of the Middle Ages*, G Bell, London, 1925

Herodotus, *The Histories*, (trans, Robin Waterfield), Oxford University Press, Oxford, 1998

BIBLIOGRAPHY

Hewins, Professor S, *The Royal Saints of Britain*, Chiswick Press, London, 1929

Hewison, James King, *The Isle of Bute in the Olden Time*, William Blackwood, Edinburgh, 1895

Higham, NJ, *The Kingdom of Northumbria*, AD 350–1100, Alan Sutton, Stroud, 1993

Hocart, AM, *Kingship*, Oxford University Press, Oxford, 1927

Hodgkin, RH, *A History of the Anglo-Saxons*, Oxford University Press, Oxford, 1952

Hulme, Edward F, *Symbolism in Christian Art*, Swann Sonnenschein, London, 1891

Hunter, Michael, *Science and Society in Restoration England*, Cambridge University Press, Cambridge, 1981

Hutchinson Encyclopedia, The, Hutchinson, London, 1997

Iznard, Guy, *Les Pirates de la Peinture*, Flammarion, Paris, 1955

Jacapo di Voragine, *Legenda Aurea (Golden Legend)*, (trans, William Caxton, 1483; ed, George V O'Neill), Cambridge University Press, Cambridge, 1972

Jackson, Samuel Macauley (ed), *The Schaff-Herzog Encyclopedia of Religious Knowledge*, Baker Book House, Grand Rapids, MI, 1953

James, BS, *Saint Bernard of Clairvaux*, Harper, New York, NY, 1957

James, John, *The Master Masons of Chartres*, West Grinstead Publishing, Leura, NSW, 1990

James, Montague R (ed), *The Apocryphal New Testament*, Clarendon Press, Oxford, 1924

Jameson, Anna, *Legends of the Madonna*, Houghton Mifflin, Boston, 1895

Jennings, Hargrave, *The Rosicrucians: Their Rites and Mysteries*, Routledge, London, 1887

Jerusalem Bible, The, Darton, Longman & Todd, London, 1996

John of Glastonbury, *Cronica sive Antiquitates Glastoniensis Ecclesie* (c1400), Boydell & Brewer, Woodbridge, 1985

Joinville, Sire Jean de, *Chronicles of the Crusades* (trans, Margaret Shaw), Penguin, London, 1976

Jonas, Hans, *The Gnostic Religion*, Routledge, London, 1992

Jones, AHM, *The Herods of Judaea*, Clarendon Press, Oxford, 1938

Josephus, Flavius, *The Antiquities of the Jews* and *The Wars of the Jews* in *The Works of Flavius Josephus*, (trans, William Whiston), Milner & Sowerby, London, 1870

Jowett, George F, *The Drama of the Lost Disciples*, Covenant Books, London, 1961

Jullian, Philippe, *The Symbolists*, Phaidon Press, London, 1973

Keating, Geoffrey, *The History of Ireland*, (trans, David Comyn and Rev PS Dinneen), 1640; reprinted by Irish Texts Society, London, 1902–14

Kemp, Martin, *Leonardo on Painting*, Yale University Press, New Haven, CT, 2001

Kenney, James F, *The Sources for the Early History of Ireland*, Four Courts Press, Dublin, 1966

King, Karen L (ed), *Images of the Feminine in Gnosticism*, Fortres Press, Philadelphia, PA, 1988

Kingsland, William, *The Gnosis or Ancient Wisdom in the Christian Scriptures*, Allen & Unwin, London, 1937

Knight, Christopher, and Robert Lomas, *The Hiram Key*, Century, London, 1996

Kramer, Heinrich, and Sprenger, James, *The Malleus Maleficarum*, (trans, Rev Montague Summers), Dover Publications, New York, NY, 1971

Kramer, Samuel Noel, *The Sacred Marriage Rite*, Indiana University Press, Bloomington, AL, 1969

Lacordaire, Père, *St Mary Magdalene*, Thomas Richardson, Derby, 1880

Lea, Henry Charles, *History of Sacerdotal Celibacy in the Christian Church*, Watts & Co, London, 1867

Levine, Sue A, *The Northern Foreportal Column Figures of Chartres Cathedral*, Verlag Peter Lang, Frankfurt, 1984

Lewis, H Spencer, *The Mystical Life of Jesus*, Ancient and Mystical Order Rosae Crucis, San Jose, CA, 1982

Lewis, Rev Lionel Smithett, *Joseph of Arimathea at Glastonbury*, AR Mobray, London, 1927

Livius, Titus (c59 BC–AD 17), *Ab Urbe Condita*, Harvard University Press, Cambridge, MA, 1919, and Bristol Classical Press, Bristol, 1998

Loomis, Roger Sherman, *The Grail: From Celtic Myth to Christian Symbolism*, University of Wales Press, Cardiff, 1963

Lucie-Smith, Edward, *Symbolist Art*, Thames & Hudson, London, 1972

Lutterworth Dictionary of the Bible (ed, Watson E Mills), Lutterworth Press, Cambridge, 1994

BIBLIOGRAPHY

Macmillan Encyclopedia, The, Macmillan, London, 1996

MacNeill, Eoin, *Celtic Ireland*, (Martin Lester, Dublin, 1921), Academy Press, Dublin, 1981

Malory, Sir Thomas, *Mort D'Arthur*, New York University Books, New York, NY, 1961

Malvern, Marjorie, *Venus in Sackcloth*, Southern Illinois University Press, Carbondale, IL, 1975

Martin, Malachi, *The Decline and Fall of the Roman Church*, Secker & Warburg, London, 1982

Matarasso, PM (trans), *The Quest of the Holy Grail* – from the *Queste del Saint Graal*, Penguin, London, 1976

Matthaei Parisiensis, *Chronica Majora*, Longman, London, 1874 – reprinted Matthew Paris, *The Chronicles of Matthew Paris*, Palgrave Macmillan, London, 1984

Mead, GRS (trans), *Pistis Sophia: a Gnostic Miscellany* (1921), reprinted Kessinger, Kila, MT, 1992

Michell, John, *The City of Revelation*, Garnstone, London 1971

— *Dimensions of Paradise*, Thames and Hudson, London, 1988

Milik, JT, *Ten Years of Discovery in the Wilderness of Judaea* (trans, J Strugnell), SCM Press, London, 1959

Nag Hammadi Library, The (trans, James M Robinson and the Coptic Gnostic Project), Institute for Antiquity and Christianity, EJ Brill, Leiden, 1977

Nathan Bailey's Universal Etymological Dictionary, T Cox at The Lamb, Royal Exchange, London, 1721

Nennius, *Historia Brittonium* (trans, John Morris), Phillimore, Chichester, 1980

Newsome, David, *The Convert Cardinals*, John Murray, London, 1993

Oldenbourg, Zoé, *Massacre at Montségur* (trans, Peter Green), Pantheon, New York, NY, 1961

Osman, Ahmed, *The House of the Messiah*, Harper Collins, London, 1992

Oxford Annotated Bible (eds Herbert G. May and Bruce M. Metzger), Oxford University Press, Oxford, 1962

Oxford Compact English Dictionary (Oxford Word Library: OWL Micrographic), Oxford University Press, Oxford, 1971

Oxford Concise English Dictionary (ed, Della Thompson), Oxford University Press, Oxford, 1995

Pagels, Elaine, *The Gnostic Gospels*, Weidenfeld and Nicolson, London, 1980

Pennick, Nigel, *Sacred Geometry*, Turnstone, Wellingborough, 1980

Perowne, Stewart, *The Life and Times of Herod the Great*, Hodder & Stoughton, London, 1956

— *The Later Herods*, Hodder & Stoughton, London, 1958

Petrie, WM Flinders, *Researches in Sinai*, John Murray, London, 1906

Picknett, Lynn, and Clive Prince, *Turin Shroud: In Whose Image?* Bloomsbury, London 1994

Pierce, Don, *How to Decorate Mats*, Cameron, San Raphael, CA, 1985

Pincus-Witten, R, *Occult Symbolism in France*, Garland, London, 1976

Pope, Marvin H, *Song of Songs*, Garden City/Doubleday, New York, NY, 1977

Porter, JR, *The Illustrated Guide to the Bible*, Duncan Baird, London, 1995

— *Jesus Christ*, Duncan Baird, London, 1999

Qualls-Corbett, Nancy, *The Sacred Prostitute*, Inner City Books, Toronto, 1988

Recht, Rolland, *Les Bâtisseurs des Cathédrales Gothiques*, Éditions les Musées de la Ville de Strasbourg, Strasbourg, 1989

Rees, Alwyn and Brinley, *Celtic Heritage*, Thames & Hudson, London, 1961

Rees, Rev WJ Rice, *Lives of the Cambro-British Saints*, Welsh MSS Society/Longman, London, 1853

Reichert, B (ed), *Acta capitulorum generalium ordinis praedicatorum*, The Vatican, Rome, 1898

Ruhemann, Helmut, *The Cleaning of Paintings*, Hacker Art Books, New York, NY, 1982

Ricci, Carla, *Mary Magdalene and Many Others*, Fortress Press, Minneapolis, MN, 1994

Richey, Margaret Fitzgerald, *Studies of Wolfram Von Eschenbach*, Oliver & Boyd, London, 1957

Ritmeyer, Leen and Kathleen, *Secrets of Jerusalem's Temple Mount*, Biblical Archaeological Society, Washington, DC, 1998

Runciman, Steven, *A History of the Crusades*, Cambridge University Press, Cambridge, 1951

Ruvigny & Raineval, Melville Henry Massue, Marquis de, 1868–1921, *The Jacobite Peerage, Baronetage, Knightage & Grants of Honour* (1921), facsimile reprint Charles Skilton, London, 1974

BIBLIOGRAPHY

Sackville-West, V, *Saint Joan of Arc*, Michael Joseph, London, 1936

Schonfield, Professor Hugh J, *The Original New Testament*, Waterstone, London, 1985

— *The Passover Plot*, Element Books, Shaftesbury, 1985

Scott, John, *The Early History of Glastonbury*, Boydell Press, London, 1981

Septuagint with Apocrypha, The (trans, Sir Lancelot CL Brenton), Samuel Bagster, London, 1851

Seward, Desmond, *The Monks of War*, Paladin/Granada, St Albans, 1974

Shaw, R Cunliffe, *Post-Roman Carlisle and the Kingdoms of the North-West*, Guardian Press, Preston, 1964

Sinclair, Andrew, *The Sword and the Grail*, Crown, New York, NY, 1992

Skeels, Dell, *The Romance of Perceval*, University of Washington Press, 1966

Skene, William Forbes, *Chronicles of the Picts and Scots*, HM General Register, Edinburgh, 1867

— *Celtic Scotland*, David Douglas, Edinburgh, 1886–90

Smallwood, EM, *The Jews Under Roman Rule*, EJ Brill, Leiden, 1976

Smith, Dr William, *Smith's Bible Dictionary*, (1868 revised), Hendrickson, Peabody, MA, 1998

Smith, Morton, *The Secret Gospel*, Victor Gollancz, London, 1974

Spence, Keith, *Brittany and the Bretons*, Victor Gollancz, London, 1978

Spong, John Shelby *Born of a Woman*, HarperSanFrancisco, San Francisco, CA, 1992

Staley, Edgcumbe, *King René d'Anjou and his Seven Queens*, John Long, London, 1912

Starbird, Margaret, *The Woman with the Alabaster Jar*, Bear, Santa Fe, 1993

— *The Goddess in the Gospels: Reclaiming the Sacred Feminine*, Bear & Co, Santa Fe, NM, 1998

Stein, Walter Johannes, *The Ninth Century*, Temple Lodge, London, 1991

Steinberg, Leo, *Leonardo's Incessant Last Supper*, Zone Books, New York, NY, 2001

Stokes, Whitley (ed), *Félire Óengusso Céli Dé (The Martyrology of Oengus the Culdee)*, Dublin Institute for Advanced Studies, Dublin, 1984

Stoyanov, Yuri, *The Hidden Tradition in Europe*, Arkana/Penguin, London, 1994

Strong, James (ed), *The Exhaustive Concordance of the Bible*, Abingdon Press, New York, NY, 1890

Sumption, Jonathan, *The Albigensian Crusade*, Faber & Faber, London, 1978

Tacitus, *The Histories*, (trans, Kenneth Wellesley), Penguin, London, 1995

— *The Annals of Imperial Rome* (trans, Michael Grant), Penguin, London, 1996

Taylor, Gladys, *Our Neglected Heritage*, Covenant Books, London, 1974

Taylor, John W, *The Coming of the Saints*, Covenant Books, London, 1969

Thiering, Barbara, *Jesus the Man*, Transworld, London, 1992

— *Jesus of the Apocalypse*, Transworld/Doubleday, London, 1996

Thompson, JM, *The French Revolution*, Basil Blackwell, Oxford, 1964

Thorpe, Lewis (trans,), *The Life of Charlemagne*, Penguin, London, 1979

Tolstoy, Count Nikolai, *The Quest for Merlin*, Hamish Hamilton, London, 1985

Torjesen, Karen Jo, *When Women Were Priests*, HarperSanFrancisco, San Francisco, CA, 1995

Unterman, Alan, *Dictionary of Jewish Lore and Legend*, Thames & Hudson, London, 1997

Vasari, Giorgio, *Le Vite de' Piú Eccelenti Architetti, Pittori, et Scultori Italiani*, Firenza, 1550

Vermes, Geza, *The Dead Sea Scrolls in English*, Penguin, London, 1995

— *The Complete Dead Sea Scrolls in English*, Penguin, London, 1998

Von Eschenbach, Wolfram, *Parzival* (ed, Hugh D Sacker), Cambridge University Press, Cambridge, 1963

Wade-Evans, Arthur W, *Welsh Christian Origins*, Alden Press, Oxford, 1934

Waite, Arthur Edward, *The Hidden Church of the Holy Grail*, Rebman, London, 1909

Walker, Barbara G, *The Woman's Encyclopedia of Myths and Secrets*, HarperSanFrancisco, San Francisco, CA, 1983

Wallace-Hadrill, JM, *The Long Haired Kings*, Methuen, London, 1962

BIBLIOGRAPHY

Warren, FE, *The Liturgy of the Celtic Church*, Oxford University Press, Oxford, 1881

Watson, WJ, *The History of the Celtic Place Names of Scotland*, William Blackwood, Edinburgh, 1926

White, Michael, *Isaac Newton, the Last Sorcerer*, Fourth Estate, London, 1998

Wijngaards, John, *No Women in Holy Orders?* Canterbury Press, Norwich, 2002

Wilken, Robert L, *The Christians as the Romans Saw Them*, Yale University Press, New Haven, CT, 1984

William of Malmesbury, *The Antiquities of Glastonbury*, Talbot/JMF Books, Llanerch, 1980

Williams, Taliesin, with Iolo Morganwg, Thomas Price, Owen Jones, and the Society for the Publication of Ancient Welsh Manuscripts. Abergavenny, *Iolo Manuscripts*, W Rees, Llandovery and Longman & Co., London, 1848

Wilson, AN, *Jesus*, Sinclair Stevenson, London, 1992

Wilson, R McL, *The Gospel of Philip: Translated from the Coptic Text*, AR Mowbray, London, 1962

Wilson, Colin, and John Grant, *The Directory of Possibilities*, Webb & Bower, Exeter, 1981

Windeatt, Barry (ed), *The Book of Margery Kempe*, Longman, London, 1999

Wojcik, Jan W, *Robert Boyle and the Limits of Reason*, Cambridge University Press, Cambridge, 1997

Wolters, Al, *The Copper Scroll*, Sheffield Academic Press, Sheffield, 1996

Yadin, Yigael, *The Temple Scroll*, Weidenfeld & Nicolson, London, 1985

Yates, Frances A, *The Rosicrucian Enlightenment*, Routledge, London, 1972

Zuckerman, Arthur J, *A Jewish Princedom in Feudal France*, Columbia University Press, New York, NY, 1972

PICTURE CREDITS

Thanks must go to those below for courtesies in respect of the following photographic illustrations and copyright images:

1, 7, 13, 15, 18, 20, 24, 26, 27, 28, 29, 30, 31, 32, 33, 34, 35, 36, 41, 46, 47, 49, 50, Bridgeman Art Library, London. 21, 12, Art Magick <http://www.artmagick.com/>. Entropic Fine Art <http://www. entropic-art.com/> Peter Robson Studio. 9, 11, Galleria degli Uffizi, Florence. 48, Colin Palmer <www.buyimage.co.uk> 01279 757917. 14, Russian Orthodox Convent of St Mary Magdalene, Jerusalem. 51, John G. Johnson Collection, Philadelphia Museum of Art. 10, Gotische Basilika St Maria Magdalena, Tiefenbronn. 2, 8, 52, 53, Private Collections. 5, 16, 17, 25, 37, 38, 39, 40, 44, 45, Brendon Arts Archive. 3, 4, 22, 23, 42, 43, Lorna Doone Studio, Deering Guild Series. 6, Congregation des Soeurs de Saint-Thomas de Villeneuve.

While every effort has been made to secure permissions, if there are any errors or oversights, we apologize and will make suitable acknowledgement in any future edition of this book.

DAN BROWN AND *THE DA VINCI CODE*

From its launch in March 2003, Dan Brown's worldwide best-seller, *The Da Vinci Code*, has given rise to a widespread public interest in Mary Magdalene and the dynastic heirs of Jesus. It has also created a new tourism focus, with a great many people now visiting the sites and locations of the story.

That Jesus and Mary Magdalene were married and had offspring is hardly news to readers such as my own. Their marriage, their children and their descendants were detailed ten years ago in *Bloodline of the Holy Grail* (and have been updated in *The Magdalene Legacy*), but these things have now emerged as wholly new revelations to the readers of fictional novels. It is possible that the impact would not have been so great, however, if Dan Brown had not stated in his book's Introduction that *The Da Vinci Code* is based on certain historical facts – something which is not a common aspect of novelistic writing. By virtue of this, his readers were immediately intrigued, and have become increasingly fascinated by the blend of fact and fiction in his story. What the author has not done, of course, is to explain in his narrative where one gives way to the other. He states in interview that *The Da Vinci Code* is just a novel, but this has led to a somewhat unsatisfactory situation as far as the press, media and academia are concerned. It has made it possible for many to insist that everything in the book is fictitious, whereas others are claiming far more factual substance than the book actually contains. Even the novel's lead character, the Harvard symbologist Robert Langdon, has his own official website, as if he truly exists.

Although Dan Brown has stated in media appearances that he does not claim the theories discussed by his fictional characters to be factual, he does rather contradict this in the book by stating, 'All descriptions of artwork, architecture, documents and secret rituals in this novel are accurate'. The reality is, however, that in a great many instances they are not accurate in terms of being generally acknowledged or proven. They are only accurate by way of extraction from other recently published books by authors whose theories are challenged and debated by the establishments concerned.

As researchers and journalists know only too well, there is always potential for there to be differences between 'fact' and 'truth'. That a footballer scored a goal in a particular match can be considered a fact. But commentators (according to which team they might support) would argue about how that goal came to be scored. In such instances, their truths would be differently presented because they subject the fact to opposing interpretations. It is precisely the same with all documented history because history is not comprised of events; it is a compiled record of events. Such records are necessarily subject to matters of opinion and the writers' vested interests. History was never carved in stone; it is an ever-flowing process, which is why dogmatic teaching can always be challenged. But one cannot challenge dogma and then replace it with another dogma. One can only replace dogma with alternative opinions and different interpretations, thereby widening the scope of choice. In this regard, Dan Brown's opinion of his own work has now mellowed somewhat. Having initially claimed that certain aspects of *The Da Vinci Code* were 'accurate', he now states on his website that 'interpreting those ideas is left to the reader'.

By mentioning the titles of certain non-fiction publications in the course of his story, Dan Brown has encouraged a new readership into that market, and this is good news for writers of the revisionist genre. But there are pitfalls for those who are not conversant with such literature, in that the individually cited books do not necessarily agree with each other in all respects. What they have within them are particular items which, when removed from their contexts, are eminently suited to *The Da Vinci Code* plot. In order to facilitate this, Dan Brown has ignored the fact that some published information has now been disproved or superseded by way of ongoing research. His discussion, for example, of Leonardo's mural of *The Last Supper* is entirely misleading because he relates it specifically to the way the painting looked after a cleaning in 1954. He stipulates this particular date as being entirely relevant to his novel's conclusions. What he failed to take into account, however, was a subsequent and far more thorough conservation procedure commissioned in 1978. When finally unveiled in 1999, *The Last Supper* was seen to be markedly different to the heavily overpainted artwork that features in *The Da Vinci Code*.

Alongside Dan Brown's discussion of Leonardo's work, he makes a number of historically based assertions which similarly ignore the research of recent years. This would not matter in something that is presented as fictional, but it does matter if readers are led to understand it as documented truth. Paramount in his story is an organization called the

Priory of Sion, and Dan Brown states in his Introduction that this currently extant secret society has existed since the time of the Crusades. This was indeed thought to be the case twenty or more years ago when *The Da Vinci Code*'s source reference was published, but it is now known to be quite wrong. Historically, there have been at least four known societies with similar names: the Order of Sion, the Prieuré Notre Dame de Sion, the Order of the Realm of Sion and the Priory of Sion. But these orders and societies were not in any way connected in terms of their interests or objectives. They did not constitute a continuous movement, and there is no such society in existence today. The last (the only one actually called the Priory of Sion) was not founded until 1956, and it folded in 1984 when its secretary's fraudulent activities were exposed in the French press.

This then is the paradox of *The Da Vinci Code*: the author set the scene for a novel with some content that was erroneously said to be factual – but had he not done this, the book might not have achieved its phenomenal sales success. As a result, the more important aspects of its underlying content would not now be subjects of such widespread interest and debate. It is a case, therefore, where the end can perhaps be said to justify the means.

The Da Vinci Code is an absorbing tale of murder, mystery and religious conspiracy – a fast-moving thriller set in France and Britain. It focuses on real locations such as the church of St Sulpice and the Louvre in Paris, Rosslyn Chapel in Scotland, and Temple Church and Westminster Abbey in London. Attention is also drawn to the monastery of Santa Maria delle Grazie in Italy. These have all been sites of long-standing fascination for those interested in art, religion, history and architecture, but they now have a new visitor audience of people who were not previously in these categories. They are the Dan Brown readers whose passion is to become acquainted with the high points of action in the novel, and this has clearly benefited the British and European tourist industries.

The Louvre and Santa Maria delle Grazie are the locations of famous paintings by Leonardo da Vinci, including *The Virgin of the Rocks*, *Mona Lisa* and *The Last Supper*, each of which features in the story. Dan Brown uses these paintings to establish the notion that Leonardo incorporated secret information within his artwork, and it is in this regard that he makes his most significant errors by way of using unreliable source information.

As discussed in *The Magdalene Legacy*, many artists of the Renaissance era produced allegorical work. But, in respect of Mary Magdalene, there are far better examples than anything attempted by Leonardo da Vinci. Dan Brown suggests that Leonardo surreptitiously introduced Mary Magdalene into *The Last Supper* by omitting the apostle John in order to keep thirteen figures at the table. But he would have had no need to do this. Other artists, such as Fra Angelico, Giotto di Bondone and Gerard David, included her blatantly and openly – not only at the Last Supper, but even alongside Jesus at the wedding in Cana. The premise of *The Da Vinci Code* is that, by seating Mary Magdalene next to Jesus, Leonardo was highlighting their marital status. This is an interesting theory, but one which is thoroughly disproved by Leonardo's own notes and sketches for the painting.

They not only make it clear that the character in question is John, but also give a detailed description of the youthful, somewhat feminine, attributes that he would apply to the figure's portrayal.

Prior to, and during the Renaissance, there was no secret made of Mary's relationship with Jesus. The writings of King René d'Anjou and others of the era confirm that even King Louis XI (1461–83) was insistent about her dynastic position in the royal lineage of France. As recently published by the Dominican Historical Institute in Rome, the gnostic Cathars of Provence firmly believed that 'Mary Magdalene was in reality the wife of Christ'. It is in such contexts that *The Da Vinci Code* loses the academic impact which it could have achieved because Dan Brown's research was actually too superficial. Instead of citing primary sources, and acknowledged historical writings to support his book's content about Jesus and Mary Magdalene, the author elected to cite only recently published mass-market editions. By virtue of this, no matter how factual might be the underlying premise of *The Da Vinci Code*, it fails to provide any weighty evidence of its claims.

Santa Maria delle Grazie, the home of Leonardo's *The Last Supper*, is a Dominican establishment and, from 1295, Mary Magdalene has been the Mother Protectress and Patron Saint of the Order. Dominican artwork of the Renaissance portrays Mary in many non-biblical environments, especially depictions of her voyage to France and her association with Bishop Lazarus of Marseilles. Franciscan and other monastic artwork was similarly contrived, and Mary Magdalene appears in all manner of scenes from the Nativity to an audience with Emperor Theodosius in Rome. Such portrayals were not just acceptable, they were expected in an environment that held the Magdalene in such high esteem. If Leonardo had wanted to include her in his famous mural, then he could have done so with impunity. The art-related premise of *The Da Vinci Code* is full of historical substance, but the examples that Dan Brown elected to use are so hypothetically based that they undermine an otherwise well-constructed plot and leave it wide open to criticism from the art establishment. It is unfortunate, therefore, that of all the novel's facts and fictions, the most significantly presented feature of the narrative – *The Last Supper* theory of Mary taking the place of John – emerges as its most inadequate element of fiction.

Laurence Gardner

INDEX

Abdias, Bishop of Babylon 27–8
Abishag 33, 203
Abraham 76, 188, 212, 265
Acts 29, 60, 68–9, 89, 131, 167,
    186, 209, 211, 217, 226, 254, 303
Adam 26, 173
Adamnan of Iona 289, 291
Ado, St 90
Adonijah 33, 203
Aedàn of Dalriada 287–8,
    289–90, 291, 292, 293, 294
Aethelfrith of Bernicia 292,
    293–4
Agnes, St 57
Aix-en-Provence 238
Albertus Magnus 122
Albi-gens 142, 144, 387
alchemy 59, 122, 383
Alexander VI, Pope 367
allegory 44, 59
American Revolution 378–9, 383
Aminadab 276, 277
Andrew, St 49, 153
Andrews, William Eusebius 158
Angelico, Fra 303, 387
 Last Supper fresco 347, 387
 Noli me tangere fresco 50, 387
angels 77
Angles 285, 291, 292–3, 294
Anglican Church 178
Ann, mother of Mother Mary 84,
    300
Anna, daughter of Joseph of
    Arimathea 261, 276, 278, 283
Annals of Imperial Rome 39
Anne of Austria 112
Anne of Brittany 113
Antioch 92, 219
Antiochus IV of Syria 72

Antiquities of the Jews, The 39, 66,
    139, 156, 190, 215, 263
Aphrodite 33, 50, 58, 224
Apocalypse de Saint Jean, L' 63–4
Apocalypse of Peter, The 87
Apostle's Creed 82
Apostolic Church Order 174
Apostolic Constitutions 40, 86,
    167, 171–2, 175, 185, 189
Aragona, Tullia d' 367
Aristobulus (Arwystli Hen)
    89–90, 260, 261
Arius (Libyan priest) 81
Ark of the Covenant 119, 122,
    123, 377–8
Armageddon 61–2
Arnolfini, Giovanni 349–50, 352
Arthur, King 265, 289–93, 294
Arthurian romance 203, 242,
    243, 262–4, 278, 288, 296–7
ArtWatch International 337
Arum Lily 327–8
Arundel, William Earl of 16
Arviragus of Siluria 251–2, 253,
    256, 278
Ascension 27, 43, 210–11
Ashburnham, Bertram, 5th Earl
    of 384
Askew, Anthony 114
Astarte 58
Atbash 128–9
Athanasius of Alexandria 167
Attila the Hun 93
Audley, Thomas Lord 18
Augustus 35, 156
Aurelius the Ambrosius 285–6,
    291
Avallachs 263, 283
Avallonian dynasty 243, 295

Baciccio, Il (Giovanni Battista Gaulli)
 The Three Marys at the Empty Sepulchre 302
Baedàn mac Cairill 291
Bakewell, Joan 42
Baphomet 125, 128–30
baptisms, mass 239–40
Barcilon, Pinin Brambilla 335, 338, 339
Bayley, Harold 46
Beli Mawr 283
Bellagambe, Jean
 St Ann Immaculately Conceiving 84
Bellini, Giovanni
 Sacred Allegory 362–4
Bellotti, Michelangelo 332–3
Benedict XI, Pope 122–3
Benjamin of Tudela 103
Berazzi, Stefano 334
Bernard de Clairvaux 19, 32, 104, 105, 116–17, 119, 143, 204, 265
Bertrand de Blanchefort 120
Bethlehem ('House of Bread') 244
Bethlehem of Judaea 216
Bézu 120, 122–4, 246, 376–7, 379, 383
Bistea Neptunis 275, 276
Black Madonna 31–2, 76, 91, 96
Bloodline of the Holy Grail (Gardner) 21, 208
Boaz and *Jachin* 242
Body in Question, The 42–3
Bolland, Jean 222
Bonaparte, Lucien 113
Bonhomme, André 370, 371
Boniface VIII, Pope 107–8, 109, 118–19, 122, 130

Book of Enoch 70–1, 78
Book of Hours 57
Book of Margery Kempe 18–19
Books of the Saviour 114
Borras, Nicolás
 St Mary Magdalene with St Dominic and St Bernard 117
Bossi, Guiseppe 345
Botticelli, Sandro 57
 The Birth of Venus 50, 224, 389
 Madonna of the Book 50, 59
 Madonna of the Magnificat 59, 242
 Madonna of the Pomegranate 49–50, 59, 242
Boudet, Henri 377
Boudicca (Boadicea) 284
Boyle, Robert 383, 384
Brân the Blessed 260, 261, 276, 278, 283
bread symbolism 244–6
Brittany 243, 283, 295–7
Bruegel, Pieter the Elder
 The Numbering at Bethlehem 355
Brychan of Brecknock 285
Brychan II 286
Byzantine Empire 92
Byzantium 84, 92

Cadwaladr of Wales 294
Caesarius of Arles 133–4
Cairill of Antrim 286, 291
Camelyn, Battle of 292
Camlanna, Battle of 292
Candlemas ritual 91
Capernaum synagogue 15
Capgrave, John 253, 280
Caput Mortuum 121–2
Caractacus the Pendragon 86, 251, 260, 261, 278
Caravaggio

Mary Magdalene 50

The Rest on the Flight into Egypt 299

Carlisle 288, 289, 292

Carolingians 97

Carolus Martel 97

Carpocrations 137

Carreño de Miranda, Juan
  La Messe de fondation de l'ordre des Trinitaires 361

Cassian, John 91, 109, 147–8, 149, 244

Cassianites 91, 101, 103–4, 147, 222

Castiglione, Baldassare 303–4

Cathars 141–4

Catherine of Siena 146

Catholic Church 11, 38, 53, 81, 93–5, 145, 171, 280 *see also* Church/Church of Rome

Catholic Encyclopedia 6, 111, 229, 297

Catholicism 38, 48

Catholics 9, 23–4, 78, 82–3, 121, 143, 179

Catus Decianus 90

Cauchon, Pierre 392

Cavenaghi, Luigi 334

Caxton, William 16

Celtic Church 52, 87, 88, 93, 243, 290

Ceretic of Strathclyde 284, 285

Cesare Baronius 88, 90, 250

Cesare Minvielle 123

Cesi, Bartolommeo
  The Vision of Saint Ann 300

Champaigne, Philippe de
  The Last Supper 345

Charlemagne 97, 102, 158

Charles, Duc de Lorraine 383

Charles I of Anjou 107

Charles II of Naples 105–6, 107–8, 146, 378

Charles VI 386, 391

Charles VIII 112

Charles IX 112

Chartres Cathedral 58, 121, 204, 212

Chaumeil, Jean Luc 372, 373

Chenamy, Jeanne de 349, 352

Chérisey, Philippe de 372, 373, 379

Childeric III 97

Chonomore, Lord of Brittany 296

Chrétien de Troyes 243, 266–7

Christian, first use of term 219

Christianity
  in Britain 88, 260–1, 279–81
  corruption by Church of Rome 60, 169–70
  emergence of Mary's 'virginity' 40–1
  Filioque debate 82–3
  portrayals of Jesus 298
  roots in Judaism 265
  veneration of Mary Magdalene 56
  see also Pauline Christianity

Christians
  called *Nazara/Nasrani* 68
  persecution by Romans 28, 90–1, 132, 186, 227, 279
  in Roman catacombs 297
  unsupported by orthodox Jews 36

Chronicles 242, 265

Church/Church of Rome 41, 62, 177, 183, 250, 254, 266, 364
  Apostolic Succession 83, 86–7, 278
  Black Madonna dilemma 32

Cardinals, instigation of 92
Cassian's denunciation of 91
Cathars, annihilation of 144
Christianity, corruption of 60, 169–70
Desposyni, problem with 37–8
dogma 148–9
Easter/Eostre debate 52–4
foundation 17, 22, 35, 60, 186, 297
Grail, condemnation of 277
Gospels, interference with 136–7, 166
Joan of Arc, attitude to 392
and Mary Magdalene
  connection with portrayals 146–7, 364–9
  denigration of 1–2, 5–6, 174
  fabrication of penitence 7, 8–9
  official image of 57
  perception of threat 21
  suppression of legacy 20–1, 170–1, 204–5
Merovingians, deposition of 96–7
non-canonical Gospels, suppression of 153–4
papal succession 86–7
Pope John XXIII's reforms 23–4
propaganda, use of 20
René d'Anjou, discrediting of 392
Revelation, attitude to 30–1, 60
saintly women with boxes, dislike of 361–2
spiritual/political conflict 22–3
split from Eastern Byzantine Church 83
women, views on 166–7, 169, 170–6
X cross as heresy 49

Church Fathers 40, 56, 88, 186, 188, 368–9
circumcision 39, 160–1
Clarke, Kenneth 323
Claudia Rufina Britannica 261
Clement V, Pope 123
Clement of Alexandria 35, 40, 131, 137–8, 169, 170, 177, 185, 188–9, 234
Cleopatra VII 13, 72
Cleve, Joos van
  The Holy Family 355
Clothilde of Burgundy 96, 275
Clovis, King 96, 133, 275
Codex Sinaiticus 135, 177
Codex Vatanicus 42, 135, 177
Coel Hen 284
Coel II of Colchester 277
Colbert Traill, Seignelay de 384
Colchester 278, 284
Coleman, Christopher B 100
Columba, St 288, 289
Commandery of Carcassonne 377, 378–9
Congregatio Propaganda Fide 20
Constantine the Great 17, 22, 28, 35–7, 62, 81, 87, 91, 95, 97, 100, 147, 161–2, 170, 224, 277–8, 297
Conte de Graal – Roman de Perceval 266–7
Coptic language 114, 126, 151
Corinthians 171, 196
Council of Basle 255
Council of Carthage 30, 147, 154, 167, 177
Council of Constantinople 82
Council of Ephesus 82
Council of Hippo 167
Council of Nicaea 36, 37, 81, 88, 186, 189

Council of Pisa 255–6
Council of Toledo 83
Council of Trento 168
Council of Troyes 19, 117
Council of Trullo 38
courtesans 366–9
Cousin, Jean
 Eva Prima Pandora 362
Cressy, Hugh 88–9, 110, 249
cross symbolism 48–50
Crucifixion 1–2, 13, 20, 27, 53,
 64, 126, 162, 206, 208–9, 229,
 232, 234, 298, 440–50
Crusades 84, 104, 370
Cunedda 284–5
Cuspius Fadus 263
Cymbeline 283–4
Cyrenius, Governor of Syria 156,
 157

Da Vinci Code, The (Brown) 21, 44,
 51, 209, 266, 305–6, 308–9, 313,
 317, 320, 321, 326, 330, 336,
 339, 340–3, 370, 381, 382, 385
Dali, Salvador 63–4
 Life of Mary Magdalene 64, 272
Damasus I, Pope 177
Daniel, Book of 69, 71
David, King 15, 26, 77, 96, 199,
 207, 244, 245
David, House of 27, 73–4, 77,
 102–3, 191, 231, 265, 266
David, Gerard 197
 The Rest on the Flight to Egypt
 302
Day of Judgement 61–2
De Sancto Joseph ab Arimathea
 223, 251, 253, 264
Dead Sea Scrolls 48, 61, 67–8, 85,
 125, 126, 127–8, 132, 139, 156,
 160, 212, 214, 216

Community Rule (Manual of
 Discipline) 125, 238, 343–4
Copper Scroll 71, 125, 216
Habakkuk Pesher 125
Messianic Rule 198
Scroll of the Rules 85, 194
Temple Scroll 162
War Scroll 62, 78, 125, 198
del Acqs, House 241, 243, 276
Desposyni 25–30, 34–5, 37–8, 48,
 63, 86–7, 88, 89, 90, 96, 99,
 101, 102–3, 142, 153–4, 166,
 206, 228, 243, 250, 264, 271,
 276, 283, 393
Deuteronomy 127, 162, 172
Dialogue of the Saviour, The 149
Dianothus, Abbot of Bangor
 93–4
Diatessaron, The 178
Dionysius calendar 158
Divine Comedie, La 63
Dominicans 108, 109, 111, 122,
 145–6
Domitian 28
Donation of Constantine 95,
 97–101, 102, 116, 281, 359
Dondaine, Antoine 141
Dorotheus of Tyre 89, 90
Dossiers Secrets, Les 379–80
Douai Bible 179
dove symbolism 58, 297
Dun Baedàn, Battles of 286–7,
 291
Dunstan, St 252
Dürer, Albrecht 357
 *Apocalypse of Saint John the
 Divine* 59–60
 Last Supper 347
 The Meeting of Anna and Joachim
 83

Easter 52–5
Eastern (Byzantine) Orthodox
    Church 9, 54, 83, 92, 189–90
Edouard de Bar 388
Edward I 266
Edward III 390
egg symbolism 52–5
Eleanor, Queen 104
Eleazar Ben Jair 228
Eleazer Annas 157
Eleutherius 279–80, 281, 282
Elias 77
Elizabeth (mother of John the
    Baptist) 69, 73, 78–9, 213
Elizabeth I 178
Elliot, John 179
Elphinstone, Lord 384
Emrys of Powys 288
'engrailing' 50
Eochaid Find 291
Eostre 52–3, 54
Epiphanius 39, 189
Erasmus, Desiderius 99
Essenes 36, 65–8, 72–3, 127, 132,
    157, 190, 209, 216, 245, 276
 marriage customs 73–81, 190–3
Eucharia (mother of Mary
    Magdalene) 16
Eucharist 45, 48, 272
Eurgain, Queen 260
Eurgen, Queen 276, 277
Eusebius of Caesaria 34, 88, 188,
    251
Eve 31, 173, 361–2
Exodus 45, 127, 199, 210, 245, 286
Ezekiel, Book of 45, 49, 183

Fagan and Dyfan 280
Faramund, King 275
Feeding of the Five Thousand
    240

Felix, Governor of Jerusalem
    226–7
Fibonacci Series 314
Filioque Article 83
fish and fisher symbolism
    238–40, 275–6, 297
Fisher Kings 222, 238–43, 257,
    275, 276, 277, 359
Flamel, Nicolas 119, 383, 389
Flavius Josephus 12–13, 29, 39,
    65–7, 73, 76, 79, 132, 139, 190,
    191, 211, 263
Flavius Titus 228
fleur-de-lis 96, 355, 356, 358
Foret, Joseph 63
Franco, Veronica
    367
François I 112, 315
Franklin, Benjamin 377, 378–9,
    383
Freculphus, Bishop of Lisieux
    223, 251
French Bibles 46
French Revolution 19, 113, 145,
    316

Gabràn, Prince 286–7
Gabriel/Abiathar 69–70, 71, 73,
    75, 77–8, 79, 80, 190, 192, 211
Gaddi, Taddeo
 Expulsion from the Temple 300
Galahad du Lac 263–4, 265, 267
Galatians 39
Galilee 12, 13, 76, 132
Gaston de la Pièrre Phoebus 123
Genesis 31, 32, 45, 127, 160, 183,
    206, 209, 212, 265
Geneva Bible 178
Gentiles 36, 76, 89, 195, 214, 225,
    239, 240
Gentilis de Foligno 123

George II 379
Gerard de Roussillon 104
Gheradini, Lisa di Anton Maria
  di Noldo 311–12
Ghirlandaio 300
  The Adoration of the Shepherds
  299
Gilbert of Holland 265
Gildas I Albanicus 223
Gildas II Badonicas 88, 110, 247,
  251, 260–1, 280, 286–7
Gilead 265
Giordano, Luca 5
Giotto di Bondone 57, 58, 146,
  197, 300, 303
  Voyage to Marseilles 225
Glastonbury 51, 251–2, 254, 256,
  258–9, 279, 280, 284, 392
Gnostics 87, 93, 114, 142, 238
Godefroi de Bouillon 382
gold, monatomic 119–20, 244–6,
  383
Golden Mean 307–10
Gospel of John 4, 5, 6, 8, 10, 13,
  40, 45, 54, 131, 133, 138–9,
  140, 164, 165, 167, 180, 193,
  194, 195, 199–200, 201, 214,
  215, 217, 223, 229, 230–1,
  232–3, 240, 244, 247, 257, 281,
  341, 342, 343, 363
  authorship 235–7
Gospel of Luke 6, 8, 10, 13, 15,
  26, 27, 39, 40, 66, 69, 73–4,
  74–5, 78–9, 131, 132, 133, 135,
  139, 156, 157, 158–9, 160, 161,
  163–4, 165, 167, 180–1, 183,
  187, 190–1, 197, 199–200, 208,
  214, 217, 229, 233, 239–40,
  268, 360
Gospel of Mark 5, 10, 11, 12, 13,
  16, 39, 40, 47, 59, 131–3, 139,
  141, 163, 164, 165, 167,
  199–200, 209, 210, 232, 233,
  240, 247, 268, 269
  corruption by Clement 135–8,
  170, 188
  spurious verses added 135–6,
  166
Gospel of Mary Magdalene 83,
  151–2, 166, 168, 169, 251
Gospel of Matthew 12, 13, 15, 26,
  27, 39, 40, 66, 68, 69, 73, 74–5,
  80, 131, 132, 139, 141, 155,
  156, 158–9, 163, 164–5, 167,
  180, 182, 190–1, 192, 193,
  199–200, 207, 209, 215, 216,
  232, 233, 239, 245, 268, 270
Gospel of Nicodemus 253
Gospel of Peter 150–1, 166, 167–8
Gospel of Philip 11, 39, 150, 166,
  167–8, 169, 170, 231, 251
Gospel of Thomas 167–8, 169
Gospels 1–2, 20, 81, 114, 178
  cryptic information 216–17
  differences in presentation 162
  discrepancies 155–6
  Eschatological Knowledge 127
  selection 167–76
  translatory confusion 41, 74–5,
  157, 179–82
Great Bible 178, 179
Greek language 13, 44, 47, 114,
  126, 131, 132, 151, 160–1, 182,
  225, 275
Gregory I, Pope 6, 10
Gregory XIII, Pope 84
Gregory XV, Pope 20
Gregory of Tours 253
Guadermaris, Henri de 225
Guidon de Montanor 123
Guilhelm de Toulouse 102–3,
  144

Guillaume d'Arbley 124
Guillaume de Tonneins 145
Gwenddolau, King 288
Gwynedd, House of 285
Gwyr Llew of Carlisle 290, 295

haloes 298
Hamilton, Gavin 323
Harbison, Craig 352, 354
Hasidic Jews 70
Hasidim 72
Hasmonaeans 13, 16, 72, 266
Hebrew alphabet 128
Hebrews, Book of 191, 194, 211, 212
Hegesippus 27, 28, 222
Helena, St 455-7
Helena-Salome, wife of Simon Lazarus 137, 220, 223, 235
Heliand 241-2
Hengest 285
Henri de Montfort 123
Henry II 252
Henry V 390-1
Henry VI 17, 386
Henry VIII 18, 110
Hernoul of the Franks 358-9
Herod, House of 231
Herod I, the Great 71, 155, 157, 158
Herod of Chalcis 29, 90, 156, 220, 254
Herod-Agrippa I 29, 90, 140, 156, 186, 220
Herod-Agrippa II 29, 90, 156, 220, 227
Herod-Antipas 28, 140, 156, 214-15
Herod-Archelaus 29, 156
Herodias 90, 214
Herodotus 98

Hieros Gamos 184-5, 202, 203, 207
hierodulai 183, 184-5, 223
High History of the Holy Grail (*Perlesvaus*) 241, 262, 267, 288
Hilary of Poitiers 88, 251
Hippolytus 56, 89, 145, 261
Hiram of Tyre 246
Historia Certaminis Apostolici 27-8
History of a Mystery, The (BBC) 373-4
Hoel I 295
Holbein, Hans 341
Holy Grail 45-6, 58, 184, 271-2, 276-7
  Grail romance 45, 241-2, 256, 262-7, 295, 387
  Three Tables of 458-71
  see also 'engrailing'; *Sangréal*
Holy Grail (Tennyson) 272
Holy Roman Empire 96-7
Holy Spirit 32, 58, 83, 143, 360
Horsa 285
Howard, Henry, Earl of Suffolk 323
Hugues de Payens 116, 117
Hugues de Piraud 124

Ignatius of Antioch 137
Imbolc 91
Inanna the Great 183-4
Innocent III, Pope 142
Inquisition(s) 48, 49, 109, 123, 143, 301
Irenaus of Lyons 40, 169, 173, 279
Irish Gaels 286-7, 291
Isaiah, Book of 45, 125, 363
Ishtar 58, 183
Isidore of Seville 251
Israel 44, 76, 198-9, 213
Israelites 27, 45, 53, 62, 71, 76, 210, 245

Jacapo di Voragine 15–16, 19, 55
Jacob-Israel 76
Jacques de Molay 123
Jairus priests 15, 78
James Boanerges 29, 220, 254–5, 340
James of Alphaeus (James the Lesser) 255
James the Just (brother of Jesus) 35, 37, 39, 41, 89, 169, 215, 219, 220, 226, 227, 248, 254, 277
 called Ilid 260
 identified as Joseph of Arimathea 248–50
James VII (II) Stuart 378, 384, 385
Jeanne de Bar 389
Jefferson, Thomas 377
Jehanne de Laval 387, 393
Jeremiah, Book of 67
Jerome, St 41, 97, 177
Jerusalem 16, 34–5, 42, 52, 66, 72, 89, 92, 219, 220, 228 see also Temple at Jerusalem
Jerusalem (Blake) 257
Jesse 45, 363–4
Jesus 59, 76, 95, 149, 226
 admittance to the priesthood 210–11, 212
 artistic portrayal 4, 45, 59, 298, 339, 356, 359–60, 363
 bloodline see Desposyni
 brothers and sisters 37–41
 childhood 215–16
 date of birth 156–62
 Davidic ancestry 77, 81, 191, 248
 Essene affiliations 66, 73
 as 'fisher' 238–41
 and India 451–4

 initiation into Order of Melchizedek 211–15
 later life and death 230
 and Mary Magdalene
  anointing by 5–6, 8, 91, 139, 180, 197, 198–204, 208
  marriage to 20–1, 35, 138–9, 141, 150, 166, 196–7, 198–206, 208, 219, 272–3
  presence at tomb 1, 40, 54, 136, 151, 162–7, 236
  raising of 15–16
  relationship with 1, 2, 126, 149–50
 as Messiah 81, 193, 198–9, 207, 214
 as a mortal man 81, 82, 173, 431–4
 Nazarene affiliations 68–9, 73
 ossuaries 41–3
 Pistis Sophia 115–16
 raising of Lazarus 131–3, 136–41
 trial 435–40
 Trinity Dispute 36–7, 81–3
 as vine 45, 363
 washing of apostles' feet 281
 wedding at Cana 193–6
 wine symbolism 45
 as 'Word of God' 217
 see also Ascension; Crucifixion; Last Supper; Nativity; Passion; Resurrection
Jesus II Justus 218, 226, 230, 257–9
 marriage and fatherhood 230–1
Jesus III (Galains) 231, 257
Jewish custom 76, 157, 159, 172, 194–5
Jewish names, in Grail legends 264–6

Jewish New Year 159
Jewish Revolt 12, 68, 72, 117,
    131–2, 284
Jewish sects 36, 65–6
Jews 76, 143, 213–14
  expulsion from England 266
  mass suicide 228
Jews of Narbonne 102
Joachim, father of Mother Mary
    84, 300
Joan of Arc 385, 390, 391–2
Joanna, sister of Jesus 39–40, 164
Job, Book of 127
John, Duke of Bavaria 350
John XXIII, Pope 22, 23–4
John Chrysostom 189
John de Celia 18
John Hyrcanus 72
John Mark (St Mark) 131, 220,
    231, 233
John of Glastonbury 242, 252
John the Baptist 69, 213–15, 218,
    231, 248
John Boanerges the Divine 230,
    233–4, 340, 387
Joinville, Lord of 104–5
Jonathan Annas 226
Joseph, father of Jesus 26, 39, 40,
    229
  annunciation 69, 73, 75, 78
  artistic portrayal 299–300, 303
  Davidic inheritance 73–4, 77, 78
  and Essene marriage customs
    74–5, 79–81, 190–3
  as 'master of the craft' 74, 246
Joseph of Arimathea 162, 223, 246,
    247–56, 261–2, 267, 272, 284
  identified as James the Just
    248–50
Josephes 226, 227, 253, 257,
    262–4, 267, 276

Joses, brother of Jesus 34, 39, 40
Joshua, Book of 13
Joseph Caiaphas 131
Josue, son of Josephes 257, 263
Judah, House of 26, 45, 77, 96–7,
    103, 209, 240, 248, 363
Judas, brother of Jesus 39
Judas Iscariot 200, 331
Judas Maccabaeus 265–6
Jude, brother of Jesus 27, 169
Judges 263
Julia, Paul's helper 175
Julius II, Pope 365, 367
Julius Africanus 27–8, 228
Julius Caesar 71
Justinian I, Pope 368
Justinian II, Pope 38

Kabbalah 129
Katherine de Valois 390
Keith, George 384
Kemp, Martin 352
Kenneth MacAlpin 294
King James Bible 179
Kings 33, 199, 203, 207, 242
Knights Hospitallers 116
Knights Templars 19, 21, 116–20,
    122–5, 128–30, 204, 246, 267,
    376–7, 379, 382, 390
Koran 68
Kramer, Samuel Noah 203

labyrinths 121
Lacordaire, Jean Baptiste Henri
    Dominique 19, 110, 111
Lancelot 264
Lanfranco, Giovanni 31
Last Supper 47, 85, 174, 184,
    233–4, 272, 281, 343–4
  artistic portrayals 51–2, 330–5,
    337–47

INDEX

Lazurus *see* Simon Zelotes
Lazarus of Marseilles 57
Légenda Aurea 16
Leggenda di Sant Anna Madre della Gloriosa Vergine, Maria e di San Gioacchino 83–4
Leo I, Pope 92–3
Leo IX, Pope 101
Léon d'Acqs 295
Leonardo da Vinci 305–29, 383, 389
  Adoration of the Magi 335–7
  Head of a girl 321
  The Last Supper 51–2, 324, 330–5, 337–47
  Madonna of the Rocks 317, 322–6, 389
  Mona Lisa 3–4, 305–17, 324, 330
  The Virgin and Child with Saint Ann 300
  Virgin of the Rocks 317–22, 348
    third version 326–9
  Vitruvian Man 309–10
Leviticus 53, 159, 160
Lewis, Lionel S 254
Library at Alexandria 110, 177
Life of St Columba 289, 291
Life of St Mary Magdalene (de Voragine) 15, 16–17
Life of St Mary Magdalene (Rabanus Maurus) 17–18, 221
Light and Darkness 61–2
Linus, Prince 86, 261
Lippi, Fra Filippo 320, 387, 389
Litany of Loreto 48
Lluan of Brecknock 290
Llud, King 283
Llyr (Lear), King 283
loaves symbolism 240
Lomazzo, Paolo 332

Lorraine, Maximilien de 383–4, 385
Lost Secrets of the Sacred Ark (Gardner) 26, 119, 245
Louis VII 104, 119, 382
Louis IX 104–5, 106
Louis XI 19, 96, 112, 393
Louis XII 112
Louis XIII 112–13, 315
Louis XIV 113, 381
Louis XVI 113–14
Louis de Bar 389
Louis de Grimoard 123
Lucius, King 278–82
Luther, Martin 179

Maccabees 16, 72
Maelgwyn of Gwynedd 287
Maeluma mac Baedàn 293
Magdala (Magdal Nunaiya) 12
Magdalen College, Oxford 17
Magdalene, meaning of name 12–16, 183
Magdalene Basilica, Tiefenbronn 57
Magdalene College, Cambridge 18
Malory, Thomas 211, 212, 243, 262–3
Manning, Henry Edward 100
Marcantonio, Franceschini 2–3
Marcus 47
Marcus Aurelius 279
Margaret of Austria 353, 359
Mariette, Pierre Jean 366
Marseilles 91, 223, 225, 250
Martha of Bethany 6, 56, 115, 133–5, 137, 140, 174, 187, 221, 390
Martin, Malachi 22, 23, 24–5, 34
Martini, Simone 146

Mary, relevance of name 10–11
Mary, mother of Jesus
 annunciation 69, 73, 75, 78
 artistic portrayal 58, 300–2
 before and after Crucifixion/
  Resurrection 40, 208–9
 and Essene marriage customs
  74–5, 79–81, 190–3
 Immaculate Conception 84–5,
  300
 later life and date of death 229
 spurious virginity 38–9, 40–1, 80
Mary, sister of Jesus 39–40
Mary Jacob Cleophas (Mary the
  Gypsy) 56, 223–4, 247, 389
Mary Magdalene 1–2, 143, 231,
  247
 Abishag association 32, 204
 and academia 16–20
 and alabastron ('alabaster jar')
  268–74, 361
 in apocryphal scriptures 2,
  83–4, 149–54, 165–6, 170
 artistic portrayal 2–7, 50, 52,
  51–8, 63–4, 117, 146–7, 197,
  222, 225, 268–74, 297, 298,
  302–3, 303–4
  distinction from Mother Mary
  301–2
  Ecstasy portrayals 244
  Last Supper conjecture 51–2,
  338–9, 340–1, 344–7
  Penitent Magdalene 2–3, 366
  Virgin of the Rocks 326–9
 authorship of Gospel of John
  235–7
 Black Madonna status 31, 76
 canonisation 7, 145
 and the Church
  connection with portrayals
  146–7, 364–9

 denigration of 1–2, 5–6, 174
 fabrication of penitence 7, 8–9
 official image of 57
 perception of threat 21
 suppression of legacy 20–1,
  170–1, 204–5
 death 238, 254, 262
 dedication of Glastonbury
  chapel 258–9
 del Acqs associations 242–3
 Dominicans and 145–6
 emblems 51–8
 flight to Provence 29, 30–1, 63,
  110, 115, 220, 221–5
 Grail associations 46, 48, 50
 as *hierodule* 184
 as Holy Balm 393
 and Jesus
  anointing of 5–6, 8, 91, 139,
  180, 197, 198–204, 208
  marriage to 20–1, 35, 138–9,
  141, 150, 166, 196–7, 198–206,
  208, 219, 272–3
  raising by 15–16
  relationship with 1, 2, 126,
  149–50
  at tomb of 1, 40, 54, 136, 151,
  162–7, 236
 as Mistress of the Waters 101,
  238
 monastic involvement with 19,
  101, 147
 Nazarene associations 76, 169
 as *Notre Dame de Sion* 389
 origins in Galilee 15, 76
 parentage 15–16
 Peter's dislike of 169
 in *Pistis Sophia* 115–16, 133,
  145
 pregnancies and births 30,
  206–7, 226

Priory of Sion, alleged link 370, 373, 380–1, 385
and raising of Lazarus 133, 136, 138–9, 140
relics 101–8, 111–14, 118–19, 130, 388, 389
René d'Anjou and 386–90, 393–4
role in *Desposynic* campaign 221
as 'sinner' 8–11, 180, 220–1
skull 107, 121
Sophia inheritance 29, 31, 114, 116, 130, 205
'whore' allegations 33, 182–5, 368–9
Mary of Bethany
identified as Mary Magdalene 6, 7, 8–9, 10
Mary Tudor 178
Massue, Melville Henri 384
Master of Flémalle
The Marriage of Mary 355
Matthew Annas 149, 248
Mazza, Guiseppe 333
Medici, House of 320, 389
Medici, Giuliano Lorenzo di 312
Medici, Lorenzo 312
Melchizedek *see* Michael Zadok
Memling, Hans
The Adoration of the Magi 299–300
Meroveus 275–6
Merovingians 96–7, 98, 242–3, 264, 275, 295, 358, 359, 462–4
Messiahs 198–9, 214
Messianic line 207, 277
Miathi 291, 292
Micah, Book of 15
Michael Cerularis, Patriarch of Constantinople 101
Michael Zadok (Melchizedek) 70, 71, 77, 212, 245

Michaelis of Provence 145
Michelangelo
Doni Tondo 299
Middle Ages 46, 50, 56, 95, 99, 141, 157, 224, 266, 272, 277
miracles 194
Modred 293
monastic scholars 109–11
Montfort, Simon de 142
Moors (Saracens) 101–2, 254
Moretto, Alessandro
The Nativity 299
Morgaine (Morgan le Fay) 243, 295, 296
Morte d'Arthur 243, 262–3
Mortier, Fra 146
Moser, Lukas 57, 225
The Sea Voyage 225
Moses 77, 210, 245
Mother Goddess 48, 226
Mount Sinai 210, 244
Murator 100
Myrrophore 297

Nag Hammadi Library 126, 147, 151
Napoleon Bonaparte 316, 333
Nascien of the Medas 263–4, 275, 276–7
Nativity 132, 155–9, 180–2, 299
Nazarenes 17, 35–6, 39, 68–9, 73, 76, 93, 169, 171, 172, 173–4, 186–7, 188, 219, 220, 227, 228
Nebuchadnezzar 71, 117
Nennius 289, 291
Nero 28, 86, 132, 227
Nestorius 82
New Testament 28, 37, 78, 128, 147–8, 150, 154, 160, 177 *see also* Gospels; individual Books
Newton, Isaac 383

Nicephorus, Patriarch of
    Constantinople 89, 90
Nicholas I, Pope 83
Nicholas V, Pope 98
Nicholas of Cusa 98
Nicodemus 257
Noble Order of the Guard of St
    Germain 385
Noli me tangere 107, 236, 357–8
 artistic portrayal 5, 50, 365, 387
Notre Dame Gothic cathedrals
    110, 121, 204
Numbers 96

Odoacer 92
Old Testament 15, 33, 45, 71, 96,
    127 *see also* individual Books
Olympias of Constantinople
    189–90
On the Origin of the World 32
Or de Rennes L' 372
Order of Melchizedek 211–15,
    238
Order of the Realm of Sion 384
Order of the Sangréal 384
Ordré de Notre Dame de Sion 382
Origen of Alexandria 32, 169, 189
ORMEs (Orbitally Rearranged
    Monatomic Elements) 120, 246
Ormus 120, 121, 122, 246, 383
ossuaries 41–3
Otto III 98

Pagès, Aimée 313
Pallas (Pelles) 276
Pandora 361–2
Papal Infallibility 85
paper making 46
Paris, Matthew 18, 254
Parzifal 45, 267
Paschal II, Pope 104
Passion 40, 357

Passover 53–4, 159–60, 161
Patrick, St 94, 252
Paul, St 28, 29, 36, 39, 60, 68–9,
    77, 86, 89, 90, 132, 167, 169,
    170–1, 173, 174, 175–6, 185,
    186, 219, 226–7, 230, 261
 and female ministry 185–8
Paul VI, Pope 22, 24, 84, 174–5
Pauline Christianity 169–70, 173,
    227
Pellicioli, Mauro 334, 343
Pendragons 283–4
Penni, Gianfrancesco 365
Pepin, King 102, 359
Perceval 262
Peruggia, Vincenzo 316
Perugino, Pietro
    The Family of the Virgin 300
Peter, St 20, 28, 29, 35, 49, 60, 86,
    115, 132, 152–3, 165, 167–8,
    169, 170, 175, 180, 186, 219,
    227, 232–3, 281, 341–2
Pharisees 65, 66, 73, 131, 193
Phebe, Paul's helper 175, 187,
    189
Philalethes, Erenaeus 383
Philip, St 169, 223, 251, 253
Philippe II 142
Philippe IV 108, 119, 122–5,
    376–7, 390
Philippe Augustus 104
Philippe d'Alsace 267
Philosophers' Stone 119–20, 122,
    383
Photius, Patriarch of
    Constantinople 83
Picts 285, 292, 294
Pierre de Lamanon 146
Pièrre Yorick de Rivault 123
Pilgrim Fathers 179
Pistis Sophia (Askew Codex)
    114–16, 133, 145, 147, 169

Pius IX, Pope 84
Pius XII, Pope 23, 84
Piviot, Jacques 352
Plantard, Pierre 370, 371–2, 373–4, 379, 380, 381
Plato 207
Pliny the Younger 189
Pontano, Teobaldo 146
Pontius Pilate 39, 139, 162–3, 213, 220, 247, 249
Pozzo, Cassiano dal 312
Precepts of Ecclesiastical Discipline 167, 170
Predis, Ambrogio de 318, 322, 324, 325
Predis, Evangelista de 318, 322
Pre-Raphaelite Brotherhood 271–2
Prieuré Notre Dame de Sion 382–4, 385, 388–9
Priory of Sion (*Prieuré de Sion*) 370–4, 379–81, 385
Priscilla the martyr 175
Priscus of Thrace 275
Protestants 9, 178
Protevangelion of James 39, 83
Provost, Jan
  The Sacred Allegory 76, 360, 361
Psalms 44, 48, 129, 209
Pythagoras 66

'Q' 149
Quested, Digby 308
Qumrân 61, 67, 71–3, 126–7, 172, 190, 210, 211, 216, 228, 245, 246

Rabanus Maurus 16, 17, 19, 29, 55, 110, 221, 247
Radclyffe, Charles 383
Rainier de Larchant 124
Raphael (angelic distinction) 71, 77

Raphael (Raffaello Sanzio) 303–4, 313, 364–5, 368
  The Knight's Dream 303
  Sposalizio 303
Rapunzel 55–6
Reinhardt, Carl 151
Remy, St 96
Renaissance 55, 97, 99, 271, 302–3, 350, 354, 355, 361, 364, 368, 387
René d'Anjou 386–90, 391
  Marie Madeleine Preaching to the King and Queen of Marseilles 387
Rennes-le-Château 372–3, 374–8
Resurrection 1, 10, 20, 27, 40, 50, 53, 54, 162–7, 208, 232, 234
Revelation (*Apocalypse*) 28–9, 30–1, 33, 54, 59–60, 61–2, 184, 207, 230–1, 271, 350–1, 356, 387
Rhydderch of Strathclyde 288, 292
Ribera, Jusepe de 57
Richard II 84
Richard Coeur de Lion 104
Robert de Boron 253, 267
Robin Hood legends 224
Romano, Giulio 365
Romans
  conflict with Zealots 227–8
  crushing of Israelites 27
  installation of Herod 71
  persecution of Christians 28, 90–1, 132, 186, 227, 279
  withdrawal from Britain 284
Romans, Book of 74, 90, 175, 187
Rome 33, 63, 131–2, 169, 227, 297, 365
  collapse of Empire 82, 92
Romulus Augustulus 92
Rosicrucians 378

Rossellino, Antonio
  Madonna 314–15
Rossetti, Dante Gabriel 55, 271–2
  The Holy Grail 58
  Mary Magdalene at the Door of Simon the Pharisee 272–4
  Mary Nazarene 271
  Seed of David altarpiece 271
Rosslyn Chapel 50–1, 386
Rosslyn Hay manuscript 386
Royal Society, London 378–9, 383
Royal Syths 55
Rufus Pudens 261
Ruheumann, Helmut 323

Sadducees 65, 66, 73
Saint Clairs (Sinclairs) 50, 389
Saint Sulpice church 380, 381
Salimbeni, Ventura
  Exaltation of the Eucharist 360
Salome *see* Helena-Salome; Sarah-Salome
Salome, daughter of Herodias 90, 215
San Gallo, Francesco da
  Saint Ann and the Madonna 300
Sandys, Frederick 55, 271
Sangréal 48, 142, 183, 203, 241, 271, 277, 393
Santiago de Compostela 254–5
Sarah-Salome (Sarah the Black), sister of Jesus 31–2, 40, 115, 133, 163, 169, 223, 224, 247
Saul, King 198
Saunière, Bérenger 372–3, 374–8
Saunière, Jacques 382
Saxons 252, 285, 294
Scanatoria, Lucrezia 368
Schonfeld, Johann Heinrich
  L'Adoration de la Sainte Trinité 360–1

Schonfield, Hugh 128–30
Schwartz, Lillian 308
Scotland 49, 97, 123, 256, 294, 379
Scots 256, 286–7, 289–93, 294, 379
Second World War 335, 386
Septimania (Septimanian Midi) 102, 103, 143, 243, 264, 295
Septimius Serverus 90
Septuagint Bible 245
Seracini, Maurizio 336
Serpent Rouge, Le 380–1
Sforza, Ludovicio 309, 322, 330
Shulamites 33
Sicambrians 276
Silvestri, Oreste 334
Simeon the Essene 229
Simon, brother of Jesus 39
Simon Zelotes (the leper, the Pharisee, Simon Lazarus) 5, 6, 8, 29, 89, 90, 135, 139–40, 169, 199, 209, 213, 219, 220–1, 222, 223, 235
  disciple whom Jesus loved 234–5
  identified as Lazarus 139
  raising of 131–2, 136–41
Sinclair, William 386
Smith, Morton 136–7
Sol Invictus 35, 53
Solomon, King 33, 96, 199, 203, 207, 245–6, 265
Song of Inanna 183, 184
Song of Solomon 32–3, 101, 150, 184–5, 202, 203–4, 242, 328
Sophia 29, 31, 32, 33, 114, 116, 129–30, 182, 205
Souchet, Jean-Baptiste 121
Souéges, Thomas 145
Spong, John Shelby 195–6

St Maximus la Sainte-Baume 91, 101–2, 103, 104–8, 109, 111–14, 118, 145–6, 222, 223, 388
Stafford, Henry 18
Stampa, Gaspara 367
Steinberg, Leo 331–2
Stendhal, Henri 333
Stephen, Pope 102
Strange, Robert 384
Stuart, Charles Edward (Bonnie Prince Charlie) 378–9
Stuart (Stewart), House of 275, 378, 384
Sumer 183, 202
Sylvester, Bishop 34–5, 87, 100
Sylvester II, Pope 98
Synod of Whitby 52–3, 93
Synoptic Gospels 131, 234
Syro the Jairus 15–16, 33, 78

Taitan 178
Talmud 12, 68
Tamar 209, 230, 327
Temple at Jerusalem 36, 66, 72, 116, 117–18, 157, 228, 242
Tennyson, Alfred Lord 272
Tertullian 170, 172, 185, 187
Thaddaeus 29, 149, 169, 220
Theobald of Cambridge 103
Theodosius I 82, 110, 253, 254, 368
Theodosius II 93
Theophilus, Bishop 110
Therapeutate 72, 172, 190, 245, 246
Thiering, Barbara 216
Thomas Aquinas 122, 146–7
Thomas the apostle 167–8, 169, 230
Thucydides 98
Tiberius 54–5, 88, 214, 261
Timothy, Epistle of 173, 175, 188, 261

Titus 28
Tolleme le Feintes 263
Tourangeau, Sancelrien 120
Trinity Debate 37, 81–2, 92
Trophimus of Arles 223
Troubadours 48, 144, 277
Tyndale, William 178

Uccello, Paolo 387
unicorns 48
Urban VI, Pope 84

V-glyph 48
Vaga, Perino del 365
Valentinus 47
Valla, Lorenzo 98–9
van de Weiden, Rogier
  Mary Magdalene Reading 356
  St Luke Drawing the Madonna 355
Van Dyck
  Repose in Egypt 300
van Eyck, Hubert 351, 352
van Eyck, Jan 387
  The Arnolfini Marriage 348–58
  The Crucifixion 358
  Ghent Altarpiece 350–1
  Giovanni Arnolfini 353–4
  The Three Marys at the Tomb of Jesus 358
van Eyck, Margaretta 350–2, 353
  Madonna 351–2
  Madonna and Mary Magdalene with a Donor 351
Vandals 92
Vannozza dei Cattanei 367
Vasari, Giorgio 311, 312–13, 332, 365, 368
Vatican 22–4, 37, 83, 90, 92, 95, 96, 147, 178, 375, 377
Vatican Archive 41, 100, 135, 269
Vatican Councils 23, 85

Venerable Bede of Jarrow 280, 288
Vermes, Geza 74
Verrocchio, Andrea del 389
Vespasian 27, 97
Vézelay hoax 104, 118–19
Vilars Dehoncort of Picardy 121
Vincent of Beauvais 242
vine symbolism 44–6, 297, 363
Visigoths 92
Vita emeritica beatae Maria Magdalenae 222
Vitruvian Man 309–10
Viviane I of Avallon 243, 290
Viviane II del Acqs 243, 264, 276, 290, 296
Vortigern of Powys 284, 285
Vulgate Bible 97, 99, 177, 178, 179
Vulgate Cycle 267, 272

Waleran the hermit 241–2, 266
Wales 260, 283, 285–6, 294
Warren, Charles 117–18
Wars of the Jews 12–13, 80, 190
watermarks 46
Weale, WH James 349, 352, 353
Welch, Evelyn 352

Whistler, James AM
  Whistler's Mother 4
William de Nogaret 123, 124
William of Malmesbury 253
William of Waynflete 17
wine symbolism 45–6, 47–8
Witcombe, Christopher 364
Wolfram von Eschenbach 45, 267
women
  female ministry 56, 185–90
  veneration by chivalry 277
  views of Church on 166–7, 169, 170–6
Wycliffe, John 178

X symbol 48–9

Ygerna del Acqs (Igraine) 290, 295
Yolande D'Aragon 389
Ywain (Eógain) 295

Zacharias 69, 73, 78–9, 213
Zachary, Pope 95–7, 100
Zadok the Priest 191, 199
Zealots 139, 220–1, 227–8
Zechariah, Book of 101, 207

THE LEARNING CENTRE
TOWER HAMLETS COLLEGE
POPLAR CENTRE
POPLAR HIGH STREET
LONDON E14 0AF

Also by Laurence Gardner and available from HarperElement

The Shadow of Solomon

The Lost Secret of the Freemasons Revealed

The Freemasons are often said to be the world's most influential secret society, and the story of this enigmatic fraternity is wrapped in mystery and intrigue. Their involvement in shaping world events has stretched over centuries, but who are the Freemasons, and what is their history and purpose?

For Freemasons, Dan Brown readers and others who might wonder what secrets lie behind this mysterious and influential fraternity, *The Shadow of Solomon* is the definitive insider's account of the startling truth behind Masonic history, and the centuries-long search that the fraternity has undertaken to find its own lost secrets. Laurence Gardner, a past Grand Lodge of England master mason, opens the door on the inner sanctum of the Masonic Temple and exposes the conflicts and intrigues that have guarded the real secret of Freemasonry for centuries – a secret that has potentially shattering implications for what we think we might know about history and cutting-edge science.

Bloodline of the Holy Grail

The Hidden Lineage of Jesus Revealed

Did Jesus marry and have children with Mary Magdalene?
If so, what happened to his family?
Are descendants of Jesus still alive today?

This extraordinary account of the Messianic bloodline
encompasses some of the most colourful and sacred territory of the past 2,000 years. Granted privileged access to royal
and suppressed archives, Gardner now reveals documented
proof of the hidden heritage of Jesus in the West and new
findings on the discovery of the Holy Grail. Coupled with
all the adventure of Arthurian romance, *Bloodline of the Holy
Grail* has a cutting edge that exposes one of the greatest con-
spiracies ever told.

'A controversial and uniquely comprehensive book of
Messianic descent, compiled from the most
intriguing histories ever written.'

Publishing News

'This book, provocative as it may be, is not a work of
fiction, but the product of years of painstaking
research. Committed Christians will find it casts
fascinating light on the origins of their beliefs.'

Daily Mail